Book Markets
for
Children's Writers

Writer's Institute Publications

Acknowledgments

The editors of this directory appreciate the generous cooperation of the publishers who made clear their policies and practices, as well as the contributions from our instructors and students.

MARNI MCNIFF, Editor

SUSAN TIERNEY, Articles Editor

BARBARA COLE, Associate Editor

SHERRI KEEFE, Assistant Editor

MEREDITH DESOUSA, Copy Editor

ARTUR GODLEWSKI, Research Assistant

JAMES HABER, Research Assistant

Contributing Writers: Susan Anderson, Jennifer Ponte Canning, Kristen Bishop, Susan Tarrant

Cover Design: Joanna Horvath
Cover illustrations supplied by Getty Images

International Standard Book Number 978-1-889715-49-0

1-800-443-6078. www.writersbookstore.com
email: services@writersbookstore.com

Contents

Step-by-Step through the Submissions Process

This section offers step-by-step instructions for compiling a submissions package.

Contents (Cont.)

Step-by-Step through the Submissions Process

Your Publishing Strategy

strategy: the art of devising or employing
plans toward a goal

C an you imagine spending years writing and revising a picture book, novel, or nonfiction manuscript only to discover that it doesn't meet the needs of a publisher? As the writer, you may have missed the mark on any number of things, including subject matter, target audience, or differentiating yourself from the competition. If you're lucky, you may be able to address these issues with some revisions; other cases may require a complete rewrite. Writers who want to get published learn to avoid these pitfalls with the help of a good publishing strategy—one that begins long before the writing starts.

Just like any successful business, writing benefits from a bit of advance planning. As writers, we've all heard the old adage to "write what you know." Clearly, authors who are passionate and knowledgeable about a subject are high on any editor's wanted list, but there's another key ingredient to becoming a writer: Write what you can sell. Even an author who is passionate about his or her topic will produce a more marketable book if it speaks to the right audience, has a unique hook, and/or covers a subject matter that is timely and relevant. Figuring out these key ingredients ahead of time will not only help you stay focused while writing; it will also boost the marketability of your manuscript.

As a writer trying to get published, what's your strategy? To get started, review the following targets, all of which are key to tailoring your manuscript with an eye toward publication:

1 - **Target the subject.** Is your topic of personal interest and a subject you feel passionate about? An editor isn't going to be enthusiastic about a book if you're not. What type of research will make it interesting and successful? Children's editors today require first-rate, primary research.

2 - **Target the quality.** Have you done your best writing? Practiced your skills, gone to writers' conferences, taken courses, joined critique groups, or in some way worked at your craft and gained the right "equipment"?

3 - **Target the audience.** Can you see it clearly? What is the age? Reading level? Interest? Voice?

4 - **Target the competition.** Are there other books on comparable subjects? If you're writing in one genre, what else is out there? Do you have a truly different slant to offer?

5 - **Target the market generally.** Is your book to be trade, mass-market, religious, crossover, regional, educational?

6 - **Target the individual publisher and editor.** What is this particular company and editor most interested in, most successful with?

We will take you step-by-step through the process of hitting some of these targets. Only you can work on the quality, but we will coach you through subject, audience, competition, and market objectives and how to reach them. You'll come nearer and nearer to a bull's-eye with every arrow—every manuscript sent flying.

Target the Subject

Whether you're finding new ideas, developing a defined project, or searching for markets for your completed manuscript, you can improve the submission process by taking time to do fundamental research. The first step is to select an idea that interests you, that you believe will appeal to readers as much as it does to you, and then collect information about it.

This idea and research development step is an important first measure toward selling your book. A good book requires authenticity if it's fiction, and accuracy if it's nonfiction. Subject research is essential in composing the best possible manuscript, whether it's historical background for a novel, geographical information on a region or city, or current data for a scientific principle. Finding and refining your idea with research will strengthen your work, and poise it to sell.

<u>Research resources.</u> The Web gives writers access to libraries, research studies, museums, associations, businesses, and a seemingly endless supply of miscellaneous sites available through myriad search engines. There are also additional resources available through your local library, many of which can be accessed from home with the use of your library card. Look at:

• online encyclopedias that might provide links to more detailed pages on other sites;
• university libraries online;

- government resources like the Library of Congress, the Smithsonian, NASA;
- museum sites, such as the Metropolitan Museum of Art in New York, the British Museum, and many other world-class museums;
- the sites of smaller, more focused museums, historical sites, even corporations;
- organizations that range from the social to the arts to sports, from the local to the universal;
- journalism and research-oriented sites that lead to "experts" for interviews.

Some sites provide information about the existence of material that you'll need to get physically from the library or another source. Other sites, however, provide actual content— text, photos, and data—online.

People are good research sources—and can be cited as such. There may be subject-area experts in your community; or, to explore a topic more generally, subscribe to a listserv about your topic to get a variety of viewpoints and opinions.

<u>**Accuracy and annotations**</u>. Websites have links to other sites. Follow the trail, the links, and keep clear notes on where you go and what you learn, so you don't lose important resources or unintentionally plagiarize. Keep a running bibliography for your submission package; even if you don't need it, it's useful for back-up and additional research. Be sure to check the *Book Markets for Children's Writers'* listings for indications of the kind of bibliographical or other research annotations targeted editors require. (See, for example, the bibliography on page 38.)

It's important to become knowledgeable about screening information that appears on the Internet. Anyone with some computer know-how can create a website, so be sure to check the credentials of every source. You can be fairly sure of the accuracy of information presented on those sites affiliated with credible organizations such as the National Education Association, NASA, the Museum of Natural History, and other educational institutions, government bodies, museums, etc.

<u>**Fiction and research.**</u> Even fiction writers may need to do some research. Is your story set in a seaside town you recall

Subject Research on the Internet

Whether you're in search of an idea or searching for information about an idea, the Internet is an excellent starting point for research. The list below provides a sampling of sites on a variety of topics that could be useful for mining information.

- EE-Link, http://eelink.net/ – provides annotated links to 5,800 environmental education resources on the Internet, in 300 categories.
- Encyclopedia Mythica, www.pantheon.org – an award-winning Internet encyclopedia of mythology, folklore, and religion.
- Footage.net, www.footage.net - includes thousands of "stock, archival and news footage collections." Registration is free.
- Guinness World Records, www.guinnessworldrecords.com – the ultimate authority on world records, this website contains records pertaining to all subject areas.
- Historical Voices, www.historicalvoices.org – a database of spoken word collections from the twentieth century, in audio format.
- Hoax Museum Blog, www.museumofhoaxes.com – a blog from the Museum of Hoaxes that identifies modern "dubious-sounding claims"; also contains an archive of articles about notorious deceptions throughout history.
- Mysteries of History, www.usnews.com/usnews/doubleissue/mysteries/index.htm – created for people who continue to wonder about things like how the stones got to Stonehenge, this site contains essays about intriguing historical mysteries of all kinds.
- Secrets of the Spies, www.cbsnews.com/htdocs/spies/framesource.html – CBS News created this interactive website that includes a timeline, espionage terminology, information about famous double agents, and more.
- 20 Things You Didn't Know About . . . http://discovermagazine.com/ – a collection of interesting nuggets of information about a variety of topics, ranging from sports and money to lab accidents and . . . nothing.
- Virtual Religion Index, http://virtualreligion.net/vri/ – an annotated list of religion-related websites created by the Rutgers University Religion Department.

from childhood? What's the weather like there when your story is set? Do you need inspiration for character names for a contemporary or historical story? Internet sites such as www.newspaper-archive.com allow you to search newspapers from as far back as 1759, and are a treasure trove for interesting stories and characters. And of course, turn to print, too. Through your local library you have access to networks of other libraries that will help you borrow virtually any book you need.

Target the Audience

Developing ideas means not only putting thought and research into your topic or story, but also gathering information about the readers. Who will read this story? Who is the ultimate market? What grabs the reader?

Experts. Search out "experts" who can help you learn which books kids are reading at which ages, or what parents or educators are reading, if they're your projected audience. Talk to children's librarians and teachers about the kinds of stories and topics that currently, or universally, appeal to young readers. Ask them about curriculum needs, especially for nonfiction. Go to bookstores and speak to managers who specialize in children's books. Online, go to library and reading sites, like those for the American Library Association (ALA) and the International Reading Association (IRA).

Developmental stages. Find out what's happening developmentally at a given age, what's being studied at school, what interests spark your audience. Talk to scout leaders, coaches, and music teachers. Observe and talk to the children themselves, especially about books if you can. Go to children's websites to see the topics they cover, and watch television programming and read young people's magazines to learn more about contemporary youth culture.

Age ranges. Browse through the listings in *Book Markets for Children's Writers* to look at the ages covered and review the sample titles. Or start with the Category Index (page 576) and look under "preK" or "middle grade" or "young adult." Review the publishers listed and request their catalogues or visit their websites. Catalogues are generally free upon request with a stamped, self-addressed, 9x12 envelope. See how many titles are published in what genres, for what age ranges; it should give you a sense of that publisher's subjects and style.

Age-Targeting Resources

- **American Library Association (ALA) and International Reading Association (IRA):** The lists of books for children compiled by these two organizations will help direct you to age-appropriate writing (www.ala.org and www.reading.org). The ALA also lists "Great Sites!" for children, which helps writers focus in on kids' interests.

- **American Academy of Pediatrics:** Try the AAP's (www.aap.org) You and Your Family page, or the publications page.

- **Bright Futures:** Available on this organization's website (www.brightfutures.org) are downloads of tip sheets on developmental stages, and a variety of resources on juvenile and adolescent health and behavioral development.

- **Child & Family WebGuide:** Created by Tufts University, this website (www.cfw.tufts.edu/) evaluates and describes hundreds of child development articles and sites on the Internet. Topics may be searched by age range, popularity, or area of interest.

- **Search Institute:** This nonprofit organization's website (www.search-institute.org) highlights 40 developmental assets for children from grades 6 to 12.

Finding Child and Teen Sites

- **KidsClick!:** A librarian-generated list of more than 600 sites for children (www.kidsclick.org). Categories include facts & reference, weird & mysterious, religion & mythology, machines & transportation, and more.

- **KidSpace (and TeenSpace) @ the Internet Public Library:** This ALA-recommended site contains links to sites on numerous subjects, from math to science to sports and recreation (www.ipl.org/div/kidspace and www.ipl.org/div/teen); sponsored by the School of Information at the University of Michigan.

- **ReadKiddoRead:** Well-known author James Patterson and children's literature specialist Judy Freeman highlight great reads for kids on this website (www.readkiddoread.com).

You might also need or want to buy a book to advance your research into what a particular segment of children is reading. Amazon.com or Barnesandnoble.com, along with other sites that help you buy books or locate out-of-print titles, have become essential tools for writers. Not only do they help you locate children's books you know you want, they give you information on readership ages. Reverse the process and begin your search at one of these sites with a designated age range and see what titles come up. Lots of humor? Nonfiction, but not the fiction you expected? Does this help you in thinking about what you want to write?

Target the Competition & General Markets

A competitive title analysis is an important part of your research. Becoming familiar with publishers' current offerings is a good way to figure out how your book can stand out from the rest. A thorough analysis will also show editors that you have the ability to judge your own book accurately.

Competitive titles. A submission package that includes information about competitive titles will have a definite advantage. It will show editors your professionalism, research skills, and dedication to your work. If you use the research well, it will indicate to the editor that you know what that particular company publishes and why your book will fit its list. Doing your competitive title research, the questions you'll need to ask are:

- What books are in print that are similar to my idea?
- Who are the publishers, and what kinds of companies are they?
- When were the competing titles published?
- How are they different in slant, format, audience, etc., from mine?
- If one or more are not different, how will I reslant my idea to make my title more distinct?

This is where you'll need to strike a balance between selecting a subject or a story that has been widely published and the challenge of giving it a new twist. The same subjects will come up over and over again, and there's a reason—a large segment of four-year-olds are always interested in trucks and always will be, for example. But how do you write another picture book on trucks and make sure it's distinct?

Competition Research Form

Title	Author	Publisher	Pub. Date	Description/Differences from My Book
Little Trucks, Big Jobs	Robert Maass	Henry Holt	August 2007	Focuses on small trucks
Trucks Roll!	George Ella Lyon	Atheneum/Richard Jackson Books	March 2007	Focuses on trucks as big and powerful, with closeup drawings
Mega Trucks	(no author listed)	Scholastic	June 2008	An introduction to the "biggest trucks in the world"; has interactive questions

Some subjects are ripe for a new spin, particularly if it's been a few years since the last book on that topic was published. To do competition research, you might check:

- bookstores, where you can ask for a list of all the books on a given subject

- *Book Markets for Children's Writers*, for an overview of companies publishing competitive books

- online booksellers, with subject and age searches

- libraries, for catalogues and the *Subject Guide to Children's Books in Print*

- publisher websites and publisher catalogues

If there are many competing titles in your subject area, focus on just four or five that you consider to be leading competitors and describe them in detail. Some online booksellers such as Amazon.com offer sales rankings, reviews, and commentary to guide you.

Market types. Use *Book Markets for Children's Writers'* Category Index to generate a list of companies that publish in the category of your book and to start you thinking about the marketplace in general. You may want to use a form like the one on page 13. Are the companies with competitive titles generally educational, trade, religious, special interest? Do they have a strong backlist of older titles that they continue to support?

The individual publisher listings in *Book Markets for Children's Writers* also give you information on how many books a company publishes each year and how many it accepts from new authors. You're another step closer to selecting the publishers to whom you'll send your submission.

Target the Publisher & Editor

Book Markets for Children's Writers is an ideal resource for aligning your work with a publisher who is looking for it. The listings in *Book Markets for Children's Writers* are updated annually, with an emphasis on finding exactly what the editor needs now.

Turn again to the Category Index on page 576, or leaf through the listings themselves, and write down those publishers with interests similar to your own, especially those you didn't find in your earlier research. You've done this in researching the field and competition as a whole, but now you need to focus on the publishers you will pursue for your book. Here's how the listings break down and how to use them best.

- **Publisher's Interests:** Does the publisher you have in mind produce books for the trade, mass market, or school and library? Does it publish fiction and/or nonfiction? Does it have a specialization, such as history, regional subjects, educational? Is your book compatible with the publisher's profile? Don't stretch to make a match—make it a close one—but if you believe you can slant your book solidly toward a publisher's needs, work toward that in pulling together your proposal. If you've written fiction that just can't be reshaped, be honest, and find a different publisher whose needs are a better fit.

- **Freelance Potential:** How many books did the publisher produce last year? Of the books published, how many came from unpublished writers? (For an idea of your odds, compare the number of submissions the publisher received last year to the number of titles it published.) What age range does it focus on? Are there particular topics or types of books it specializes in? What genres did the company publish, in fiction or nonfiction?

- **Editor's Comments:** This section reveals a publisher's current needs, and the types of manuscripts it *doesn't* want to see. It may also give you insight into preferred style or other editor preferences.

You can also keep up with current needs through many of the trade publications like *Children's Writer* newsletter (www.childrenswriter.com or 1-800-443-6078) and *Publishers Weekly* (www.publishersweekly.com/). *PW* offers special feature issues on children's publishing every spring and fall, as well as an online newsletter, *Children's Bookshelf,* that covers the children's publishing industry.

Industry Insider

You can do more than subject research online; there are also many resources useful for getting the scoop on publishers, editors, and the latest new books. Blogs are a good source for news on the children's publishing industry in general. Find your favorite blogs and follow one or two for a good overview of the industry from a writer's point of view—or an editor's.

Blogs for industry trends:

- www.JacketFlap.com – a children's book resource and social networking site for people in the children's book industry

- http://editorialanonymous.blogspot.com/ – editorial questions are answered by an anonymous children's book editor

- www.ypulse.com – this media and marketing blog offers insight on how best to reach tweens and teens

- www.cynthialeitichsmith.com – a blog from author Cynthia Leitich Smith covering children's book news, interviews, reviews, booklists, and more

Narrow your choices to 6 to 12 publishers and request their catalogues, along with their writers' guidelines. Ask a final set of questions—those in the sidebar on page 19.

You're about to pull together your submissions package. First, review the writers' guidelines, if a company has them. Read the *Book Markets for Children's Writers'* listing closely for specifications, and follow them exactly. Suppose you have completed a nonfiction book on robotics you'd like to propose to Boyds Mills Press. The Boyds Mills guidelines for submission of a nonfiction manuscript require a detailed bibliography; they also *highly recommend* an expert review and a competitive analysis of similar books on the market. You could send your submission with a bibliography only, but you'd be starting off at a disadvantage—another writer may have sent in an expert review and a competitive analysis as well. Follow any publisher's guidelines as best you can; they not only help to streamline the submission process, they also help editors to identify worthwhile submissions—both of which help you.

About Agents

Writers of books at some point face the question of whether or not to look for an agent. Some successful writers never work with an agent, while others prefer to find a strong representative for their work to deal with the business side. Some publishers will not accept unsolicited materials except through an agent. But a good manuscript will find its home with or without an agent, if you are committed to finding the right publisher to match your work.

How to find an agent: Look at listings in *Literary Marketplace* (LMP), or contact the Association of Authors' Representatives or go to its website (www.aar-online.org) for its member list. Other resources include the SCBWI Agents Directory (offered free to members) and the *2010 Guide to Literary Agents* (F & W Publications), which provides the names and specialties of agents around the world. If you'd prefer surfing the Web, the *Guide*'s editor's blog (www.guidetoliteraryagents.com/blog) is a wealthy resource, offering current information on agent needs and a wide variety of subjects related to working with and submitting to agents. Another site, Agent Query (www.agentquery.com/), is a free searchable database of agents that also includes specific information about each, including past and present clients and special interests. Be sure that any agent you contact works with writers for children.

What an agent does: An agent will review your work editorially before deciding to represent you, but the primary work of an agent is to contact publishers, market your material, negotiate for rights and licenses, and review financial statements. Although you don't need to be published to get an agent, most agents agree that an author should demonstrate commitment to the craft and a professional approach to writing in order to be considered for representation.

(continued on following page)

About Agents (continued)

How to contact an agent: If the agent has a website, go online for specific contact requirements. If not, send a well-written, professional cover letter describing your work and background, accompanied by an outline or synopsis and sample chapter. Most agents will accept simultaneous submissions, as long as you inform them them you're querying other agents, and perhaps publishers, as well. Remember to tailor your query to individual agents just as you would to a publisher.

Fees: Be careful about agent fees. Increasingly, some will charge for readings and critiques, even without taking you on as a client. Compare the fees and the comissions to similar agents if you do enter into a contract. A typical rate is 15 percent for domestic sales, 20 percent for foreign.

What you need to know: Once you have an agent interested in representing you, compile a list of questions to ask him or her before getting on board. These might include:

- Why do you like my work?
- What should I expect of you, and you of me?
- What are the terms of the contract, including its duration?
- What is your track record, i.e. how many books have you sold?
- How does communication between us take place, via phone, email, or both?
- What can I do to help sell my work?
- What is required to end the agreement if it doesn't work out?

Take Close Aim

When you've narrowed your targeted publishers to a short list, review the individual publishers' catalogues closely or go to their websites (indicated in the listings) to find out about their overall list and specific titles—dates of publication, slant, format. With even greater focus now as you sight your target, ask:

- Is this a large house, a smaller publisher, or an independent press with 10 or fewer books published yearly?

- How many books are on its backlist?

- What audience does the publisher target?

- Are most books single titles, or does the publisher focus on series books?

- Does it aim for one or two age groups, or does it feature books for all age groups?

- Does the publisher use the same authors repeatedly, or are many different authors featured?

- Are newer authors also represented?

- Is there a mix of fiction and nonfiction books, or is there more of one than the other?

- Is there a range of subject matter? Does my book fit in their range?

- Does the publisher specialize in one or more types of books, such as picture books or easy-to-reads? Is my book one of these, or not?

- Are there books similar to yours? Too similar and too recent, so the publisher might not want duplication?

- Would your book fit in with others this house has published?

- What are the specific requirements of the writers' guidelines and how will I meet them?

Query Letters
Step-by-Step

First impressions are crucial in publishing, whether it's to engage your reader in the first chapter of a book, or to catch an editor's attention with an intriguing pitch. While the overall quality of your book will ultimately cinch the sale, the first hurdle is to present your project in the best light by way of a query letter.

Many editors request query letters in place of complete manuscripts. Query letters are brief (usually one page) but significant. A good query should capture the editor's interest and give a sense of your treatment of a topic. It should also convince him or her that you are the best person to write this book.

But a good query still has more work to do: It also provides important information about you as the author. A professional, well-written query lets the editor know if you've mastered the idea of a "hook," have a good grasp of your project's theme and/or plot points, and understand how and why your work is a good fit for the publisher.

The best advice:

• Be succinct, positive, enthusiastic, and interesting.

• Briefly describe your book proposal.

• Identify the publisher's needs by indicating your familiarity with titles on their list.

• Outline your qualifications to write the book.

Review the query letter samples on pages 29, 30, and 33. Note each of the following elements:

Opener: A direct, brief lead that:

• captures and holds the editor's interest (it could be the first paragraph of your book);

• tells what the subject is and conveys your particular angle or slant;

• reflects your writing style, but is at all times professional; you need not be overly formal, but do not take a casual tone.

Subject: A brief description of your proposed manuscript and its potential interest to the publisher.

Specifications: If applicable, include the following:

- your manuscript's word length;

- number and type of illustrations;

- a brief indication of the research and interviews to be done; if this list is extensive, include it on a separate page with a reference to it in your query;

- market information and intended audience; again, if you've done more extensive competition research, attach it separately.

Reader Appeal: A brief description of why your target audience will want to read your proposed book.

Credits: If you have publishing credits, list them briefly, including the publisher and the date. List magazine credits as well. Don't tell the editor you've read your book to your child's class, or that several teachers have encouraged you to send it in, or that you've taken a writing course. If you have particular qualifications that helped you write the book (e.g., you run obedience classes and have written a book on dog training), say so. Many publishers request résumés. If you're attaching one in your submissions package, your query should mention relevant credits, and then refer to the résumé.

Marketing is a primary concern in publishing, and many publishers are more willing to take a chance on an author with previous writing experience and/or professional credentials. To build up your author "platform," get smaller pieces published in a variety of outlets and network with other professionals whenever possible.

Closing: Let the publisher know if this is an exclusive or simultaneous submission.

Queries are often required for nonfiction submissions, but in the past were very uncommon in fiction. Most editors preferred to see complete manuscripts or several chapters and a synopsis for novels and early reader fiction. That has changed somewhat in recent years; some editors want a query for fiction before they'll read anything more. Here are some of the distinctions in the queries and packages for nonfiction and fiction:

Nonfiction Query Package

A nonfiction package may include:

- a query or cover letter (see page 27 for which to use);

- a synopsis (see page 34);

- a detailed outline (topical or chapter) that describes each chapter's contents (see page 36);

- alternatively, a proposal that incorporates the synopsis, outline, and other information, such as the target audience (see page 37);

- representative chapters;

- a bibliography consisting of the books, periodicals, and other sources you have already used to research the project, and those that you will use, including expert sources and interviews (see page 38);

- a résumé (see page 39).

Fiction Query Package

A fiction query package may also contain any or all of the following:

- one- to two-page synopsis that briefly states the book's theme and the main character's conflict, then describes the plot, major characters, and ending;

- chapter-by-chapter synopsis consisting of one to two paragraphs (maximum) per chapter, describing the major scene or plot development of each chapter. Keep the synopsis as brief as possible. You may either single space or double space a synopsis (see page 35);

- the first three chapters (no more than 50 pages). Check the *Book Markets for Children's Writers'* listing and publisher's guidelines carefully, as some editors prefer to see only the first chapter.

Query Letter Checklist

Use this checklist to evaluate your query letter before you send it with the rest of your book proposal.

Basics:
- ☐ Address the letter to the current editor, or as directed in writers' guidelines or market listings (for example, Submissions Editor or Acquisitions Editor).
- ☐ Spell the editor's name correctly.
- ☐ Proofread the address, especially the numbers.

Opening:
- ☐ Create a hook—quote a passage from your manuscript, give an unusual fact or statistic, ask a question.

Body:
- ☐ Give a brief overview of what your book proposal is about, but do not duplicate the detailed information you give in the outline or synopsis.
- ☐ List your special qualifications or experience, publishing credits/organization memberships, and research sources.
- ☐ State whether you can or cannot supply artwork.

Closing:
- ☐ Provide a brief summation.
- ☐ Let the publisher know if this is an exclusive or simultaneous submission.

Last steps:
- ☐ Proofread for spelling and punctuation errors, including typos.
- ☐ Sign the letter.

Cover Letters

A cover letter accompanies a submitted manuscript and provides an overview of your fiction or nonfiction submission, but it does not go into the same level of detail as a query letter. A cover letter is a professional introduction to the materials attached. If you are attaching a large package of materials in your submission—a synopsis, outline, competition research, résumé, for example—you don't need a full-blown query, but a cover letter.

Cover letters range from a brief business format, stating, "Enclosed is a copy of my manuscript, (Insert Title), for your review" to something more. In a somewhat longer form, the letter may include information about your personal experience with the topic; your publication credits, if you have them; potential sources for artwork; and, if relevant, the fact that someone the editor knows and respects suggested you submit the manuscript.

A cover letter is always included when a manuscript is sent at the request of the editor or when it has been reworked following the editor's suggestions. The cover letter should remind the editor that he or she asked to see this manuscript. This can be accomplished with a simple phrase along the lines of "Thank you for requesting a copy of my manuscript, (Insert Title)." If you are going to be away or if it is easier to reach you at certain times or at certain phone numbers, include that information as well. Do not refer to your work as a book; it is a manuscript until it is published.

Many submissions are rejected because query and/or cover letters are poorly written and contain grammatical errors. Make sure your package is error-free, cleanly presented and readable, and includes an SASE (self-addressed, stamped envelope) for the publisher's reply.

Proposals

A proposal is a collection of information with thorough details on a book idea. Arguably, a query alone is a proposal, but here we'll consider the various other components that may go into a proposal package. Always consult—and follow to the letter—writers' guidelines to see what a publisher requires.

__Query or cover letter.__ The descriptions on pages 20–24 should help you construct your query or cover letter.

__Synopsis.__ A brief, clear description of the fiction or nonfiction project proposed, conveying the essence of the entire idea. A synopsis may be one or several paragraphs on the entire book, or it may be written in chapter-by-chapter format. Synopses should also convey a sense of your writing style, without getting wordy. See the samples on pages 34 and 35.

__Outline.__ A formally structured listing of the topics to be covered in a manuscript or book. Outlines may consist of brief phrases, or they may be annotated with one- or two-sentence descriptions of each element. See the sample on page 36.

Note that synopses are more common for fiction than outlines. Both outlines and synopses are sometimes used to describe nonfiction, but not necessarily both in the same proposal package.

__Competition/market research.__ The importance of researching other titles in the marketplace that might be competitive to yours was discussed earlier (pages 12–14). The presentation of this information to the editor might be in synopsis form or presented as an annotated bibliography.

__Bibliography.__ Bibliographies are important in nonfiction submissions, yet considerably less so with fiction, except possibly when writing in a genre such as historical fiction. A well-wrought bibliography can go a long way toward convincing an editor of the substance behind your proposal. Include primary sources, which are a necessity in children's nonfiction; book and periodical sources; Internet sources (but be particularly careful these are well-established); and expert sources you've interviewed or plan to interview. For format, use a style reference such as *Chicago Manual of Style, Modern Language Association*

(MLA) Handbook, or one of the major journalist references by organizations such as the *New York Times* or Associated Press. See the sample on page 38.

Résumé/publishing credits. Many publishers request a list of publishing credits or a résumé with submissions. The résumé introduces you to an editor by indicating your background and qualifications. An editor can judge from a résumé if a prospective writer has the necessary experience to research and write material for that publishing house. The résumé that you submit to a publisher is different from one you would submit when applying for a job, because it emphasizes writing experience, memberships in writing associations, and education. Include only those credentials that demonstrate experience related to the publisher's editorial requirements, not all of your work experience or every membership. In the case of educational or special interest publishers, be sure to include pertinent work experience.

No one style is preferable, but make sure your name, address, telephone number, and email address (if you have one) appear at the top of the page. Keep your résumé short and concise—it should not be more than a page long. If you have been published, those credits may be included on the one page, or listed on a separate sheet. See the sample on page 39.

Sample chapters or clips. As well-written as a query or even a synopsis might be, nothing can give an editor as clear a sense of your style, slant, and depth of the work you are proposing, or can do, than sample chapters or clips of published work. One of the obvious dilemmas of new writers is that they may not have clips, or they may be few and not suitable to a given proposal. But sample chapters, almost always the first and perhaps one or two others that are representative, help an editor make a judgment on your abilities and the project, or determine how to guide you in another direction—and toward a sale.

Query Letter v. Cover Letter

When to use a query letter:

- [ ] Always when a query is the specific requirement in the publisher's writers' guidelines.

- [ ] When you are including no other attached information; the query should be specific, but not exceed a single page.

- [ ] When you are attaching some additional materials, such as a synopsis or sample chapter.

When to use a cover letter:

- [ ] When an editor has requested that you send a specific manuscript and it is attached. The cover letter is a polite, professional reminder to the editor.

- [ ] When you have had previous interactions with an editor, who will know who you are. Perhaps you've written something for the editor before, or you had a conversation at a conference when the editor clearly suggested you send your work.

- [ ] When your proposal package is comprehensive, and explains your book completely enough that a cover letter is all that is needed to reiterate, very briefly, the nature of the proposal.

How to Write a Synopsis

H ow often have you decided to buy a book (or not buy it) based on its jacket or flap copy? This promotional copy has similar qualities to the synopsis, a boiled-down version of your book, anywhere from one to five pages, that highlights the major plot points and characters. In essence, the synopsis is an important sales tool that should convince an editor to take a chance on your work.

Whether your book is fiction or nonfiction, the synopsis does the same job: It informs editors of the complete plot of your fiction book or the complete scope of your nonfiction book, and helps them to determine if they are interested in reviewing the manuscript. Note that the description is *complete*. Although a query letter for fiction usually only alludes to the ending for purposes of enticing the editor, a synopsis should answer all questions and show an editor that your project has a well thought-out story arc.

A **fiction synopsis** should describe:
- What your characters want
- What obstacles they face in getting what they want
- How they solve the problem

A **nonfiction synopsis** should describe:
- The main point of the book
- The content of your supporting argument
- Why you are the best person to write the book

Writing a synopsis often poses a challenge: How much detail should you include? As you write about the pivotal scenes or major points of your manuscript, try to strike a balance between including too much detail and not enough. For example, avoid in-depth character descriptions or detailed accounts of every scene, but do mention a particular characteristic if it will help the reader to better understand the character's actions. A synopsis that is all generalizations will do little to entice the editor and/or make your manuscript stand out.

Remember, the synopsis should show off your skills as a writer and storyteller, so the same techniques you used to write the story are just as handy for crafting a synopsis that sells.

Sample Query Letter – Fiction

Street Address
City, State Zip
Telephone Number
Email Address
Date

Beth Parker
Mountain Press Publishing
P.O. Box 2399
Missoula, MT 59806

Dear Ms. Parker:

Opener/ Hook — Would you be willing to look at my 32-page picture book manuscript entitled *Where's Blind Tom Today?* It is the true story of a horse that played a role in building the transcontinental railroad from Omaha, Nebraska, to Promontory Point, Utah. This tale about an obscure, all-American "horse hero" has child appeal and would be marketable to adult "trainiacs" at the nearly 300 railroad museums in the United States with bookstores/gift shops. It is <u>not</u> anthropomorphized, and the title's query was the telegraph operators' way of asking how many miles of track had been laid each day.

Synopsis

Market Analysis — Currently, there are no children's books about Blind Tom on the market. Other titles about the building of the railroad are chapter books for older readers, such as *The Transcontinental Railroad* by Elaine Landau (Franklin Watts, 2005) and *Railroad Fever* (National Geographic Books, 2004). *Full Steam Ahead* by Blumberg and *10-Day Mile* by Fraser were both published in 1996 and are now out of print.

Experience — I have several nonfiction books in stores now. *Patriots in Petticoats: Heroines of the American Revolution* (Random House) was named one of the best children's books of 2005 by the Bank Street College of Education in New York. *Lewis & Clark: A Prairie Dog for the President* (Random Step Into Reading) has sold more than 130,000 copies and is recommended by the Lewis & Clark Trail Association.

I am a professional member of the Society of Children's Book Writers and Illustrators, Women Writing the West, the Albuquerque chapter of Sisters in Crime, Southwest Writers, the Alamos Historical Society, and the New Mexico Book Association.

Sincerely,

Shirley Raye Redmond

Sample Query Letter – Nonfiction

Street Address
City, State Zip
Telephone Number
Email Address
Date

Morning Glory Press
6595 San Haroldo Way
Buena Park, CA 90620

Dear Ms. Lindsey:

Opener/ Hook

Reading is the cornerstone of education. Children who read well are more likely to be successful students. Parents want their children to become good readers, but they often don't know the steps to take to make this dream a reality. My 5,200-word self-help manuscript, *Listen to Me, I Can Read: Tips Mom and Dad Can Use to Help Me Become a Lifelong Reader*, is a practical guide for parents to use with children from birth to young adulthood. The humorous text is written from the perspective of a child. The advice is divided into four categories: baby and toddler, preschooler, little kid reader, and big kid reader.

Subject/ Reader Appeal

Credits/ Special Experience

I worked as a classroom teacher and later as a librarian in an elementary school for twenty-seven years. Recently, I have conducted workshops on literacy, instructing parent volunteers, teaching assistants, and teachers. I am also an author of children's picture books and make numerous school presentations. If this manuscript is accepted for publication, I will market it through schools, workshops, and educational conventions.

Parents often request information, such as the tips in this manuscript, to use with their children, and teachers request the same information to pass along to parents. Several markets exist for this type of book. Many hospitals give packages to parents of newborns. This book would be a great addition to those packages. When children enter kindergarten and preschool, parents are invited to an open house in which they are given educational packages. Head Start programs, Montessori schools, and day care centers may also be interested, as well as gift shops. I know of no other book on the market that deals with the subject of literacy using the fresh approach of this manuscript: a child appealing to the parents. The federally funded "No Child Left Behind Act" requires schools to make literacy a top priority. Many schools would endorse this book.

Closing

If this manuscript meets your editorial needs, please contact me at the following:

Sincerely,

Nancy Kelly Allen

Sample Cover Letter – Nonfiction

Street Address
City, State Zip
Telephone Number
Email Address
Date

Attn: Children's Book Division
Tate Publishing
127 East Trade Center Terrace
Mustang, OK 73604

To Whom It May Concern:

Opener/ Subject

Have you ever watched a dog while it sleeps? Do you wonder if a dog has dreams just like you and I? Enclosed is a story that offers a humorously entertaining approach to this interesting question. Every page of this book allows for vibrant illustrations that will surely appeal to any child's imagination.

Market/ Appeal

    The title of my story is *WHAT DO DOGS DREAM ABOUT?* It contains 150 words with a projected target age of 4–8 years. Professional artwork from an established artist is available depending on your interest in the style depicted in the attached, rough illustrations.

Closing

    Thank you for considering my manuscript. I am enclosing a self-addressed, stamped envelope for your convenience in replying.

Sincerely,

Mike Dyson

Enc: SASE

Sample Cover Letter – Fiction

Street Address
City, State Zip
Telephone Number
Email Address
Date

Karen Fisk
Associate Children's Book Editor
Tilbury House Publishers
2 Mechanic Street #3
Gardiner, ME 04345

Dear Ms. Fisk:

Opener/ — Enclosed please find my 1,030-word picture book entitled THE LUNCH
Hook THIEF. It is a contemporary realistic story about an eleven-year-old boy
named Rafael who gets justifiably angry with "the new kid" at school who
steals lunches. However, this story is really about learning how to make a
Synopsis — friend rather than punish an enemy. I think it will be a good fit for your list,
appealing to children and parents both as a story and as a "lesson" in looking
beyond appearances.

Closing — Thank you for taking the time to read my work. Please feel free to contact me
if you are interested. Enclosed is an SASE for your reply only. It is not necessary to return the manuscript.

Sincerely,

Experience — Anne C. Bromley
Member, SCBWI San Diego Chapter

Enc: manuscript
    SASE

Sample Query Letter – Fiction

Street Address
City, State Zip
Telephone Number
Email Address
Date

Emma Dryden, Associate Publisher
Margaret K. McElderry Books
Simon & Schuster Children's Publishing Division
1230 Avenue of the Americas
New York, NY 10020

Dear Ms. Dryden,

Opener/ Subject

I would very much like you to meet Jamie and Kyle, two brothers with a solid friendship and a shared passion for their make-believe cowboy world. Just when the boys think their backyard "cattle drive" is under control, the neighbors' dog invades their territory. While Bogie's friendly presence is fun at first, the dog proceeds to hog the cowboys' bedrolls, and sinks his teeth into Kyle's favorite toy. How will the boys handle this "coyote" in their midst? And how will they protect their ranch from another invasion?

Synopsis

This picture book, COWPOKES, COWS AND COYOTES, portrays kids making their own fun and cooperating in creative ways. And tarnation! It's just full o' fun cowboy words to boot! I am very hopeful that you would find it has the right tone and matches the quality of other books on your list. I should alert you that this is a multiple submission, but I will have it under consideration by just a few publishers at any one time.

perience

I have published articles in *Boys' Quest*; *Wee Ones*; *Cecil Child*; *Babybug*; and *Dragonfly Spirit*.

Closing

My manuscript is complete and ready to be sent should you be interested in looking at it. I have enclosed an SASE for your convenience.

Sincerely,

Lisa Bierman

Sample Synopsis – Nonfiction

Name   Address, Telephone, Email

Storms

Chapter One: How Storms Form

Defines a storm as a mass of rapidly moving air that redistributes
energy from the sun's heat. Discusses air currents, including the Jet Stream,
and their patterns of movement across the Earth. Explains that storms begin
when warm, moist air meets cold, dry air and discusses the role that the
sharp boundary, or front, formed at this meeting place has in the creation of
storms.

Chapter Two: Rainstorms, Snowstorms, and Thunderstorms

Provides information about clouds and their moisture, explaining how
rain, snow, and hail are produced. Describes the processes by which thunder
and lightning are created. Talks about weather forecasting and storm
watches and warnings. Discusses how winds influence the severity of
storms, identifying the terms gale, blizzard, and cyclone.

Chapter Three: Hurricanes and Typhoons

Explains that hurricanes and typhoons are tropical cyclones. Talks about
the formation of hurricanes and typhoons as well as "the eye of the storm."
Discusses the effects of these storms on the environment. Gives examples
of major hurricane damage and reports on scientists' attempts to study and
predict the severity of hurricanes. As part of this discussion, provides
information about the hurricane naming system, the Saffir-Simpson
Damage-Potential Scale, hurricane watches and warnings, and hurricane
safety.

Chapter Four: Tornadoes

Defines the term tornado and reports that they are the product of
middle-latitude storms as opposed to tropical storms. Describes the
formation of a tornado and mentions some of the most significant tornadoes
in history. Discusses scientists' attempts to study and predict the severity of
tornadoes, providing information about storm chasers, the Fujita Tornado
Intensity Scale, tornado watches and warnings, and tornado safety.

Sample Synopsis – Fiction

TWO MOON PRINCESS
by Carmen Ferreiro

Wishing to be the heir her father the king has always wanted, Princess Andrea trains to be a knight. But the king laughs at her efforts and sends her to her mother to be made into a lady. Andrea sulks. She finds the ladies' company boring, their manners puzzling. To make matters worse, the queen, offended by Andrea's behavior, forbids her to attend the ball that her sisters claim would have changed her view of the world. Andrea has had enough, and when that very night she learns of the existence of a parallel universe, she happily leaves her parents' castle and crosses the door into the other world: present day California.

Andrea loves California and wants to stay forever. But when by mistake she returns to her kingdom and brings a Californian boy with her, the balance of her world is upset and war breaks out. Andrea leaves the castle once more in search of the enemy king, don Julian. While she tries to convince him to negotiate, don Julian is shot trying to protect her. Bound by her conscience to save his life, Andrea defies her father and, swallowing her pride, asks her mother for help.

In a desperate effort to end the war, Andrea puts her life at risk by taking don Julian back to his kingdom. Although her plan succeeds and she has gained her parents' respect, Andrea is haunted by the cruelties of the battle she has witnessed and her grief for don Julian. She questions her wish to be a warrior, and finally accepts her role as a lady. However, the unexpected arrival of don Julian at the castle shatters her apathy and reawakens her dreams. But this time Andrea knows that leaving will not solve her problems, and she refuses to run away. Instead she confronts her mother and openly fights for the right to be herself.

Sample Outline – Nonfiction

SWEAT THE SMALL STUFF:
STRATEGIES FOR WINNING SCIENCE PROJECTS
Outline

INTRODUCTION

CHAPTER 1: "Why Do I Have to Learn This Stuff?"
The Benefits of Participating in Science Research and Science Fairs
Opportunities Beyond School or Local Competition

CHAPTER 2: In the Beginning
Questions to Ask Yourself to Evaluate a Topic
Pitfalls to Avoid: Is My Project Possible? Is It Safe?
ISEF Categories

CHAPTER 3: There's a Method to this Madness
Basic Definitions of the Elements of a Project
Keeping an Exact Record—the Logbook
Recording the Results

CHAPTER 4: Who, What, Where, When, and How
How to Write Your Research Paper
Knowing When to Stop
Putting It Together in One Page: The Abstract

CHAPTER 5: Murphy's Law of Science Research: If Anything Can Go Wrong, It Will
Establishing a Timeline
Using Proper Safety
Have a Back-up Plan

CHAPTER 6: What's Green, Glows in the Dark, and Is Growing on My Project?
Using Sterile Technique
Inoculation Techniques
Precautions When Working with Biological Hazards

CHAPTER 7: Data Isn't Just a Star Trek Character
Statistics

CHAPTER 8: Misteaks, Mistaxe, Mistackes, Mistakes
Common Errors

Sample Proposal – Nonfiction

Name
Address
City, State Zip
Date

Proposal for Millbrook Press
"Invisible Invaders: New and Dangerous Infectious Diseases"

By the middle of the 20th century, it seemed like most infectious diseases were a thing of the past. However, over the past 30 years, nearly three dozen new or re-emerging infectious diseases have started to spread among humans. Each year, 1,500 people die of an infectious disease, and half of those people are children under five years old. In the United States alone, the death rate from infectious disease has doubled since 1980.

Invisible Invaders: New and Dangerous Infectious Diseases will be an addition to the Medical Library, the Millbrook/Twenty-First Century Press series on health issues. The Centers for Disease Control and Prevention and the National Institute of Allergy and Infectious Diseases have identified 35 emerging or re-emerging diseases as serious threats to human health. The book will cover the infectious diseases with the greatest real and potential impact to Americans. It will discuss why so many infectious diseases are threatening world health and where the diseases come from. The alarming appearance of new strains of organisms that are becoming ever more resistant to antibiotics will be covered, as will the potential use of deadly microbes and bioterrorism.

One children's book about epidemics that was published in 2000 blithely announced the eradication of smallpox in the world. Yet today, the government is making contingency plans to vaccinate millions of Americans should a bioterrorist release a deadly virus. Other books fail to mention Hantavirus, West Nile Virus, or Severe Acute Respiratory Syndrome, diseases recently threatening the health and lives of Americans. Clearly, a new children's book on the subject of infectious diseases is needed.

Invisible Invaders will consist of about 25,000 words, or approximately 115 pages of text interspersed with art. It will be written for children ages 7–10 to fit into the Medical Library series format. Each section will include information about the origin and spread of the disease, its symptoms, and treatment. With knowledge comes the power to help prevent or avoid these diseases, so the text will also cover appropriate steps that young readers can follow to decrease their risk. Case studies and pertinent sidebars enhance the text.

The author will use the latest information from prestigious organizations like the CDC, World Health Organization, National Institutes of Health, the American Public Health Association, the Infectious Diseases Society of America, and the Institute of Medicine.

Sample Bibliography

Bibliography

Blind Tom

<u>The Great and Shining Road: The Epic Story of the Transcontinental Railroad</u>
John Hoyt Williams
Times Books, Random House, NY 1988

<u>The Horse in America</u>
Robert West Howard
Follett Publishing Company
Chicago and New York, 1965

<u>The American Heritage History of Railroads</u>
Oliver Jensen
Bonanza Books, NY 1975

<u>American Railroads</u>
John F. Stover
University of Chicago Press
2nd edition 1997

<u>American Railroads of the Nineteenth Century: A Pictorial History in Victorian Wood Engravings</u>
Jim Harter
Texas Tech Univ. Press, Lubbock, 1998

<u>Nothing Like It in the World</u>
Stephen Ambrose
Simon & Schuster, NY 2000

Sample Résumé

Ann Purmell
Address
Telephone Number
Email

Experience

- Writer of inspirational and children's literature.
- Freelance journalist and feature writer for *Jackson Citizen Patriot* (Michigan), a Booth Communications daily. Affiliate newspapers throughout Michigan carry my articles.
- Freelance writer for *Jackson Magazine,* a monthly business publication.
- Guest lecturer for Children's Literature and Creative Writing classes at Spring Arbor College, Spring Arbor, Michigan.
- Performs school presentations for all grade levels.

Publications/Articles

Published numerous articles, including:

- "Prayers to the Dead," *In Other Words: An American Poetry Anthology* (Western Reading Services, 1998).
- "Promises Never Die," *Guideposts for Teens* (June/July 1999). Ghost-written, first-person, true story.
- "Teaching Kids the Financial Facts of Life," *Jackson Citizen Patriot* (July 20, 1999). An interview with Jayne A. Pearl, author of *Kids and Money.*
- "New Rules for Cider? Small Presses Might Be Put Out of Business," *Jackson Citizen Patriot* (December 12, 1999).
- "Jackson Public Schools Prepare for Change: Technology, Ideas Shaping Education," *Jackson Magazine* (December 1999). An interview with Dan Evans, Superintendent of Jackson Public Schools.

Education

- B.S., Nursing, Eastern Michigan University.
- Post-B.A. work, elementary education, Spring Arbor College.
- Highlights Foundation Chautauqua Conference, summer 1999.

Sample Manuscript Pages

Title Page

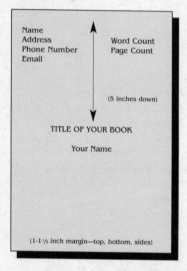

Name
Address
Phone Number
Email

Word Count
Page Count

(5 inches down)

TITLE OF YOUR BOOK

Your Name

(1-1½ inch margin—top, bottom, sides)

New Chapter

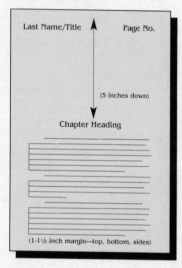

Last Name/Title

Page No.

(5 inches down)

Chapter Heading

(1-1½ inch margin—top, bottom, sides)

Following Pages

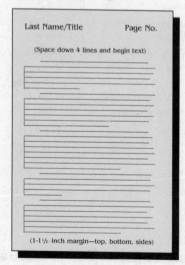

Last Name/Title

Page No.

(Space down 4 lines and begin text)

(1-1½ inch margin—top, bottom, sides)

Manuscript Preparation

Prepare and mail your manuscript according to the following guidelines:

- Use high-quality 8½x11 white bond paper.

- Double-space manuscript text; leave 1- to 1½-inch margins on the top, bottom, and sides. (See page 40.)

- Send typewritten pages or letter-quality printouts. You may send a computer disk if the publisher requests one.

- *Title Page.* In the upper left corner, type your name, address, phone number, and email address.

  In the upper right corner, type your word count, rounded to the nearest 10 to 25 words. For anything longer than a picture book, you may also type the number of pages. (Don't count the title page.) Center and type your title (using capital letters) about 5 inches from the top of the page with your byline two lines below it.

  Start your text on the next page. (Note: if this is a picture book or board book, see pages 43–44.)

- *Following Pages.* Type your last name and one or two key words of your title in the upper left corner, and the page number in the upper right. Begin new chapters halfway down the page.

- *Cover Letter.* Include a brief cover letter following the guidelines on page 24.

Mailing Requirements

- Assemble pages unstapled. Place cover letter on top of title page. Mail in a 9x12 or 10x13 manila envelope. Include a same-sized SASE marked "First Class." If submitting to a publisher outside the U.S., enclose an International Reply Coupon (IRC) for return postage.

- To ensure that your manuscript arrives safely, include a self-addressed, stamped postcard the editor can return upon receipt.

- Mail your submissions First Class or Priority. Do not use certified or registered mail.

Email Submissions

Publishers are increasingly open to receiving submissions and queries through email; in some cases it is their preferred method of submission. Whatever your personal preference may be, read the publishers' guidelines carefully to determine the best way to contact them. If you do submit by email, prepare your query as carefully as if it was a traditional "mail in." Pay special attention to style and presentation, elements that are often overlooked in email submissions. Other things to consider are:

- *__File attachments.__* Some publishers prefer that the body of the email be used as a cover letter, with supporting documents—including the synopsis, outline, etc.—attached as separate files. In other cases, queries may be included in the main body of the email.

- *__Electronic format.__* Rich text format (RTF) and Microsoft Word are most commonly used for sending documents electronically; postscript and PDF files are also sometimes accepted. If you're not computer savvy, take time to learn what these options are and what your target publisher wants.

- *__Contact information.__* Don't forget to include your contact information—traditional mailing address and telephone as well as email address—in the body of your email, as well as the full title of your work. If your email has attachments, briefly describe the attachments by file name as part of your cover letter.

- *__Subject line.__* To ensure that your email is read, follow the publisher's guidelines for describing the content of your message, which sometimes includes the title of your work and/or your name, i.e. 'Submission—My Bestseller,' or the word 'Query,' as well as other information.

Email queries should be shorter than traditional "paper" queries, so that they fit on an editor's computer screen with minimal scrolling. To make sure your message is readable in most email programs: 1) use block-style paragraphs rather than indents, 2) break up large paragraphs into smaller chunks for easy reading, and 3) avoid using any special fonts or formatting.

Picture Book Submissions

Most editors will accept a complete manuscript for a picture book without an initial query. Because a picture book text may contain as few as 20 words and seldom exceeds 1,500 words, it is difficult to judge if not seen in its entirety. Do not submit your own artwork unless you are a professional artist; editors prefer to use illustrators of their own choosing.

Prepare the manuscript following the guidelines for the title page on page 40. Drop down four lines from the byline, indent, and begin your manuscript on the title page. Type it straight through as if it were a short story. Do not indicate page breaks.

Keep in mind that description is conveyed largely through illustrations, not text. Keep descriptive details to a minimum, and make sure that your manuscript provides a variety of lively illustration opportunities.

The average picture book is 32 pages, although it may be as short as 16 pages or as long as 64 pages, depending on the age of the intended audience. To make a dummy for a 32-page book, take eight sheets of paper, fold them in half, and number them as the sample indicates; this will not include the end papers. (Each sheet makes up four pages of your book.) Lay out your text and rough sketches or a brief description of the accompanying illustrations. Move these around and adjust your concept of the artwork until you are satisfied that words and pictures fit together as they should.

Do not submit your dummy unless the editor asks for it. Simply submit your text on separate sheets of paper, typed double-spaced, following the format guidelines given on page 40. If you do choose to submit artwork as well, be sure to send copies only; editors will rarely take responsibility for original artwork. Be sure to include a self-addressed, stamped envelope (SASE) large enough for the return of your entire package.

Picture Book Dummy

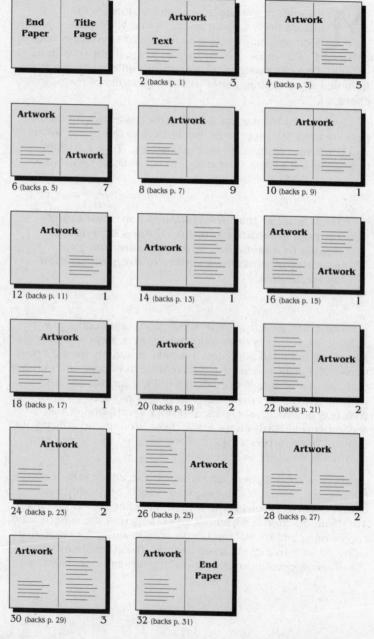

End Paper	Title Page

1

Artwork / Text / Artwork
2 (backs p. 1)   3

Artwork
4 (backs p. 3)   5

Artwork / Artwork
6 (backs p. 5)   7

Artwork
8 (backs p. 7)   9

Artwork
10 (backs p. 9)   1

Artwork
12 (backs p. 11)   1

Artwork
14 (backs p. 13)   1

Artwork / Artwork
16 (backs p. 15)   1

Artwork
18 (backs p. 17)   1

Artwork
20 (backs p. 19)   2

Artwork
22 (backs p. 21)   2

Artwork
24 (backs p. 23)   2

Artwork
26 (backs p. 25)   2

Artwork
28 (backs p. 27)   2

Artwork
30 (backs p. 29)   3

Artwork / End Paper
32 (backs p. 31)

44

Step-by-Step through the Business of Publishing

Book Contracts

Once an editor is interested in buying your work, he or she will send a book contract for your review and signature. While book contracts vary in length and precise language from publisher to publisher, the basic provisions of these contracts are generally similar. All writers should understand publishing contract standards, know enough to acknowledge an offer as appropriate, and recognize when there may be room to negotiate. Remember, the agreement isn't complete until you sign the contract.

In Plain English

The best advice for your first contract reading is not to let the legal terminology distract you. A book contract is a complex legal document that is designed to protect you and the publisher. It defines the rights, responsibilities, and financial terms of the author, publisher, and artist (when necessary).

Because some publishers issue standard contracts and rarely change wording or payment rates for new writers, you may not need an agent or a lawyer with book-publishing experience to represent you in the negotiation of the contract. But if you choose to negotiate the contract yourself, it is advisable that you read several reference books about book contracts and have a lawyer, preferably with book-contract experience, look it over prior to signing the agreement.

In either case, you should be familiar enough with the basic premises of the contract to communicate what items you would like to change in the document. For your protection, reread the contract at every stage of negotiation.

In the following section, you'll find a primer on the basic provisions of a book contract. If a statement in your contract is not covered or remains unclear to you, ask the editor or an attorney to "translate" the clauses into plain English.

Rights and Responsibilities

A standard book contract specifies what an author and a publisher each agree to do to produce the book and place it in the marketplace. It explicitly states copyright ownership, royalty, advance, delivery date, territorial and subsidiary rights, and other related provisions.

Grant of Rights

A clause early in the contract says that, on signing, the author agrees to "grant and assign" or "convey and transfer" to the publisher all or certain specified rights to a book. You thus authorize, or license, the publisher to publish your work.

Subsidiary rights are negotiated in a contract. These rights include where a book is distributed, in what language it is printed, and in what format it is published. While most publishers want world English-language rights, some publishers will consent to retaining rights only in the United States, the Philippines, Canada, and U.S. dependencies. With the United Kingdom now part of the European Community, more and more publishers want British publication rights, in English, so they can sell books to other members of the European Community.

Other subsidiary rights often included in contracts are:

Reprint Rights: These consist of publishing the work in magazines (also known as serial rights), book club editions, and hardcover or paperback versions.

Mechanical Rights: These cover audio and video cassettes, photocopying, filmstrips, and other mechanical production media.

Electronic or Computer Rights: These include rights to cover potential use on software programs, multimedia packages, CD-ROMs, online services, etc.

Dramatic Rights: These include versions of the work for film, television, etc.

Translation Rights: These allow a work to be printed in languages other than English.

If you don't have an agent, you may want to assign a publisher broad rights since you may not have the necessary connections or experience to sell them on your own.

If possible, seek a time limit that a publisher has to use subsidiary rights. That way certain rights will revert to you if the publisher has not sold them within a specific period.

Copyright Ownership

According to the Copyright Term Extension Act of 1998, you now own all rights to work you created during or after 1978 for your lifetime plus 70 years, until you choose to sell all or part of the copyright in very specific ways. According to this law, your idea is not copyrighted; it is your unique combination of words—how you wrote something—that this law protects and considers copyrighted. A separate clause in a book contract states that you retain the copyright in your name.

Once you complete your manuscript, your work is protected. You don't need to register your work, published or unpublished, with the United States Copyright Office. In most contract agreements, a publisher is responsible for registering the published version of your work. Writers who provide a copyright notice on their submitted manuscript may be viewed as amateurs by many editors. However, registration does offer proof of ownership and a clear legal basis in case of infringement. If you decide to register your work, obtain an application form and directions on the correct way to file your copyright application. Write to the Library of Congress, Copyright Office, 101 Independence Ave. S. E., Washington, DC 20559-6000 or download them in Adobe Acrobat format at: www.copyright.gov/forms. Copyright registration fees are currently $45 for paper applications; $35 for online filing.

If you have registered your unpublished manuscript with the Library of Congress, notify your publisher of that fact once your book is accepted for publication.

Manuscript Delivery

A publishing contract sets a due date by which you must complete and deliver an acceptable manuscript of the length specified in your contract. This clause allows a publisher time to request editorial changes, permits editing of the manuscript with your review and approval, establishes editorial schedules, and indicates how many author's alterations (also known as editorial changes) you may make without cost after the book has been typeset.

Warranty and Indemnification

You will be asked to ensure that the manuscript is your original work; that it contains nothing libelous, obscene, or private; and that it does not infringe on any copyright. The clause also stipulates that the author must pay the publisher's court costs and damages should it be sued over the book. This should not be an issue to the author who has exercised reasonable caution and written in good faith.

Though publishers are often reluctant to change this provision, you should still seek to limit the scope of warranty clauses. Include the phrase "to the best of the writer's knowledge" in your warranty agreement. Don't agree to pay for client's damages or attorney's fees and put a ceiling on your liability—perhaps the fee agreed upon for the assignment.

Also remember that many publishers carry their own insurance and can sometimes include writers under their house policy.

Obligation to Publish

The publisher agrees to produce and distribute the book in a timely manner, generally between one and two years. The contract should specify the time frame and indicate that if the publisher fails to publish the book within that period, the rights return to you (reversion of rights) and you keep any money already received.

Option

The option clause requires the author to offer the publisher the first chance at his or her next book. To avoid a prolonged decision-making process, try to negotiate a set period for the publisher's review of a second book, perhaps 60 or 90 days from submission of the second manuscript. Also stipulate that the publisher acquire your next book on terms to be mutually agreed upon by both parties. In this way, you have room to negotiate a more favorable deal.

Payment

Calculations for the amount of money an author receives as an advance or in royalties are fairly standardized.

Advance: An advance is money the writer receives in a lump sum or installments when a manuscript is accepted or delivered. It is like a loan paid "against" royalties coming from anticipated profits.

Royalty: A royalty is a percentage of sales paid to the author. It is based either on a book's retail price or on net receipts (the price actually received by the publisher), and it may be fixed or arranged on a sliding scale. For example, standard royalty may be 10% for the first 5,000 copies, 12.5% for the next 5,000 copies, and 15% thereafter. Royalties range anywhere from 2% to 10% or higher, depending on the publisher and the author's publishing history.

Depending on the extent of artwork and who supplied it to the publisher, author and artist may divide royalties or the artist may be paid a flat fee.

Accounting Statements: The publisher must provide the author with earning statements for the book. Most companies provide statements and checks semiannually, three or more months after each accounting period ends. Be sure to determine exactly when that is. For example, if the accounting periods end June 30 and December 31, you should receive statements by October 1 and April 1.

Flat Rate: Instead of paying royalties, some book packagers and smaller publishers offer a fixed amount or flat rate in return for all rights or as part of a work-for-hire agreement. This amount is paid upon completion of the book.

Traditionally, work-for-hire means that the publisher becomes the 'author' of the work for copyright purposes. More prevalent among school and library publishers and book packagers, this type of agreement has advantages and disadvantages that you should weigh before signing.

Before You Sign . . .

The explanations presented here include suggestions for a reasonable and (we hope) profitable approach to your book contract. Every situation presents distinct alternatives, however. Your agreement with a publisher must be undertaken in good faith on both sides and you should feel comfortable with the deal you strike. When in doubt, consult an expert for advice.

You can find additional information about copyrights and publishing law in *The Copyright Handbook: What Every Writer Needs to Know* (ninth ed.) by Stephen Fishman (Nolo Press, 2006), *The Writer's Legal Guide* (third edition) by Tad Crawford (Allworth Press, 2002), and *Every Writer's Guide to Copyright and Publishing Law* by Ellen Kozak (Owl Books, 2004).

A Note About Self, Subsidy, and Co-op Publishing Options

When you self-publish your book, you assume the cost of and responsibility for printing and distributing your book. In contrast, subsidy presses handle—for a fee—the production and, to some degree, the marketing and distribution of a writer's book. Co-op or joint-venture publishers assume responsibility for marketing and distribution of a book, while the author pays some or all of the production costs.

A newer incarnation of self-publishing is print on demand (POD), a type of printing technology that allows companies to print and bind your book in a matter of minutes. This makes it easy and cost-effective to publish books individually or in small lots, rather than investing in print runs of hundreds of books—letting you publish your work on a shoestring. POD books, however, are more expensive to produce than books done by traditional offset printing.

Another technology that's appeared as a result of the Internet boom is electronic books. Authors can publish their work without the cost of printing and binding by distributing their books in the form of computer files—Adobe PDF files are typically used.

Aside from the actual production of your book, marketing is an integral part of the self-publishing process. Many large booksellers—and consumers—are wary of buying self-published titles, making sales and marketing an even bigger hurdle. Self-published authors must handle all marketing and promotional tasks on their own, which can be complex and costly. The most common marketing options include targeted direct mail advertising, web advertising, and sending out review copies. Electronic books benefit from services such as Booklocker.com, which distributes ebooks for a modest fee.

Based on your own needs and expectations, you may choose to try one of these approaches. If you do, exercise caution. Be sure you understand the terms of any contract, including exactly how much you will be required to pay, the marketing and distributing services the publisher is promising (if any), and the rights you are retaining. Also, check out *Dan Poynter's Self-Publishing Manual: How to Write, Print, and Sell Your Own Book* (16th edition, Para Publishing, 2007) for a good overview of self-publishing. If you decide to take this route, it is advisable to consult a lawyer before entering into any arrangement.

Postage Information

When you send a manuscript to a publisher, always enclose a return SASE with sufficient postage; this way, if the editor does not want to use your manuscript, it can be returned to you. To help you calculate the proper amount of postage for your SASE, here are the U.S. postal rates for first-class mailings in the U.S. and from the U.S. to Canada based on the May 2009 increase.

Ounces	8½x11 Pages (approx pgs)	U.S. 1st-Class Postage Rate	U.S. to Canada
5	21–25	$1.56	$2.07
6	26–30	1.73	2.33
7	31–35	1.90	2.59
8	36–40	2.07	2.85
9	41–45	2.24	2.85
10	46–50	2.41	2.85
11	51–55	2.58	2.85
12	56+	2.75	3.83

How to Obtain Stamps

People living in the U.S., Canada, or overseas can acquire U.S. stamps through the mail from the Stamp Fulfillment Service Center: call 800-STAMP-24 (800-782-6724) to request a catalogue or place an order. For overseas, the telephone number is 816-545-1000. You pay the cost of the stamps plus a postage and handling fee based on the value of the stamps ordered, and the stamps are shipped to you. Credit card information (MasterCard, VISA, and Discover cards only) is required for fax orders. The fax number is 816-545-1212. If you order through the catalogue, you can pay with a U.S. check or an American money order. Allow 3–4 weeks for delivery.

Frequently Asked Questions

How do I request a publisher's catalogue and writers' guidelines?

Write a brief note to the publishing company: "Please send me a recent catalogue and writers' guidelines. If there is any charge please enclose an invoice and I will pay upon receipt." The publisher's website, if it has one, offers a faster and less expensive alternative. Many companies put their catalogues, or at least their latest releases and their writers' guidelines, on the Internet.

Do I need an agent?

There is no correct answer to this question. Some writers are very successful marketing their own work, while others feel more comfortable having an agent handle that end of the business. It's a personal decision, but if you decide to work through an agent, be an "informed consumer." Get a list of member agents from the Association of Authors' Representatives, 676A 9th Avenue, #312, New York, NY 10036 or check it out online at www.aar-online.org.

I need to include a bibliography with my book proposal. How do I set one up?

The reference section of your local library can provide several sources that will help you set up a bibliography. A style manual such as the *Chicago Manual of Style* will show you the proper format for citing all your sources, including unpublished material, interviews, and Internet material.

What do I put in a cover letter if I have no publishing credits or relevant personal experience?

In this case you may want to forego a formal cover letter and send your manuscript with a brief letter stating, "Enclosed is my manuscript, (Insert Title), for your review." For more information on cover letters see page 24.

I don't need my manuscript returned. How do I indicate that to an editor?

With the capability to store manuscripts electronically, some writers keep postage costs down by enclosing a self-addressed stamped postcard (SASP) saying, "No need to return my manuscript. Please use this postcard to advise me of the status of my manuscript. Thank you."

Do I need to register or copyright my manuscript?

Once completed, your work is automatically protected by copyright. When your manuscript is accepted for publication, the publisher will register it for you.

Should I submit my manuscript on disk?

Do not send your manuscript on disk unless the publisher's submission guidelines note that this is an acceptable format.

When a publisher says "query with sample chapters," how do I know which chapters to send? Should they be chapters in sequence or does that matter? And how many should I send?

If the publisher does not specify which chapters it wishes to see, then it's your decision. Usually it's a good idea to send the first chapter, but if another chapter gives a flavor of your book or describes a key action in the plot, include that one. You may also want to send the final chapter of the book. For nonfiction, if one chapter is more fully representative of the material your book will cover, include that. Send two to three but if the guidelines state "sample chapter" (singular), just send one.

How long should I wait before contacting an editor after I have submitted my manuscript?

The response time given in the listings can vary, and it's a good idea to wait at least a few weeks after the allocated response time before you send a brief note to the editor asking about the status of your manuscript. If you do not get a satisfactory response or you want to send your manuscript elsewhere, send a certified letter to the editor withdrawing your work from consideration and requesting its return. You are then free to submit the work to another publishing house.

A long time ago, in 1989, I was fortunate enough to have a picture book published. If I write a query letter, should I include that information? It seems to me that it may hurt more than it helps, since I have not published anything since that.

By all means include it, though you need not mention the year it was published. Any publishing credit is worth noting, particularly if it is a picture book, because it shows you succeeded in a highly competitive field.

How do I address the editor, especially if she is female (e.g., Dear Miss, Dear Ms., Dear Mrs., Dear Editor-in-Chief, or what)?

There is no accepted preference, so the choice is really yours, but in general Ms. is used most frequently. Do use the person's last name, not his or her first. Before you decide which title to use, make sure you know if the person you are addressing is male or female.

If a publisher does not specify that "multiple submissions" are okay, does that imply they are not okay?

If a publisher has a firm policy against multiple submissions, this is usually stated in its guidelines. If not mentioned, the publisher probably does not have a hard and fast rule. If you choose to send a multiple submission, make sure to indicate that on your submission. Then it's up to the publisher to contact you if it prefers not to receive such submissions.

Publishing Terms

Advance: initial payment by publisher to author against future sales

Agent: professional who contacts editors and negotiates book contracts on author's behalf

All rights: an outright sale of your material; author has no further control over it

Anthropomorphization: attributing human form and personality to things not human, for example, animals

Backlist: list of publisher's titles that were not produced this season but are still in print

Beginning readers: children ages 4 to 7 years

Book contract: legal agreement between author and publisher

Book packager/producer: company that handles all elements of producing a book and then sells the final product to a publisher

Book proposal: see **Proposal**

Caldecott Medal: annual award that honors the illustrator of the current year's most distinguished children's book

CD-ROM: (compact-disc read-only memory) non-erasable electronic medium used for digitalized image and document storage

Clean-copy: a manuscript ready for typesetting; it is free of errors and needs no editing

Clip: sample of a writer's published work. See also **Tearsheet**

Concept book: category of picture book for children 2 to 7 years that teaches an idea (i.e., alphabet or counting) or explains a problem

Contract: see **Book contract**

Co-op publishing: author assumes some or all of the production costs and publisher handles all marketing and distribution; also referred to as "joint-venture publishing"

Copyedit: to edit with close attention to style and mechanics

Copyright: legal protection of an author's work

Cover letter: brief introductory letter sent with a manuscript

Disk submission: manuscript that is submitted on a computer disk

Distributor: company that buys and resells books from a publisher

Dummy: a sample arrangement or "mock-up" of pages to be printed, indicating the appearance of the published work

Electronic submission: manuscript transmitted to an editor from one computer to another through a modem

Email: (electronic mail) messages sent from one computer to another via a modem or computer network

End matter: material following the text of a book, such as the appendix, bibliography, index

Final draft: the last version of a polished manuscript ready for submission to an editor

First-time author: writer who has not previously been published

Flat fee: one-time payment made to an author for publication of a manuscript

Front matter: material preceding the text of a book, such as title page, acknowledgments, etc.

Galley: a proof of typeset text that is checked before it is made into final pages

Genre: category of fiction characterized by a particular style, form, or content, such as mystery or fantasy

Hard copy: the printed copy of a computer's output

Hi/lo: high-interest/low-reading level

Imprint: name under which a publishing house issues books

International Reply Coupon (IRC): coupon exchangeable in any foreign country for postage on a single-rate, surface-mailed letter

ISBN: International Standard Book Number assigned to books upon publication for purposes of identification

Letter-quality printout: computer printout that resembles typed pages

Manuscript: a typewritten, or computer-generated document (as opposed to a printed version)

Mass-market: books aimed at a wide audience and sold in supermarkets, airports, and chain bookstores

Middle-grade readers: children ages 8 to 12 years

Modem: an internal or external device used to transmit data between computers via telephone lines

Ms/Mss: manuscript/manuscripts

Newbery Medal: annual award that honors the author of that year's most distinguished children's book

Outline: summary of a book's contents, usually nonfiction, often organized under chapter headings with descriptive sentences under each to show the scope of the book

Packager: see **Book Packager**

Pen name/pseudonym: fictitious name used by an author

Picture book: a type of book that tells a story primarily or entirely through artwork and is aimed at preschool to 8-year-old children

PreK: children under 5 years of age; also known as preschool

Proofread: to read and mark errors, usually in typeset text

Proposal: detailed description of a manuscript, usually nonfiction, and its intended market

Query: letter to an editor to promote interest in a manuscript or idea

Reading fee: fee charged by anyone to read a manuscript

Reprint: another printing of a book; often a different format, such as a paperback reprint of a hardcover title

Response time: average length of time for an editor to accept or reject a submission and contact the writer with a decision

Résumé: short account of one's qualifications, including educational and professional background and publishing credits

Revision: reworking of a piece of writing

Royalty: publisher's payment to an author (usually a percentage) for each copy of the author's work sold

SAE: self-addressed envelope

SASE: self-addressed, stamped envelope

Self-publishing: author assumes complete responsibility for publishing and marketing the book, including printing, binding, advertising, and distributing the book

Simultaneous submission: manuscript submitted to more than one publisher at the same time; also known as a multiple submission

Slush pile: term used within the publishing industry to describe unsolicited manuscripts

Small press: an independent publisher that publishes a limited or specialized list

Solicited manuscript: manuscript that an editor has asked for or agreed to consider

Subsidiary rights: book contract rights other than book publishing rights, such as book club, movie rights, etc.

Subsidy publishing: author pays publisher for all or part of a book's publication, promotion, and sale

Synopsis: condensed description of a fiction manuscript

Tearsheet: page from a magazine or newspaper containing your printed story or article

Trade book: book published for retail sale in bookstores

Unsolicited manuscript: any manuscript not specifically requested by an editor; "no unsolicited manuscripts" generally means the editors will only consider queries or manuscripts submitted by agents

Vanity press: see **Subsidy publishing**

Whole language: educational approach integrating literature into classroom curricula

Work-for-hire: work specifically ordered, commissioned, and owned by a publisher for its exclusive use

Writers' guidelines: publisher's editorial objectives or specifications, which usually include word lengths, readership level, and subject matter

Young adult: children ages 12 years and older

Young reader: the general classification of books written for readers between the ages of 5 and 8

Gateway to the Markets

Hungry for More: Exploring Middle-Grade & YA Series Fiction

By Sarah Cloots

H arry Potter. Gossip Girl. Diary of a Wimpy Kid. The Twilight books. It's no secret that series fiction for both middle-grade and young adult readers is hot. But not all stories and characters are suitable for series, and not all series have such wild success. As Laura Arnold, Editor at HarperCollins, notes, a property with series potential, whether aimed at a middle-grade or young adult readership, "has to be high-concept enough to sustain interest for multiple books over multiple years; readers have to care about the characters enough to keep reading about them and revisiting them; and the plot has to be satisfying enough in each book as well as the overarching series plot to keep readers coming back for more."

Middle-Grade Series: The Basics

Middle-grade books are generally aimed at readers aged 8 to 12, in grades 3 to 6. A step up from chapter books, middle-grade novels are "usually a little heftier, at least in subject matter if not in page count, and not always illustrated," says Arnold. But Rachel Orr, a literary agent at Prospect Agency and former editor, says that middle-grade books can vary greatly in reading level and writing style. Some middle-grade series, such as Dan Gutman's Baseball Card Adventures (HarperCollins) and Jake

Bell's The Amazing Adventures of Nate Banks (Scholastic), are written with reluctant readers—mainly boys—in mind. "These stories are fast-paced with lots of action, which is great for reluctant readers," says Orr, "and the subjects are high-concept as well."

Certain houses, including HarperCollins, use the term *tween* interchangeably with *middle-grade*, but Arnold says, "Some people consider tween to be more girly." Still others, like Orr, think of tween as a bit higher in both age (ages 10 to 13, grades 5 to 7) and subject matter.

"If the book ventures into romance," says Orr, "I'd automatically call it tween, and the characters in tween books might also be a little older. In one tween series I'll be pitching soon, Summer Job, by Jodi Rothman Moore, the main character has just turned 16, whereas I don't think characters in middle-grade books are usually over the age of 14. Kids definitely like to read *up*, but (the character age) still needs to be at an appropriate level. The main character in the first Summer Job book definitely thinks and acts on the young side, which is why this is tween and not YA."

The Craft and the Pitch

"The biggest challenge in middle-grade writing is finding a genuine voice. If you don't have the ability to write in a sincere middle-grade voice, the whole novel is seriously challenged, because kids can smell that insincerity from a mile away," says Arnold. "That's probably the number-one reason I have to reject manuscripts." Arnold feels that it's sometimes easier for writers to get the teen voice down because they were teens more recently. She warns: "Don't talk down to readers. They don't think of themselves as babies."

Some genres present more challenges than others for middle-grade readers. As a result, Orr believes, creating a solid mystery series for this age group is difficult. A series "has to be enough of a mystery for the reader to care, but nothing too scary or gruesome." She also cites the task of maintaining consistency in characters and setting, especially since characters in middle-grade series usually stay the same or age only slightly. "Joe Stoshack, the hero of Dan Gutman's Baseball Card Adventures, has been 13 for more than 10 years now. It's been spring in some books, and fall in others, yet he never ages. How very Peter Pan of him!" remarks Orr.

Maintaining characters, setting, and story lines speaks to the question of whether to pitch an idea as a series from the get-go. According to Arnold, "If you have ideas for sequels, it never hurts to outline them briefly to your agent or editor. Just be prepared for their opinion. If they don't feel it's strong enough to sustain multiple books, they'll probably tell you. But the thing is, publishers like series. It's a way for the book's audience to grow from one book to the next." ·

Orr says, "So much of a series depends on the author's vision, so I definitely think if an author has a true (and reasonable) vision for a middle-grade series, then he or she should present it to an editor as such—as long as the author is flexible and is willing to alter the vision"—and willing to keep it at one stand-alone book if that's what is recommended. Above all, "If a book is envisioned as part of a series from the beginning, it still needs to stand on its own with a solid resolution that doesn't rely on the reader reading the rest of the series."

What the Industry is Looking For

One of the best qualities of middle-grade series is their wide range of possible subjects and approaches. "Fantasy, adventure, sports, friendship, coming-of-age—there are so many different types of books that this age wants to read," says Arnold. "Middle-grade is always going to be a meaty area to bite into because there are so many options as far as genres go, and because of the wonderful school and library market support in (our mutual) efforts to get kids to read."

But Orr warns against trying to write to fit a trend. "I always encourage my clients to write what they're really passionate about. There's always the danger of jumping on the bandwagon in a saturated subject: By the time something becomes a trend, it's too late. But if you're

---

"What's going to be the Baby-sitters Club of the 2010s? That's something I'm keenly interested in."

---

really interested in writing to the trend, then I would suggest seeing what subjects are popular and making the logical leap." She points to how fairies followed the princess trend, and in YA zombies seem to be following vampires. "Also, keep an eye out for the trickle-down effect," she says. "If something is really big in YA, chances are it will be big in middle-grade in a year or two."

Arnold predicts publishers' next moves will include "trying to serve the tweens, the *Hannah Montana* crowd. What's going to be the Baby-sitters Club of the 2010s? That's something I'm keenly interested in." She says she would love to acquire a girl friendship series "with some sort of unique hook and a wonderful, warm voice. I see so many *mean girls* submissions and it makes me kind of sad. I know that girls do struggle with that in middle school, but I wish I could find something more active and engaging."

Orr feels that in today's market, an idea that is high-concept—that has appeal to a wide audience, with characters and settings that are, well, *popular*—has a better chance of becoming a successful middle-grade series than something that's character-driven. As far as what she's looking for as an agent: "I'm keeping my eye out for sports, mysteries, and school stories (which editors seem to be wanting), as well as series with multicultural characters."

Young Adult Series: The Basics

YA books are generally designated as directed to ages 12 and up, with the racier books (those with mature language, mentions of alcohol or drugs, and possibly sex) labeled 14 and up. Some houses, such as the Simon

Pulse imprint of Simon & Schuster, take things one step further with a 16 and up category. Jen Klonsky, Editorial Director of Simon Pulse, cites books such as Elizabeth Scott's *Living Dead Girl* and the works of Jason Myers (*Exit Here*) and Nina Malkin (*Swoon*) as examples of this category.

YA is synonymous with *teen*, say most in the industry. "YA seems like more of an industry term, sometimes confusing to others, so usually I just say I work in teen books, which sounds cooler anyway," says Lexa Hillyer, Editor at Penguin's Razorbill imprint.

While Klonsky points out that *young adult* could at times indicate a target audience of the 18- to 25-year-old crowd (like many of the novels published by MTV Books), she says at Pulse they generally use the terms teen and YA interchangeably.

Greg Ferguson, Editor at Egmont USA, says that some think of the young adult label as describing a more literary novel, and teen as more commercial. He also notes that there is some resistance from children's publishers to do books featuring young adults of college age. "I think it's because it's believed—and most likely true—that readers of that age are hesitant to go into children's sections to buy their books," Ferguson says. Therefore, YA generally does not feature protagonists older than 18—and it is important to keep in mind that most readers will be younger than the protagonist they are reading about.

A YA book with a teen protagonist can be differentiated from an *adult* book with a teen main character. Hillyer points to relatability and immediacy. "Typically, for me, the difference is the voice. Does the voice really speak to a teen? Not just whether it's accessible or easy to read, but does it have the kind of attitude toward life that a teen could relate to? For instance, a very nostalgic or jaded or satirical tone might fall flat for a teen who doesn't have the same kind of life experience the author is trying to convey in the book. The level of self-awareness in the book can make the difference, too. I think writing a good teen book usually requires immediacy, whereas you can create more distance between the reader and the story in an adult book," says Hillyer.

Klonsky agrees: "It's really the voice and perspective that differentiates these two. For example, *Prep*, by Curtis Sittenfeld (Random House) features a teenager but the voice felt, to me, like an adult looking back on her prep school years." Indeed, the book was marketed as an adult book. In contrast, the YA *Looking for Alaska*, by John Green (Dutton), "feels like a more solidly teen perspective. Yet both feature teens in prep school."

She emphasizes the importance of "finding a unique voice that's not preachy and doesn't bring with it the weight of adult perspective. Also, don't fall into the trap of sliding around the ages of your characters without re-examining the voice/issues/sensibilities. What works for a 14-year-old protagonist and 12-year-old reader does not translate to a 17-year-old protagonist and a 15-year-old reader," Klonsky says.

For YA series, Ferguson asks himself whether a story in a series "can be told more effectively in one book rather than two books or three books, etc." He highlights the importance of a high concept, plot, and strong characters, but says whichever aspect dominates a particular series, it should be what drives the overarching story, and the book or books should fully explore the story "without running on for the sake of making it into a series."

The Craft and the Pitch

Many of the challenges in writing YA series can be logistical, says Hillyer. "How can you properly *plant seeds* in the earlier books for later developments in the series? How can you create characters who have satisfying mini-arcs, i.e., they grow in each book but also have a bigger ongoing journey to make that can last them through multiple books? How do you raise the stakes at the end of one book so that readers really feel the need to read the next? On top of that, it's a particular challenge with teens because if they start reading the series at age 12, you probably have them for four or five years max and then they move on." A key ingredient for a successful series, Hillyer notes, is a strong character (or set of them) who you want to stick with for many books. Ideally there is also some *addictive* element—"action, suspense, mystery, melodrama"—that a reader comes to expect from each book in the series.

Ferguson believes that the biggest challenge in a YA series is coming up with a fresh idea "and then fully executing it. There are so many books being published now, so it's really about coming up with a unique twist, character, or voice to make your idea interesting."

Be open to variations for a set of books, too. Hillyer advises, "It's great to have a series plan from the get-go if that's what you're aiming for with your story, but also to be open to serialization for the kinds of books that work as stand-alone novels but seem to beg for more exploration of the character or world."

Klonsky explains that series come about in all kinds of ways. "Quite often we ask an author to expand on a single title or add a third title to a two-book series. That's how Lisa McMann's *Fade* came about. If an author has an idea that feels rich and epic enough to require more than one book to execute it, she should envision it as a series from the start, but it should be plotted out carefully," Klonsky says.

A series idea can come from the author, editor, or agent, says Ferguson, who warns, "One common mistake is submissions that are firm on being a series rather than whatever amount of books is best to tell the story"— whether it is one or ten.

What the Industry is Looking For

It appears that some of the strongest YA trends of the last few years will continue. "As long as there are *Twilight* movies to be made, I think the paranormal genre will be successful because Stephenie Meyer's books will drive the market," says Ferguson. "There is the possibility that this genre will be over-published—maybe some people would say that has already happened—but teens' appetite for this type of story seems strong."

Klonsky concurs: "The books that seem to be connecting most strongly right now with our readers are the dark books, whether realistic fiction or paranormal. On our list we've had great success with Lisa McMann's *Wake* and *Fade*; L. J. Smith's Night World series; Nancy Holder and Debbie Viguie's Wicked series; Lisa Schroeder's paranormal verse novels; and *Go Ask Alice* remains a backlist staple. All of these tackle

tough, emotional issues, and feature tough characters and/or *regular* characters who find themselves in challenging and even life-threatening situations." She continues, "That said, I think coming-of-age novels like Elizabeth Scott's, and those of Deb Caletti (such as *The Secret Life of Prince Charming*) will always sell strongly, as they mirror the lives of their readers and can explore dark, tough issues—abandonment, identity, rejection, betrayal—as well." Here we definitely see a difference in subject matter and tone from most middle-grade books.

Like most editors, Hillyer is hesitant to talk about trends, but says, "In general I do think there's a bit of a trend away from the sort of brand-name-dropping, voyeuristic, rich-kid stuff that glutted the market a few years back—probably due to the simple fact that the country's interest in those kinds of stories tends to rise and fall along with the economy. In the '90s it was all about edginess, disturbing content, *real* people in *real* situations, rather than glamour and exotic lifestyles. So perhaps there's a little more interest in that again. But one reason I don't like to predict trends is that there are always exciting, phenomenal exceptions."

Klonsky points out that when it comes to series, Pulse is not really looking for drawn-out, ongoing stories. "We're more interested in limited series (two to three books) that contain an overarching story, as opposed to stand-alone books featuring the same characters and setting. There's so much competition out there, so we're strategically thinking: Would readers be more likely to follow a dramatic arc if there was an end in sight? Also, it's challenging to maintain a level of tension and drama that's consistent over a long stretch, and having no end date makes it difficult to pace the plot and emotional journey of the characters," she says.

Hillyer feels that YA series have changed dramatically over the years—for the better. "There's a much greater demand for them, a whole market where there didn't use to be one," she says. "And teens who read from the YA section are older—it's not just for 12-year-olds anymore. Kids who read adult books also read YA, so they have sophisticated sensibilities: They want convincing voices and characters with depth and believable plot twists and complex approaches to the subject matter."

The advice Hillyer gives YA-series authors is just as applicable to writers of middle-grade books: "The biggest mistake I run into is an author talking down to teens or trying to teach a lesson. Not to say that teen books can't be wholesome or have strong moral codes—they can. Just that the average book-buying teen, as far as I can tell, looks for entertainment and intriguing subject matter. I know the last thing I wanted when I was a teen was yet another adult voice telling me what I should and shouldn't be doing. There are parents, teachers, and plenty of others to fill that role. Given the kind of fun a teen can have watching TV or movies or hanging out online, books really have to compete to seem exciting."

Finally, Hillyer makes an important point for all children's writers: "Another mistake is thinking writing for teens is easier than writing for an adult. Why would this be the case? You still have to have phenomenal prose and something compelling to say in a new way. Sometimes the demands are greater—the audience probably has a shorter attention span so you have to be that much more engaging upfront." Especially when writing for worldly, seen-it-all teens, "they are probably less willing to take leaps and make assumptions, which means the author has to actually do the work of justifying everything that happens to the characters and tying it all together."

In other words, series fiction should be as smart as the readers for whom it is written.

Folktales and Fairy Tales: Old Stories with a New Twist

By Chris Eboch

"Folktales and fairy tales aren't selling" goes the conventional wisdom in recent years. That so-called wisdom is off. While the market is down for traditional picture book retellings, fairy tales have found a new home in novels for middle-grade and young adult readers. You might say that fairy tales have grown up.

Reka Simonsen, Senior Editor at Henry Holt and Company Books for Young Readers, says, "Fairy tales and folktales for younger kids are hard to publish successfully these days. That doesn't seem to be true of novels for young adult readers, though. There are enough books, authors, and long-term fans to have turned the novel-length fairy tale into a subgenre of its own, a particular type of fantasy that's especially popular with adolescent girls." Most popular are versions that give the classic tales a new twist—"a different setting or a stronger female lead character, for example."

Heather Tomlinson, author of *The Swan Maiden* and *Aurelie*, twists a traditional story in her new book, *Toads and Diamonds* (all from Holt). She says, "In Charles Perrault's original tale, a fairy rewards one girl with the gift of speaking jewels and flowers while condemning her older sister to spew toads and snakes when she talks. I wondered what would happen if the two gifts were equally valuable—and equally dangerous."

Tomlinson points to "many successful novels and series drawing on fairy tale roots. But I think writers can increase their chances of success by retelling a lesser-known story, or finding a really fresh angle on a familiar one."

"Books, authors, & long-term fans have turned the novel-length fairy tale into a subgenre, one especially popular with adolescent girls."

Deva Fagan was inspired by a traditional archetype for her novel, *Fortune's Folly* (Holt). "I was thinking about how many myths and fairy tales involve a prophecy that must be fulfilled by the hero, and wondering what might happen if that prophecy was actually a big lie," Fagan says. "I think one of the keys to success was finding a story that had what I like to call a spark." *Fortune's Folly* succeeded because of a twist that took the story in a new direction and made it stand out.

Maggie Stiefvater also works fairy tales into stories for teenagers in novels such as *Lament* and *Ballad* (both published by Flux). Andrew Karre, Stiefvater's editor and now Editorial Director at Carolrhoda Books, notes, "A book like *Lament* uses a lot of existing *faerie* lore and mythology, but it is a very contemporary story. I approach faery YA this way: If you take any number of aspects of adolescence—self-centeredness, the feeling of immortality, obsession with beauty—and exaggerate them, you pretty naturally arrive at faeries."

Stiefvater points to "market evidence that proves that editors still want unique retellings. Jackson Pearce sold a retelling of Little Red Riding Hood, *Sisters Red* (Little, Brown), for a nice chunk of change; Amanda Marrone did a recent retelling of Snow White, *Devoured* (Simon Pulse); and Elizabeth Bunce's historical retelling of Rumpelstilt-

More Fairy-Tale Inspired Novels

Beastly and *A Kiss in Time*, Alex Flinn (HarperTeen)
Impossible, Nancy Werlin (Dial)
Stolen, Vivian Vande Velde (Marshall Cavendish)
The Thirteenth Princess, Diane Zahler (HarperCollins)
Wildwood Dancing, Juliet Marillier (Knopf)

skin, *A Curse Dark as Gold* (Arthur A. Levine), has done enormously well and won several awards."

At Bloomsbury Children's Books USA, Editor Margaret Miller says, "In middle-grade and teen (novels), there are almost no traditional fairy tale retellings, but many wonderful *inspired-by* novels. We've had great success with E. D. Baker's *The Frog Princess* and Shannon Hale's *The Goose Girl*, among others. But for these books to succeed, the author needs to truly reinvent the tales, bringing the characters to vivid life."

Simonsen admits, "Some people in publishing and bookselling are getting pretty tired of fantasy of all kinds, including fairy tale novelizations. I think that response is mostly from the people who never liked these kinds of books anyway. Fantasy has been the bestselling genre for the past decade and it's still going strong, so clearly kids are not sick of it. It's a crowded market, so it can be hard to stand out, but there is definitely a big fan base for fairy tale novelizations."

For the Younger Set

Picture book folktales face greater challenges, including recent market changes. "It used to be that you could publish picture books with 1,500, even 2,000 words," says Lise Lunge-Larsen, author of *The Adventures of Thor the Thunder God* (Houghton Mifflin). "That is a perfect length for some of the best folktales," which can lose complexity and depth if shortened. Publishers now prefer much shorter stories.

When published, folktales may have trouble reaching their readers for some possibly unexpected reasons. Because of the potential for beautiful illustration, folktales are often published in picture book format—but the story level may appeal most to elementary school children who want to be seen reading chapter books. Lunge-Larsen also points out, "Folktales are classified as nonfiction, and in many libraries, get shelved away from the picture books." They may thus go unnoticed.

Finally, says Lunge-Larsen, "Publishers want new and fresh stories. As soon as they hear *folktale*, I believe many of them think 'quaint relics from the past,' and don't give the story a fair read. Yet children relish and long for repetition, for predictability and hearing the same stories over and over again."

Despite the challenges, authors find homes for their stories because of their quality, newness, and universality. Miller says, "Traditional fairy tales will always have a place in picture books, although the market is competitive enough that the books that do well tend to be by big-name illustrators."

For the best chance of a sale, author Susan VanHecke says the story must feel *today*. "Can the tale be updated with a different setting, modern characters, or a tweak of the plot?" In the original folktale behind *An Apple Pie for Dinner* (Marshall Cavendish), a generic old woman wanted to make a dumpling. "For my retelling, I gave the woman a name and a persona," says VanHecke, "and updated the old-fashioned dumpling to a more modern pie."

David LaRochelle literally flipped a traditional story with his picture book *The End* (Arthur A. Levine Books), and the first editor to see the manuscript bought it. LaRochelle adds, however, "I've been marketing a folktale of mine for years now without any luck. I think the main difference between the two is that *The End* was a twist on the fairy tale theme: The story is told backwards, beginning with 'And they all lived happily ever after' and ending with 'Once upon a time.' For a fairy tale or a folktale to get noticed, it has to be more than just well-written; it has to have something unique about it."

Think Small

Despite a tight publishing market, small and regional presses are still looking for folktales, especially unusual ones. Naomi C. Rose focused on a less familiar culture when she wrote and illustrated *Tibetan Tales from the Top of the World* (Clear Light). "I've found niche publishers and publishers focused on the school and library markets to be willing to consider my books," she says. "The publisher who bought my books of Tibetan folktales did so mostly for the cultural aspect."

Elizabeth O. Dulemba fell in love with the Jack tales of the southern Appalachians. She says, "When Raven Tree Press approached me to illustrate *Paco and the Giant Chile Plant* (written by Keith Polette), introducing Jack to Latino culture, I jumped at it—I even took Spanish lessons! My first picture book as both author and illustrator is the bilingual adaptation of another classic Jack tale, *Soap, soap, soap ~ Jabón, jabón, jabón.*"

Raven Tree Publisher Dawn Jeffers says, "We love the

idea of taking a classic fairy tale and adding a twist. Comparing and contrasting the original to the new version allows kids to be educated and entertained at the same time. We find our fractured fairy tale line is very popular as companion pieces to the originals. Our word count is generally lower than in the originals and illustrations are more contemporary. We plan to continue publishing more classics with a twist."

Other small publishers may be open to folktale adaptations. Shen's Books looks for multicultural stories, particularly about Asia and Latin America. Pelican Publishing focuses on Louisiana and the Gulf Coast, while Rising Moon Books focused on the Southwest (Rising Moon and its companion imprints, now owned by Cooper, are reportedly not now publishing new titles, however). The Jewish Publication Society and Kar-Ben Publishing specialize in Jewish themes. "Of course, it takes an engaging, well-written story to open doors anywhere," Dulemba notes.

Added Value

Even when folktales are retold in a traditional way, they can work—and sell—because of additional creative materials, whether in format or add-on educational material. Judy Goldman, a citizen of Mexico, will have a title combining fiction and nonfiction with *As Our Ancestors Say* (Charlesbridge, scheduled for 2012). "Randi Rivers, my editor, read one of my stories and proposed a different book: One with several stories from different parts of Mexico as well as nonfiction information about each of the native groups that tells the stories."

Rose explains about her Tibetan stories, "Each book includes information about Tibet, and the stories are told in Tibetan as well as in English. These cultural additions create a lot of enthusiasm among educators and parents. I also include songs and chants."

VanHecke's *An Apple Pie for Dinner* has an author's

note about the original story, and a kid-friendly recipe for apple pie. She includes bonus material on her website (www.anapplepiefordinner.com), with "fun apple pie facts, links to apple-info sites, an 'Apple Pie for Dinner' song, read-aloud narration, and other goodies for kids, parents, and teachers."

Turning Old to New

New wine in old wineskins is the creative key to entering the folktale and fairy tale market, for readers of every age. "The images and the plots of the old folktales are so compelling that they will never go out of style," Lunge-Larsen says. "Writers should feel like the story-tellers of old, free to retell an old tale in their own voice and updated to suit our times."

Natalie M. Rosinsky, author of *Write Your Own Fairy Tale* and *Write Your Own Folktale* (Compass Point Books), advises, "Think globally. Examine every continent and the multiple cultures that may thrive within a country to find tales or ideas for tales that intrigue you." Set a story in a new location. Change the point of view. Use humor.

Any and every story needs a unique identity ultimately, and something more. "Your characters have to sing," Stiefvater says. "We'll read Sleeping Beauty one thousand times over if the characters are brilliant and different every time."

Picture Book & Concept Book Nonfiction for All Ages

By Katherine Swarts

Picture books aren't all fairy tales and funny stories, and illustrated books aren't reserved for children under eight. Most history, geography, and science books for older elementary and middle-grade readers fill about half the available page space with visual elements.

When written for younger children, fact-oriented titles often take the form of *concept books*, most familiar in the form of ABC and 1-2-3 texts. But concept books can cover a wide range of topics and be aimed at a wide range of ages. Older concept books might focus on the periodic table; anthropological or zoological classifications; or the differences between planets and asteroids, among endless others. The one element all concept books have in common is that they explain a specific idea or system whose definitions go beyond the physical.

The one quality all picture books have in common is that they are heavily illustrated. Beyond that, again the potential subjects are endless, and the writer's approach depends on the expected audience.

What's the Difference?

"Picture book length and vocabulary depends on the age for which the book is intended," says Paul McMahon, Managing Editor of Paulist Press. "Writers should always test out their stories with the age group for which they are writing."

"If you are not knowledgeable about accepted language levels and word choices for different ages," advises Joni Sussman, Publisher at Kar-Ben Publishing, "ask a librarian to suggest the best books for children of a particular age. Then peruse the books, counting pages, words per page, and syllables per word." She also advises writers not to forget that "children listening to a story can actually absorb more sophisticated language and concepts than very young readers who must sound out words while at the same time absorb the content."

Kathleen Hayes, now Editor of *Highlights High Five* and a former librarian, says, "The vocabulary used in books to be read aloud can be much more elaborate" than the vocabulary in read-it-yourself books for readers of the same age. "Illustrations can help support comprehension, but ultimately, it's the interaction between the skilled reader and the child that ensures understanding." Whoever does the reading, "concept books for young children are more likely to present isolated facts, while books for older children cover subjects more exhaustively. First- and second-graders need short, simple sentence structure and vocabulary that is carefully defined within the body of the text. Books for older children can use more complex structure and vocabulary, though a dense page of text can be off-putting for any young reader."

As for the concepts themselves, "books for very young children focus on basic concepts, which are handled overtly," says Sussman. "Our concept board books might involve teaching colors through holiday symbols: a red apple for Rosh Hashanah, a yellow candle for Hanukkah. Concept books for older children might teach values such as giving to charity," perhaps through true stories of people who exemplify or learned such values.

Smarter Than You Might Think

Elementary and middle-school readers can handle far more sophisticated topics than writers often expect—if the text is presented appropriately. "Include any background that readers need to understand plot, setting, or ideas," says Louise E. May, Editor in Chief of Lee & Low Books. "Our book *Honda: The Boy Who Dreamed of Cars,* about the founder of the Honda Motor Company, uses descriptive language to make car mechanics accessible to young readers." Be careful, however; too much expla-

---

Long after youngsters are reading on their own, comprehension level can differ from reading level.

nation can easily disrupt the flow of a text. The best way to avoid trouble is through sidebars or appendices, and be sure to identify them as such in your manuscript. "Backmatter allows you to convey interesting background," says May. "Glossaries with phonetic pronunciations are very helpful in books that contain unfamiliar names, languages, or concepts."

Even long after youngsters are reading on their own, comprehension level can still differ from reading level. Typical English-language abilities can also vary widely among ethnic and socioeconomic groups. In today's multicultural-minded society, choosing age-appropriate vocabulary and sentence length "is much more difficult than it used to be," says Doris Wenzel of Mayhaven Publishing, "but in a way, that is liberating. I read books to children in schools, and I see a wide variety of understanding as we become a more multifaceted population."

Not only readers, but writers should be free from pressure to overstretch their abilities. All illustrated-book writers should think long and hard before suggesting that they also do illustrations. Unless you are a professional artist or photographer, don't even mention pictures in the initial inquiry. "It's rare to find a good writer who is also a good enough photographer (or artist) to meet modern publishing standards," says Deborah Burns, Acquiring Editor for Storey Publishing's juvenile line. "Photos have to be incredibly sharp, clear, well-composed, and rich in color or contrast." Drawings must be perfectly consistent

More Nonfiction Concept & Picture Books

America, A Book of Opposites, W. Nikola-Lisa (Lee & Low)
Brave Dogs, Gentle Dogs, Cat Urbigkit (Boyds Mills Press)
The Barefoot Book of Monsters, Fran Parnell, illus., Sophie Fatus (Barefoot)
Counting in the Taiga, Lisa Beringer McKissack, Fredrick L. McKissack, Jr. (Enslow Publishers)
The Bug in a Jug Wants a Hug (A Short Vowel Sounds Book), Brian P. Cleary (Millbrook Press)
Eye See You (Storey Publishing)
Move!, Steve Jenkins and Robin Page (Houghton Mifflin)

with each other, and their style must be an excellent match for the text.

Publishers normally hire the illustrators. Publishers also decide what sort of illustration will work best. "When we acquire a manuscript," says Sussman, "we create an art profile based on considerations such as setting and time frame. We then determine whether the manuscript is best suited to art or to photos."

That's not to say writers can't offer suggestions once a publisher is interested, or that texts should be composed without a thought to visual elements. "I'd encourage all picture book writers to think visually," says Emily Lawrence, Associate Editor of Aladdin Books. "There's no need for wordy, detailed descriptions if the picture will show the reader what something looks like; so keep your words to a minimum and have a concrete idea of how you want your book to look." (Note that Aladdin is currently buying only fiction, and accepts agented and requested submissions.)

Don't Get Singsong

Next to offering to supply illustrations, probably the most common beginner's mistake in picture and concept book writing (especially when aiming at younger audiences) is assuming that such books should be written in rhyme.

"It's very hard to write a good rhyming book," says Sussman. "The text often suffers because the author tries to find a rhyming word rather than the right word to convey meaning, or uses a word that rhymes great but throws off the meter (overall beat). Both word choice and meter have to be perfect."

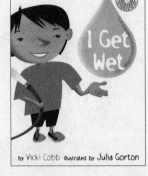

by Vicki Cobb illustrated by Julia Gorton

"Verse must scan rhythmically and be easy to read aloud," agrees Vicki Cobb, author of more than 85 science and other nonfiction books for children.

"A rhyming text can hijack the goal of the book," says Hayes. "Children may focus on the rhyme and miss the underlying concept." When in doubt, stick to prose. If you are a poet at heart and really want to try verse, "don't select too complicated a topic," advises Sussman. "Rhyme itself is a complicating factor; elaborate stories become difficult to follow with rhyme getting in the way."

As simple as concept books can be, do not choose the most obvious approach; odds are that other writers have proposed the same idea until no editor can look at it without groaning. "Anyone can match up animal names with letters of the alphabet," says Kim Duncan-Mooney, U.S. Editor of Barefoot Books. "Any book worth adding to the market must be something special, different but not gimmicky."

Choosing the best format is indeed hard work, "tough for the first-time author—and for us," says Wenzel. "Sometimes, if we like the theme, we will accept a manuscript and then help the author identify problem areas." Don't, however, expect extensive editing assistance from publishers, especially big ones. Not only are most editorial staffs overworked already, but they prefer to work with diligent and thorough writers, and a well-prepared manuscript is your best advertisement.

Best Books

Among books that have succeeded, every editor and writer has favorites from his or her professional experience. "*Alef-Bet Yoga for Kids*, a book of photos of children doing yoga poses that mimic the letters of the Hebrew alphabet, includes outlines of the Hebrew letters behind the children" demonstrating the positions, says Sussman. "It's a very clever concept. Children can use yoga poses and the Hebrew alpahbet at the same time and can then spell their Hebrew names or Hebrew words in yoga poses. We used photos because we wanted readers to be able to easily copy the poses."

"*What Bluebirds Do*, by Pamela F. Kirby, is a wonderful example of how clear, informative photographs amplify and explain text," says Hayes. "There is not a hint of fictionalization, but the text reads as a story" because it was based on the author's direct observations "of a pair of bluebirds in her backyard. *You Can't Do That, Amelia!*, by Kimberly Wagner Klier, is an excellent example of a carefully researched, accessible biography" of Amelia

Improve Your Informational Writing

Nancy Carol Willis is the founder of Birdsong Books, which publishes children's natural science books. She offers tips to help your informational writing:

● "The magic number for sentence length seems to be 17 words. Children read slower than adults; so let's help by breaking a long sentence into two shorter sentences. Vary sentence structure (subject/verb/object) and keep introductory phrases short. I may be old-fashioned, but I still like to see correct punctuation."

● "Writing in the present tense really grabs my attention. It feels fresh and immediate and sets up opportunities to show, not tell. Use vivid images to paint a picture in your reader's mind and make it easy to imagine what's being described. Include sensory details to expand the reader's experience beyond the purely visual."

● "Even though Birdsong Books titles include glossaries, I'm a strong proponent of using vocabulary words in context. Example: 'It's the June summer solstice, the shortest night of the year' (to nocturnal raccoons). Similes can help explain words or concepts. To describe navigation among migrating robins, say: 'To guide them, the birds use rivers, mountains, and coastlines like road maps.'"

● "In my experience, children have difficulty comprehending numbers (length/weight/area) and statistics (population/area/percent). So whenever possible, use kid-friendly comparisons such as, 'If you hold a nickel, that's how much a newly hatched robin weighs,' or 'Each (newborn raccoon) weighs two ounces, about as much as a candy bar.'"

● "None of the above-mentioned tips matter if the writing lacks a clear focus, logical order, or easy flow. Read your manuscript aloud. If you stumble over a word, change it. Your final edits should examine individual words for precision, clarity, and alliteration."

Earhart. "*We Are One: The Story of Bayard Rustin*, by Larry Dane Brimner, reproduces historical photos on a large scale; the text can be used by all ages to gather information about civil-rights leader Bayard Rustin. *Drive*, by Nathan Clement, is a wonderful example of a concept book for the very young: Striking graphic illustrations and minimal text tell the story of a boy's father who drives a freight truck; and in the end, the reader, like the boy, is glad to see Dad safely home from work."

Among titles meant to be read to children, says Cobb, "The best picture books promote interactivity between reader and listener," says Cobb. "In my Science Play books (including *I Get Wet* and *I Face the Wind*), I built interactivity into the text by suggesting activities that move the concepts along to non-intuitive conclusions."

"*Night of the Lighted Freedom*, by Dana Marquess, inspired by the author's wheelchair-using brother and her time along the east coast," says Wenzel, "deals with very real children and giant fireflies." Marquess's book is technically fiction, but then, the line between nonfiction and fiction is frequently blurred in concept and picture books. Even with straightforward collections of fact, including some story-like elements makes a better book—assuming the writer interweaves story and facts skillfully. "I always remember a description from *Edward Eager*," says Hayes, "about nonfiction books that 'pretend to be a story.' If you think you must create a story to trick your reader into learning about your topic, it probably won't work."

One skill that does work no matter how many actual pictures in a book is an author's ability to write text that draws pictures in readers' minds. So think visually; choose descriptive and specific words; and read similar books to learn from the pros. And pick a topic you love: "Be genuinely interested in the information!" as Hayes puts it. If you want kids to enjoy reading your book, make sure you enjoy writing it.

Listings

How to Use the Listings

On the following pages are over 590 profiles of publishers involved in the wide range of children's publishing. More than 50 publishers and contest listings are new to the directory. These publishing houses produce a variety of material from parenting guides, textbooks, and classroom resources to picture books, photo-essays, middle-grade novels, and biographies.

Each year we update every listing through mailed surveys and telephone interviews. While we verify everything in the listing before we go to press, it is not uncommon for information such as contact names, addresses, and editorial needs to change suddenly. Therefore, we suggest that you always read the publisher's most recent writers' guidelines before submitting a query letter or manuscript.

If you are unable to find a particular publisher, check the Publishers' Index beginning on page 610 to see if it is cited elsewhere in the book. We do not list presses that publish over 50% of their material by requiring writers to pay all or part of the cost of publishing. While we cannot endorse or vouch for the quality of every press we list, we do try to screen out publishers of questionable quality.

To help you judge a publisher's receptivity to unsolicited submissions, we include a Freelance Potential section in each listing. This is where we identify the number of titles published in 2009 that were written by unpublished writers, authors new to the publishing house, and agented authors. We also provide the total number of query letters and unsolicited manuscripts a publisher receives each year.

Use this information and the other information included in the listing to locate publishers that are looking for the type of material you have written or plan to write. Become familiar with the style and content of the house by studying its catalogue and a few recent titles.

Elva Resa Publishing

! — New Listing

Who to Contact

8362 Tamarack Village, Suite 119-106
St. Paul, MN 55125

Publisher: Christy Lyon

Publisher's Interests
Elva Resa publishes books for military families, including children's books. Its children's imprint, Alma Little, is a general interest children's publisher offering everything from picture books to middle-grade novels.
Website: www.elvaresa.com; www.almalittle.com

— Profile of Publisher & Readership

Freelance Potential
Published 4 titles (2 juvenile) in 2009. Of the 4 titles, 1 was by an unpublished writer and 1 was by an author who was new to the publishing house. Receives 360–3,600 queries each year.

— Number of Unsolicited Submissions Published & Received

- **Fiction:** Publishes story picture books, 4–10 years. Genres include contemporary and historical fiction, and stories about family members in the military.
- **Nonfiction:** Publishes early picture books, 0–4 years. Topics include self-help, current events, and military resources. Also publishes activity books and books for adults.
- **Representative Titles:** *The Wishing Tree* by Mary Redmond is the story of a girl who deals with her father's deployment by writing her thoughts on yellow ribbons and tying them to tree branches. *Perch, Mrs. Sackets, and Crow's Nest* by Karen Pavlicin finds a boy who makes the most of his summer at his grandmother's house, finding wonder and fun in everything.

— Recent Titles to Study

Submissions and Payment
Guidelines and catalogue available at website. Elva Resa: query with outline. Accepts email queries to submissions@elvaresa.com. Alma Little: accepts targeted submissions only, see www.almalittle.com for details. Responds in 3 weeks. Publication in 12–18 months. Royalty; advance. Flat fee.

Editor's Comments
We are interested in good resources for military teens and pre-teens, and general interest middle-grade novels. All submissions should demonstrate a knowledge of our mission.

— Editor's Current Needs & Tips for Writers

Website

Categories of Current Titles

How to Submit

Icon Key

! New Listing   🖱 E-publisher   🌐 Overseas Publisher

✍ Accepts agented submissions only

✖ Not currently accepting submissions

A & B Publishers Group

223 Duffield Street
Brooklyn, NY 11201

Managing Editor: Wendy Gift

Publisher's Interests

The children's books in this publisher's catalogue celebrate cultural diversity and self-identity. Fiction and nonfiction titles are featured for beginning to young adult readers.
Website: www.anbbooks.com

Freelance Potential

Published 24 titles in 2009: 6 were reprint/licensed properties. Of the 24 titles, 3 were by authors who were new to the publishing house. Receives 500 unsolicited mss yearly.

- **Fiction:** Publishes story picture books, 4–10 years; middle-grade books, 8–12 years; and young adult novels, 12–18 years. Genres include contemporary, multicultural, and inspirational fiction; fairy tales; and humor.
- **Nonfiction:** Publishes toddler books and early picture books, 0–4 years; easy-to-read books, 4–7 years; and story picture books, 4–10 years. Topics include holidays, biography, culture, and gifted education.
- **Representative Titles:** *Nappy Hair* by Carolivia Herron is the story of a girl who learns that being different can be fun, too. *Five Notable Inventors* by Wade Hudson presents the fascinating facts behind the inventions of African Americans, including hair products, shoe machinery, and traffic signals. *When I Look in the Mirror* by Sopoeia Greywolf helps young readers understand positive self-image and self-knowledge.

Submissions and Payment

Guidelines available. Send complete ms. Accepts hard copy and simultaneous submissions if identified. SASE. Responds in 2–3 months. Publication period varies. Royalty; advance.

Editor's Comments

We are interested in books that promote self-esteem, embrace the world's diverse cultures, and help young readers prepare for real life. Of particular interest are topics that have not been overdone and that will appeal to children.

Abdo Publishing

8000 West 78th Street, Suite 310
Edira, MN 55439

Editor-in-Chief: Paul Abdo

Publisher's Interests

Abdo Publishing is dedicated to producing quality nonfiction books for children of all ages. Its titles are known for grade-appropriate language that promotes reading success and are designed to be visually appealing to young readers.
Website: www.abdopublishing.com

Freelance Potential

Published 480 titles in 2009. Of the 480 titles, 28 were by authors who were new to the publishing house. Receives 120 queries yearly.

- **Nonfiction:** Publishes early picture books, 0–4 years; easy-to-read books, 4–7 years; story picture books, 4–10 years; chapter books, 5–10 years; middle-grade books, 8–12 years; and young adult books, 12–18 years. Topics include animals, nature, travel, geography, sciences, social studies, sports, history, leisure, and multicultural and ethnic subjects. Also publishes biographies.
- **Representative Titles:** *Leaders of the American Revolution* by Linda R. Wade introduces readers to the war's powerful leaders, daring soldiers, and battles; part of the American Revolution series. *All Aboard America* by Julie Murray & Sarah Tieck (6–9 years) takes children on an educational journey to America's national landmarks.

Submissions and Payment

Guidelines and catalogue available at website. Query with résumé. No unsolicited mss. Accepts hard copy. SASE. Response time varies. Publication on January 1 and September 1 of each year. Flat fee.

Editor's Comments

We are always looking for qualified writers knowledgeable about any of the topics we publish. Be sure to include your experience on the topic you wish to write about when submitting your query.

Abrams Books for Young Readers

Harry N. Abrams Inc.
115 West 18th Street, 6th Floor
New York, NY 10011

Editor: Maggie Lehrman

Publisher's Interests
The titles from Abrams Books for Young Readers show that it's never too early to introduce children to such sophisticated pursuits as fine arts and poetry. For more than a decade, that's just what Abrams has been doing, with a catalogue of storybooks and nonfiction titles for children from preschool through junior high.
Website: www.hnabooks.com

Freelance Potential
Published 30 titles in 2009: 1 was developed from an unsolicited submission and 29 were by by agented authors. Receives 1,200 queries yearly.

- **Fiction:** Publishes early picture books, 0–4 years; easy-to-read books, 4–7 years; story picture books, 4–10 years; middle-grade books, 8–12 years; and young adult books, 12–18 years. Genres include folklore, folktales, and stories about animals, nature, and the environment.
- **Nonfiction:** Publishes easy-to-read books, 4–7 years; story picture books, 4–10 years; and middle-grade books, 8–12 years. Topics include animals, history, art, and relationships.
- **Representative Titles:** *All In a Day* by Cynthia Rylant (4+ years) illuminates all the possibilities a day offers, while also delivering a gentle message of good environmental stewardship. *Library Mouse: A Friend's Tale* by Daniel Kirk (6–9 years) tells of the literary partnership between a boy and a mouse. *City I Love* by Lee Bennett Hopkins (4–8 years) is an illustrated collection of urban-themed poetry.

Submissions and Payment
Agented authors only. Guidelines and catalogue available at website. Royalty; advance.

Editor's Comments
Please note that we will review agent-submitted nonfiction only. We're overloaded with fiction at this time.

Absey & Company

23011 Northcrest Drive
Spring, TX 77389

Editor-in-Chief: Edward Wilson

Publisher's Interests

For 10 years, Absey & Company has focused on publishing strong literary works in the genres of fiction, poetry, and language arts. Its children's list includes fiction as well as educational nonfiction for ages 4 through 18, while its adult list includes books for teachers and books about writing. **Website: www.absey.biz**

Freelance Potential

Published 5–10 titles (1–2 juvenile) in 2009. Of the 5–10 titles, 4–7 were by unpublished writers and 4–9 were by authors who were new to the publishing house. Receives 10,000 queries yearly.

- **Fiction:** Publishes story picture books, 4–10 years; chapter books, 5–10 years; and young adult books, 12–18 years. Genres include historical fiction, adventure, and suspense. Also publishes stories about animals.
- **Nonfiction:** Publishes educational titles, 0–18 years. Topics include history, religion, language arts, and biography. Also publishes activity books, poetry collections, and books for adults.
- **Representative Titles:** *Regular Lu* by Robin Nelson tells the story of a little mouse named Lu, who learns—in a dramatic way—that his real value in life is being who he is, no matter how small. *Saving the Scrolls* by Mary Kerry (YA) is a historical novel featuring the younger sister of Queen Cleopatra as she fights to save important scrolls from a burning library.

Submissions and Payment

Guidelines and catalogue available at website. Query with outline/synopsis and 2–3 sample chapters. Accepts hard copy. No simultaneous submissions. SASE. Responds in 6–9 months. Publication in 1 year. Payment policy varies.

Editor's Comments

Please be advised that we do not open nor download documents from unknown sources.

ACTA Publications

5559 West Howard Street
Skokie, IL 60077

Acquisitions Editor: Andrew Yankech

Publisher's Interests

Originally formed as a publisher of Catholic books and resources, ACTA Publications produces a wide array of materials for those who are seeking the Christian way in all aspects of their lives. Children's books and self-help titles for adults are included in its catalogue.
Website: www.actapublications.com

Freelance Potential

Published 20 titles in 2009: 1 was developed from an unsolicited submission and 2 were by agented authors. Of the 20 titles, 3 were by unpublished writers and 4 were by authors who were new to the publishing house. Receives 120 queries yearly.

- **Nonfiction:** Publishes story picture books, 4–10 years; and young adult books, 12–18 years. Also publishes books for adults, parents, and Christian educators. Topics include religion, parenting, divorce, grief, self-help, and history.
- **Representative Titles:** *Little Lucy's Family* by Eleanor Gormally tells how Lucy was adopted from her home in Russia and became a part of her new family. *Animals of the Bible from A to Z* by Alice Camille depicts 26 animals from the Bible and their significance.

Submissions and Payment

Guidelines and catalogue available at website. Query with table of contents, sample chapter, and market analysis. Accepts hard copy and simultaneous submissions if identified. SASE. Responds in 3–6 weeks. Publication in 9–12 months. Royalty, 10%.

Editor's Comments

Writers who do not first study our website to become familiar with our products often waste their time, as their submissions usually don't fit our needs. If your book is for "everyone," it is probably not for us.

Action Publishing

P.O. Box 391
Glendale, CA 91209

Submissions Editor

Publisher's Interests
This independent publisher features quality children's picture books, juvenile and young adult fiction, and nonfiction titles for all ages.
Website: www.actionpublishing.com

Freelance Potential
Published 6 titles (4 juvenile) in 2009. Of the 6 titles, 1 was by an author who was new to the publishing house. Receives 1,100–1,200 queries yearly.

- **Fiction:** Publishes early picture books, 0–4 years; easy-to-read books, 4–7 years; story picture books, 4–10 years; chapter books, 5–10 years; middle-grade books, 8–12 years; and young adult books, 12–18 years. Genres include fantasy and adventure.
- **Nonfiction:** Publishes middle-grade books, 8–12 years; and young adult books, 12–18 years. Topics include nature, the environment, and humor. Also publishes titles for parents.
- **Representative Titles:** *The Family of Ree* by Scott E. Sutton tells of a wizard and his assistant who learn a valuable lesson about protecting the environment and all of its creatures. *Merrywinkle* by Anne Fewell introduces young children to Santa's big brother, who helps Santa bring the Christmas spirit to the town of Noggenhorn.

Submissions and Payment
Guidelines and catalogue available at website. Send complete ms for picture books. Query with outline and sample chapter or send complete ms for all others. Accepts hard copy. SASE. Response time and publication period vary. Royalty; advance.

Editor's Comments
Most of our titles are acquired through agents, however, we make our best effort to review unsolicited manuscripts provided they follow the conditions outlined on our website.

Active Parenting Publishers

1955 Vaughn Road, Suite 108
Kennesaw, GA 30144

Product Development Manager: Molly Davis

Publisher's Interests
The mission of this publisher is to support parents who are
striving to improve their parenting skills, build their children's character, and educate their children about contemporary social issues. In addition to books, it also produces
multimedia training programs.
Website: www.activeparenting.com

Freelance Potential
Published 4 titles in 2009. Receives 120 queries, 96 unsolicited mss yearly.

- **Fiction:** Publishes concept books, 0–4 years; story picture
  books, 4–10 years; middle-grade books, 8–12 years; and
  young adult books, 12–18 years. Offers stories about self-
  esteem and social issues.
- **Nonfiction:** Publishes concept books, 0–4 years; story picture
  books, 4–10 years; middle-grade books, 8–12 years; and
  young adult books, 12–18 years. Topics include gifted and
  special education, social issues, and parenting. Also publishes
  self-help titles.
- **Representative Titles:** *Teen Dads: Rights, Responsibilities,
  and Joys* by Jeanne Warren Lindsay (YA) contains tips to help
  young fathers accept their role. *Cyber Bullying* by Robin M.
  Kowalski et al. presents critical prevention strategies for
  addressing the new media of bullying.

Submissions and Payment
Guidelines available. Catalogue available at website. Query
or send complete ms. Accepts hard copy and email submissions to cservice@activeparenting.com. SASE. Response time
and publication period vary. Royalty. Flat fee.

Editor's Comments
We are open to all parenting subjects and social issues, and
welcome projects that will give parents, educators, counselors, and children effective tools for navigating those issues.

Adams Media Corporation

57 Littlefield Street
Avon, MA 02322

Book Proposals

Publisher's Interests
This publisher's catalogue is filled with a wide selection of practical and meaningful nonfiction titles that inspire, inform, and impact the lives of readers. Its books cover a broad range of contemporary topics including parenting, business, personal finance, and travel.
Website: www.adamsmedia.com

Freelance Potential
Published 252 titles (1 juvenile) in 2009.

- **Nonfiction:** Publishes young adult books, 12–18 years. Topics include animals, careers, hobbies, health, fitness, social issues, relationships, and contemporary issues. Features humor as well as inspirational, self-help, exam-prep, and how-to books. Also publishes books for adults on business, cooking, home improvement, parenting, personal finance, women's issues, weddings, travel, and writing.
- **Representative Titles:** *The Everything Father-to-Be Book: A Survival Guide for Men* by Kevin Nelson is packed with helpful information and advice for the nervous first-time father. *365 Ways to Boost Your Brain Power: Tips, Exercises, and Advice* by Carolyn Dean et al. offers nutrition and exercise tips for bettering the brain.

Submissions and Payment
Guidelines and catalogue available at website. Query with table of contents and brief author biography. Accepts hard copy. SASE. Responds only if interested. Publication period varies. Royalty.

Editor's Comments
We are always looking for great book proposals whether they come directly from authors or literary agents. We welcome submissions from first-time authors. Please refer to our website for submission guidelines as well as for information on "Call for Stories."

Aladdin Paperbacks

Simon & Schuster Children's Publishing Division
1230 Avenue of the Americas
New York, NY 10020

Editorial Assistant: Alyson Heller

Publisher's Interests
This imprint of Simon & Schuster publishes hardcover and paperback original fiction and nonfiction for children from preschool through the tween years.
Website: www.simonandschuster.com

Freelance Potential
Published 90 titles in 2009. Of the 90 titles, 4 were by unpublished writers and 18 were by authors who were new to the publishing house. Receives 200+ queries yearly.

- **Fiction:** Publishes easy-to-read books, 4–7 years; story picture books, 4–10 years; chapter books, 5–10 years; and middle-grade books, 8–12 years. Genres include contemporary and historical fiction, suspense, mystery, fantasy, and adventure.
- **Nonfiction:** Publishes easy-to-read books, 4–7 years; and middle-grade books, 8–12 years. Topics include America's national monuments and natural wonders; childhood biographies of world figures; and humor.
- **Representative Titles:** *Jay Leno's How to Be the Funniest Kid in the Whole Wide World* by Jay Leno (7–12 years) contains hundreds of jokes and bits of advice for any kid trying to find his funny bone. *Eloise Visits the Zoo* by Lisa McClatchy (4–6 years) features the beloved character Eloise taking a trip to the zoo with Nanny and Weenie to see the animals she loves.

Submissions and Payment
Agented authors only. Guidelines available. Query with proposal. Accepts hard copy. SASE. Response time, publication period, and payment policy vary.

Editor's Comments
We look for books that have an emphasis on quality recreational reading in all genres, with a particular interest in school stories, action-adventure, humor, and coming-of-age stories. Our target audience is kids ages 4 to 14. We highly recommend having an agent represent you and your work.

ALA Editions

American Library Association
50 East Huron Street
Chicago, IL 60611

Editorial Assistant: Eugenia Chun

Publisher's Interests

ALA Editions publishes professional resources for librarians on such topics as library administration, copyright law, new technologies, and children's services, among many others. Its parent organization, the American Library Association, has been supporting librarians for more than 100 years.
Website: www.ala.org/editions

Freelance Potential

Published 30–35 titles in 2009: 1 was by an author who was new to the publishing house. Receives 50 queries yearly.

- **Nonfiction:** Publishes professional resources for the library information services community. Topics include school services; acquisitions and collection development; library studies, issues, and trends; reference services and resources; technology; digital library operations and services; library administration and management; budgeting; fundraising; buildings and facilities; and children's programming.
- **Representative Titles:** *Booktalking Bonanza* by Betsy Diamant-Cohen & Selma K. Levi offers 10 kid-tested, ready-to-use multimedia models for enlivening traditional booktalks. *Leadership for Excellence* by Jo Ann Carr, ed. shares the best practices of successful school library media specialists.

Submissions and Payment

Guidelines available at website. Query with outline, 300-word synopsis, table of contents, brief author bio, and writing sample. Accepts hard copy. SASE. Responds in 6–8 weeks. Publication in 7–9 months. Royalty.

Editor's Comments

Most of our titles are published in book format, but electronic publishing projects are also being considered. Please provide brief notes on the major print and electronic resources that address your topic, or a large part of it. Be sure to read our guidelines for complete submission instructions.

Alaska Northwest Books

Graphic Arts Publishing
P.O. Box 10306
Portland, OR 97296-0306

Executive Editor: Tim Frew

Publisher's Interests
This imprint of the regional publisher Graphic Arts Publishing produces children's fiction and nonfiction books on Alaskan subjects and themes. It accepts books for all age levels.
Website: www.gacpc.com

Freelance Potential
Published 4 titles in 2009: 1 was developed from an unsolicited submission.

- **Fiction:** Publishes early picture books, 0–4 years; easy-to-read books, 4–7 years; chapter books, 5–10 years; middle-grade books, 8–12 years; and young adult books, 12–18 years. Genres include adventure, nature, and the environment, and historical and contemporary fiction—all with Alaskan themes.
- **Nonfiction:** Publishes early picture books, 0–4 years; easy-to-read books, 4–7 years; middle-grade books, 8–12 years; and young adult books, 12–18 years. Topics include animals, crafts, hobbies, history, sports, the environment, and nature—all with Alaskan themes.
- **Representative Titles:** *Runaways on the Inside Passage* by Joe Upton (10+ years) is a novel of adventure as two young twins discover that winter sailing in Alaska is filled with peril. *Aurora: A Tale of the Northern Lights* by Mindy Dwyer (3+ years) introduces children to the wonders of the aurora borealis. *Baby Animals of the North* by Katy Main (3–5 years) features some of Alaska's young creatures.

Submissions and Payment
Guidelines and catalogue available at website. Query with outline/synopsis, table of contents, and 1–2 chapters. Send ms for picture books. Accepts hard copy. SASE. Responds in 6 months. Publication period and payment policy vary.

Editor's Comments
Anything about Alaska, its people, or its culture will be of interest to us.

Ambassador Books

91 Prescott Street
Worcester, MA 01605

Acquisitions Editor: Paul McMahon

Publisher's Interests
This Christian publisher focuses on books that speak equally to readers' spirituality and intellect. Its children's catalogue is comprised of books that introduce children to Jesus and godly living, and books that use the Bible as a basis for navigating life. It also publishes parenting books.
Website: www.ambassadorbooks.com

Freelance Potential
Published 8 titles in 2009. Receives 2,000 queries yearly.

- **Fiction:** Publishes easy-to-read books, 4–7 years; story picture books, 4–10 years; and middle-grade books, 8–12 years. Genres include inspirational, religious, historical, and regional fiction; adventure; mystery; and suspense. Also publishes books about spirituality in sports.
- **Nonfiction:** Publishes easy-to-read books, 4–7 years; story picture books, 4–10 years; and middle-grade books, 8–12 years. Topics include religion, sports, and regional subjects. Also publishes self-help titles.
- **Representative Titles:** *Frank is a Chihuahua* by Kevin Morrison is the story of a chihuahua raised by coyotes who suddenly realizes he is different and doesn't quite fit in. *The Lion Who Wouldn't Roar* by John Powers presents a story about a quiet lion and the sheep who need him as parable about finding our unique gifts.

Submissions and Payment
Guidelines available. Catalogue available at website. Query with outline/synopsis, 3 sample chapters, author biography, and market analysis. Send complete ms for picture books only. Accepts hard copy. SASE. Responds in 2 months. Publication in 1 year. Royalty, 8% of net.

Editor's Comments
We look for children's books that can convey a message of Jesus along with a great tale or inspirational information.

AMG Publishers

6815 Shallowford Road
Chattanooga, TN 37421

Acquisitions: Rick Steele

Publisher's Interests

This company is the publishing arm of an evangelical mission and relief agency. It focuses on nonfiction titles for young adults and adults that are intended to help readers understand the Gospel. Bible study resources and books on parenting, relationships, and discipleship are offered, as well as contemporary and fantasy fiction with Christian themes for middle-grade kids and young adults.
Website: www.amgpublishers.com

Freelance Potential

Published 25 titles (4 juvenile) in 2009. Of the 25 titles, 3 were by unpublished writers and 4 were by authors new to the publishing house. Receives 2,500 queries yearly.

- **Fiction:** Publishes middle-grade books, 8–12 years; and young adult books, 12–18 years. Genres include fantasy fiction with Christian themes.
- **Nonfiction:** Publishes Bible study materials, inspirational and motivational books, Bible reference books, and books on parenting, family life, and contemporary issues.
- **Representative Titles:** *Preparing My Heart for Motherhood* by Ann Marie Stewart presents a Bible study that centers around preparing for motherhood and discerning what it means to love your husband and prepare your heart for the love that is to come. *Life Principles from the Women of Acts* by Xavia Arndt Sheffield examines the lives of the women who were essential to the survival of early Christianity.

Submissions and Payment

Guidelines and catalogue available at website. Query. Accepts email queries to ricks@amgpublishers.com. Response time and publication period vary. Royalty; advance.

Editor's Comments

We're looking to add American history-themed fiction, Bible studies, and young adult fiction to our list.

Amulet Books

Harry N. Abrams Inc.
115 West 18th Street, 6th Floor
New York, NY 10011

Editor: Maggie Lehrman

Publisher's Interests
Overwhelmed by the large volume of unsolicited manuscripts it has received in recent years, Amulet Books now
accepts proposals through literary agents only. This imprint
of Harry N. Abrams publishes picture books, graphic novels,
fiction, and nonfiction for readers ages 8 through 18.
Website: www.amuletbooks.com

Freelance Potential
Published 30 titles in 2009: each was by an agented author.
Receives 1,200 queries yearly.

- **Fiction:** Publishes middle-grade books, 8–12 years; and young
  adult books, 12–18 years. Genres include contemporary, historical, and science fiction; fantasy; mystery; suspense; and
  humor. Also publishes graphic novels.
- **Nonfiction:** Publishes middle-grade books, 8–12 years; and
  young adult books, 12–18 years. Topics include multicultural
  and ethnic issues, animals, natural history, the environment,
  history, and self-help.
- **Representative Titles:** *My Life in Pink & Green* by Lisa Green-
  wald (10–14 years) is the story of a seventh-grade girl who
  comes up with a plan to resuscitate her family's pharmacy,
  while helping the environment at the same time. *Operation
  Redwood* by S. Terrell French (8–12 years) tells how a ragtag
  group of kids tries to save an ancient forest from a greedy corporation. *The Girls* by Tucker Shaw (YA) is a modern retelling
  of the classic play *The Women*, set at an Aspen prep school.

Submissions and Payment
Guidelines and catalogue available at website. Agented
authors only; no unsolicited mss or queries. Royalty; advance.

Editor's Comments
We suggest you study the guidelines on finding an agent
and/or publisher detailed in this directory and others. Our
roster includes several bestselling and award-winning authors.

Andersen Press

20 Vauxhall Bridge Road
London SW1V 2SA
United Kingdom

Submissions Editor

Publisher's Interests
Home of Elmer, the patchwork elephant, Andersen Press specializes in picture books for young children. It also publishes middle-grade and young adult fiction.
Website: www.andersenpress.co.uk

Freelance Potential
Published 87 titles in 2009: 10 were by agented authors. Receives 1,200 unsolicited mss yearly.

- **Fiction:** Publishes early picture books, 0–4 years; easy-to-read books, 4–7 years; story picture books, 4–10 years; chapter books, 5–10 years; middle-grade books, 8–12 years; and young adult books, 12–18 years. Genres include historical and contemporary fiction, humor, adventure, fantasy, folktales, horror, mystery, suspense, and romance. Also publishes stories about animals and sports.
- **Representative Titles:** *Minty and Tink* by Emma Chichester Clark (0–5 years) is a picture book about a little girl who wants to keep her baby brother's birthday gift: a talking toy bear named Tink. *Pirates Ahoy!* by Sophie Smiley (7–9 years) recounts the seaside adventures of a boy with Down syndrome and his family.

Submissions and Payment
Guidelines and catalogue available at website. Send complete ms for picture books. Query with synopsis and 3 sample chapters for longer works. Accepts hard copy. SAE/IRC. Responds in 2 months. Publication period and payment policy vary.

Editor's Comments
Please take note of our word limits: Picture books run under 1,000 words; books in our "Tigers" series of juvenile fiction run 3,000–5,000 words; and our novels for older children run 15,000–50,000 words. We are unable to acknowledge receipt or give editorial guidance on the material we reject.

Annick Press

15 Patricia Avenue
Toronto, Ontario M2M 1H9
Canada

Submissions Editor: Katie Hearn

Publisher's Interests

Annick Press is concerned strictly with children's books from Canadian authors. It publishes some picture books, but it is primarily interested in juvenile and young adult fiction and nonfiction. Its nonfiction list covers subjects such as history and pop culture, while its fiction books often have characters dealing with social issues affecting young people.
Website: www.annickpress.com

Freelance Potential

Published 26 titles (20 juvenile) in 2009: 15 were by unpublished writers and 25 were by authors who were new to the publishing house. Receives 5,000 queries yearly.

- **Fiction:** Publishes story picture books, 4–10 years; middle-grade books, 8–12 years; and young adult books, 12–18 years. Genres include contemporary fiction and humor.
- **Nonfiction:** Publishes middle-grade books, 8–12 years; and young adult books, 12–18 years. Topics include culture, history, and contemporary issues.
- **Representative Titles:** *Drusilla the Lucky Duck* by Errol Broome (6–10 years) is the story of young girl's pet duckling, and the lengths she goes to in order to stop Drusilla from becoming dinner. *Dancing Feathers* by Christel Kleitsch (8–11 years) finds a young Ojibway girl learning to balance her people's traditional values with those of the mainstream.

Submissions and Payment

Canadian authors only. Guidelines available at website. Query with synopsis and sample chapter. Accepts email queries to annickpress@annickpress.com. Response time, publication period, and payment policy vary.

Editor's Comments

We are not accepting picture books at this time. Please check our website for the most current information about our submission requirements.

Atheneum Books for Young Readers

1230 Avenue of the Americas
New York, NY 10020

Editorial Director: Caitlyn Dlouhy

Publisher's Interests

High-quality books in all genres and on a variety of topics comprise the catalogue of this Simon & Schuster imprint. Fiction and nonfiction titles are considered.
Website: www.simonandschuster.com

Freelance Potential

Published 70 titles in 2009: 42 were by agented authors. Of the 70 titles, 7 were by unpublished writers. Receives 30,000 queries yearly.

- **Fiction:** Publishes concept books, toddler books, and early picture books, 0–4 years; story picture books, 4–10 years; chapter books, 5–10 years; middle-grade books, 8–12 years; and young adult books, 12–18 years. Genres include fantasy, graphic novels, mysteries, adventure, and historical fiction.
- **Nonfiction:** Publishes story picture books, 4–10 years; chapter books, 5–10 years; middle-grade books, 8–12 years; and young adult books, 12–18 years. Topics include the environment, science, nature, sports, history, and multicultural issues. Also publishes biographies.
- **Representative Titles:** *DogFish* by Gillian Shields (3–7 years) is a humorous picture book that creates the perfect pet by blending the mom-friendly aspects of a goldfish with the kid-friendly aspects of a dog. *The Hand You're Dealt* by Paul Volponi (YA) features a teen who gets involved in poker as a way to feel closer to his late father, but then realizes that the environment might be too much for him.

Submissions and Payment

Guidelines available. Query with outline/synopsis. Accepts hard copy. SASE. Responds in 3 months. Publication period varies. Royalty.

Editor's Comments

We will consider all books as long as they are engaging, creative, and original.

Autism Asperger Publishing Co.

15490 Quivira Road
Overland Park, KS 66221

Submissions: Kirsten McBride

Publisher's Interests

Focusing strictly on autism and Asperger Syndrome, this publisher is interested in books that speak to teachers, parents, and children on the autism spectrum.
Website: www.asperger.net

Freelance Potential

Published 30 titles (5 juvenile) in 2009: 5 were developed from unsolicited submissions. Of the 30 titles, 25 were by unpublished writers and 25 were by authors who were new to the publishing house. Receives 240 queries yearly.

- **Nonfiction:** Publishes easy-to-read books, 4–7 years; middle-grade books, 8–12 years; and young adult books, 12–18 years. Also publishes books for teachers and parents. Topics include autism spectrum disorders, special education, and parenting.
- **Representative Titles:** *Learn to Move, Moving Up!* by Jenny Clark Brack provides sensorimotor, theme-based lesson plans that include literacy and curriculum suggestions for incorporating them into elementary school schedules. *Why Does Lizzie Cover Her Ears?* by Jennifer Veenendall uses a fictional first-grader dealing with sensory modulation difficulties as a way of introducing children to the disorder.

Submissions and Payment

Guidelines and catalogue available at website. Query with table of contents, sample chapters, and author profile. Accepts hard copy. Availability of artwork improves chance of acceptance. SASE. Responds in 3–6 months. Publication in 8 months. Royalty, 10%.

Editor's Comments

We accept proposals for books on effective strategies and techniques that can be easily implemented in school, clinic, and home settings. We also consider books targeting individuals with autism spectrum disorders.

Avalon Books

160 Madison Avenue
New York, NY 10016

Editor: Faith Black

Publisher's Interests

Avalon Books publishes family-friendly fiction. Its list is suitable for teens, but geared toward adults. It specializes in romance (contemporary and historical), mystery, and Westerns that are free of violence, profanity, and sex.
Website: www.avalonbooks.com

Freelance Potential

Published 60 titles in 2009. Of the 60 titles, 38 were by unpublished writers and 13 were by authors who were new to the publishing house. Receives 2,400 queries yearly.

- **Fiction:** Publishes titles for young adults and adults. Genres include career romance, historical romance, mystery, suspense, and Westerns.
- **Representative Titles:** *Stuck* by Elisabeth Rose features two people who get stuck in an elevator, then find their lives intertwined forever. *Pushin' Up Daisies* by Carolyn Brown is a historical romance featuring a widowed hotel owner and the detective investigating the disappearance of her abusive brother-in-law. *Dead Man's Money* by V. S. Meszaros follows the Wild West adventures of two witnesses to a stage coach robbery as they try to outrun the deadly Bodine Gang.

Submissions and Payment

Guidelines and catalogue available at website. Query with 2- to 3-page synopsis and first 3 chapters. Accepts hard copy and simultaneous submissions if identified. SASE. Response time and publication period vary. Royalty; advance.

Editor's Comments

Since 1950, the underlying principle of our company has been to publish books with good stories and wholesome entertainment. We will not accept any book with profanity, premarital sex, or sexual tension of any kind. It is the author's job to heighten the romantic atmosphere by developing love stories with tenderness, emotion, and perception.

Avari Press

P.O. Box 285
Smoketown, PA 17576

Managing Editor: Adam J. Barkafski

Publisher's Interests
Fantasy literature, medieval studies, and nonfiction books
are the specialty of this award-winning publisher. It looks for
exceptional writing that educates as well as entertains.
Website: www.avaripress.com

Freelance Potential
Published 10 titles (2 juvenile) in 2009: 8 were developed
from unsolicited submissions and 2 were by agented
authors. Of the 10 titles, each was by an unpublished writer.
Receives 360 queries yearly.

- **Fiction:** Publishes young adult books, 12–18 years. Also
  publishes titles for adults. Genres include high fantasy and
  historical fiction.
- **Nonfiction:** Publishes young adult books, 12–18 years. Topics
  include online gaming resources and history.
- **Representative Titles:** *Griffin's Daughter* by Leslie Ann Moore
  is the story of a young woman's struggle to make her way in a
  world that has trouble accepting her. *Griffin's Shadow* by
  Leslie Ann Moore, the sequel, is a story of courage and love in
  the face of adversity.

Submissions and Payment
Guidelines and catalogue available at website. Query with
brief biography, synopsis, and sample chapters. Accepts
hard copy, email submissions to editorial@avaripress.com
(no attachments), and simultaneous submissions if identified. SASE. Responds in 8–10 weeks. Publication in 7
months. Royalty; advance.

Editor's Comments
We welcome submissions of epic fantasy literature, historical
fiction based on medieval times, nonfiction medieval studies, scholarly work on fantasy topics, and books on fantasy
role-playing games and virtual communities. We do not
publish science fiction, erotica, poetry, or children's books.

Ave Maria Press

P.O. Box 428
Notre Dame, IN 46556

Acquisitions Department

Publisher's Interests
Publishing continually since 1865, first as a magazine and then as a book publisher, Ave Maria serves a predominantly Catholic readership with religious books and materials for religious education ministry.
Website: www.avemariapress.com

Freelance Potential
Published 39 titles in 2009. Of the 39 titles, 6 were by authors who were new to the publishing house. Receives 200 queries yearly.

- **Nonfiction:** Publishes young adult books, 12–18 years. Also publishes titles for teachers, ministers, and parents. Topics include catechism, Christian living, parenting, prayer, relationships, religion, sacraments, spirituality, and youth ministry.
- **Representative Titles:** *A Teen's Game Plan for Life* by Lou Holtz (YA) presents a common-sense message for teens striving to set goals for their lives. *Activities for Catholic School Teaching* by James McGinnis is a resource guide for teachers and youth ministers that offers teens a chance to put into action the Church's body of social teaching.

Submissions and Payment
Guidelines and catalogue available at website. Query with résumé, synopsis, table of contents, introduction, and 1–2 sample chapters; or send complete ms. Accepts hard copy and simultaneous submissions if identified. SASE. Responds in 6–8 weeks. Publication in 1 year. Payment policy varies.

Editor's Comments
We do not accept fiction, poetry, biography, or autobiography, nor do we publish accounts of personal conversions or private revelations. Note that college-level texts and scholarly works are also inappropriate for our publishing program. Please be sure to read our guidelines for more information on what to include in a submission package.

Avocus Publishing

4 White Brook Road
P.O. Box 89
Gilsum, NH 03448

Submissions Editor

Publisher's Interests

Serving homeschoolers and educators in the independent
school system, Avocus Publishing specializes in parenting
and educational books that address curricula development,
classroom teaching, and gifted and special education.
Website: www.avocus.com

Freelance Potential

Published 2 titles (1 juvenile) in 2009: 1 was developed
from an unsolicited submission and 1 was a reprint/licensed
property. Of the 2 titles, 1 was by an author who was new to
the publishing house. Receives 48 queries yearly.

- **Nonfiction:** Publishes chapter books, 5–10 years; middle-
  grade books, 8–12 years; and young adult books, 12–18
  years. Also publishes books for teachers and parents. Topics
  include gifted and special education, curriculum, and educational issues.
- **Representative Titles:** *The Courtroom in the Classroom* by
  Donald Grace is the first in a series of books that address
  issues of concern in independent schools. *Casualties of Privi-
  lege: Essays on Prep Schools' Hidden Culture* by Louis Crosier
  reveals the other side of prep school education with observations from former students.

Submissions and Payment

Guidelines and catalogue available at website. Query with
synopsis, intended audience, and several sample chapters.
Accepts hard copy. SASE. Response time and publication
period vary. Royalty; advance.

Editor's Comments

Submissions should be well researched and cover an important challenge or issue in today's independent schools. We
pride ourselves on being careful in developing our evalua-
tions and that simply takes time. Please be patient while we
review your submission.

Bahá'í Publishing Trust

415 Linden Avenue
Wilmette, IL 60091

Director of Acquisitions: Terry Cassiday

Publisher's Interests

This is the publishing arm of the national governing body of
the Bahá'í faith in the United States. It publishes trade books
for children and adults about the faith's teachings and
beliefs. Books for children appear under its Bellwood Press
imprint.
Website: http://books.bahai.us

Freelance Potential

Published 10–15 titles (4 juvenile) in 2009: 10 were developed from unsolicited submissions. Of the 10–15 titles, 8
were by unpublished writers. Receives 96 queries, 60 unsolicited mss yearly.

- **Fiction:** Publishes story picture books, 4–10 years; and chapter books, 5–10 years. Genres include contemporary and historical fiction centered on the Bahá'í faith.
- **Nonfiction:** Publishes young adult books, 12–18 years. Topics
  include Bahá'í teachings, history, identity, church members,
  and social issues.
- **Representative Titles:** *In Grandfather's Barn* by William Sears
  is a humorous novel that recounts the author's adventures
  growing up in a small town and learning what it means to live
  with compassion for others. *Maggie Celebrates Ayyam-i-Ha* by
  Patti Rae Tomarelli is a picture book that tells the simple story
  of one child's joyous celebration of Ayyam-i-Ha.

Submissions and Payment

Guidelines available with 9x12 SASE. Catalogue available at
bahaibookstore.com. Query with clips; or send complete ms.
Accepts email to acquisitions@usbnc.org. Responds to
queries in 1–2 weeks, to mss in 2–3 months. Publication in
18 months. Royalty, 10%.

Editor's Comments

We welcome books that give accurate information about the
youngest of the independent world religions.

Baker's Plays

45 West 25th Street
New York, NY 10010

Managing Editor: Roxane Heinze-Bradshaw

Publisher's Interests
Geared to school, family, and faith-based groups, Baker's Plays publishes one-act and full-length plays and musicals in a variety of genres, as well as nonfiction material.
Website: www.bakersplays.com

Freelance Potential
Published 50 titles (40 juvenile) in 2009. Receives 1,000+ queries, 500 unsolicited mss yearly.

- **Fiction:** Publishes one-act and full-length plays, monologues, and skits for children's, high school, and family theater groups. Genres include comedy; mystery; folktales; fairy tales; and multicultural, religious, and historical fiction. Also publishes holiday plays, the classics, and musicals.
- **Nonfiction:** Publishes textbooks and theater resource materials for drama students and teachers. Topics include improvisation, teaching theater, acting techniques, theatrical history, and play writing.
- **Representative Titles:** *Eleanor for President* by Merritt Ierley offers an insightful look into how history could have been re-written if Eleanor Roosevelt ran for president. *A Father's Secret* by Alexandra Dennett tells the story of a young girl who discovers a long-held secret that quickly changes her world.

Submissions and Payment
Guidelines available. Query with script history, reviews, and sample pages or synopsis; or send complete ms. Prefers email submissions to publications@bakersplays.com (Microsoft Word or PDF attachments); will accept hard copy and simultaneous submissions if identified. SASE. Responds to queries in 1 month; to mss in 2–6 months. Publication period and payment policy vary.

Editor's Comments
Anthologies or collections of one-act plays are much preferred, as are plays that have already been produced.

Bancroft Press

P.O. Box 65360
Baltimore, MD 21209

Editor: Bruce Bortz

Publisher's Interests
Bancroft Press is a general interest book publisher focused on quality writing and understanding of the subject matter at hand. The majority of its children's and young adult catalogue is fiction, but some nonfiction adult titles appeal to young adult readers.
Website: www.bancroftpress.com

Freelance Potential
Published 4–6 titles (3–4 juvenile) in 2009. Of the 4–6 titles, 3 were by unpublished writers and 3 were by authors who were new to the publishing house. Receives 5,000 queries, 10,000 unsolicited mss yearly.

- **Fiction:** Publishes middle-grade books, 8–12 years; and young adult books, 12–18 years. Genres include mystery, history, sports, and contemporary and multicultural fiction. Also publishes novels for adults.
- **Nonfiction:** Publishes young adult books, 12–18 years. Topics include sports and biography. Also publishes parenting and financial self-help books for adults.
- **Representative Titles:** *Butterflies in May* by Karen Hart (YA) is a realistic novel about a teenage girl's traumatic experiences with an unintended pregnancy. *Glory for Sale* by Jon Morgan (YA) profiles the "new" NFL as one of back room deals and publicly funded stadiums.

Submissions and Payment
Guidelines and catalogue available at website. Query with cover letter, résumé, and 4 or 5 sample chapters; or send complete ms with cover letter and résumé. Accepts hard copy. SASE. Responds in 6 months. Publication period varies. Royalty, 80%; advance, $750–$5,000.

Editor's Comments
We do not publish fiction for young children (under eight years) or poetry. Other than that, anything goes!

B & H Publishing Group

127 Ninth Avenue North
MSN 164
Nashville, TN 37234

Submissions

Publisher's Interests

B & H is a publisher of Christian living books on topics such as parenting, homeschooling, history, and youth-related subjects. It also publishes fiction, as long as the story embraces a Christian theme.
Website: www.broadmanholman.com

Freelance Potential

Published 100 titles in 2009. Receives 300 unsolicited mss each year.

- **Fiction:** Publishes story picture books, 4–10 years. Genres include historical, contemporary, and Christian fiction with biblical themes.
- **Nonfiction:** Publishes concept books and toddler books, 0–4 years; easy-to-read books, 4–7 years; story picture books, 4–10 years; middle-grade books, 8–12 years; and young adult books, 12–18 years. Topics include religion and contemporary social issues. Also publishes traditional and retold Bible stories, self-help books, and parenting titles.
- **Representative Titles:** *Five Conversations You Must Have with Your Daughter* by Vicki Courtney offers advice for mothers preparing to have important discussions with their daughters on topics such as sex and self-esteem. *Simple Student Ministry* by Eric Geiger & Jeff Borton provides a blueprint to transform a church youth program into a simpler, results-oriented spiritual development process.

Submissions and Payment

Guidelines available. Send complete ms. Accepts hard copy and simultaneous submissions if identified. SASE. Responds in 3 months. Publication in 12–18 months. Royalty; advance.

Editor's Comments

Although we are not currently accepting submissions for children's fiction, we are open to a variety of nonfiction topics that affect young people or parents.

Barefoot Books

2067 Massachusetts Avenue
Cambridge, MA 02140

Submissions Editor

Publisher's Interests

"Celebrating art and story," Barefoot Books publishes books
for children up to the age of 12 that celebrate the vital role
of imagination in their lives. Stories that honor diversity, balance art and language, and introduce early learning themes
can be found in its catalogue.
Website: www.barefootbooks.com

Freelance Potential

Published 35–40 titles in 2009. Of the 35–40 titles, 2 were
by unpublished writers and 7 were by authors who were new
to the publishing house. Receives 2,000 unsolicited mss
each year.

- **Fiction:** Publishes concept books, 0–4 years; story picture
  books, 4–10 years; and middle-grade books, 8–12 years.
  Genres include fairy tales, folklore, folktales, multicultural and
  ethnic fiction, and stories about nature and the environment.
- **Representative Titles:** *Mama Panya's Pancakes* by Mary &
  Rich Chamberlain (4–10 years) tells a heartwarming story
  about life in Kenya and the rewards for sharing. *Arthur of
  Albion* by John Matthews (7–10 years) presents the best
  known stories of King Arthur and his court.

Submissions and Payment

Guidelines and catalogue available at website. Send complete ms with artwork, if applicable. Accepts hard copy.
SASE. Responds in 4–6 months if interested. Publication
period and payment policy vary.

Editor's Comments

We take our inspiration from the many different cultures
around the word. Our books focus on themes that encourage independence of spirit, an enthusiasm for learning, and
a sharing of the world's diversity. Please study our website
first. If you feel your manuscript is compatible with our catalogue of books, feel free to send it along.

Behler Publications

22365 El Toro Road, Box 135
Lake Forest, CA 92630

Editor: Lynn Price

Publisher's Interests

Through its nonfiction catalogue of self-help books and biographies, Behler Publications shares "personal journeys with social relevance." It also considers fictional works in which a character's personal growth is key to the story.
Website: www.behlerpublications.com

Freelance Potential

Published 12 titles in 2009. Receives 2,400 queries yearly.

- **Fiction:** Publishes young adult books, 12–18 years. Genres include contemporary, Western, and science fiction; fantasy; and romance. Also publishes titles for adults.
- **Nonfiction:** Publishes young adult books, 12–18 years. Topics include self-help, biography, health, fitness, and education. Also publishes parenting titles.
- **Representative Titles:** *Kosher* by Kim Beam (YA) depicts a 12-year-old boy's crisis of faith as his bar mitzvah approaches. *Fostering Hope* by Shane Salter (YA–Adult) chronicles the author's journey from an abandoned preschooler to a prominent child advocate. *The Hollows of Candlewick* by Scot R. Stone (YA–Adult) is a fantasy novel about a king who must face the simultaneous threats of violent weather, a vengeful enemy, a mysterious mangler, and treasonous subjects; third in the Snowtear Wars series.

Submissions and Payment

Guidelines and catalogue available at website. Query with outline/synopsis, first 30 pages, and author bio. Accepts hard copy and email to acquisitions@behlerpublications.com (Microsoft Word attachments). SASE. Response time and publication period vary. Royalty, 10%.

Editor's Comments

We seek timeless literature that touches all the emotional and physical aspects of life. Please note that we are currently focused on increasing our nonfiction list.

Behrman House

11 Edison Place
Springfield, NJ 07081

Editorial Department

Publisher's Interests

This publisher specializes in textbooks and other educational resources for the Jewish religious school classroom. It accepts material for children in all grade levels, including preschool. It also publishes books of a Jewish nature on any topic.

Website: www.behrmanhouse.com

Freelance Potential

Published 10 titles (8 juvenile) in 2009. Receives 50 queries, 50 unsolicited mss yearly.

- **Nonfiction:** Publishes early picture books, 0–4 years; chapter books, 5–10 years; middle-grade books, 8–12 years; and young adult books, 12–18 years. Topics include Judaism, religion, theology, prayer, holidays, the Bible, the Holocaust, history, liturgy, Hebrew, and ethics.
- **Representative Titles:** *Jewish & Me: Fall Holidays* by Sunny Yudkoff & Dena Neusner (preK–K) introduces the Jewish fall holidays to young students through age-appropriate text and craft projects. *Pass the Torah, Please* by Cheri Ellowitz Silver (grades 4–6) puts a fresh face on Jewish history by combining first-person monologues from more than 20 Jewish leaders with historical and political background.

Submissions and Payment

Guidelines and catalogue available at website. Prefers complete ms with author bio and table of contents; will accept query with at least 2 sample chapters. Accepts hard copy and simultaneous submissions if identified. SASE. Responds in 3 months. Publication in 18 months. Royalty, 5–10%; advance, $1,500. Flat fee.

Editor's Comments

Please note that although textbooks are our main focus, we will consider books on any Jewish subject, as long as they have educational value.

Benchmark Books

Marshall Cavendish
99 White Plains Road
Tarrytown, NY 10591

Editor: Michelle Bisson

Publisher's Interests

Benchmark Books publishes school library nonfiction series for children in kindergarten through twelfth grade. This imprint of Marshall Cavendish puts an emphasis on visually appealing and authoritative series in a variety of curriculum areas, from history and social studies to math and the arts. **Website: www.marshallcavendish.us**

Freelance Potential

Published 250 titles in 2009. Of the 250 titles, 5 were by authors who were new to the publishing house. Receives 200+ queries yearly.

- **Nonfiction:** Publishes easy-to-read books, 4–7 years; chapter books, 5–10 years; middle-grade books, 8–12 years; and young adult books, 12–18 years. Topics include animals, mathematics, science, social studies, history, world cultures, American studies, human behavior, the arts, and health.
- **Representative Titles:** *Graphing in the Desert* by Jennifer Roy & Gregory Roy (grades 2 and up) reinforces the ability to read and create graphs; part of the Math All Around series. *Following Freedom's Star: The Story of the Underground Railroad* by James Haskins & Kathleen Benson (grades 6 and up) presents a vivid account of how escaped slaves found their way north; part of the Great Journeys series.

Submissions and Payment

Query with table of contents and sample chapter. Accepts hard copy. SASE. Responds in 6–8 months. Publication in 9–18 months. Flat fee.

Editor's Comments

Our motto is "Opening New Worlds for Readers." Writers should be aware that although we publish curriculum-based nonfiction book series, we are not interested in staid, dull writing. Our books should enlighten, engage, and educate our readers.

Bess Press

3565 Harding Avenue
Honolulu, HI 96816

Submissions Editor

Publisher's Interests
This regional publisher is interested in Hawaii-related fiction and nonfiction for children, as well as textbooks and educational materials designed to meet the needs of kindergarten through grade 12 teachers in Hawaii and the Pacific Islands.
Website: www.besspress.com

Freelance Potential
Published 10–12 titles in 2009: 3 were developed from unsolicited submissions. Of the 10–12 titles, 1 was by an unpublished writer and 1 was by an author who was new to the publishing house. Receives 100 unsolicited mss yearly.

- **Fiction:** Publishes story picture books, 4–10 years. Genres include regional fiction, folklore, and folktales about Hawaiian life and culture.
- **Nonfiction:** Publishes concept books, 0–4 years; story picture books, 4–10 years; middle-grade books, 8–12 years; and young adult books, 12–18 years. Topics include Hawaiian and Pacific Island culture, language, natural history, and literature. Also publishes activity books and biographies.
- **Representative Titles:** *How Six Little Ipu Got Their Names* by Debi Brimmer & Julie Coleson is an imaginative look into the life story of a hula implement. *Kamehameha and His Warrior Kekuhaupio* (grades 9–12) by Stephen L. Desha teaches students about the epic tale of the two men.

Submissions and Payment
Guidelines and catalogue available at website. Query for K–12 textbooks. Send complete ms for all other children's books. Accepts hard copy and simultaneous submissions if identified. SASE. Responds in 4–6 months. Publication in 6–18 months. Royalty, 5–10%.

Editor's Comments
Please note that we are not seeking juvenile or young adult novels, or Asian language textbooks.

Bethany House Publishers

11400 Hampshire Avenue South
Bloomington, MN 55438

Submissions Editor

Publisher's Interests
Specializing in the Christian youth market, Bethany House publishes many bestselling fiction series as well as nonfiction titles that deal with personal growth and contemporary issues relevant to today's youth. Inspirational books for parents of teens are also featured.
Website: www.bethanyhouse.com

Freelance Potential
Published 89 titles (11 juvenile) in 2009: 80 were by agented authors. Of the 89 titles, 3 were by unpublished writers and 7 were by authors who were new to the publishing house.

- **Fiction:** Publishes young adult books, 12–18 years. Genres include inspirational, contemporary, and historical fiction.
- **Nonfiction:** Publishes devotionals, personal growth titles, and books dealing with contemporary issues.
- **Representative Titles:** *The Mandie Collection: Volume Five* by Lois Gladys Leppard (8–12 years) follows this popular character as she embarks on several exciting adventures during her coming of age in the South. *The Big Book of Animal Devotions* by William L. Coleman (8–12 years) uses animals and other creatures of God to illustrate character-development lessons straight from the Bible.

Submissions and Payment
Guidelines available at website. Query through agent only. Not currently accepting unsolicited mss. Responds in 9–12 weeks. Publication period varies. Royalty; advance.

Editor's Comments
We're reviewing agented queries only at this time. For the coming year, we'd like to see more middle-grade and young adult nonfiction, including devotionals, personal growth titles, and books that deal with contemporary issues. We look for well-planned, thoughtfully developed books with an outstanding ability to communicate with youth.

A & C Black

38 Soho Square
London W1D 3HB
United Kingdom

Submissions Editor

Publisher's Interests
In business for two centuries, A & C Black has seen it all—
and published it all. Its children's catalogue spans early
childhood through middle school, emerging readers through
young adult novels, technology through art. Titles are marketed to bookstores, schools, and libraries.
Website: www.acblack.com/childrens

Freelance Potential
Published 80 titles in 2009. Receives few unsolicited mss
each year.

- **Fiction:** Publishes easy-to-read books, 4–7 years; chapter
  books, 5–10 years; middle-grade books, 8–12 years; and
  young adult books, 12–14 years. Genres include contemporary
  and historical fiction, myths and legends, humor, science fiction, and drama. Also publishes poetry.
- **Nonfiction:** Publishes easy-to-read books, 4–7 years; chapter
  books, 5–10 years; middle-grade books, 8–12 years; and young
  adult books, 12–14 years. Topics include art, design, technology,
  geography, history, music, physical education, sports, science,
  and social issues. Also publishes reference books and teacher
  resources.
- **Representative Titles:** *The Honourable Ratts* by Karen
  Wallace (8–11 years) tells the story of a distinguished yet
  diminutive family that lives beneath the floorboards of an old
  mansion; part of the Black Cats series. *100 Most Dangerous
  Things on the Planet* by Anna Claybourne tells children how to
  survive such situations as a shark attack or a tornado.

Submissions and Payment
Guidelines available. Send complete ms. Accepts hard copy.
SAE/IRC. Responds in 2 months. Publication period and pay-
ment policy vary.

Editor's Comments
Most of our titles are organized into series, whether they be
written directly for children or for teachers.

Bloomsbury Children's Books

175 Fifth Avenue, 8th Floor
New York, NY 10010

Submissions Editor

Publisher's Interests

Though fiction is the main interest of this publisher, it does produce a small number of nonfiction titles. It publishes high-quality books for children of all ages, from babies through high school students.
Website: www.bloomsburyusa.com

Freelance Potential

Published 72 titles in 2009: 71 were by agented authors. Of the 72 titles, 9 were by unpublished writers. Receives 2,500 queries yearly.

- **Fiction:** Publishes concept books, toddler books, and early picture books, 0–4 years; easy-to-read books, 4–7 years; story picture books, 4–10 years; chapter books, 5–10 years; middle-grade books, 8–12 years; and young adult books, 12–18 years. Genres include adventure, fantasy, mystery, contemporary and science fiction, and multicultural themes.
- **Nonfiction:** Publishes early picture books, 0–4 years; middle-grade books, 8–12 years; and young adult books, 12–18 years. Topics include multicultural and ethnic subjects.
- **Representative Titles:** *Monsters Are Afraid of the Moon* by Marjane Satrapi (4–7 years) is a story about a girl who hangs the moon in her room to ward off monsters, only to learn that the lack of moonlight outside has consequences. *Prison Ship* by Paul Dowswell (YA) is the story of a sailor who is sent to a prison camp.

Submissions and Payment

Guidelines and catalogue available at website. Query with synopsis and sample chapter (or first 10 pages). Accepts hard copy and simultaneous submissions. No SASE. Responds if interested. Publication period varies. Royalty; advance.

Editor's Comments

We will contact you if we're interested in your proposal, but please note that we cannot return your materials.

Blue Dolphin Publishing

P.O. Box 8
Nevada City, CA 95959

Editor: Paul M. Clemens

Publisher's Interests

This publisher specializes in books about health, spirituality, and psychology, with the goal of helping people "grow in their social awareness and conscious evolution." Its children's list ranges from biography to science to folktales.
Website: www.bluedolphinpublishing.com

Freelance Potential

Published 24 titles (7 juvenile) in 2009: 5 were by agented authors and 4 were reprint/licensed properties. Of the 24 titles, 18 were by authors who were new to the publishing house. Receives 3,600 queries and unsolicited mss yearly.

- **Fiction:** Publishes easy-to-read books, 4–7 years; story picture books, 4–10 years; middle-grade books, 8–12 years; and young adult books, 12–18 years. Genres include contemporary, inspirational, spiritual, multicultural, and historical fiction; and folktales.
- **Nonfiction:** Publishes middle-grade books, 8–12 years; and young adult books, 12–18 years. Topics include science, nature, health, and biography. Also publishes self-help books for adults.
- **Representative Titles:** *To Find a Friend* by Brian Jones (4–7 years) is an easy-to-read book about making friends. *This Strange Quantum World & You* by Patricia Topp (9+ years) suggests a few simple experiments to show how the energy and material parts of our universe may work.

Submissions and Payment

Guidelines and catalogue available at website. Query or send complete ms. Accepts hard copy, disk submissions, and simultaneous submissions if identified. SASE. Responds to queries immediately, to mss in 3–6 months. Publication in 9–12 months. Royalty, 10%.

Editor's Comments

Manuscripts that arrive smelling like cigarette smoke may not receive the completely positive reception they deserve.

Blue Sky Press

Scholastic Inc.
557 Broadway
New York, NY 10012-3999

Editorial Director: Bonnie Verburg

Publisher's Interests
Helping children around the world to learn and grow, this imprint of Scholastic features a wide selection of fiction and nonfiction books.
Website: www.scholastic.com

Freelance Potential
Published 10–15 titles in 2009. Receives 3,000 queries each year.

- **Fiction:** Publishes toddler books and early picture books, 0–4 years; easy-to-read books, 4–7 years; story picture books, 4–10 years; chapter books, 5–10 years; middle-grade books, 8–12 years; and young adult books, 12–18 years. Genres include historical, contemporary, and multicultural fiction; folklore; fairy tales; fantasy; humor; and adventure.
- **Nonfiction:** Publishes story picture books, 4–8 years; and middle-grade books, 8–12 years. Topics include nature, the environment, and history.
- **Representative Titles:** *Into the Volcano* by Don Wood (8+ years) follows two brothers on an expedition that takes them on a wild boat ride to an erupting volcano. *Camping Catastrophe!* by Abby Klein (4–8 years) tells of a camping trip where everything goes wrong, from a collapsed tent to a swarm of angry bees; part of the Ready, Freddy series.

Submissions and Payment
Accepts queries from previously published authors only. Query with synopsis and publishing credits. Send complete ms for picture books. Accepts hard copy. SASE. Responds in 6–12 months. Publication in 2–5 years. Royalty, 5% hardcover trade; advance.

Editor's Comments
We believe that literacy is the cornerstone of a child's intellectual, personal, and cultural growth. We are looking for products that educate, entertain, and motivate.

Borealis Press Ltd.

8 Mohawk Crescent
Nepean, Ontario K2H 7G6
Canada

Senior Editor: Frank M. Tierney

Publisher's Interests
Known for its quality fiction and nonfiction books about
Canadian people and history, Borealis Press produces a
selection of books for school-age children.
Website: www.borealispress.com

Freelance Potential
Published 28 titles in 2009. Of the 28 titles, 10 were by
authors who were new to the publishing house. Receives
200–300 queries yearly.

- **Fiction:** Publishes story picture books, 4–10 years; and young
  adult books, 12–18 years. Genres include fantasy and multicultural and ethnic fiction.
- **Nonfiction:** Publishes reference titles about Canadian history.
  Also offers drama, poetry, and books with multicultural themes.
- **Representative Titles:** *Freckles: A Child's Life* by Ardith
  Trudzik depicts a girl's experience in her struggle through adolescence to self-understanding. *Mimikej and the Far Too Big
  Moccasins* by Barbara Little tells how a young girl searches for
  a way to replace her moccasins. *The Tale of the Giant Pigeon*
  by Manfred J. von Vulte tells of a red tabby cat and his search
  for an elusive pigeon.

Submissions and Payment
Guidelines and catalogue available at website. Query with
outline/synopsis and sample chapter. Accepts hard copy and
disk submissions. No simultaneous submissions. SAE/IRC.
Responds in 3–4 months. Publication in 1–2 years. Royalty,
10% of net. Flat fee.

Editor's Comments
We specialize in Canadian authored or oriented material.
Please send only submissions you are reasonably certain are
consistent with what we usually publish. We like children's
books that are fun, but that also have a connection to the
beauty of nature and life.

Boyds Mills Press

815 Church Street
Honesdale, PA 18431

Manuscript Submission

Publisher's Interests

Publishing children's books that enlighten and entertain is the specialty of Boyds Mills Press, which reaches its audience primarily through bookstores, schools, and libraries.
Website: www.boydsmillspress.com

Freelance Potential

Published 100 titles in 2009: 20 were developed from unsolicited submissions, 50 were by agented authors, and 20 were reprint/licensed properties. Of the 100 titles, 8 were by unpublished writers and 20 were by authors who were new to the publishing house. Receives 2,600 queries, 15,000 unsolicited mss yearly.

- **Fiction:** Publishes concept, toddler, and early picture books, 0–4 years; easy-to-read books, 4–7 years; story picture books, 4–10 years; chapter books, 5–10 years; middle-grade books, 8–12 years; and young adult books, 12–18 years. Genres include adventure stories, and multicultural and ethnic fiction.
- **Nonfiction:** Publishes early picture books, 0–4 years; easy-to-read books, 4–7 years; story picture books, 4–10 years; chapter books, 5–10 years; and middle-grade books, 8–12 years. Topics include history, science, and nature.
- **Representative Titles:** *Pippa at the Parade* by Karen Roosa (2–4 years) shares the fun things a young girl gets to do when she spends the day at a parade. *Armadillo Trail* by Stephen R. Swinburne (7–9 years) follows the trail of four armadillo pups as they leave their burrow and travel northward.

Submissions and Payment

Guidelines available at website. Query with outline; or send complete ms. Accepts hard copy. SASE. Response time, publication period, and payment policy vary.

Editor's Comments

We recommend including an expert's review of your nonfiction manuscript.

Boynton/Cook Publishers

Heinemann
361 Hanover Street
Portsmouth, NH 03801-3912

Proposals

Publisher's Interests
Boynton/Cook, part of the Heinemann publishing family, produces professional resources for middle-grade through college-level English teachers. It also publishes writing and language arts textbooks for students.
Website: www.boyntoncook.com

Freelance Potential
Published 10 titles in 2009. Receives 1,000 queries yearly.

- **Nonfiction:** Publishes professional books for writing and language arts teachers. Also publishes a select number of textbooks for college students. Topics include literature, rhetoric, communications, composition, writing, and style.
- **Representative Titles:** *Plagiarism: A How-Not-to Guide for Students* by Barry Gilmore is a handbook for helping students avoid plagiarism in their writing. *Students Teaching, Teachers Learning* by Amanda Branscombe et al., eds. presents a research project that shows how classroom dynamics change and more active learning takes place for both teacher and student when collaboration is involved.

Submissions and Payment
Guidelines and catalogue available at website. Query with table of contents, sample illustrations (if applicable), chapter summaries, and 3 sample chapters. Prefers email queries to proposals@heinemann.com; will accept hard copy and simultaneous submissions if identified. SASE. Responds in 6–8 weeks. Publication in 10–12 months. Royalty.

Editor's Comments
We are constantly on the lookout for new voices and visions, and welcome proposals from unpublished authors. Our books generally either present new or little-known material—including recent research and innovative practices—or treat familiar material in an original manner. In your proposal, be sure to address how your book satisfies this description.

Butte Publications

P.O. Box 1328
Hillsboro, OR 97123-1328

Acquisitions Editor

Publisher's Interests
Butte Publications specializes in educational books that serve readers of all ages who are deaf or hard of hearing. It also publishes a large number of informational and resource books for educators and professionals who work with the deaf, those in the speech and language fields, and early intervention specialists.
Website: www.buttepublications.com

Freelance Potential
Published 5 titles (2 juvenile) in 2009. Receives 20 queries each year.

- **Nonfiction:** Publishes resources and educational books on signing, interpreting, vocabulary, reading, writing, language skills, and lipreading. Also publishes parenting titles.
- **Representative Titles:** *The Silent Garden: Raising Your Deaf Child* by Paul W. Ogden provides parents of deaf children with crucial information on the greater possibilities afforded their children today. *Literacy and Your Deaf Child: What Every Parent Should Know* by David A. Stewart & Bryan R. Clark gives parents the tools to ensure that their child becomes a proficient reader and writer; also provides information about hearing aids and sign language.

Submissions and Payment
Guidelines and catalogue available at website. Query with table of contents, market analysis, and 2 sample chapters. Accepts hard copy. SASE. Responds in 3–6 months. Publication in 1 year. Royalty.

Editor's Comments
We expect our authors to be well credentialed in the area about which they are writing. Please let us know your background when you query. We are interested in a variety of subjects that would be useful to deaf persons, their families, and the professionals who work with them.

Calkins Creek

815 Church Street
Honesdale, PA 18431

Manuscript Submissions

Publisher's Interests
American history is the focus of Calkins Creek, an imprint
of Boyds Mills Press. Its fiction and nonfiction books, from
story picture books to chapter books, appeal to children and
young adults.
Website: www.calkinscreekbooks.com

Freelance Potential
Published 7 titles in 2009. Receives 600 unsolicited mss
each year.

- **Fiction:** Publishes story picture books, 8+ years; chapter
  books, 5–10 years; middle-grade books, 8–12 years; and
  young adult books, 12–18 years. Genres include historical
  fiction.
- **Nonfiction:** Publishes story picture books, 4–10 years; chapter
  books, 5–10 years; middle-grade books, 8–12 years; and
  young adult books, 12–18 years. Topics include U.S. history.
- **Representative Titles:** *The White Ox* by Ruth Hailstone (8+
  years) tells the story of Emily Swain Squires' journey as she
  leaves England and sails for her new home in America. *Voyages* by Neil Waldman (10+ years) follows a young Abraham
  Lincoln on his travels as he shares his deepest thoughts and
  struggles with the pressing ethical question of whether slavery
  should be abolished.

Submissions and Payment
Guidelines available at website. Query or send complete ms
with detailed bibliography for both historical fiction and nonfiction. Accepts hard copy. SASE. Response time and publication period vary. Royalty.

Editor's Comments
Keep in mind that good children's nonfiction has a narrative
quality—a story line—that encyclopedias do not. Please consider whether the subject and the language will appeal to
children and young adults.

Candlewick Press

99 Dover Street
Somerville, MA 02144

Associate Publisher: Liz Bicknell

Publisher's Interests
This employee-owned company has published some of today's most recognizable children's books, including *Guess How Much I Love You* by Sam McBratney, *Where's Waldo?* by Martin Handford, and *The Tale of Despereaux* by Kate DiCamillo.
Website: www.candlewick.com

Freelance Potential
Published 175 titles (170 juvenile) in 2009: 26 were developed from unsolicited submissions and 115 were by agented authors. Of the 175 titles, 1–2 were by unpublished writers and 4–5 were by new authors. Receives 300 queries yearly.

- **Fiction:** Publishes concept books, toddler books, and early picture books, 0–4 years; easy-to-read books, 4–7 years; story picture books, 4–10 years; chapter books, 5–10 years; middle-grade books, 8–12 years; and young adult books, 12–18 years. Genres include contemporary, multicultural, historical, and science fiction; fantasy; adventure; mystery; and humor.
- **Nonfiction:** Publishes concept books and early picture books, 0–4 years; story picture books, 4–10 years; middle-grade books, 8–12 years; and young adult books, 12–18 years. Topics include history, nature, the environment, politics, geography, biography, and music.
- **Representative Titles:** *The Girl Who Wanted to Dance* by Amy Ehrlich (6–10 years) depicts the call to self-expression and the pain of those left behind. *Footprints on the Moon* by Mark Haddon (4–8 years) recalls the author's boyhood wonder at witnessing the first lunar landing.

Submissions and Payment
Accepts submissions from agented authors only.

Editor's Comments
We publish only those books we believe in, only those books that speak to children, and only those that have both words and art of the highest quality.

Capstone Publishers

Fiction Division
7825 Telegraph Road
Bloomington, MN 55438

Editorial Director: Michael Dahl

Publisher's Interests

This publisher has two imprints that offer a wide variety of
fiction books for children. Picture Window Books specializes
in picture books, easy readers, and chapter books that
weave lyrical text with dazzling art illustrations. Stone Arch
Books presents contemporary and engaging fiction in a number of genres, including graphic novels, for young adults.
**Website: www.picturewindowbooks.com or
www.stonearchbooks.com**

Freelance Potential

Published 200 titles in 2009. Receives 1,200 queries yearly.

- **Fiction:** Publishes early picture books, 0–4 years; easy-to-read
  books, 4–7 years; story picture books, 4–10 years; chapter
  books, 5–10 years; middle-grade books, 8–12 years; and
  young adult books, 12–18 years. Genres include adventure,
  fantasy, horror, mystery, suspense, and graphic novels.
- **Representative Titles:** *Nuclear Distraction* by Chris Everheart
  (grades 3–8) is a story about a break-in at a nuclear power
  plant and the trouble that ensues. *The Day Mom Finally
  Snapped* by Bob Temple (grades 1–3) is a humorous story
  about a mother who is so angry she has smoke coming out
  of her ears.

Submissions and Payment

All work is assigned. Writers' guidelines available. Query with
clips and résumé. No unsolicited mss. Accepts hard copy.
SASE. Responds in 3–5 months. Publication period varies.
Flat fee.

Editor's Comments

All of our work is assigned. Please do not send unsolicited
mss. We are looking for younger books as well as books for
the tween set, especially realistic fiction, fantasy, horror,
mystery, and adventure. Our graphic novels are safe; no violence or inappropriate subjects.

Capstone Publishers

Nonfiction Division
151 Good Counsel Drive
Mankato, MN 56001

Editorial Director: Kay M. Olsen

Publisher's Interests

The nonfiction division of this publishing company presents children's books at a variety of reading and interest levels that are curriculum-aligned and easy to read. Its mission is to help kids learn to read and read to learn.
Website: www.capstonepress.com

Freelance Potential

Published 400 titles in 2009. Of the 400 titles, 30 were by authors who were new to the publishing house. Receives numerous queries yearly.

- **Nonfiction:** Publishes concept books and early picture books, 0–4 years; easy-to-read books, 4–7 years; chapter books, 5–10 years; middle-grade books, 8–12 years; and young adult books, 12–18 years. Topics include animals, arts and crafts, social studies, geography, health, science, math, technology, and sports. Also publishes biographies, graphic nonfiction, and bilingual English/Spanish titles.
- **Representative Titles:** *Coyotes* by Patricia J. Murphy (grades K–1) introduces the characteristics, behaviors, and habitat of coyotes. *Memorial Day* by Helen Frost (grades K–1) explains how and why this holiday came to be celebrated in the United States.

Submissions and Payment

All work is assigned. Guidelines available. Catalogue available at website. Query with résumé and 3 writing samples, indicating areas of interest. Accepts hard copy. SASE. Responds in 3–5 months. Publication period varies. Flat fee.

Editor's Comments

We develop an annual list of approximately 350 series titles in-house and assign book topics to writers on a work-for-hire basis. We look for writers with solid research and writing skills. Currently, we are interested in hearing from those who have experience writing about science topics.

Carolrhoda Books

Lerner Publishing Group
241 First Avenue North
Minneapolis, MN 55401

Fiction Submissions Editor

Publisher's Interests
Award-winning picture books and intermediate and young
adult fiction and nonfiction books are the specialty of this
imprint of Lerner Publishing. The company accepts only
targeted submissions at this time.
Website: www.lernerbooks.com

Freelance Potential
Published 20–25 titles in 2009.

- **Fiction:** Publishes story picture books, 4–10 years; middle-
  grade books, 8–12 years; and young adult books, 12–18
  years. Genres include contemporary, historical, and multicultural fiction; and mystery.
- **Representative Titles:** *Mousetraps* by Pat Schmatz (YA) is the
  story of two former best friends who meet up again in high
  school only to discover how much each has changed. *Class
  Three at Sea* by Julia Jarman (5–9 years) tells the story of
  students on an ocean field trip who are captured by pirates
  and later rescued by some new friends from the sea. *Silver
  World* by Cliff McNish (9–13 years), the final book in the Silver
  Sequence, finds the children of Coldharbour faced with the
  challenge of defeating a mysterious creature who intends to
  destroy the Earth.

Submissions and Payment
Guidelines available at website. Accepts targeted submissions only. Visit the website for a list of needs aimed at
specific reading levels in specific subject areas, and for
complete submission information.

Editor's Comments
We like books with thoroughly researched content crafted
into a well-written story that will engage readers. Please
review our website. You will find detailed information in our
submissions guidelines, along with suggestions for how best
to market your submission.

Carson-Dellosa Publishing Co., Inc.

P.O. Box 35665
Greensboro, NC 27425-5665

Submissions Editor: Donna Walkush

Publisher's Interests

Learning materials for teachers of kindergarten through grade eight are the foundation of this publishing company's catalogue. Resource books, activity books, and student workbooks for math, reading, social studies, and Christian education are among the offerings.

Website: www.carsondellosa.com

Freelance Potential

Published 100 titles in 2009. Receives 150 queries yearly.

- **Nonfiction:** Publishes supplementary educational material, including activity books, resource guides, classroom material, and reproducibles; preK–grade 8. Topics include reading, language arts, mathematics, science, the arts, social studies, English Language Learners (ELL), early childhood, and crafts. Also publishes Christian titles.
- **Representative Titles:** *First-Rate Reading* (grade K) helps early readers recognize sounds, decode text, read aloud with fluency, and comprehend the author's message. *American Women Achievers* (grades 3–5) takes a look at the life stories of such notables as Amelia Earhart, Sacagawea, and Oprah Winfrey.

Submissions and Payment

Guidelines available at website. Query with outline, market analysis, and sample pages. Accepts hard copy and simultaneous submissions if identified. SASE. Responds in 10–12 weeks. Publication in 1–2 years. Flat fee.

Editor's Comments

Fiction, including children's storybooks, trade books, and novels, is not accepted. Keep in mind that we can only use a small percentage of the submissions we receive each year and we also develop book ideas in-house, so we may already have projects in various stages of development that are similar in nature to yours.

Cartwheel Books

Scholastic Inc.
557 Broadway
New York, NY 10012

Editor: Jeff Salane

Publisher's Interests

This imprint of Scholastic focuses on fiction and nonfiction books for children up to the age of 10. It accepts submissions by previously published or agented authors only.
Website: www.scholastic.com

Freelance Potential

Published 100+ titles in 2009: 20+ were reprint/licensed properties. Of the 100+ titles, 3–4 were by authors who were new to the publishing house. Receives 1,000 queries yearly.

- **Fiction:** Publishes concept books, toddler books, and early picture books, 0–4 years; easy-to-read books, 4–7 years; story picture books, 4–8 years; and chapter books, 5–10 years. Publishes humor and short stories about friendship, family, and animals.
- **Nonfiction:** Publishes concept books, toddler books, and early picture books, 0–4 years; easy-to-read books, 4–8 years; and story picture books, 4–10 years. Topics include science and math.
- **Representative Titles:** *I Love Snow!* by Hans Wilhelm (4–8 years) is a learn-to-read book about a little white dog that embarks on a snow adventure. *The Best Thanksgiving Ever!* by Teddy Slater (4–8 years) tells the story of a turkey clan that gathers together for a holiday feast. *I Spy Phonics Fun* by Jean Marzollo (4–8 years) pairs easy-to-read riddles with fun photographs to create a phonics program.

Submissions and Payment

Accepts submissions from agents and previously published authors only. Send complete ms. Accepts hard copy. SASE. Responds in 3–6 months. Publication period and payment policy vary.

Editor's Comments

We publish books in a variety of formats. The text length and difficulty should be appropriate to the format.

Marshall Cavendish Children's Books

99 White Plains Road
Tarrytown, NY 10591

Publisher: Margery Cuyler

Publisher's Interests
This self-described "boutique publisher" prides itself on choosing high-quality fiction and artwork. It currently seeks contemporary middle-grade and young adult fiction, as well as "fun, quirky" picture books. 5% self-, subsidy-, co-venture, or co-op published material.
Website: www.marshallcavendish.us/kids

Freelance Potential
Published 70 titles in 2009: 6 were developed from unsolicited submissions and 14 were by agented authors. Of the 70 titles, 5 were by unpublished writers and 23 were by authors who were new to the publishing house. Receives 2,400 queries and unsolicited mss yearly.

- **Fiction:** Publishes early picture books, 0–4 years; easy-to-read books, 4–7 years; story picture books, 4–10 years; chapter books, 5–10 years; middle-grade books, 8–12 years; and young adult books, 12–18 years. Genres include contemporary, multicultural, and ethnic fiction; drama; fantasy; humor; mystery; suspense; and stories about sports and nature.
- **Representative Titles:** *Silly Tilly* by Eileen Spinelli (3–7 years) recounts the eccentric exploits of a barnyard goose. *Watersmeet* by Ellen Jensen Abbott (YA) is a fantasy about a teenage girl who confronts prejudice, war, and family secrets.

Submissions and Payment
Guidelines and catalogue available at website. Query with first 3 chapters and synopsis for novels; send ms for picture books. Accepts hard copy. SASE. Responds in 6–8 months if interested. Publication in 2 years. Payment policy varies.

Editor's Comments
We love finding new talent! Our spirit is quirky and creative, never preachy. Please note that we do not publish nonfiction, historical fiction, or poetry, and that we accept chapter books only in series, and with strong central characters.

Cedar Fort

2373 West 700 S.
Springville, UT 84663

Acquisitions Editors: Jennifer Fielding & Lee Nelson

Publisher's Interests
Although this publisher targets the Latter-day Saints market, its uplifting and edifying books embrace basic Christian beliefs and are suitable for many other readers.
Website: www.cedarfort.com

Freelance Potential
Published 140 titles (14 juvenile) in 2009.

- **Fiction:** Publishes middle-grade books, 8–12 years; and young adult books, 12–18 years. Genres include religious, contemporary, and historical fiction; fantasy; and adventure stories.
- **Nonfiction:** Publishes young adult books, 12–18 years. Topics include history, religion, self-help, and LDS doctrine. Also publishes books for adults.
- **Representative Titles:** *Sneezles and Wheezles* by Marion Passey is a silly story about a simple sniffle that turns into sneezes of monstrous breezes. *Call Me Little Echo Hawk* by Terry Echohawk follows a young girl as she discovers the story and heritage behind her last name, and motivates readers to learn and be proud of the heritage of their ancestors. *Choose to Believe, Live to Receive* by Lori Riddle (YA) uses stories from prominent Church leaders to inspire teens to be firm and steadfast in their LDS faith, even when it isn't easy.

Submissions and Payment
Guidelines and catalogue available at website. Send complete ms with submission form available at website. Accepts hard copy. SASE. Responds in 2–3 months. Publication period varies. Royalty; advance.

Editor's Comments
While we do publish a large number of LDS-related books, we also serve the national market, and are therefore looking for general interest books as well—especially for children. All of our books, however, must carry an uplifting message and should be in line with our Christian beliefs.

Charlesbridge

85 Main Street
Watertown, MA 02472

Submissions Editor

Publisher's Interests
Charlesbridge offers children's nonfiction that focuses on nature, science, social studies, and multicultural topics. Its fiction features lively, plot-driven stories with strong characters.
Website: www.charlesbridge.com

Freelance Potential
Published 44 titles in 2009: 1 was developed from an unsolicited submission and 5 were by agented authors. Receives 180 queries, 2,400 unsolicited mss yearly.

- **Fiction:** Publishes concept books, toddler books, and early picture books, 0–4 years; easy-to-read books, 4–7 years; story picture books, 4–10 years; chapter books, 5–10 years; and middle-grade books, 8–12 years. Genres include contemporary fiction, folktales, and nature stories.
- **Nonfiction:** Publishes concept books, toddler books, and early picture books, 0–4 years; easy-to-read books, 4–7 years; story picture books, 4–10 years; chapter books, 5–10 years; and middle-grade books, 8–12 years. Topics include nature, history, social studies, science, music, and multicultural themes.
- **Representative Titles:** *Emma's Question* by Catherine Urdahl (5–8 years) uses gentle humor and simple explanations to describe what is happening to young Emma's sick grandmother. *Unite or Die* by Jacqueline Jules (8–11 years) traces the challenges facing the colonies after the American Revolution.

Submissions and Payment
Guidelines available at website. Query with synopsis and 3 chapters for books longer than 30 pages; send complete ms for shorter works. Accepts hard copy. No simultaneous submissions. Responds in 3 months if interested. Publication in 2–5 years. Royalty.

Editor's Comments
At this time, we are not actively seeking alphabet books, board books, activity books, or multimedia works.

Chelsea House

132 West 31st Street, 17th Floor
New York, NY 10001

Managing Editor: Justine Ciovacco

Publisher's Interests
Chelsea House specializes in curriculum-based nonfiction books for students in middle school and high school. Its catalogue includes social studies, geography, science, health, and high-interest titles, as well as biographies. It is an imprint of Infobase Publishing.
Website: www.chelseahouse.com

Freelance Potential
Published 300+ titles in 2009: 5 were developed from unsolicited submissions. Of the 300+ titles, 30 were by authors who were new to the publishing house. Receives 240+ queries yearly.

- **Nonfiction:** Publishes middle-grade books, 8–12 years; and young adult books, 12–18 years. Genres include careers, geography, government and law, health, the arts, pet care, sports, transportation, literary criticism, religion, mythology, science, and social studies. Also publishes biographies.
- **Representative Titles:** *Tito Puente* by Tim McNeese (grades 6–12) explains the life and legacy of this Afro-Cuban songwriter and musician; part of the Great Hispanic Heritage series. *African Mythology A to Z* by Patricia Ann Lynch (grades 5–8) describes key stories, characters, themes, and other aspects of the myths of African peoples; part of the Mythology A to Z series.

Submissions and Payment
Guidelines available. All books are assigned. Query with résumé and clips or writing samples for new series ideas only. Accepts hard copy and email queries to jciovacco@aol.com. SASE. Response time and publication period vary. Flat fee.

Editor's Comments
Authors should have college or professional degrees in the subjects they cover, or be thoroughly familiar with their topics.

Chicago Review Press

814 North Franklin Street
Chicago, IL 60610

Senior Editor: Jerome Pohlen

Publisher's Interests

In addition to general nonfiction and parenting titles, Chicago Review Press publishes a line of activity books with "more depth and substance than is usually found in children's nonfiction." Topics range from art and architecture to math, science, history, and literature.
Website: www.chicagoreviewpress.com

Freelance Potential

Published 60 titles (7 juvenile) in 2009. Receives 1,500 queries yearly.

- **Nonfiction:** Publishes early picture books, 0–4 years; story picture books, 4–10 years; middle-grade books, 8–12 years; and young adult books, 12–18 years. Topics include art, architecture, math, science, history, biography, geography, engineering, multicultural and ethnic issues, dream analysis, and outdoor activities. Also publishes books for parents.
- **Representative Titles:** *Abraham Lincoln for Kids* by Janis Herbert (9+ years) chronicles the 16th president's life and times through 21 activities. *African Crafts* by Lynne Garner (8–12 years) shows children how to recreate the clothing, masks, pottery, and music of Ghana and West Africa. *Amazing Rubber Band Cars* by Mike Rigsby (9+ years) provides instructions for building wind-up racers, models, and toys.

Submissions and Payment

Guidelines and catalogue available at website. Query with table of contents, 1–2 sample chapters, and market analysis. Accepts hard copy and simultaneous submissions if identified. SASE. Responds in 8–10 weeks. Publication in 18 months. Royalty, 7–10%; advance, $1,500–$5,000.

Editor's Comments

While we do not publish original fiction or poetry, we are always on the lookout for fun and interesting books on popular science.

Children's Book Press

965 Mission Street, Suite 425
San Francisco, CA 94103

Editorial Submissions

Publisher's Interests
This is a nonprofit publisher of multicultural and bilingual literature for children of elementary school age. It is interested in books that present the diversity, traditions, and experiences of cultures around the world.
Website: www.childrensbookpress.org

Freelance Potential
Published 5 titles in 2009. Receives 1,200 unsolicited mss each year.

- **Fiction:** Publishes story picture books, 4–10 years. Genres include contemporary, ethnic, and multicultural fiction; and humor. Also publishes stories about immigration, family life, and relationships.
- **Representative Titles:** *Quinito, Day and Night* by Ina Cumpiano (4–8 years) follows a young boy throughout his day, whether it's playing outside or reading inside. *Animal Poems of the Iguazu* by Francisco X. Alarcon (6+ years) lets the animals of a magical rainforest in South America speak for themselves—in verse. *The Barber's Cutting Edge* by Gwendolyn Battle Lavert (6+ years) is the story of a young African American boy and the barber who becomes his friend and mentor.

Submissions and Payment
Guidelines and catalogue available at website. Send complete ms. Accepts hard copy and simultaneous submissions if identified. SASE. Responds in 2–3 months. Publication in 18–24 months. Royalty; advance.

Editor's Comments
We look for stories that let readers feel a culture through words and pictures, and for characters and storylines that are true to the culture. Most importantly, we look for books that children—of any culture—will love to read again and again. All books must reflect a minority culture or employ a multicultural voice.

Children's Press

Scholastic Library Publishing
90 Sherman Turnpike
Danbury, CT 06816

Editor-in-Chief

Publisher's Interests
Well known for its highly successful and long-running nonfiction series, Children's Press publishes titles that correlate to core curricula topics from preschool through middle school. It is an imprint of Scholastic.
Website: www.scholastic.com

Freelance Potential
Published 352 titles in 2009. Receives 2,000 queries yearly.

- **Nonfiction:** Publishes concept books, 0–4 years; easy-to-read books, 4–7 years; story picture books, 4–10 years; chapter books, 5–10 years; and middle-grade books, 8–12 years. Topics include animals, arts, culture, economics, geography, history, the human body, the military, science, social studies, sports, and transportation. Also publishes biographies.
- **Representative Titles:** *Ancient World* by Katherine Gleason (5–10 years) takes a look at the people, leaders, and customs of the ancient world; part of the True Tales series. *Life in the Grasslands* by Catherine Chambers (grades 2–4) introduces readers to the animals and habitats of the grasslands; part of the What on Earth? series. *Apache Helicopters* (grades 3–7) is designed to get reluctant readers interested with high-interest subjects; part of the Torque series.

Submissions and Payment
Accepts submissions through literary agents only. Query with outline/synopsis and sample chapters. Accepts hard copy. SASE. Responds in 2–6 months. Publication in 1–2 years. Flat fee.

Editor's Comments
We are committed to providing the best products that will turn young readers into lifelong learners. We are looking for submissions that offer original ideas, are useful to educators working in mainstream settings, and fit the direction and goals of Children's Press.

Christian Ed. Publishing

9260 Trade Place #100
San Diego, CA 92126

Assistant Editor: Janet Ackelson

Publisher's Interests
This non-denominational evangelical publishing company produces Christ-centered curriculum material for use in Bible study classes, Christian education, and vacation Bible schools. It also produces teacher resources and program kits.
Website: www.christianedwarehouse.com

Freelance Potential
Published 84 titles in 2009. Of the 84 titles, 2 were by authors who were new to the publishing house. Receives 50 queries yearly.

- **Fiction:** Publishes religious fiction, preK–grade 12.
- **Nonfiction:** Publishes Christian education titles, Bible-based curriculum materials, and Bible club materials, grades K–12. Also publishes church-wide special event programs and Bible-teaching crafts and activities.
- **Representative Titles:** *LittleKidsTime: My Great Big God* (2–5 years) is a year-in-a-box Sunday school program designed to answer big questions from little thinkers. *Growing a Healthy Children's Ministry* by Steve Alley guides Christian education leaders through the steps of developing an effective ministry to kids.

Submissions and Payment
Catalogue available at website. Guidelines and application available via email request to jackelson@cehouse.com. All work is done on assignment. Response time varies. Publication in 12–18 months. Flat fee; $.03 per word.

Editor's Comments
We work with freelance writers on a work-for-hire basis. Please follow our guidelines and application process if you would like to be considered for an assignment. We seek writers who love the Lord, relate well to the revelent age group, and have experience working with children in a faith-based setting.

Christian Focus Publishing

Geanies House, Fearn by Tain
Ross-shire 1V20 ITW
Scotland

Children's Editor: Catherine Mackenzie

Publisher's Interests

This nondenominational publisher presents a children's catalogue full of Bible stories, biographies, and fiction.
Website: www.christianfocus.com

Freelance Potential

Published 100+ titles (50 juvenile) in 2009: 6 were developed from unsolicited submissions, 6 were by agented
authors, and 4 were reprint/licensed properties. Of the 100+
titles, 14 were by authors who were new to the publishing
house. Receives 1,200+ queries, 600+ mss yearly.

- **Fiction:** Publishes toddler books and early picture books, 0–4
  years; easy-to-read books, 4–7 years; story picture books,
  4–10 years; chapter books, 5–10 years; middle-grade books,
  8–12 years; and young adult books, 12–18 years. Genres
  include contemporary Christian fiction.
- **Nonfiction:** Publishes toddler books, 0–4 years; easy-to-read
  books, 4–7 years; story picture books, 4–10 years; chapter
  books, 5–10 years; middle-grade books, 8–12 years; and
  young adult books, 12–18 years. Topics include Bible stories,
  biographies, and devotionals.
- **Representative Titles:** *Rescue and Redeem* by Mindy & Bran-
  don Withrow (9–14 years) tells how the modern church seeks
  to rescue and redeem God's global people to a new life in
  Christ. *John Calvin: After Darkness Light* by Catherine Mackenzie presents a biography of this historical figure.

Submissions and Payment

Guidelines available at website. Query with synopsis and
3 chapters. Send complete ms for works under 10 chapters.
Accepts email to Catherine.Mackenzie@christianfocus.com.
Response time, publication period, and payment policy vary.

Editor's Comments

Our bright, fun books help children discover God and
become enthusiastic about reading the Bible.

Christopher-Gordon Publishers

1420 Providence Highway, Suite 120
Norwood, MA 02062

Publisher: Susanne F. Canavan

Publisher's Interests

An independent publisher, this company specializes in professional enrichment materials for teachers, administrators, and curriculum developers. It focuses on literacy, math, science, technology, educational administration, and topics of universal interest to educators.
Website: www.christopher-gordon.com

Freelance Potential

Published 6 titles in 2009: 1 was developed from an unsolicited submission. Receives 72–144 queries yearly.

- **Nonfiction:** Publishes professional enrichment material for educators. Topics include literacy, administration, classroom management, general education, teaching skills, mathematics, self-development, science, technology, supervision, literature, education law, and cognitive thinking.
- **Representative Titles:** *Teaching Writing Using Blogs, Wikis, and Other Digital Tools* by Richard Beach et al. contains examples of activities using various digital tools to teach writing in the classroom. *Real-World Supervision: Adapting Theory to Practice* by Sally J. Zepeda, ed. provides a look at contemporary research topics and issues of practice in today's realm of instructional supervision.

Submissions and Payment

Guidelines and catalogue available at website. Query with résumé, sample chapter, synopsis, table of contents, book length, and market and competition analysis. Accepts hard copy. SASE. Response time varies. Publication in 18 months. Royalty; advance.

Editor's Comments

Many of our authors are leading educators as well as recognized writers and researchers. We believe in working closely with educators to produce quality materials that reflect the best of the teaching profession.

Chronicle Books

Children's Division
680 Second Street
San Francisco, CA 94107

Children's Division Editor

Publisher's Interests
A publisher of children's books for all ages, Chronicle Books is dedicated to offering exceptional works that are instantly recognizable for their spirit, creativity, and value.
Website: www.chroniclebooks.com

Freelance Potential
Published 170 titles (90–100 juvenile) in 2009. Receives 240 queries, 12,000 unsolicited mss yearly.

- **Fiction:** Publishes concept books, toddler books, and early picture books, 0–4 years; easy-to-read books, 4–7 years; story picture books, 4–10 years; chapter books, 5–10 years; middle-grade books, 8–12 years; and young adult books, 12–18 years. Genres include contemporary, historical, and science fiction; adventure; and humor.
- **Nonfiction:** Publishes concept books, toddler books, and early picture books, 0–4 years; easy-to-read books, 4–7 years; story picture books, 4–10 years; chapter books, 5–10 years; middle-grade books, 8–12 years; and young adult books, 12–18 years. Topics include art, crafts, nature, geography, and history.
- **Representative Titles:** *Duck! Rabbit!* by Amy Krouse Rosenthal (3+ years) is a clever tale about the age-old optical illusion. *52 Fun Things to Do in the Car* by Lynn Gordon features games, art activities, and puzzles.

Submissions and Payment
Guidelines and catalogue available at website. Query with synopsis and 3 sample chapters. Send complete ms for toddler books and picture books. Accepts hard copy and simultaneous submissions if identified. Does not return materials. Responds in 2–3 months if interested. Publication in 2 years. Payment policy varies.

Editor's Comments
We seek submissions that are unique in bent—either in subject matter, writing style, or illustrative technique.

Claire Publications

Tey Brook Centre, Unit 8
Great Tey, Colchester C06 2EB
United Kingdom

Managing Director: Noel Graham

Publisher's Interests
This international publisher is interested in books and products designed to support teachers and help make learning fun for students. Its list covers all subjects, including science, math, language arts, technology, special needs, and learning difficulties.
Website: www.clairepublications.com

Freelance Potential
Published 5 titles in 2009: 1 was by an agented author and 1 was a reprint/licensed property. Of the 5 titles, 1 was by an author who was new to the publishing house. Receives 60 queries, 60 unsolicited mss yearly.

- **Nonfiction:** Publishes books and activity kits, preK–grade 12. Topics include mathematics, English, ESL, science, languages, design and technology, early education, special needs, gifted education, and homeschooling.
- **Representative Titles:** *The Outdoor Classroom* by Gerard Victor (7–12 years) is filled with hands-on activities that science teachers can use to encourage their students to become more aware of their environment. *Mathematics for Teddy Bears* by Elizabeth Graham (5–9 years) is a collection of activities using Teddy Bear counters to teach number, length, weight, capacity, area, science, and design.

Submissions and Payment
Catalogue available at website. Query with résumé and clips; or send complete ms. Accepts hard copy and email submissions to mail@clairepublications.com. SAE/IRC. Response time varies. Publication in 1 year. Royalty, 10%.

Editor's Comments
We would like to hear from teachers who have created programs and activities that have been successful in their own classrooms. You do not have to be a teacher, but you should be knowledgeable about education concepts.

Clarion Books

Houghton Mifflin Company
215 Park Avenue South
New York, NY 10003

Vice President/Publisher: Dinah Stevenson

Publisher's Interests
Favoring historical, multicultural, and scientific topics, this imprint of Houghton Mifflin publishes fiction and nonfiction for children of all ages.
Website: www.clarionbooks.com

Freelance Potential
Published 40 titles in 2009: 4 were developed from unsolicited submissions, 30 were by agented authors, and 4 were reprint/licensed properties. Receives 720 queries, 3,600 unsolicited mss yearly.

- **Fiction:** Publishes toddler books and early picture books, 0–4 years; easy-to-read books, 4–7 years; story picture books, 4–10 years; chapter books, 5–10 years; middle-grade books, 8–12 years; and young adult books, 12–18 years. Genres include adventure, folklore, fairy tales, and historical, multicultural, and science fiction.
- **Nonfiction:** Publishes easy-to-read books, 4–7 years; story picture books, 4–10 years; chapter books, 5–10 years; middle-grade books, 8–12 years; and young adult books, 12–18 years. Topics include animals, nature, science, history, holidays, biography, and multicultural and ethnic issues.
- **Representative Titles:** *Those Darn Squirrels!* by Adam Rubin (4–8 years) is a funny take on the classic man vs. squirrel conflict over backyard birdfeeders. *Mars and the Search for Life* by Elaine Scott (9–12 years) looks at the possibility of life—past and future—on the red planet.

Submissions and Payment
Guidelines available. Send complete ms for picture books. Query for other material. Accepts hard copy. No SASE. Responds only if interested. Publication in 2 years. Royalty.

Editor's Comments
We look for manuscripts and illustrations that are sure to delight young children.

Clear Light Publishing

823 Don Diego
Santa Fe, NM 87505

Publisher: Harmon Houghton

Publisher's Interests
Clear Light Publishing produces fiction and nonfiction books for adults and children that address Native Americans, Southwestern Americana, and Eastern philosophy and religion.
Website: www.clearlightbooks.com

Freelance Potential
Published 15–20 titles in 2009: each was developed from an unsolicited submission. Of the 15–20 titles, 5 were by unpublished writers and 5 were by authors who were new to the publishing house. Receives 180 unsolicited mss yearly.

- **Fiction:** Publishes story picture books, 4–10 years; middle-grade books, 8–12 years; and young adult books, 12–18 years. Genres include historical, regional, multicultural, and inspirational fiction.
- **Nonfiction:** Publishes middle-grade books, 8–12 years; and young adult books, 12–18 years. Topics include animals, nature, history, religion, multicultural subjects, folktales, social issues, health, and fitness. Also publishes biographies.
- **Representative Titles:** *Pueblo Girls: Growing Up in Two Worlds* by Marcia Keegan is the story of two girls who enjoy their American lifestyle, yet also relish their Indian heritage. *Children's Book of Yoga* by Thia Luby introduces children to yoga through games and exercises that involve mimicking animals and plants.

Submissions and Payment
Guidelines and catalogue available at website. Send complete ms with formal proposal. Accepts hard copy and simultaneous submissions if identified. Availability of artwork improves chance of acceptance. SASE. Responds in 3 months. Publication in 1 year. Royalty.

Editor's Comments
We do not hire illustrators, so any children's book sent without illustrations will be returned to you.

Concordia Publishing House

3558 South Jefferson Avenue
St. Louis, MO 63118-3968

Senior Editor: Peggy Kuethe

Publisher's Interests

As the publishing arm of the Lutheran Church in Missouri,
Concordia Publishing House produces books and other
materials that spread the Word of God. Its list includes nonfiction titles for young readers that "reflect the glory of God
in our lives and show children His love."
Website: www.cph.org

Freelance Potential

Published 20 titles (10 juvenile) in 2009: 1 was developed
from an unsolicited submission, 1 was by an agented author,
and 4 were reprint/licensed properties. Of the 20 titles, 1
was by an unpublished writer and 4 were by authors who
were new to the publishing house. Receives 1,500 queries
each year.

- **Nonfiction:** Publishes early picture books, 0–4 years; easy-to-
  read books, 4–7 years; and story picture books, 4–10 years.
  Topics include faith, religious holidays, prayer, spirituality,
  Bible studies, devotionals, and biography. Also publishes religious education resources.
- **Representative Titles:** *Easter ABCs* by Isabel Anders (2–5
  years) is an alphabetical retelling of the Easter story. *God
  Made It for You!* by Charles Lehmann (5–8 years) is the story
  of creation. *Amos Fortune, Free Man* by Elizabeth Yates (8–12
  years) is the story of an African prince who was sold into slavery as a teenager.

Submissions and Payment

All work is assigned. Query or send résumé. No unsolicited
mss. Accepts hard copy. SASE. Response time, publication
period, and payment policy vary.

Editor's Comments

All works must be Christ-centered, with explicit reference to
the Gospel. No series or stand-alone fiction submissions for
children or youth will be accepted.

Contemporary Drama Service

Meriwether Publishing Ltd.
885 Elkton Drive
Colorado Springs, CO 80907

Associate Editor: Arthur Zapel

Publisher's Interests

This publisher of theater arts books specializes in plays for youngsters from the middle grades through college. In addition to dramas, musicals, and monologues for school performance, it also publishes skits for Sunday school classrooms. **Website: www.meriwetherpublishing.com**

Freelance Potential

Published 85 titles in 2009: 65 were developed from unsolicited submissions. Of the 85 titles, 68 were by unpublished writers and 17 were by authors who were new to the publishing house. Receives 420–480 queries yearly.

- **Fiction:** Publishes middle-grade plays, 8–12 years; and young adult plays, 12–18 years. Genres include drama, musicals, folktales, farce, fantasy, novelty plays, skits, adaptations, parody, social commentary, prevention plays, Christian dramas, and creative worship resources.
- **Nonfiction:** Publishes middle-grade books, 8–12 years; and young adult books, 12–18 years. Topics include public speaking, acting, improvisation, and theater arts.
- **Representative Titles:** *Hey, Girlfriend!* by Kimberly McCormick provides 75 insightful monologues for girls to perform. *Comedy Scenes for Student Actors* by Laurie Allen offers several short sketches based on real-life dilemmas.

Submissions and Payment

Guidelines and catalogue available at website. Query with outline/synopsis. Accepts hard copy and simultaneous submissions if identified. SASE. Responds in 6 weeks. Publication in 6 months. Royalty. Flat fee.

Editor's Comments

Please note that we are not currently publishing for the elementary level except for Sunday school plays for churches. These should be one-act non-royalty plays or short sketches with religious themes, to 30 pages.

Corwin Press

2455 Teller Road
Thousand Oaks, CA 91320

Editorial Director: Robert D. Clouse

Publisher's Interests
Corwin Press' publishing credo is "helping educators do their work better." To that end, it publishes practical resources for school administrators, teachers, specialists, teacher educators, and advanced-level students.
Website: www.corwinpress.com

Freelance Potential
Published 260 titles in 2009. Receives 1,000+ queries yearly.

- **Nonfiction:** Publishes resource books and manuals for educators, grades K–12. Topics include administration, assessment, evaluation, professional development, curriculum development, classroom practice and management, gifted and special education, bilingual learning, counseling, school health, and educational technology.
- **Representative Titles:** *Literacy Beyond Picture Books* by Dorothy Dendy Smith et al. is a step-by-step guide that shows secondary school teachers how to match learning disabled students with appropriate texts and develop units that encourage literacy learning. *Mental Health in Schools* by Howard S. Adelman & Linda Taylor describes a new approach to school-based mental health services.

Submissions and Payment
Guidelines and catalogue available at website. Query with prospectus, including alternative titles, rationale, and market analysis. Accepts hard copy. SASE. Response time varies. Publication in 7 months. Royalty.

Editor's Comments
To interest us, your book should be based on theory and research, draw on real-world examples and practices, and be filled with practical, hands-on advice that can be replicated in the classroom or school. We expect our writers to be accomplished professionals in their fields. All of our books are peer-reviewed to ensure applicability and quality.

Coteau Books

2517 Victoria Avenue
Regina, Saskatchewan S4P OT2
Canada

Managing Editor: Nik L. Burton

Publisher's Interests

Coteau publishes fiction for teens and middle readers, as well as novels, short story collections, and poetry of literary merit. It works with Canadian authors only.
Website: www.coteaubooks.com

Freelance Potential

Published 14 titles (7 juvenile) in 2009: each was developed from an unsolicited submission. Receives 120–144 queries, 480–600 unsolicited mss yearly.

- **Fiction:** Publishes chapter books, 5–10 years; middle-grade books, 8–12 years; and young adult books, 12–18 years. Genres include regional, historical, and contemporary fiction; mystery; suspense; and humor.
- **Representative Titles:** *Katie Be Quiet* by Darcy Tamayose (11+ years) is the story of a young girl dealing with the death of her father, bullies, her mother's weird friends, and a mystery. *Ghost Voyages IV: Champlain and Cartier* by Cora Taylor (8+ years) finds Jeremy taking new seafaring adventures, this time with Canadian explorers Samuel de Champlain and Jacques Cartier; part of the Ghost Voyages series.

Submissions and Payment

Canadian authors only. Guidelines available at website. Query with summary, writing samples, and CV; or send complete ms. Accepts hard copy. No simultaneous submissions. SAE/IRC. Responds in 2–3 months. Publication in 1–2 years. Royalty, 10%.

Editor's Comments

We do not publish children's picture books. Don't send us a web address where we can read your work; we won't do it. The best way to determine if your work will catch the eye of our editors is to check out the kinds of books we have already published—at our website, at a bookstore, or at your library.

Cottonwood Press

109-B Cameron Drive
Fort Collins, CO 80525

President: Cheryl Miller Thurston

Publisher's Interests

Most of the materials published by Cottonwood Press are written for teachers of English and language arts in grades five through twelve. These books include classroom ideas and ready-to-use activities that teachers can reproduce.
Website: www.cottonwoodpress.com

Freelance Potential

Published 3 titles in 2009: 1 was developed from an unsolicited submission. Of the 3 titles, 1 was by an author who was new to the publishing house. Receives 120 queries, 96–120 unsolicited mss yearly.

- **Nonfiction:** Publishes classroom materials for teachers, grades 5–12. Topics include English and language arts.
- **Representative Titles:** *Write What You See* by Hank Kellner (grades 7–12) provides a variety of photographs and writing prompts to motivate students. *Phunny Stuph* by M. S. Samston (grades 7–12) contains reproducible proofreading exercises that use humor. *AbraVocabra* by Amy Rider (grades 6–9) helps students broaden their vocabulary with 24 lists of 12 practical words they are likely to encounter in everyday life.

Submissions and Payment

Guidelines available at website. Query with sample pages; or send complete ms. Accepts hard copy and simultaneous submissions if identified. SASE. Responds in 4–6 weeks. Publication in 6–12 months. Royalty, 10%.

Editor's Comments

We are not interested in variations of the same old games and ideas you see everywhere. (If we see one more game on homonyms, for example, we may scream.) We also do not use word-search puzzles. We love to use materials with a humorous, lighthearted, offbeat, or down-to-earth approach, the kind of material that real teachers can use with real kids, the kind that requires thought and creativity from students.

Covenant Communications

920 East State Road
P.O. Box 416
American Fork, UT 84003-0416

Submissions Editor

Publisher's Interests
The children's and adult books from this publisher support the values of the Church of Jesus Christ of Latter-day Saints.
Website: www.covenant-lds.com

Freelance Potential
Published 50 titles in 2009: 49 were developed from unsolicited submissions and 1 was by an agented author. Of the 50 titles, 25 were by unpublished writers and 37 were by authors who were new to the publishing house. Receives 1,200 unsolicited mss yearly.

- **Fiction:** Publishes concept books, toddler books, and early picture books, 0–4 years; chapter books, 5–10 years; middle-grade books, 8–12 years; and young adult books, 12–18 years. Genres include adventure, humor, suspense, science fiction, and inspirational and historical fiction.
- **Nonfiction:** Publishes concept books and toddler books, 0–4 years. Topics include history, religion, and regional subjects. Also publishes biographies, activity books, novelty and board books, photo-essays, and reference titles.
- **Representative Titles:** *Do What Is Right: 52 Fun Motivators for LDS Families* by Douglas J. & Laurie H. Wilcox presents fun and creative ways to teach kids to do what is right. *Contentment: Inspiring Insights for LDS Mothers* by Maria Covey Cole offers perspective on the trials and joys of raising a family with stories, Scripture verses, and quotes from prophets.

Submissions and Payment
Guidelines and catalogue available at website. Send complete ms with synopsis. Accepts disk submissions and email to submissions@covenant-lds.com. SASE. Responds in 3 months. Publication in 6–12 months. Payment policy varies.

Editor's Comments
We look for original and insightful work that will appeal to a broad range of LDS readers.

The Creative Company

P.O. Box 227
Mankato, MN 56002

Editor: Aaron Frisch

Publisher's Interests

Most of this company's catalogue features nonfiction children's books, organized into series, that are marketed directly to schools and libraries. Yet it also publishes four to five picture books for the trade market each year.
Website: www.thecreativecompany.us

Freelance Potential

Published 120 titles in 2009: 6 were developed from unsolicited submissions and 3 were by agented authors. Of the 120 titles, 1 was by an unpublished writer and 4 were by authors who were new to the publishing house. Receives 120 queries, 360 unsolicited mss yearly.

- **Fiction:** Publishes story picture books, 4–12 years. Features a wide range of genres.
- **Nonfiction:** Publishes chapter books, 5–10 years; middle-grade books, 8–12 years; and young adult books, 12–18 years. Topics include science, sports, music, history, zoology, architecture, geography, and biography.
- **Representative Titles:** *Full Color* by Etienne Delessert is a picture book that brings strange but friendly creatures to life in a playful celebration of colors. *Dolphins* by Jason Skog looks at the habitats, physical characteristics, behaviors, relationships with humans, and threatened status of these mammals; part of the Living Wild series.

Submissions and Payment

Guidelines available. Send complete ms for picture books. Query with outline and sample pages for series (4–8 titles). Accepts hard copy. SASE. Responds in 3–4 months. Publication in 2 years. Flat fee.

Editor's Comments

We prefer nonfiction submissions over fiction, as our annual picture book publishing list is very small. Each series should generally include four to eight titles.

Creative Education

P.O. Box 227
Mankato, MN 56002

Senior Editor: Aaron Frisch

Publisher's Interests

With a primary market of school and public libraries, Creative Education publishes nonfiction children's books, organized in series, for children up to age 12. Covering a range of topics—such as geography, science, and art—it also publishes a number of picture books.
Website: www.thecreativecompany.us

Freelance Potential

Published 120 titles in 2009: 6 were developed from unsolicited submissions. Of the 120 titles, 2 were by authors who were new to the publishing house. Receives 240 queries each year.

- **Nonfiction:** Publishes easy-to-read books, 4–7 years; middle-grade books, 8–12 years; and young adult books, 12–18 years. Also publishes books in series, 5–12 years. Topics include science, sports, art, music, history, zoology, architecture, and geography.
- **Representative Titles:** *A Desert Food Chain* by A. D. Tarbox (grades 5 and up) introduces readers to the food chain of this ecosystem; part of the Nature's Bounty series. *Gravity* by Joy Frisch-Schmoll (grades 1 and up) explains the concept of gravity in an easy-to-understand format; part of the Simple Science series.

Submissions and Payment

Guidelines available. All work is done on a work-for-hire basis. Query with ms sample. Accepts hard copy. No simultaneous submissions. SASE. Responds in 4–6 months. Publication in 2 years. Flat fee.

Editor's Comments

We are looking for series proposals, generally four to eight titles per series, rather than single manuscripts. We do not publish single, stand-alone books or fiction. There are no subject restrictions.

Creative Learning Press

P.O. Box 320
Mansfield Center, CT 06250

Editor: Kris Morgan

Publisher's Interests

Specializing in "products for high-end learning," Creative Learning Press publishes how-to books for gifted children, along with inspiring resources for their teachers and parents. It also offers activities for download at its website.
Website: www.creativelearningpress.com

Freelance Potential

Published 4 titles in 2009. Receives 100 queries, 100 unsolicited mss yearly.

- **Nonfiction:** Publishes textbooks, educational materials, how-to books, teaching resources, and audio cassettes for grades K–12. Topics include science, mathematics, language arts, geography, history, research skills, business, fine arts, and leadership.
- **Representative Titles:** *Looking for Data in All the Right Places* by Alane J. Starko & Gina D. Schack assists educators in teaching students to gather and analyze data from the real world. *The Elements of Pop-Up* by David A. Carter & James Diaz teaches aspiring paper engineers every technique used in the process, as well as the medium's history. *Super Sentences* by Susan Winebrenner (grades 3–12) introduces new vocabulary words through sentence translation.

Submissions and Payment

Guidelines and catalogue available at website. Query with sample pages; or send complete ms with résumé and artwork. Accepts hard copy and email submissions to clp@ creativelearningpress.com. SASE. Responds in 1 month. Publication period varies. Royalty.

Editor's Comments

Our goal is to help teachers discover all they can do in their classrooms. We look for lessons and activity books that stimulate gifted students to think critically and be curious about the world around them.

Creative Teaching Press

15342 Graham Street
Huntington Beach, CA 92649

Idea Submissions

Publisher's Interests
Creative Teaching Press publishes a wide variety of class-room materials for preschool through grade eight, including teacher resources, books for emergent readers, and charts.
Website: www.creativeteaching.com

Freelance Potential
Published 84 titles (48 juvenile) in 2009: 14 were developed from unsolicited submissions. Of the 84 titles, 4 were by unpublished writers and 4 were by authors who were new to the publishing house. Receives 240–300 queries, 120–240 unsolicited mss yearly.

- **Fiction:** Publishes easy-to-read books, 4–7 years. Themes include ethnic, multicultural, and social issues; ethics and responsibility; fantasy; phonics; fluency; and writing.
- **Nonfiction:** Publishes easy-to-read books, 4–7 years; and chapter books, 5–10 years. Topics include history, social issues, science, and mathematics. Also publishes supplemental resource books for teachers.
- **Representative Titles:** *Early Childhood Centers* by Dr. Margaret Allen (preK–K) provides creative activities and standards charts to identify key learning objectives. *Strategies for Struggling Readers* (grades 3–5) offers activities rooted in a brain-based approach to learning.

Submissions and Payment
Guidelines and catalogue available at website. Prefers complete ms; will accept query with outline/synopsis. Accepts hard copy and simultaneous submissions if identified. SASE. Response time varies. Publication period and payment policy vary.

Editor's Comments
New ideas developed by teachers are always of interest to us. While we do publish a line of books for emergent readers, we do not typically publish children's books.

Critical Thinking Company

P.O. Box 1610
Seaside, CA 93955

President: Michael Baker

Publisher's Interests

Since 1958, this company has been publishing lessons that sharpen the mind as they teach standards-based reading, writing, mathematics, science, and history to children.
Website: www.criticalthinking.com

Freelance Potential

Published 20 titles (3 juvenile) in 2009: 10 were developed from unsolicited submissions. Of the 20 titles, 2 were by unpublished writers and 5 were by authors who were new to the publishing house. Receives 60 unsolicited mss yearly.

- **Fiction:** Publishes concept books, 0–4 years. Features stories that promote development of critical thinking skills.
- **Nonfiction:** Publishes concept and early picture books, 0–4 years; easy-to-read books, 4–7 years; and chapter books, 5–10 years. Topics include general thinking skills, grammar, spelling, vocabulary, reading, writing, mathematics, science, and history. Also publishes activity books, 8–18 years.
- **Representative Titles:** *Mathematical Reasoning: Beginning 1* (3 years) teaches kindergarten math concepts to toddlers, focusing on the numbers 1–5. *James Madison Critical Thinking Course* by William O'Meara & Daniel Flage (grades 7–12) engages children in crime-related scenarios to develop essential critical reading and reasoning skills.

Submissions and Payment

Guidelines available. Send complete ms. Accepts hard copy and Macintosh and DOS disk submissions. SASE. Responds in 6–9 months. Publication in 1–2 months. Royalty, 10%.

Editor's Comments

We design critical thinking into our reading, writing, math, science, and history lessons so children carefully analyze what they are learning. Deeper analysis produces deeper understanding, which results in better grades and higher test scores. Children learn to apply these skills throughout their lives.

Crossway Books

Good News Publishers
1300 Crescent Street
Wheaton, IL 60187

Editorial Administrator: Jill Carter

Publisher's Interests
Nonfiction Christian books and Bibles for children and adults alike are the focus of this evangelical publisher, which includes many key church leaders and teachers on its list of authors. Its titles focus on the critical issues facing Christians today, as well as the application of Christian truth to daily life.
Website: www.crossway.org

Freelance Potential
Published 70 titles (5 juvenile) in 2009: 6 were by agented authors and 1 was a reprint/licensed property. Of the 70 titles, 3 were by unpublished writers and 15 were by authors who were new to the publishing house. Receives 240 queries, 120 unsolicited mss yearly.

- **Nonfiction:** Publishes children's Bibles. Also publishes books on Christian issues for parents and young adults.
- **Representative Titles:** *A Family Guide to the Bible* by Christin Ditchfield guides parents and teachers through each of the 66 books of the Bible so they can confidently introduce their children to the Scriptures. *Do You Want a Friend?* by Noel Piper (3–7 years) tells the story of a boy looking for friends in his new town while discovering that Jesus is the best friend of all.

Submissions and Payment
Guidelines available. Accepts submissions from agented authors only. Responds in 6–8 weeks. Publication in 12–18 months. Payment policy varies.

Editor's Comments
We publish only nonfiction books written from an evangelical Christian perspective, and we review submissions from agented authors only. Items sent without permission will not be returned. Please refer to our website for additional information about the types of books we seek.

Crown Books for Young Readers

1745 Broadway, Mail Drop 9-3
New York, NY 10019

Assistant Editor: Allison Wortche

Publisher's Interests

Crown Books, an imprint of Random House, publishes a variety of fiction and nonfiction titles for children of all ages. Its offerings range from picture books to young adult novels.
Website: www.randomhouse.com/kids

Freelance Potential

Published 75 titles in 2009: 2 were developed from unsolicited submissions and 65 were by agented authors. Of the 75 titles, 6 were by unpublished writers and 27 were by new authors. Receives 1,200 queries, 3,600 unsolicited mss yearly.

- **Fiction:** Publishes story picture books, 4–10 years; middle-grade books, 8–12 years; and young adult books, 12–18 years. Genres include historical and contemporary fiction.
- **Nonfiction:** Publishes story picture books, 4–10 years; middle-grade books, 8–12 years; and young adult books, 12–18 years. Topics include science, nature, sports, history, and social issues.
- **Representative Titles:** *Kofi and His Magic* by Maya Angelou employs colorful photos to depict the life of a young boy in Africa. *Shipwreck at the Bottom of the World* by Jennifer Armstrong relays the true-life adventure of Ernest Shackleton and the crew of the *Endurance*.

Submissions and Payment

Guidelines and catalogue available at website. Query for nonfiction and novels. Send complete ms and cover letter for picture books. Accepts hard copy and simultaneous submissions if identified. No SASE; materials are not returned. Responds in 6 months if interested. Publication period varies. Royalty; advance.

Editor's Comments

We're looking for quality books for children of all ages, toddler to young adults, ranging from board books to picture books to novels to nonfiction.

CSS Publishing Company

517 South Main Street
Lima, OH 45804

Managing Editor: Becky Allen

Publisher's Interests
CSS is a religious publisher of books, lesson programs, and pamphlet series serving the needs of pastors, worship leaders, religious educators, and parish program planners in the broad Christian mainline of the American church. It accepts preaching and lectionary-based resources, children's lessons, material for use in parish education and various ministries, pastoral aids such as resources that assist in counseling, and dramas and pageants for all age groups.
Website: www.csspub.com

Freelance Potential
Published 75 titles in 2009: 50 were developed from unsolicited submissions. Of the 75 titles, 12 were by unpublished writers and 12 were by authors who were new to the publishing house. Receives 120–240 queries, 120 unsolicited mss yearly.

- **Nonfiction:** Publishes Christian education materials, program planners, children's sermons, and parenting titles. Topics include religious education, prayer, worship, and family life.
- **Representative Titles:** *Teaching the Mystery of God to Children* by Judy Gattis Smith identifies and reaffirms the spiritual experiences young people are already having, and provides suggestions for reflecting on those experiences in Christian education class. *Six Presents From God* by Gary Houston presents sermons and children's lessons for Advent and Christmas.

Submissions and Payment
Guidelines available at website. Prefers queries; will accept complete ms. Accepts hard copy and simultaneous submissions if identified. SASE. Responds in 8 months. Publication in 1 year. Payment policy varies.

Editor's Comments
We are interested in anything that provides pastors and religious educators with fresh ideas to invigorate their parishes.

Da Capo Press

11 Cambridge Center
Cambridge, MA 02142

Editorial Director

Publisher's Interests
Da Capo publishes nonfiction on a variety of topics, including history, the arts, sports, parenting, children's health, and popular culture. It does not have a children's list, but many of its titles may be of interest to young adults.
Website: www.dacapopress.com

Freelance Potential
Published 70 titles in 2009: 2 were developed from unsolicited submissions and 68 were by agented authors. Receives 150 queries yearly.

- **Nonfiction:** Publishes nonfiction titles for adults. Topics include parenting, pregnancy, current events, entertainment, health, history, science, nature, multicultural issues, religion, social issues, and sports. Also publishes self-help books, humor, and biographies.
- **Representative Titles:** *Growing Up Dead: The Hallucinated Confessions of a Teenage Deadhead* by Peter Conners tells of the author's journey from straight-laced suburban teen to a full-fledged Deadhead, touring the country in a van following the Grateful Dead. *You'd Be So Pretty If . . .* by Dara Chadwick discusses mothers' body images and how their issues affect teenage daughters.

Submissions and Payment
Guidelines and catalogue available at website. Query with sample chapter, biography, and credentials. Accepts hard copy. Availability of artwork improves chance of acceptance. SASE. Responds in 1–2 months. Publication in 1 year. Royalty; advance.

Editor's Comments
Please note that we do not accept fiction, nor do we accept children's books. We are happy to receive proposals (not unsolicited manuscripts) for books *about* children, families, and parenting.

Jonathan David Publishers

68-22 Eliot Avenue
Middle Village, NY 11379

Editor: David Kolatch

Publisher's Interests

This company publishes trade nonfiction books, specializing in Judaica and sports, biographies, and reference books. Although the majority of its catalogue is devoted to adult titles, it does produce a small number of nonfiction books and Jewish-themed fiction for children.

Website: www.jdbooks.com

Freelance Potential

Published 11 titles in 2009: 5 were by unpublished writers and 8 were by new authors. Receives 1,000 queries yearly.

- **Fiction:** Publishes easy-to-read books, 4–7 years; and story picture books, 4–10 years. Genres include folktales and stories of Jewish culture.
- **Nonfiction:** Publishes easy-to-read books, 4–7 years; middle-grade books, 8–12 years; and young adult books, 12–18 years. Topics include religion, Judaica, history, culture, and multicultural issues.
- **Representative Titles:** *A Child's First Book of Jewish Holidays* by Alfred J. Kolatch (3–6 years) provides an entertaining introduction to the major Jewish holidays. *Aaron's Bar Mitzvah* by Sylvia Rouss is a story about a young girl trying to understand why her older brother no longer has time for her, until she learns about the meaning of a Bar Mitzvah.

Submissions and Payment

Guidelines available at website. Query with résumé, table of contents, synopsis, and sample chapter. No unsolicited mss. Accepts hard copy. No simultaneous submissions. SASE. Responds in 1–2 months. Publication in 18 months. Royalty; advance. Flat fee.

Editor's Comments

In addition to book projects, we accept inquiries from freelancers applying for assignments. Send us your résumé and a statement about your areas of expertise.

DAW Books

375 Hudson Street
New York, NY 10014

Associate Editor: Peter Stampfel

Publisher's Interests

Focusing specifically on the science fiction and fantasy genres, DAW Books prides itself on discovering and publishing some of the best up-and-coming writers in the field. Its titles are geared to young adults and adults and many appear as part of a series.

Website: www.dawbooks.com

Freelance Potential

Published 35 titles in 2009. Receives 1,000 unsolicited mss each year.

- **Fiction:** Publishes young adult books, 12–18 years. Genres include science fiction and fantasy.
- **Representative Titles:** *Harmony* by C. F. Bentley is a story about a new High Priestess who is looking to protect her land from the invasion of others in the galaxy. *Riders of the Storm* by Julia Czerneda follows a young woman with a secret talent who tries to negotiate peace in her divided village. *The High King's Tomb* by Kristen Britain is the third in a series about a leader looking to protect his land from the descendants of a powerful conquerer.

Submissions and Payment

Guidelines and catalogue available at website. Send complete ms. Accepts hard copy. No simultaneous submissions. SASE. Responds in 3 months. Publication in 8–12 months. Royalty; advance.

Editor's Comments

We are not interested in short stories, short story novellas, or poetry. Our books are almost never shorter than 80,000 words. If you are an unpublished writer, we welcome your submission as long as it is of professional quality. Please note that it is not necessary for you to register or copyright your work before submitting it.

Dawn Publications

12402 Bitney Springs Road
Nevada City, CA 95959

Editor: Glenn Hovemann

Publisher's Interests
This publisher produces nature awareness titles for children and adults, as well as teacher guides to nature topics. Its children's titles include those that are ideal for classroom use as well as those intended for bedtime reading.
Website: www.dawnpub.com

Freelance Potential
Published 7 titles in 2009; 6 were developed from unsolicited submissions. Of the 7 titles, 2 were by unpublished writers and 3 were by authors who were new to the publishing house. Receives 2,000+ unsolicited mss yearly.

- **Nonfiction:** Publishes easy-to-read books, 4–7 years; and story picture books, 4–10 years. Topics include the environment, conservation, ecology, rainforests, animal habitats, the water cycle, the seasons, family relationships, personal awareness, and multicultural and ethnic issues.
- **Representative Titles:** *There's a Babirusa in My Bathtub!* by Maxine Rose Schur (7–12 years) uses humorous rhymes to illuminate the lives and careers of little-known animals. *In the Trees, Honeybees!* by Lori Mortensen (4–10 years) educates readers about the inside workings of a honeybee colony.

Submissions and Payment
Guidelines and catalogue available at website. Send complete ms with author bio, synopsis, and publishing credits. Accepts hard copy and email to submission@dawnpub.com (Microsoft Word attachments; title and author in subject line). SASE. Responds in 2–3 months. Publication in 18–24 months. Royalty; advance.

Editor's Comments
We continue to seek creative nonfiction titles. Please note that many of our publications come from unsolicited submissions and first-time authors. Due to our small size, we are able to accept only a handful of submissions each year.

Deseret Book Company

57 West South Temple
Salt Lake City, UT 84101

Manuscript Acquisitions: Lisa Mangum

Publisher's Interests
The fiction, nonfiction, and activity books found in this publisher's catalogue all reflect the values espoused by the Church of Jesus Christ of Latter-day Saints.
Website: www.deseretbook.com

Freelance Potential
Published 150 titles (70 juvenile) in 2009: 9 were developed from unsolicited submissions. Of the 150 titles, 18 were by authors who were new to the publishing house. Receives 500 queries, 1,000 unsolicited mss yearly.

- **Fiction:** Publishes early picture books, 0–4 years; story picture books, 4–10 years; and young adult books, 12–18 years. Genres include fantasy; mystery; romance; and contemporary, historical, inspirational, and religious fiction.
- **Nonfiction:** Publishes early picture books, 0–4 years; story picture books, 4–10 years; chapter books, 5–10 years; and young adult books, 12–18 years. Also publishes activity, novelty, and board books, and biographies.
- **Representative Titles:** *Bright Blue Miracle* by Becca Wilhite (YA) is about a teen girl learning to cope with a new stepsister. *The Wednesday Letters* by Jason F. Wright tells the story of a wife's collection of love letters her husband wrote her each Wednesday of their marriage.

Submissions and Payment
Guidelines and catalogue available at website. Query with outline/synopsis, table of contents, and 2–3 sample chapters; or send complete ms. Accepts hard copy. SASE. Responds in 2 months. Publication in 12–18 months. Royalty, 5–12% of retail.

Editor's Comments
We're not interested in poetry, family histories, or personal journals. We want our readers to feel that they are better people for having read our books.

Dial Books for Young Readers

Penguin Group USA, Inc.
345 Hudson Street
New York, NY 10014

Submissions Coordinator

Publisher's Interests

Dial publishes creative titles for young children; stylish, character-driven novels; and nonfiction for older readers.
Website: www.penguin.com/youngreaders

Freelance Potential

Published 54 titles in 2009: 1 was developed from an unsolicited submission, 53 were by agented authors, and 14 were reprint/licensed properties. Of the 54 titles, 7 were by unpublished writers and 20 were by authors who were new to the publishing house. Receives 1,200 unsolicited mss yearly.

- **Fiction:** Publishes early picture books, 0–4 years; easy-to-read books, 4–7 years; story picture books, 4–6 years; chapter books, 5–10 years; middle-grade books, 9–12 years; and young adult books, 12–18 years. Genres include contemporary and science fiction.
- **Nonfiction:** Publishes concept books, toddler books, and early picture books, 0–4 years; easy-to-read books, 4–7 years; story picture books, 4–6 years; middle-grade books, 9–12 years; and young adult books, 12–18 years. Topics include animals, science, and social issues.
- **Representative Titles:** *Ladybug Girl and Bumblebee Boy* by Jacky Davis & David Soman (3–5 years) tells the story of two children and their great playground game. *Triple Shot Bettys in Love* by Jody Gehrman (12+ years) follows two girls through their high school crushes.

Submissions and Payment

Guidelines available at website. Send ms for picture books. Send 10 ms pages with synopsis and publishing credits for longer works. Accepts hard copy. Responds in 4 months if interested. Publication period and payment policy vary.

Editor's Comments

Our only requirement is that your book be creative, entertaining, and unique.

Didax

395 Main Street
Rowley, MA 01969

Submissions

Publisher's Interests

Its name is derived from the Greek word for "to teach," which is exactly what Didax aims to do through its educational materials. It publishes activity books, manipulatives, and software for the classroom.
Website: www.didax.com

Freelance Potential

Published 25 titles in 2009: 1 was by an author who was new to the publishing house.

- **Nonfiction:** Publishes reproducible activity books and teacher resources, preK–grade 8. Topics include math fundamentals, fractions, geometry, algebra, probability, problem-solving, the alphabet, pre-reading, phonics, word study, spelling, vocabulary, writing, reading comprehension, social studies, science, art, and character education.
- **Representative Titles:** *A Bad Case of Tattle Tongue* by Julia Cook (preK–grade 3) is a story about a boy nobody likes because he tattles too much. *101 Games for Self-Esteem* by Jenny Mosley & Helen Sonnet (grades K–6) offers activities to help children relate well to others and feel more positive about themselves. *Australian Aboriginal Culture* by Jenni Harold & Joanne Whitby (grades 5–6) teaches students about Aboriginal traditions, beliefs, language, art, clothing, and shelter using activities across several curriculum areas.

Submissions and Payment

Guidelines available at website. Query with résumé and outline. Accepts hard copy, email queries to development@didax.com, and simultaneous submissions if identified. SASE. Responds in 2 weeks. Publication in 1 year. Royalty; advance.

Editor's Comments

Almost all of our products come directly from teachers, and we are always available to consider your ideas and needs.

DK Publishing

375 Hudson Street
New York, NY 10014

Assistant Editor: John Searcy

Publisher's Interests

A division of Penguin Group USA, Inc., DK Publishing produces a wide variety of nonfiction books for children, including encyclopedias, atlases, cookbooks, sticker books, board books, and leveled readers. Licensed properties, such as *Star Wars* and *High School Musical* merchandise, are also found on its young readers list.

Website: www.dk.com

Freelance Potential

Published 363 titles in 2009: 10 were by agented authors and 96 were reprint/licensed properties. Receives 1,000 queries yearly.

- **Nonfiction:** Publishes concept books and toddler books, 0–4 years; easy-to-read books, 4–7 years; middle-grade books, 8–12 years; and young adult books, 12–18 years. Topics include animals, cars, trucks, numbers, letters, potty-training, manners, bedtime, families, cooking, nature, the human body, mythology, religion, history, geography, and science. Also publishes reference, activity, and sticker books.
- **Representative Titles:** *Big Girls Use the Potty!* (2–5 years) motivates toddlers to use the toilet with the help of stickers and a reward chart. *Greek Myths* by Deborah Lock (7–9 years) is a leveled reader that retells some of the most beloved stories from Greek mythology. *Take Me Back* (10+ years) presents a chronological exploration of the people and events that have shaped societies throughout history.

Submissions and Payment

Guidelines available. Accepts queries through literary agents only. Responds in 6 months. Publication in 2 years. Royalty, 10%; advance, varies.

Editor's Comments

We are world-renowned for our distinctive, highly visual books that inform, inspire, and entertain readers of all ages.

DNA Press

242 King Street
Pottstown, PA 19464

Acquisitions Editor: Alexander Kuklin, Ph.D.

Publisher's Interests
The books published by DNA Press all share a common thread—love of science, in one form or another. It produces nonfiction titles on scientific subjects, business, and sales and marketing; as well as science fiction and fantasy titles.
Website: www.dnapress.com

Freelance Potential
Published 8 titles (1 juvenile) in 2009: each was by an unpublished writer who was new to the publishing house. Receives 400 queries, 500 unsolicited mss yearly.

- **Fiction:** Publishes story picture books, 4–10 years; chapter books, 5–10 years; middle-grade books, 8–12 years; and young adult books, 12–18 years. Genres include science fiction, fantasy, and stories about animals.
- **Nonfiction:** Publishes chapter books, 5–10 years; middle-grade books, 8–12 years; and young adult books, 12–18 years. Topics include animals, science, technology, sports, and recreation. Also publishes books for adults.
- **Representative Titles:** *The Prometheus Project: Trapped* by Douglas E. Richards (9–13 years) is a science-laden thriller about two siblings who discover their parents are part of a mysterious science project that could get them all killed. *Toaster Pond* by Peter de Witt is a story about a group of teen friends who dive into a pond and surface in a parallel world.

Submissions and Payment
Guidelines and catalogue available at website. Query with synopsis, table of contents, and sample chapter; or send complete ms. Accepts hard copy. SASE. Responds in 3 months. Publication period varies. Royalty.

Editor's Comments
Books should embrace science or utilize scientific principles in their plots. Be sure to include a list of your publishing credits with your submission, along with a marketing plan.

Dog-Eared Publications

P.O. Box 620863
Middleton, WI 53562-0863

Publisher: Nancy Field

Publisher's Interests

This "Nature Publisher for Children" focuses on nonfiction books, puzzles, and interactive games designed to foster kids' natural interest in their environment. Though its emphasis is on nature and the environment, it also considers other ideas.
Website: www.dog-eared.com

Freelance Potential

Plans to resume publishing (1 or more titles) in 2010. Receives 240 queries, 120 unsolicited mss yearly.

- **Nonfiction:** Publishes story picture books, 4–10 years; and middle-grade books, 8–12 years. Also publishes activity books and puzzles. Topics include animals, nature, the environment, ecology, biology, and geology.
- **Representative Titles:** *Discovering Sharks and Rays* by Nancy Field explores the natural history, environmental relationships, and current plight of sharks and rays. *Leapfrogging Through Wetlands* by Margaret J. Anderson et al. teaches the importance and diversity of wetlands. *Discovering Endangered Species* by Nancy Field & Sally Machlis introduces concepts of biological diversity and the interdependence of life.

Submissions and Payment

Guidelines and catalogue available at website. Query or send complete ms with description of target audience, publication history, and résumé. Accepts hard copy. SASE. Responds in several months. Publication period varies. Royalty.

Editor's Comments

Our printing and publishing decisions are in place for the next year and a half. So while we are certainly open to new submissions, we are focusing our immediate attention on marketing our present titles. We prefer to choose the artists for books, but if you are submitting artwork, know that we are interested only in accurate depictions, not cartoons.

Dorchester Publishing

200 Madison Avenue, Suite 2000
New York, NY 10016

Editorial Assistant

Publisher's Interests

An independent publisher specializing in mass-market paperback fiction, Dorchester Publishing offers award-winning
titles in the romance, science fiction, horror, mystery, and
Western genres. It publishes adult books with crossover
appeal to young adults.
Website: www.dorchesterpub.com

Freelance Potential

Published 200+ titles in 2009: 12 were developed from
unsolicited submissions and 112 were by agented authors.
Of the 200+ titles, 18 were by unpublished writers and
25–30 were by authors who were new to the publishing
house. Receives 3,000 queries yearly.

- **Fiction:** Publishes young adult books, 12–18 years. Genres
  include contemporary and science fiction, romance, mystery,
  and paranormal activities. Also publishes books for adults.
- **Representative Titles:** *If Wishes Were Horses* by Anne McCaf-
  frey (YA) is the story of twin siblings who assist their mother,
  the village healer, in caring for war refugees. *Harp, Pipe, and
  Symphony* by Paul DiFillipo follows a man's confrontations
  with humans, fairies, and monsters.

Submissions and Payment

Guidelines and catalogue available at website. Query with
first 3 chapters. No unsolicited mss. Accepts hard copy and
email queries to submissions@dorchesterpub.com. SASE.
Responds in 6–8 months. Publication in 9–12 months.
Royalty; advance.

Editor's Comments

We're currently acquiring the following categories of
romance: futuristic, time-travel, paranormal, contemporary,
romantic suspense, and African American. Horror, Westerns,
and thrillers are also of interest. Please review our guidelines
for detailed descriptions of the plot lines we're seeking.

Douglas & McIntyre Publishing Group

201-2323 Quebec Street
Vancouver, British Columbia V5T 4S7
Canada

Editorial Board

Publisher's Interests

This publisher produces nonfiction books on subjects that are rooted in the Canadian Pacific Northwest, although it does publish some titles on general Canadian subjects. It publishes books for young children, and some nonfiction subjects that are of interest to young adult readers, such as sports, fishing, nature, history, health, fitness, and science.
Website: www.douglas-mcintyre.com

Freelance Potential

Published 60 titles (3 juvenile) in 2009.

- **Nonfiction:** Publishes easy-to-read books, 4–7 years; and story picture books, 4–10 years. Topics include art, architecture, Canadian culture, First Nations art and culture, the environment, ecology, natural science, outdoor recreation, travel, geography, health, fitness, history, military history, social and political issues, biography, cooking, sports, and British Columbia and Northern Canadian regional themes.
- **Representative Titles:** *Hockey Challenge* by Kathy Vanderlinden has readers learning about the sport and its players by answering trivia questions, solving puzzles, and matching pictures. *There's a Barnyard in My Bedroom* by David Suzuki teaches children about the science and nature that exists everywhere—from the air in the house to the sheets and pillows in your bedroom.

Submissions and Payment

Guidelines and catalogue available at website. Query with outline/synopsis, sample chapter, author bio, and required cover sheet from website. Accepts hard copy. SAE/IRC. Responds in 6–8 weeks. Publication period and payment policy vary.

Editor's Comments

Our submissions guidelines fully outline the details that we expect in your proposal. Please follow them.

Dover Publications

31 East 2nd Street
Mineola, NY 11501-3582

Editorial Department

Publisher's Interests

Books on everything from American history and wildlife to
fine art and archaeology can be found in this publisher's
children's catalogue. It also features reprints of children's
classics and activity books.
Website: www.doverpublications.com

Freelance Potential

Published 500 titles (120 juvenile) in 2009. Of the 500 titles,
15–20 were by authors who were new to the publishing
house. Receives 125 queries yearly.

- **Fiction:** Publishes reprints of children's classics and storybooks. Genres include folktales, fantasy, and fairy tales. Also
  publishes stories about animals.
- **Nonfiction:** Publishes story picture books, 4–10 years; middle-
  grade books, 8–12 years; and young adult titles, 12–18 years.
  Topics include natural history, wildlife, American history,
  Native Americans, architecture, archaeology, literature,
  hobbies, and fine art. Also publishes educational titles,
  anthologies, biographies, coloring books, posters, sticker
  books, and activity books.
- **Representative Titles:** *Experimenting with Water* by Robert
  Gardner (10–13 years) includes 21 puzzles and experiments
  that reveal interesting facts about water. *How to Draw Cats*
  by Barbara Soloff Levy (6–10 years) offers simple step-by-step
  diagrams for rendering several poses.

Submissions and Payment

Guidelines and catalogue available at website. Query with
outline, table of contents, and sample chapter. Accepts hard
copy. Submissions are not returned. Responds if interested.
Publication period and payment policy vary.

Editor's Comments

Please note that we do not accept submissions for original
fiction, music, or poetry.

Down East Books

P.O. Box 679
Camden, ME 04843

Managing Editor: Michael Steere

Publisher's Interests
This publisher has been celebrating Maine and its New England neighbors for four decades. Its children's catalogue includes fiction and nonfiction for toddlers through young adults. 5% self-, subsidy-, co-venture, or co-op published material.
Website: www.downeastbooks.com

Freelance Potential
Published 30 titles (4 juvenile) in 2009: 4 were developed from unsolicited submissions and 1 was by an agented author. Of the 30 titles, 8 were by unpublished writers and 9 were by new authors. Receives 60–120 queries, 700 mss yearly.

- **Fiction:** Publishes story picture books, 4–10 years; middle-grade books, 8–12 years; and young adult books, 12–18 years. Genres include contemporary and historical fiction, adventure, mystery, and humor.
- **Nonfiction:** Publishes toddler books and early picture books, 0–4 years; easy-to-read books, 4–7 years; and story picture books, 4–10 years. Topics include the wildlife and history of New England and Maine.
- **Representative Titles:** *Beau Beaver Goes to Town* by Frances Bloxam (4–8 years) follows the adventures of a beaver searching for a place for his lodge. *The Legend of Burial Island* by David A. Crossman (10–14 years) unveils a mystery that blows into Penobscot Island.

Submissions and Payment
Guidelines and catalogue available at website. Query with outline/synopsis and sample chapter; or send complete ms. Accepts hard copy and simultaneous submissions if identified. SASE. Responds in 8–10 weeks. Publication in 2 years. Royalty, 9–12%; advance, $300–$600.

Editor's Comments
This year we're specifically looking for art, travel, and children's picture/story books with Maine or New England themes.

Dramatic Publishing

311 Washington Street
Woodstock, IL 60098

Acquisitions Editor: Linda Habjan

Publisher's Interests

Publishing plays since 1885, Dramatic Publishing offers musicals, full-length and one-act plays, and high-quality theatric books suitable for high-school theater, children's theater, or professional or community theater projects. It accepts plays for every cast size and for all ages.
Website: www.dramaticpublishing.com

Freelance Potential

Published 37 titles (9 juvenile) in 2009. Of the 37 titles, 14 were by authors who were new to the publishing house. Receives 500 unsolicited mss yearly.

- **Fiction:** Publishes full-length and one-act plays, monologues, and anthologies. Genres include drama, humor, fairy tales, and musicals. Also publishes plays with holiday themes.
- **Nonfiction:** Publishes books and resource materials. Topics include teaching theater arts, stagecraft, stage dialects, production techniques, playwriting, and audition presentations.
- **Representative Titles:** *A Kidsummer Night's Dream* by Lynn Barlett et al. is a musical retelling of Shakespeare's classic for middle- and high-school and family audiences. *Adventures With Young King Arthur* by David Lewman & Kevin Stites finds Merlin traveling to the present in order to teach young Arthur that girls can be as smart as boys.

Submissions and Payment

Guidelines and catalogue available at website. Send complete ms with résumé, synopsis, production history, reviews, cast list, and set and technical requirements; include a CD or audio cassette for musicals. Accepts hard copy. SASE. Responds in 4–6 months. Publication in 18 months. Payment policy varies.

Editor's Comments

We are always looking for clever, engaging productions for use in school or classroom theater projects.

The Dundurn Group

3 Church Street, Suite 500
Toronto, Ontario M5E 1M2
Canada

Assistant Editor: Allison Hirst

Publisher's Interests

This award-winning publishing company features fiction and
nonfiction for young adults, with an emphasis on Canadian
history, the environment, and nature.
Website: www.dundurn.com

Freelance Potential

Published 85 titles in 2009: 10 were from unsolicited submissions, 18 were by agented authors, and 8 were reprint/
licensed properties. Of the 85 titles, 10 were by unpublished
writers and 25 were by authors who were new to the publishing house. Receives 240 queries, 600 mss yearly.

- **Fiction:** Publishes middle-grade books, 8–12 years; and young
  adult books, 12–18 years. Genres include contemporary, historical, regional, and dramatic fiction; mystery; and suspense; and
  stories about nature, the environment, and the paranormal.
- **Nonfiction:** Publishes middle-grade books, 8–12 years; and
  young adult books, 12–18 years. Topics include biography,
  current events, history, nature, the environment, the paranormal, and Canadiana.
- **Representative Titles:** *Snakes and Ladders* by Shaun Smith
  (10+ years) is the story of a teen girl pulled into a maze of
  dark secrets and shocking truths while at the family cottage.
  To Stand and Fight Together by Steve Pitt (12–18 years) tells
  how Richard Pierpoint and his unique fighting unit helped to
  quash the Rebellion of 1837.

Submissions and Payment

Guidelines and catalogue available at website. Query with
résumé, synopsis (fiction), table of contents (nonfiction), and
3 sample chapters; or send complete ms. Accepts hard
copy. SAE/IRC. Responds in 6 months. Publication in 1 year.
Royalty; advance.

Editor's Comments

We also publish fiction and nonfiction titles for adults.

Dutton Children's Books

Penguin Group USA, Inc.
345 Hudson Street
New York, NY 10014

Queries Editor

Publisher's Interests

An imprint of Penguin Young Readers Group, Dutton has something for everyone—from board books for babies to young adult novels.
Website: www.us.penguingroup.com

Freelance Potential

Published 50 titles in 2009. Of the 50 titles, 7 were by unpublished writers. Receives 1,000+ queries yearly.

- **Fiction:** Publishes concept books and early picture books, 0–4 years; easy-to-read books, 4–7 years; story picture books, 4–10 years; middle-grade books, 8–12 years; and young adult books, 12–18 years. Genres include adventure, mystery, fantasy, and humor.
- **Nonfiction:** Publishes toddler books, 0–4 years; story picture books, 4–10 years; and young adult books, 12–18 years. Topics include history and nature.
- **Representative Titles:** *Skippyjon Jones: Shape Up* by Judy Schachner (3+ years) is a board book that teaches shapes through the antics of a crazy chihuahua. *A New Beginning* by Wendy Pfeffer (6+ years) celebrates the spring equinox and explains the science behind the season. *Gods of Manhattan* by Scott Mebus (10+ years) is a novel about a young boy who sees a hidden world all around him in New York City.

Submissions and Payment

Guidelines available at website. Query. Accepts hard copy. SASE. Responds in 3–6 months. Publication in 1+ years. Royalty; advance.

Editor's Comments

Multiple submissions are fine, as long as you are not simultaneously submitting to the other hardcover imprints at Penguin Young Readers Group (Dial, Philomel, Putnam, Razorbill, Viking). You are free to submit an idea to Dutton that has been turned down by one of the other Penguin imprints, however.

E & E Publishing

1001 Bridgeway, Suite 227
Sausalito, CA 94965

Submissions Editor: Eve Bine-Stock

Publisher's Interests
E & E Publishing produces high-quality picture books and
e-books in a variety of genres for children ages four to eight.
It also publishes nonfiction books for adult readers on the
subject of writing for young children, middle-grade kids, and
young adults.
Website: www.eandegroup.com/Publishing

Freelance Potential
Published 4–5 titles (2 juvenile) in 2009. Of the 4–5 titles,
1 was by an unpublished writer and 4 were by authors who
were new to the publishing house. Receives 24 queries,
100+ unsolicited mss yearly.

- **Fiction:** Publishes concept books and early picture books,
  0–4; easy-to-read books, 4–7 years; and story picture books,
  4–10 years. Genres include adventure, fantasy, and humor.
- **Nonfiction:** Publishes titles for adults about writing books
  for children.
- **Representative Titles:** *Kitten Up a Tree* by Melanie Abel tells
  of a little boy who patiently puts out fresh milk every day in
  order to gain the trust of a kitten in a tree. *The Adventures of
  Edward the Bear and Heidi the Birdie* by Annie Applefield is an
  e-book featuring the adventures of two unlikely friends.

Submissions and Payment
Catalogue available at website. Send complete ms for picture
books. Query for longer works. Prefers email submissions to
eandegroup@eandegroup.com (Microsoft Word attachment or
pasted into body of email); will accept hard copy. SASE.
Response time and publication period vary. Royalty, 5% of
retail; non-illustrated books for adults, 10% of retail.

Editor's Comments
We'll be adding nonfiction to our children's list in the future,
so send us ideas for nonfiction for four- to eight-year-old
kids, and for readers ages nine to twelve.

Ebooksonthe.net

Write Words, Inc.
2934 Old Route 50
Cambridge, MD 21613

Publisher: Arline Chase

Publisher's Interests

Readers ages 12 and older are the target for this publisher, which accepts projects in all genres and on all subjects. It makes some of its titles available as paper books, but most of its catalogue consists of e-books. It is interested in both fiction and nonfiction.
Website: www.writewordsinc.com

Freelance Potential

Published 40–60 titles in 2009: 10 were by unpublished writers and 30 were by authors who were new to the publishing house. Receives 200–300 queries yearly.

- **Fiction:** Publishes young adult books, 12–18 years. Genres include contemporary, historical, inspirational, and science fiction; romance; and mystery.
- **Nonfiction:** Publishes young adult books, 12–18 years. Topics include self-help, inspirational stories, and biography.
- **Representative Titles:** *Lilah and the Locket* by Nikki Leigh (YA) is a murder mystery that begins with a woman finding a human bone in the sand near the Cape Hatteras Lighthouse. *Hazel and the Boys* by Shelley Rodgerson (YA) is an inspirational tale of a girl who has to move due to her father's job, and finds three "friends" in a trio of ducks.

Submissions and Payment

Guidelines and catalogue available at website. Query with author credentials, word count, synopsis, and market analysis. Accepts email queries only to arline@mail.com.
Responds in 1 week. Publication in 3 months. Royalty, 40% for e-books sold from our website, 15% for paper books; 50% of proceeds from e-books sold on subsidiary websites.

Editor's Comments

We are particularly looking for romance, mystery, and humor titles. We are increasing our e-book marketing through subsidiary sites like Mobipocket, Fictionwise, and Amazon.

Edcon Publishing Group

30 Montauk Boulevard
Oakdale, NY 11769

Editor-in-Chief

Publisher's Interests

Research-based educational materials are the specialty of
Edcon Publishing Group. Its titles are geared toward school-
age children in mainstream and special education.
Website: www.edconpublishing.com

Freelance Potential

Published 10 titles in 2009: 2 were developed from unsolicited submissions. Of the 10 titles, 2 were by unpublished
writers and 1 was by an author who was new to the publishing house. Receives 120 unsolicited mss yearly.

- **Fiction:** Publishes easy-to-read books, 4–7 years; chapter
  books, 5–10 years; middle-grade books, 8–12 years; and
  young adult books, 12–18 years. Genres include science
  fiction, adventure, multicultural and ethnic fiction, and fairy
  tales. Also publishes hi/lo fiction, 6–18 years; and activity
  books, 6–12 years.
- **Nonfiction:** Publishes chapter books, 5–10 years; and young
  adult books, 12–18 years. Topics include reading comprehension, mathematics, science, and technology. Also publishes
  educational materials for homeschooling.
- **Representative Titles:** *Sticking Up for Number One!* provides
  students with the basic skills needed to handle difficult
  situations. *Career Decision Making* includes exercises to
  help students decide their path in life; part of the Personal
  Development for Success series.

Submissions and Payment

Guidelines available with 9x12 SASE ($1.75 postage). Send
complete ms. Accepts hard copy and simultaneous submissions if identified. Submissions are not returned. Responds
in 1 month. Publication in 6 months. Flat fee, $300–$1,000.

Editor's Comments

We're currently seeking submissions for math books, as well
as environmental, "save the Earth" material.

Edupress

W5527 Highway 106
P.O. Box 800
Fort Atkinson, WI 53538

Product Development Manager: Liz Bowie

Publisher's Interests

Edupress provides teachers of preschool through grade eight with quality supplemental, standards-based educational materials that help them bring fun and excitement to their classrooms. It produces everything from activity books to games and activity card sets and even classroom decor. Its catalogue covers language arts, mathematics, science, and social studies.
Website: www.edupressinc.com

Freelance Potential

Published 165 titles in 2009. Receives 24–36 queries yearly.

- **Nonfiction:** Publishes activity books and resource materials for educators, preK–grade 8. Topics include social studies, science, curriculum coordination, language arts, early learning, math, holidays, arts and crafts, and classroom decor.
- **Representative Titles:** *Classroom Plays for Social Studies* (grades 3–6) provides plays of varying length that allow students to step into history and expand their understanding of historical events. *Reading Comprehension Practice Cards* (grades 3 and up) provide reading and comprehension opportunities for individual or shared learning.

Submissions and Payment

Guidelines and catalogue available at website. Query with résumé, targeted grade range, outline, and sample pages. Accepts hard copy and email queries to lbowie@ highsmith.com (with "Manuscript Submission" in subject line). SASE. Responds in 4–5 months. Publication in 1 year. Flat fee.

Editor's Comments

Most of the material we publish is written by authors in the educational field. Time limitations have made it necessary for us to use form letters for rejecting proposals. We are unable to provide specific comments on all submissions.

Eerdmans Books for Young Readers

2140 Oak Industrial Drive NE
Grand Rapids, MI 49505

Acquisitions Editor

Publisher's Interests

An imprint of William B. Eerdmans Publishing Company, this group publishes high-quality works of fiction and nonfiction that engage and delight young readers. Its list includes titles for babies through young adult readers.
Website: www.eerdmans.com/youngreaders

Freelance Potential

Published 15 titles in 2009: 5 were developed from unsolicited submissions, 3 were by agented authors, and 7 were reprint/licensed properties. Of the 15 titles, 2 were by unpublished writers and 9 were by new authors. Receives 1,200–1,800 unsolicited mss yearly.

- **Fiction:** Publishes toddler books and early picture books, 0–4 years; story picture books, 4–10 years; chapter books, 5–10 years; middle-grade books, 8–12 years; and young adult books, 12–18 years. Genres include multicultural and historical fiction, and stories about animals and nature.
- **Nonfiction:** Publishes early picture books, 0–4 years; and middle-grade books, 8–12 years. Topics include history, biography, religion, and social issues.
- **Representative Titles:** *A River of Words* by Jen Bryant (7+ years) is a picture book biography of the poet William Carlos Williams. *Attack of the Turtle* by Drew Carlson (9–14 years), set during the American Revolution, tells the story of the invention of the prototype of the first submarine.

Submissions and Payment

Guidelines available. Send complete ms. Accepts hard copy (marked "exclusive" on the envelope). No simultaneous submissions. SASE. Responds in 6 months. Publication period varies. Royalty.

Editor's Comments

We are actively seeking picture book biographies and works of historical fiction.

Egmont Books

239 Kensington High Street
London W8 6SA
United Kingdom

Submissions: The Reader

Publisher's Interests
This publisher offers books in a wide range of formats for children of all ages and reading levels.
Website: www.egmont.co.uk

Freelance Potential
Published 70 titles in 2009: most were by agented authors.

- **Fiction:** Publishes concept books, toddler books, and early picture books, 0–4 years; easy-to-read books, 4–7 years; story picture books, 4–10 years; chapter books, 5–10 years; middle-grade books, 8–12 years; and young adult books, 12–18 years. Genres include adventure; drama; fairy tales; fantasy; mystery; horror; humor; historical, multicultural, and inspirational fiction; and stories about nature and the environment. Also publishes activity, novelty, and board books.
- **Nonfiction:** Publishes concept books, toddler books, and early picture books, 0–4 years; easy-to-read books, 4–7 years; story picture books, 4–10 years; chapter books, 5–10 years; middle-grade books, 8–12 years; and young adult books, 12–18 years. Topics include history and humor. Also publishes activity, novelty, and board books.
- **Representative Titles:** *Mr. Gum and the Biscuit Billionaire* by Andy Stanton is a wacky tale about a cantankerous man who meets up with some eccentric characters. *Mustang Mountain: Fire Horse* by Sharon Siamon (9+ years) tells how three friends are trapped by a forest fire while searching the mountains for a missing horse.

Submissions and Payment
Guidelines available. Query with outline/synopsis and 3 sample chapters. Accepts hard copy. SAE/IRC. Responds in 6–8 months. Payment policy varies.

Editor's Comments
Our aim is to deliver great stories, outstanding quality, and lasting pleasure to children and their parents. We don't just publish children's books—we are passionate about them.

Eldridge Publishing

P.O. Box 14367
Tallahassee, FL 32317

Editor: Susan Shore

Publisher's Interests
Plays and musicals, both secular and religious, geared to schools as well as community theater, are the mainstay of this publisher.
Website: www.histage.com; www.95church.com

Freelance Potential
Published 35 titles (23 juvenile) in 2009: 30 were developed from unsolicited submissions. Of the 35 titles, 5 were by authors who were new to the publishing house. Receives 500 unsolicited mss yearly.

- **Fiction:** Publishes full-length plays, skits, and musicals for grades 6–12. Genres include classical and contemporary drama, humor, folktales, melodrama, and Westerns. Also publishes plays with religious themes, holiday plays, and adult drama for community theaters.
- **Representative Titles:** *Just Another High School Play* by Bryan Starchman is a satirical comedy that combines history and improvisation in the re-writings of several typical high school plays. *Nativity Activity* by Matthew Wilson presents a family reluctantly coming together to participate in their church's live Nativity only to discover the joys of celebrating the holiday together.

Submissions and Payment
Guidelines available. Send ms with cover letter stating play length, age ranges for actors and audience, and performance history. Include CD and sample score for musicals. Accepts hard copy and email to newworks@histage.com (Microsoft Word or PDF attachments). SASE. Responds in 2 months. Publication in 6–12 months. Royalty, 50% performances; 10% copy sales. Flat fee for religious plays.

Editor's Comments
Refer to our website for our company's distinct advantages for playwrights publishing in our secular market.

Elva Resa Publishing

8362 Tamarack Village, Suite 119-106
St. Paul, MN 55125

Publisher: Christy Lyon

Publisher's Interests
Elva Resa publishes books for military families, including children's books. Its children's imprint, Alma Little, is a general interest children's publisher offering everything from picture books to middle-grade novels.
Website: www.elvaresa.com; www.almalittle.com

Freelance Potential
Published 4 titles (2 juvenile) in 2009. Of the 4 titles, 1 was by an unpublished writer and 1 was by an author who was new to the publishing house. Receives 360–3,600 queries each year.

- **Fiction:** Publishes story picture books, 4–10 years. Genres include contemporary and historical fiction, and stories about family members in the military.
- **Nonfiction:** Publishes early picture books, 0–4 years. Topics include self-help, current events, and military resources. Also publishes activity books and books for adults.
- **Representative Titles:** *The Wishing Tree* by Mary Redmond is the story of a girl who deals with her father's deployment by writing her thoughts on yellow ribbons and tying them to tree branches. *Perch, Mrs. Sackets, and Crow's Nest* by Karen Pavlicin finds a boy who makes the most of his summer at his grandmother's house, finding wonder and fun in everything.

Submissions and Payment
Guidelines and catalogue available at website. Elva Resa: query with outline. Accepts email queries to submissions@elvaresa.com. Alma Little: accepts targeted submissions only, see www.almalittle.com for details. Responds in 3 weeks. Publication in 12–18 months. Royalty; advance. Flat fee.

Editor's Comments
We are interested in good resources for military teens and pre-teens, and general interest middle-grade novels. All submissions should demonstrate a knowledge of our mission.

Encore Performance Publishing

P.O. Box 14367
Tallahassee, FL 32317

New Plays Editor: Meredith Edwards

Publisher's Interests
Encore Performance Publishing specializes in children's plays and musicals. Inspired by Latter-day Saints doctrine, it seeks to bring wholesome family entertainment to schools and churches, while simultaneously equipping students to handle social pressures.
Website: www.encoreplay.com

Freelance Potential
Published 5–10 titles in 2009. Receives 75 queries yearly.

- **Fiction:** Publishes full-length plays and musicals, skits, and monologue collections for grades 4–12. Genres include comedy and drama with Christian, multicultural, and ethnic themes.
- **Nonfiction:** Publishes resource titles for all ages. Topics include theater arts, acting, auditions, improvisation, stage management, set design, lighting, and makeup.
- **Representative Titles:** *The Commedia Aladdin* by Lane Riosley is a slapstick version of the classic Middle Eastern tale, written for four traveling actors. *Elephans* by Jeff Goode is a musical about elephant-like creatures who must learn to communicate without words; its goal is to teach tolerance, understanding, and the importance of listening.

Submissions and Payment
Guidelines available at website. Query with synopsis and production history. Accepts email queries to newworks@encoreplay.com. Responds in 2 months. Publication in 6 months. Royalty, 50% performance, 10% script.

Editor's Comments
We're especially interested in plays and musicals for children, tweens, and teens to help them navigate the perilous waters of middle school and high school. We're looking for honest but entertaining works. Please include any reviews, production photos, or DVDs that are available.

Enslow Publishers, Inc.

40 Industrial Road
Berkeley Heights, NJ 07922

Editor-in-Chief: Dorothy Goeller

Publisher's Interests

Founded in 1976, Enslow Publishers offers historical fiction for middle-grade readers and educational nonfiction for children in kindergarten through grade 12. It is interested in books that relate to school curricula, as most are marketed to school and public libraries.
Website: www.enslow.com

Freelance Potential

Published 200 titles in 2009. Receives 240 queries yearly.

- **Fiction:** Publishes middle-grade books, 8–12 years. Genres include historical fiction.
- **Nonfiction:** Publishes easy-to-read books, 4–7 years; middle-grade books, 8–12 years; and young adult books, 12–18 years. Topics include contemporary issues, health and drug education, history, government, holidays and customs, math, science, technology, sports, and recreation. Also publishes biographies.
- **Representative Titles:** *Why Are Animals Green?* by Melissa Stewart (grades 1–3) explains animal characteristics and behavior related to being green; part of the Rainbow of Animals series. *Amazing American Women Inventors: Eight Ingenious Lives* by Jennifer Reed (grades 6 and up) explores the lives and accomplishments of some of the country's greatest female inventors; part of the Great Scientists and Famous Inventors series.

Submissions and Payment

Guidelines available. Catalogue available at website. Query with outline. Accepts hard copy. SASE. Responds in 1–6 months. Publication in 1 year. Royalty; advance. Flat fee.

Editor's Comments

We are particularly interested in books in the following categories: biography, social issues, high interest topics for reluctant readers, science, and self-help books for young people about their personal or social problems.

Facts on File

132 West 31st Street, 17th Floor
New York, NY 10001

Editorial Director: Laurie Likoff

Publisher's Interests

This imprint of Infobase Publishing produces an array of reference books and curriculum-based nonfiction titles for use in school and public libraries.
Website: www.factsonfile.com

Freelance Potential

Published 550 titles in 2009: 25 were by agented authors. Of the 550 titles, 225 were by unpublished writers and 55 were by authors who were new to the publishing house. Receives 120 queries yearly.

- **Nonfiction:** Publishes chapter books, 5–10 years; middle-grade books, 8–12 years; and young adult books, 12–18 years. Topics include history, social studies, current affairs, politics, government, multicultural subjects, math, science, and the environment. Also publishes biographies.
- **Representative Titles:** *Dawn of the Dinosaur Age* by Thom Holmes (grades 9 and up) is devoted to the prehistoric creatures of the late Triassic and early Jurassic periods; part of the Prehistoric Earth series. *Ben Roethlisberger* by Rachel A. Koestler-Grack (grades 6–12) is a biography of the Pittsburgh Steelers quarterback who won two Superbowl championships; part of the Football Superstars series.

Submissions and Payment

Guidelines and catalogue available at website. Query with résumé, sample chapter, market analysis, and marketing ideas. Accepts hard copy, email queries to editorial@factsonfile.com, and simultaneous submissions if identified. SASE. Responds in 2 months. Publication in 1 year. Royalty; advance.

Editor's Comments

You are welcome to submit a proposal that fits within an existing series, creates a new one, or is an original work designed to be a stand-alone product.

Fairview Press

2450 Riverside Avenue
Minneapolis, MN 55454

Submissions: Steve Deger

Publisher's Interests
Fairview Press publishes practical books that address the physical, emotional, and spiritual wellness of children as well as adults. Its titles are written by education professionals and cover such topics as adolescent social pressures, sex education, grief management, and pregnancy.
Website: www.fairviewpress.org

Freelance Potential
Published 6–12 titles (1 juvenile) in 2009. Receives 600 queries yearly.

- **Nonfiction:** Publishes easy-to-read books, 4–7 years; middle-grade books, 8–12 years; and young adult books, 12–18 years. Also publishes parenting titles. Topics include health; complementary, holistic, and integrative medicine; patient education; self-help; relationships; pregnancy and childbirth; sex education; reproductive health; diet and exercise; and inspiration and mindfulness.
- **Representative Titles:** *Help Me Say Goodbye* by Janis Silverman is an art therapy book for children coping with the death of someone they love. *Brave New Girls* by Jeanette Gadeberg addresses issues that girls face and offers ideas to help them be confident, healthy, and happy.

Submissions and Payment
Guidelines and catalogue available at website. Query with outline, sample chapter, and marketing plan. Accepts hard copy. SASE. Response time and publication period vary. Payment negotiated on a case-by-case basis.

Editor's Comments
We do not publish children's picture books, fiction, poetry, or personal memoirs about coping with illness. We are de-emphasizing our former focus on end-of-life issues but will consider proposals on any topic pertaining to physical, emotional, or spiritual wellness.

Faith Kidz

Cook Communications
4050 Lee Vance View
Colorado Springs, CO 80918

Senior Acquisitions Editor: Ingrid Beck

Publisher's Interests
Believing that parents and teachers are the best mentors for
guiding children into lives filled with Christian values, this
imprint of Cook Communications publishes books and other
resources for children—each containing "teachable" moments.
Website: www.cookministries.com

Freelance Potential
Published 12–15 titles in 2009: 10 were by agented authors.

- **Fiction:** Publishes early picture books, 0–4 years; easy-to-read
  books, 4–7 years; story picture books, 4–10 years; middle-
  grade books, 8–12 years; and young adult books, 12–18
  years. Publishes stories with Christian themes.
- **Nonfiction:** Publishes easy-to-read books, 4–7 years; chapter
  books, 5–10 years; and middle-grade books, 8–12 years.
  Topics include Christianity, the Bible, and life skills.
- **Representative Titles:** *Little Heart, Little Hands Prayers* introduces babies to God's love and wonder; part of the Land of
  Milk & Honey series. *But It's True* by Heather Gemmen (4–7
  years) explores the differences between telling deliciously creative stories and telling lies. *The Journey of Hannah* by Wanda
  Luttrell (8–12 years) follows four children who have recently
  immigrated to America, introducing readers to their home-
  lands while telling their inspirational stories.

Submissions and Payment
Catalogue available at website. Prefers agented submissions;
will accept résumés and writing samples. Accepts hard copy.
SASE. Response time and publication period vary. Royalty.

Editor's Comments
We look for books that can provide children—in an entertaining and enlightening fashion—with some insight into what it
means to be part of God's world. While we do accept
résumés for works that we assign, we prefer to work through
literary agents.

Farrar, Straus & Giroux

18 West 18th Street
New York, NY 10011

Children's Editorial Department

Publisher's Interests

Farrar, Straus & Giroux's Books for Young Readers division has been operating since 1954, during which time it has racked up multiple awards and published the work of such notables as William Steig and Madeleine L'Engle. It is continually adding new authors to its roster.
Website: www.fsgkidsbooks.com

Freelance Potential

Published 80 titles in 2009. Receives 800 queries, 7,500 unsolicited mss yearly.

- **Fiction:** Publishes early picture books, 0–4 years; easy-to-read books, 4–7 years; story picture books, 4–10 years; chapter books, 5–10 years; and young adult books, 12–18 years. Genres include fantasy, humor, and contemporary fiction.
- **Nonfiction:** Publishes story picture books, 4–10 years; middle-grade books, 8–12 years; and young adult books, 12–18 years. Topics include history, science, and nature.
- **Representative Titles:** *The Pout-Pout Fish* by Deborah Diesen (3–6 years) is a rhyming tale about a gloomy fish who learns to cheer up. *How I Learned Geography* by Uri Shulevitz (4–8 years) is a Caldecott Honor Book about the author's experiences during World War II.

Submissions and Payment

Guidelines available at website. Query for mss longer than 20 pages. Send complete ms for shorter works. Accepts hard copy and simultaneous submissions if identified. SASE. Responds in 2–3 months. Publication in 18–36 months. Royalty, 3–10%.

Editor's Comments

Please keep in mind that you should submit to only one of our editors at a time, and submit only one manuscript at a time. Do not expect an editor to give you specific comments; we receive far too many manuscripts for this to happen.

Feiwel & Friends

175 Fifth Avenue
New York, NY 10010

Publisher: Jean Feiwel

Publisher's Interests
Founded in 2006 by veteran publisher Jean Feiwel, this imprint of Macmillan seeks books that make a contribution to literature as well as an impact on the marketplace. It does not restrict itself to any particular niche.
Website: www.feiwelandfriends.com

Freelance Potential
Published 40 titles in 2009: each was by an agented author.

- **Fiction:** Publishes story picture books, 4–10 years; chapter books, 5–10 years; middle-grade books, 8–12 years; and young adult books, 12–18 years. Genres include humor, fantasy, thrillers, historical fiction, and stories about animals.
- **Nonfiction:** Publishes middle-grade books, 8–12 years. Topics include humor.
- **Representative Titles:** *Jake Starts School* by Michael Wright (4–7 years) is a humorous tale about a boy who is so afraid to be left "alone" on his first day of school, that his parents attend class with him. *Fairy School Dropout* by Meredith Badger (7–9 years) is the story of Elly Knottleweed-Eversprightly, who hates being a fairy. *The Girl Who Could Fly* by Victoria Forester (11+ years) is a funny, heartbreaking, and scary novel about a girl whose special talent puts her in peril.

Submissions and Payment
Agented authors only. Guidelines available. SASE. Response time, publication period, and payment policy vary.

Editor's Comments
Feiwel & Friends combines quality with substance and commercial appeal. Our list is eclectic: for children from birth to age 16; fiction and nonfiction; hardcover and paperback series and individual titles. We will not follow trends, be derivative, or look to see what the competition is doing. Feiwel & Friends is defined and guided by our principle: Our books are friends for life.

Frederick Fell Publishers

1403 Shoreline Way
Hollywood, FL 33019-5007

Submissions: Barbara Newman

Publisher's Interests
While most of its books are written for adults, Frederick Fell's catalogue includes young adult novels and career guides for students. It also features parenting titles.
Website: www.fellpub.com

Freelance Potential
Published 24 titles in 2009: 22 were developed from unsolicited submissions and 2 were by agented authors. Of the 24 titles, 9 were by unpublished writers and 3 were by authors who were new to the publishing house. Receives 1,800 queries yearly.

- **Fiction:** Publishes young adult novels, 12–18 years. Genres include inspirational and religious fiction.
- **Nonfiction:** Publishes young adult books, 12–18 years. Topics include spirituality and health. Also publishes books on parenting and child care.
- **Representative Titles:** *Quick Guide to Good Kids* by Virginia Bentz shows how parents can be a strong line of defense for their children against the dangers of the world. *School Days and the Divorce Maze* by Dr. Renae Lapin is a guide to help divorced parents who share custody manage their children's school careers.

Submissions and Payment
Guidelines and catalogue available at website. Query with synopsis, table of contents, and 2 sample chapters. Accepts hard copy and simultaneous submissions if identified. SASE. Responds in 1 month. Publication in 9–12 months. Royalty.

Editor's Comments
In your proposal, please tell us about your book's competitors and explain why yours is better. Include at least three competitive titles along with a comparison between each title, and tell us what makes yours unique. Also include your credentials and a brief biography of yourself.

Ferguson Publishing

132 West 31st Street, 17th Floor
New York, NY 10001

Editor-in-Chief: James Chambers

Publisher's Interests
Ferguson Publishing is known among librarians and guidance counselors for its career-education references aimed at middle school and high school students. Its parent company, Infobase, also publishes the Facts On File series.
Website: www.fergpubco.com

Freelance Potential
Published 60 titles (6 juvenile) in 2009: 2 were developed from unsolicited submissions. Of the 60 titles, 2 were by authors who were new to the publishing house. Receives 48–72 queries yearly.

- **Nonfiction:** Publishes middle-grade books, 8–12 years; and young adult books, 12–18 years. Topics include college planning, career exploration and guidance, and job training. Also publishes development titles and general reference books.
- **Representative Titles:** *Teaching* (grades 4–9) introduces youngsters to the roles of college professors, guidance counselors, music teachers, preschool teachers, special education teachers, and others; part of the Discovering Careers for Your Future series. *Career Opportunities in the Film Industry* by Fred & Jan Yager (grades 9 and up) provides job descriptions, salary ranges, and employment outlook for more than 80 jobs; part of the Career Opportunities series.

Submissions and Payment
Guidelines and catalogue available at website. Query with résumé, outline, and sample chapter. Accepts hard copy, email to editorial@factsonfile.com, and simultaneous submissions if identified. SASE. Responds in 3–4 weeks. Publication in 9–24 months. Payment policy varies.

Editor's Comments
Your proposal will be acknowledged by an editorial assistant within three weeks of receipt. If your proposal fits our list, an editor will contact you within one month.

David Fickling Books

31 Beaumont Street
Oxford OX1 2NP
England

Editor: Bella Pearson

Publisher's Interests

This imprint of Random House Children's Books is a bi-continental company publishing simultaneously in the USA and the UK. It produces hardcover fiction in a variety of genres for children of all ages.
Website: www.davidficklingbooks.co.uk

Freelance Potential

Published 12 titles (6 juvenile) in 2009. Of the 12 titles, 2 were by authors who were new to the publishing house. Receives 500+ queries, 1,000+ unsolicited mss yearly.

- **Fiction:** Publishes toddler books, 0–4 years; story picture books, 4–10 years; chapter books, 5–10 years; middle-grade books, 8–12 years; and young adult books, 12–18 years. Genres include contemporary, historical, and science fiction; adventure; drama; fairy tales; fantasy; humor; and romance.
- **Representative Titles:** *Sylvie and the Songman* by Tim Binding (8–12 years) is the story of a girl who uncovers an underworld of magic and evil as she hunts for her kidnapped father. *Grizzly Dad* by Joanna Harrison (4–7 years) is a picture book about a grumpy father and the young son who lets him act like a bear all day—and even joins in on the fun.

Submissions and Payment

Guidelines available at website. Query with first 3–4 chapters for fiction. Send complete ms for poetry. Accepts hard copy. SAE/IRC. Responds in 4–6 months. Publication in 1–2 years. Royalty; advance.

Editor's Comments

Any book we accept from an unpublished writer must be truly exceptional, so we prefer to consider works that are sent to us by literary agents. We suggest that you try to get an agent before sending us your query. Be sure to browse through our catalogue to get to know us; you will see that many of our titles are award winners.

Finney Company

8075 215th Street West
Lakeville, MN 55044

President: Alan E. Krysan

Publisher's Interests

With a host of materials designed to enhance education and career development, Finney Company publishes books that specialize in agriculture, career exploration and guidance, workforce development, and technical education. Its main markets include schools, libraries, and government agencies.
Website: www.finneyco.com

Freelance Potential

Published 2–3 titles in 2009: 2 were developed from unsolicited submissions. Of the 2–3 titles, 2 were by unpublished writers and 2 were by authors who were new to the publishing house. Receives 36–60 queries yearly.

- **Nonfiction:** Publishes middle-grade books, 8–12 years; and young adult books, 12–18 years. Topics include occupational guidance, careers, technical education, counseling, portfolios, skills development, applying for employment, résumé writing, and interpersonal skills.
- **Representative Titles:** *Occupational Guidance for Agriculture* by Keri Henkel et al. features in-depth descriptions of more than 170 careers in six agricultural fields. *Planning My Career* by Vincent Capozziello, Jr., stresses the importance of career development and school-to-work transitions in a world in which workers must continually evolve and plan for change.

Submissions and Payment

Guidelines available at website. Query with résumé, overview, table of contents, introduction, 3 or more sample chapters, and market description. Accepts hard copy and simultaneous submissions if identified. SASE. Responds in 10–12 weeks. Publication period varies. Royalty, 10% of net.

Editor's Comments

Please note that we will review only submissions that are educational in nature. In general, we do not publish fiction or religious material.

Fitzhenry & Whiteside

195 Allstate Parkway
Markham, Ontario L3R 4T8
Canada

Children's Book Editor

Publisher's Interests
This Canadian publisher accepts high-quality fiction and non-fiction on a variety of subjects for children of all ages.
Website: www.fitzhenry.ca

Freelance Potential
Published 10 titles in 2009: 3 were by agented authors and 2 were reprint/licensed properties. Receives 36 queries, 360 unsolicited mss yearly.

- **Fiction:** Publishes toddler books and early picture books, 0–4 years; story picture books, 4–10 years; chapter books, 5–10 years; middle-grade books, 8–12 years; and young adult books, 12–18 years. Genres include contemporary, historical, and multicultural fiction; mystery; suspense; adventure; and romance. Also publishes poetry.
- **Nonfiction:** Publishes early picture books, 0–4 years; story picture books, 4–10 years; middle-grade books, 8–12 years; and young adult books, 12–18 years. Topics include animals, history, nature, and the environment.
- **Representative Titles:** *Only a Cow* by Arlene Hamilton (4–8 years) is a heartwarming story of Lucille the cow, who wants to try something new. *Daughter of War* by Marsha Forchuk Skrypuch (14+ years) is a story of a young woman who must hide her true identity, and separate from her loved ones, in order to survive the Armenian genocide.

Submissions and Payment
Guidelines available at website. Send complete ms for picture books and poetry. Query with clips for longer work. Accepts hard copy. SASE. Responds in 3 months. Publication in 1 year. Royalty; advance.

Editor's Comments
We are interested in Canadian biographies for middle-grade readers, as well as children's fiction. We are not accepting board books, seasonal stories, or narrative poetry.

Flashlight Press

527 Empire Boulevard
Brooklyn, NY 11225

Editor: Shari Dash Greenspan

Publisher's Interests

This independent publisher is interested in children's fiction
for kids ages four to eight. Its books have universal themes
of family life, love, and social interactions.
Website: www.flashlightpress.com

Freelance Potential

Published 2 titles in 2009: both were developed from unsolicited submissions. Of the 2 titles, both were by unpublished writers who were new to the publishing house.
Receives 1,200+ queries yearly.

- **Fiction:** Publishes easy-to-read books, 4–7 years; and story
  picture books, 4–10 years. Genres include contemporary
  fiction with themes of family and social situations.
- **Representative Titles:** *I Need My Monster* by Amanda Noll is
  a unique monster-under-my-bed story for all monster-loving
  kids. *I'm Really Not Tired* by Lori Sunshine presents the
  rhyming adventure of young Sam and his stuffed bear as they
  sneak out of bed to find out what happens in their house
  while they are asleep. *Grandpa For Sale* by Dotti Enderle &
  Vicki Sansum finds a girl who, while minding the family
  antiques store, bargains with a customer who wants to purchase her napping grandfather.

Submissions and Payment

Guidelines and catalogue available at website. Query with
description of story and word count. Accepts email queries
to editor@flashlightpress.com (no attachments). Responds in
2–4 weeks. Publication period and payment policy vary.

Editor's Comments

Please remember that we publish picture books only. We're
not interested in concept books, nonfiction, chapter books,
or young adult books. We want books that explore and illuminate the touching and humorous moments of family situations and social interactions.

Floris Books

15 Harrison Gardens
Edinburgh, EH11 1SH
Scotland

Commissioning Editor: Sally Martin

Publisher's Interests
This publisher of children's fiction and adult nonfiction is reviewing submissions for its Kelpies series of Scottish children's fiction.
Website: www.florisbooks.co.uk

Freelance Potential
Published 50 titles (20 juvenile) in 2009: 5 were developed from unsolicited submissions, 10 were by agented authors, and 15 were reprint/licensed properties. Of the 50 titles, 5 were by unpublished writers and 5 were by new authors. Receives 600 queries, 300 unsolicited mss yearly.

- **Fiction:** Publishes picture books, 4–6 years; chapter books, 7–10 years; and middle-grade books, 8–12 years. Genres include contemporary, multicultural, and regional fiction; drama; and fantasy. Also publishes board books, 0–4 years; and story collections, 6–10 years.
- **Nonfiction:** Publishes books for adults. Topics include child health and development, self-help, holistic health, science and spirituality, and philosophy.
- **Representative Titles:** *Toby and the Flood* by Rebecca Price (3–6 years) is a funny story about a habitual bedwetter who finds himself having an imaginary adventure in a flood. *The Underground City* by Anne Forbes (8–12 years) blends fantasy and mystery into an adventure in a haunted desert oasis; part of the Dragonfire series.

Submissions and Payment
Guidelines available. Query or send complete ms. Agented submissions have a better chance of acceptance. Accepts hard copy. SASE. Responds to queries in 1 week, to mss in 3 months. Publication in 18 months. Royalty.

Editor's Comments
Stories for our Kelpies series should be set largely or wholly in Scotland.

Flux

2143 Wooddale Drive
Woodbury, MN 55125

Acquisitions Editor: Brian Farrey

Publisher's Interests

This imprint is dedicated solely to teen fiction, and sees the term "young adult" as a point of view rather than a reading level. It welcomes submissions from new writers.
Website: www.fluxnow.com

Freelance Potential

Published 24 titles in 2009. Receives 1,200 queries, 360 unsolicited mss yearly.

- **Fiction:** Publishes young adult books, 12–18 years. Genres include contemporary, realistic, and coming-of-age fiction; fantasy; and thrillers.
- **Representative Titles:** *The Straits* by Jeremy Craig (YA) is the story of a high school student who literally gambles on his future after a hurricane kills his mother and sister. *The Secret of the Dread Forest* by Gillian Summers (YA) continues the saga of a 16-year-old girl who has recently discovered her elfin ancestry, and must now take up residence in an enchanted forest; third in the Faire Folk trilogy. *So Punk Rock (and Other Ways to Disappoint Your Mother)* by Micol Ostow (YA) is a humorous novel about a Jewish hipster rock band.

Submissions and Payment

Guidelines and catalogue available at website. Query with synopsis and 3 chapters; or send complete ms with synopsis. Accepts email to submissions@fluxnow.com (Microsoft Word attachments). Responds in 2–6 months if interested. Publication in 18–24 months. Royalty; advance.

Editor's Comments

Please include your cover letter in the body of your email, and send your manuscript and your synopsis as two separate Microsoft Word files. The synopsis should not run more than three pages. Do not include pictures, marketing materials, résumés, or any other extra materials. And remember: Patience is a virtue.

Focus on the Family
Book Development

8605 Explorer Drive
Colorado Springs, CO 80920

Managing Editor: Kathy Davis

Publisher's Interests
This publishing arm of the nonprofit Christian organization develops books with messages that are in keeping with its ministry and goals—that is, books that present a traditional, biblical perspective on men, women, and family roles.
Website: www.family.org

Freelance Potential
Published 20 titles (6 juvenile) in 2009: each was by an agented author. Receives 180 queries yearly.

- **Fiction:** Publishes chapter books, 5–10 years. Also publishes books for adults. Genres include Christian fiction featuring family issues.
- **Nonfiction:** Publishes young adult books, 12–18 years. Also publishes books for adults. Topics include family advice, marriage, parenting, relationships, encouragement for women, and topics for seniors.
- **Representative Titles:** *Handbook on Thriving as an Adoptive Family: Real Life Solutions to Common Challenges* by David Sanford is filled with practical advice and ideas for families with adopted children. *Extreme Grandparenting: The Ride of Your Life!* by Tim & Darcy Kimmel presents humor, real stories, and practical ideas to help grandparents develop rich relationships with their children and grandchildren.

Submissions and Payment
Guidelines available. Query through literary agent only. Response time varies. Publication in 18 months. Payment policy varies.

Editor's Comments
We do not accept unsolicited material. In nonfiction, we are publishing only family advice topics; in fiction, we are publishing a limited number of adult titles and some commissioned projects for children. All material must be in keeping with our message of traditional family values.

Formac Publishing Company

5502 Atlantic Street
Halifax, Nova Scotia B3H 1G4
Canada

Submissions Editor

Publisher's Interests
Formac Publishing Company's focus is on its homeland: books by Canadian authors, with Canadian settings, for Canadian children. Most of its titles are part of a series. **Website: www.formac.ca**

Freelance Potential
Published 70 titles (25 juvenile) in 2009. Of the 70 titles, 6–7 were by authors who were new to the publishing house. Receives 80 queries yearly.

- **Fiction:** Publishes easy-to-read books, 4–7 years; chapter books, 5–10 years; and middle-grade books, 8–13 years. Genres include humor, mystery, suspense, fantasy, adventure, historical fiction, and stories about sports.
- **Nonfiction:** Publishes middle-grade books, 8–13 years. Topics include Canadian history, multicultural and ethnic issues, the environment, and sports.
- **Representative Titles:** *Lilly and the Hullabaloo* by Brenda Bellingham follows the efforts of a grade-school class to create their own version of a Caribbean carnival; part of the First Novels series. *Adrenaline High* by Christine Forsyth tells of two 16-year-old girls who get in over their heads while trying to track down one's missing mother. *Formac Pocketguide to Fossils* by Jeffrey C. Domm is a guide to the fossilized plants, insects, and animals of Canada's Maritimes region.

Submissions and Payment
Canadian authors preferred. Guidelines and catalogue available at website. Query with résumé, outline, and sample chapters. Accepts hard copy and simultaneous submissions if identified. SAE/IRC. Responds in 1–12 months. Publication in 1–2 years. Royalty.

Editor's Comments
We pride ourselves on offering books that appeal to a wide range of ages and reading abilities.

Forward Movement

300 West Fourth Street, 2nd Floor
Cincinnati, OH 45202

Editor & Publisher: Richard H. Schmidt

Publisher's Interests

An official agency of the Episcopal Church, Forward Movement publishes religious tracts, daily devotional guides, and
other books related to the life and concerns of the Anglican
Communion. While it has published children's books and
learning activities in the past, it now concentrates solely on
titles for adults.
Website: www.forwardmovement.org

Freelance Potential

Published 30 titles in 2009: 4 were developed from unsolicited submissions. Of the 30 titles, 10 were by unpublished
writers and 5 were by authors who were new to the publishing house. Receives 24 unsolicited mss yearly.

- **Nonfiction:** Publishes books for parents. Topics include
  explaining death to children, family prayer, raising children of
  faith, baptism, holy communion, and religious education.
- **Representative Titles:** *Explaining Death to Children* by Rabbi
  Earl A. Grollman helps adults articulate their theology of death
  to young people. *Home Prayers for Little Children* is a guide
  for parents that includes simple prayers and practical suggestions for helping children begin to pray.

Submissions and Payment

Guidelines and catalogue available at website. Sample pamphlet available (send 7 first-class stamps; no SASE). Send
complete ms. Accepts hard copy. SASE. Responds in 1
month. Publication period varies. Flat fee.

Editor's Comments

Of the approximately 30 new titles we publish each year,
some are booklets of up to 64 pages; the rest are tracts of
under 24 pages. We have a special need for tracts of under
eight pages. (A page runs approximately 130 to 150 words.)
Previously published material is accepted, but indicate when
and by whom it was previously published.

Frances Foster Books

Farrar, Straus & Giroux
175 Fifth Avenue
New York, NY 10010

Children's Editorial Department

Publisher's Interests

Picture books to young adult books—both fiction and nonfiction—are of interest to this imprint of Farrar, Straus & Giroux. Its titles feature interesting characters, clever writing, and an overall appeal to young readers.
Website: www.fsgkidsbooks.com

Freelance Potential

Published 70 titles in 2009. Of the 70 titles, 9 were by unpublished writers and 20 were by authors who were new to the publishing house. Receives 2,000 queries, 7,500 unsolicited mss yearly.

- **Fiction:** Publishes toddler books and early picture books, 0–4 years; easy-to-read books, 4–7 years; story picture books, 4–10 years; middle-grade books, 8–12 years; and young adult books, 12–18 years. Genres include contemporary, historical, and ethnic fiction; fantasy; adventure; and drama.
- **Nonfiction:** Publishes story picture books, 4–10 years; and young adult books, 12–18 years. Topics include history.
- **Representative Titles:** *Leaving the Nest* by Mordicai Gerstein (3–6 years) follows a baby blue jay, kitten, girl, and squirrel as they leave their safe home for the first time and discover the things that live outside their "nests." *How To Steal a Dog* by Barbara O'Connor (8–12 years) features a young girl trying to do what's right to get herself out of a desperate situation.

Submissions and Payment

Guidelines and catalogue available at website. Query with outline/synopsis and 3 sample chapters. Send complete ms for picture books. Accepts hard copy and simultaneous submissions if identified. SASE. Responds in 3+ months. Publication in 3+ years. Royalty; advance.

Editor's Comments

Please do not expect an editor to give you specific comments on your manuscript; we simply receive too many to do that.

Free Spirit Publishing

217 Fifth Avenue North, Suite 200
Minneapolis, MN 55401-1299

Acquisitions Editor

Publisher's Interests
This company publishes nonfiction, self-help books, and
learning materials for children and teens, as well as for parents and professionals who work with youth. It publishes on
the subjects of emotional and physical development, learning differences, self-esteem, and social issues.
Website: www.freespirit.com

Freelance Potential
Published 20 titles (15 juvenile) in 2009. Of the 20 titles,
1 was by an unpublished writer and 2 were by authors who
were new to the publishing house. Receives 1,095 queries,
450 unsolicited mss yearly.

- **Nonfiction:** Publishes toddler books and early picture books,
  0–4 years; easy-to-read books, 4–7 years; story picture books,
  4–10 years; middle-grade books, 8–12 years; and young adult
  books, 12–18 years. Topics include social skills, stress management, conflict resolution, character-building, relationships,
  and self-esteem. Also publishes titles about parenting, behavior issues, learning disorders, and gifted education.
- **Representative Titles:** *Ready to Play!* by Stacey R. Kaye (3–6
  years) offers healthy, lasting ways that kids can learn to play
  and share together without bickering. *Good-Bye Bully Machine*
  by Debbie Fox & Allan L. Beane (8+ years) helps kids learn
  what bullying is, why it hurts, and what they can do to end it.

Submissions and Payment
Guidelines and catalogue available at website. Query with
résumé, outline, market analysis, and 2 or more sample
chapters. Send complete ms for early childhood books.
Accepts hard copy. SASE. Responds in 2–6 months. Publication in 1–3 years. Royalty; advance.

Editor's Comments
We are very interested in material for children and teens with
learning differences.

Samuel French, Inc.

45 West 25th Street
New York, NY 10010

Editor: Roxane Heinze-Bradshaw

Publisher's Interests
This international publisher calls itself "the gateway to the world of classic, contemporary, and compelling plays and musicals" for all ages.
Website: www.samuelfrench.com

Freelance Potential
Published 100 titles in 2009: several were by unpublished writers and several were by authors who were new to the publishing house.

- **Fiction:** Publishes full-length and one-act plays, monologues, readings, and anthologies for theater groups of all ages. Genres include musicals; drama; comedy; farce; fantasy; thrillers; operettas; and religious, holiday, and Shakespearean plays.
- **Nonfiction:** Publishes books and resource materials for theater teachers and directors. Topics include acting methods, directing, stage design, lighting, theater management, auditions, comedy, improvisations, and film productions.
- **Representative Titles:** *The Awesome 80s Prom* by Ken Davenport is an audience participation comedy that features famous characters from popular 1980s movies who compete for Prom King and Queen. *China: The Whole Enchilada* by Mark Brown dares to tackle racism, human rights, and the birth of the fortune cookie.

Submissions and Payment
Guidelines available. Query with 10-page sample and links to information about previous productions. Send complete ms through literary agents only. Prefers submissions via website; will accept hard copy and simultaneous submissions if identified. SASE. Responds to queries in 1 month, to mss in 2–3 months. Publication in 1 year. Payment policy varies.

Editor's Comments
We prefer works that have been successfully produced by a prominent theater before they are published.

Friends United Press

101 Quaker Hill Drive
Richmond, IN 47374

Editor: Katie Terrell

Publisher's Interests
Friends United Press publishes works that support the mission statement of Friends United Meeting: "to energize and equip Friends through the power of the Holy Spirit to gather people into fellowships where Jesus Christ is known, loved, and obeyed as Teacher and Lord."
Website: www.fum.org/shop

Freelance Potential
Published 2 titles in 2009: 1 was developed from an unsolicited submission. Receives 50 queries yearly.

- **Fiction:** Publishes middle-grade books, 8–12 years; and young adult books, 12–18 years. Genres include historical fiction and religious fiction.
- **Nonfiction:** Publishes middle-grade books, 8–12 years; and young adult books, 12–18 years. Topics include Quaker history, theology, and biography; spirituality; peace; justice; African-American culture; and the Underground Railroad.
- **Representative Titles:** *Bracera Con Esperanza* by Elizabeth Newby is the memoir of a Mexican American migrant child, her family, and the struggles they faced. *A Peculiar People* by Joseph John Gurney conveys the author's observations of the distinguishing elements of the Quakers/Religious Society of Friends.

Submissions and Payment
Guidelines and catalogue available at website. Query with synopsis and 2–3 sample chapters. Accepts hard copy and email queries to friendspress@fum.org (Microsoft Word attachments). SASE. Responds in 3–6 months. Publication in 1 year. Royalty, 7.5%.

Editor's Comments
We are interested in fiction and nonfiction submissions, as well as curriculum material, that reflect the mission statement of Friends United Meeting.

Front Street

Boyds Mills Press, Inc.
815 Church Street
Honesdale, PA 18431

Editorial Director: Larry Rosler

Publisher's Interests
This imprint of Boyds Mills Press publishes fiction and picture books for children, novels for middle-grade readers and young adults, and nonfiction for young adults.
Website: www.frontstreetbooks.com

Freelance Potential
Published 25 titles in 2009. Receives 1,000 queries yearly.

- **Fiction:** Publishes story picture books, 4–10 years; middle-grade books, 8–12 years; and young adult books, 12–18 years. Genres include adventure; fantasy; humor; and multicultural, historical, contemporary, and science fiction.
- **Nonfiction:** Publishes young adult books, 12–18 years. Topics include contemporary issues. Also publishes novelty books, educational titles, and poetry.
- **Representative Titles:** *Morning in a Different Place* by Mary Ann McGuigan (14–17 years) is the story of a girl who discovers the true meaning of friendship and family when she chooses her best friend and mother's safety over social acceptance by her peers. *The Baseball Card Kid* by Adam Osterweil (8–12 years) is a tale of time travel, friendship, and a mint condition Honus Wagner baseball card.

Submissions and Payment
Guidelines and catalogue available at website. Query with outline/synopsis and 1 sample chapter for nonfiction, 3 sample chapters for fiction. Accepts hard copy. SASE. Responds in 3 months. Publication in 2–3 years. Royalty; advance.

Editor's Comments
We welcome submissions from published and unpublished writers alike. Please understand that the large number of submissions we receive makes our reviewing process time-consuming; therefore, we will only respond personally if we are interested in your proposal. All other submissions will receive a form letter.

Fulcrum Publishing

4690 Table Mountain Drive, Suite 100
Golden, CO 80403

Acquisitions Editor

Publisher's Interests

An independent trade publisher, Fulcrum Publishing produces fiction and nonfiction books on a variety of topics for children as well as adults, although it is currently accepting nonfiction titles only. For children, it focuses on Western culture and history, Native Americans, and books about nature and the environment.
Website: www.fulcrum-books.com

Freelance Potential

Published 35 titles (8 juvenile) in 2009. Receives 300 queries yearly.

- **Nonfiction:** Publishes easy-to-read books, 4–7 years; middle-grade books, 8–12 years; and young adult books, 12–18 years. Topics include ecology, natural history, Native American culture, outdoor recreation, and the American West.
- **Representative Titles:** *Gas Trees and Car Turds: A Kids' Guide to the Roots of Global Warming* by Kirk Johnson & Mary Ann Bonnell breaks down the complicated problem of global warming into ideas easily understood by children. *America's Deserts* by Marianne D. Wallace (8–13 years) is a detailed guide to the plants and animals of the four desert regions of North America.

Submissions and Payment

Guidelines available at website. Query with synopsis, sample chapters, résumé, and competition analysis. Accepts hard copy and simultaneous submissions if identified. No SASE. Responds in 3 months if interested. Publication in 18–24 months. Royalty; advance.

Editor's Comments

Due to the volume of material received, submissions will be recycled and you will not hear from us unless we are interested. Writers should know, however, that we do consider each and every submission.

Gibbs Smith, Publisher

P.O. Box 667
Layton, UT 84041

Senior Editor: Jennifer Grillone

Publisher's Interests
Gibbs Smith creates books that celebrate children and childhood. It offers craft and activity books as well as story and picture books for children. It also publishes books on home decorating and cookbooks for adults.
Website: www.gibbs-smith.com

Freelance Potential
Published 84 titles in 2009: Of the 84 titles, 42 were by authors who were new to the publishing house. Receives 800 queries, 2,500 unsolicited mss yearly.

- **Fiction:** Publishes easy-to-read books, 4–7 years; and story picture books, 4–10 years. Genres include adventure, Westerns, fantasy, folktales, and humor. Also publishes stories about animals, nature, and the environment.
- **Nonfiction:** Publishes activity books, 4–10 years. Topics include drawing, crafts, the outdoors, and holidays.
- **Representative Titles:** *The Big Book of Girl Stuff* by Bart King (9+ years) is filled with everything a girl needs to know, from sleepovers and diaries to shopping and boys. *Pocketdoodles for Kids* by Bill Zimmerman is a guide for drawing, coloring, and thinking that inspires doodlers not only to draw but to stretch their imaginations.

Submissions and Payment
Guidelines and catalogue available at website. Query with outline and writing samples for nonfiction. Send complete ms for picture books. Accepts email to info@ gibbs-smith.com. Responds only if interested. Publication in 1–2 years. Royalty; advance.

Editor's Comments
We view the book business as a trade and ourselves as artisans crafting books with our authors. Prospective authors should share this philosophy of publishing, as well as our goal to "enrich and inspire mankind."

Gifted Education Press

10201 Yuma Court
P.O. Box 1586
Manassas, VA 20109

Editor: Maurice D. Fisher

Publisher's Interests
For almost 30 years, Gifted Education Press has been publishing books about teaching gifted students. It reviews manuscripts written for teachers, parents, and students.
Website: www.giftededpress.com

Freelance Potential
Published 10 titles in 2009: 4–8 were developed from unsolicited submissions. Of the 10 titles, 2–5 were by unpublished writers. Receives 50 queries yearly.

- **Nonfiction:** Publishes middle-grade books, 8–12 years; and young adult books, 12–18 years. Topics include chemistry, physics, biology, mathematics, social studies, language arts, and the humanities. Also publishes educational resources for parents and teachers who work with gifted students.
- **Representative Titles:** *Heroes of Giftedness: An Inspirational Guide for Gifted Students and Their Teachers* by Maurice D. Fisher & Eugenia M. Fisher, eds. presents the biographies of 12 men and women who overcame challenges to move forward in their fields. *Energize Your Gifted Students' Creative Thinking & Imagination* by Harry T. Roman guides teachers in nurturing their gifted students' ability to solve practical and real-world problems.

Submissions and Payment
Guidelines and catalogue available at website. Query with 1-page proposal. No unsolicited mss. Accepts hard copy. SASE. Responds in 3 months. Publication in 3 months. Royalty, 10%.

Editor's Comments
We are in need of books on the topics of environmental sciences or environmental studies for gifted students; and we are always interested in books for parents. In addition to book submissions, we accept articles and brief essays for our quarterly newsletter.

The Globe Pequot Press

246 Goose Lane
Guilford, CT 06437

Editorial Administrator: Melanie Bugbee

Publisher's Interests
The Globe Pequot Press is well known for its books on travel, outdoor recreation, adventure, and regional topics. Its books for children and parents focus on animals, nature, the environment, and fun outdoor activities.
Website: www.globepequot.com

Freelance Potential
Published 440 titles in 2009: many were developed from unsolicited submissions, were by agented authors, or were reprint/licensed properties. Of the 440 titles, 75 were by authors who were new to the publishing house. Receives 300+ queries yearly.

- **Nonfiction:** Publishes story picture books, 4–10 years; middle-grade books, 8–12 years; and young adult books, 12–18 years. Topics include animals, pets, nature, history, the environment, travel, conservation, and regional subjects. Also publishes biographies.
- **Representative Titles:** *How To Build Treehouses, Huts and Forts* by David Stiles is filled with fun projects for kids and their parents to build in their own backyards, including some to build in the snow. *Budgee Budgee Cottontail* by Jo Mora is a tale, told in verse, about Budgee's encounters with animal friends and foes.

Submissions and Payment
Guidelines and catalogue available at website. Query with author biography, synopsis, table of contents, sample chapter, and market analysis. Accepts hard copy. SASE. Responds in 3 months. Publication in 18 months. Royalty, 8-12%; advance, $500–$1,500.

Editor's Comments
We're looking for more regional travel and outdoor recreation subjects, particularly material that will engage both children and their parents.

David R. Godine, Publisher

9 Hamilton Place
Boston, MA 02108

Editorial Department

Publisher's Interests

This publishing house chooses eclectic works that many other publishers may not accept, but that deserve publication nonetheless. Its children's list includes fiction and nonfiction for readers ages five to ten. It accepts queries through literary agents only. 3% self-, subsidy-, co-venture, or co-op published material.
Website: www.godine.com

Freelance Potential

Published 30 titles in 2009: each was by an agented author. Of the 30 titles, 7 were by authors who were new to the publishing house. Receives 1,000 queries yearly.

- **Fiction:** Publishes story picture books, 4–10 years; and chapter books, 5–10 years. Genres include mystery, Westerns, historical fiction, and stories about animals and nature.
- **Nonfiction:** Publishes story picture books, 4–10 years; and chapter books, 5–10 years. Topics include study skills, camping, crafts, activities, history, and biography.
- **Representative Titles:** *Electra to the Rescue: Saving a Steamship and the Story of Shelburne Museum* by Valerie Biebuyck brings children the true story of a woman who collected things that embodied the American tradition of craftsmanship. *Lucy's Summer* by Donald Hall & Michael McCurdy is a tale of growing up in rural America during simpler, more wholesome times, when a parade and getting a penny toy were big events.

Submissions and Payment

Guidelines and catalogue available at website. Query through literary agent only. Accepts hard copy. SASE. Response time, publication period, and payment policy vary.

Editor's Comments

Please note that we are a small publishing house, and we must be very selective in the books we publish.

Goodheart-Willcox

18604 West Creek Drive
Tinley Park, IL 60477-6243

Editor, Family & Consumer Sciences: Teresa Dec

Publisher's Interests
This educational publisher specializes in books on family
and consumer sciences, technology and technical trades,
business, marketing, and career planning. It produces textbooks, supplements, and multimedia resources for teachers,
schools, businesses, and individuals.
Website: www.g-w.com

Freelance Potential
Published 10 titles in 2009. Receives 100+ queries yearly.

- **Nonfiction:** Publishes textbooks, professional development
  books for teachers, and how-to titles. Topics include life management, personal development, family living, child care, child
  development, parenting, consumer education, food and nutrition, housing and interiors, technical trades, fashion, career
  education, and professional development. Also publishes
  instructor's guides, resource guides, and software.
- **Representative Titles:** *Planning Activities for Child Care*
  by Caroline Spang Rosser is a curriculum guide for all professionals involved in child care for preschoolers. *Teen Life* by
  Martha Dunn-Strohecker & Deborah Tippett is a textbook
  designed to help young teens learn about themselves, their
  friends, families, communities, and environment; includes
  lessons on daily living skills and decision-making.

Submissions and Payment
Guidelines available. Catalogue available at website. Query
with résumé, outline, sample chapter, and list of illustrations. Accepts hard copy. SASE. Responds in 2 months.
Publication in 2 years. Royalty.

Editor's Comments
If you are considering sending us a proposal, please send
for our author's guide. It is a detailed documentation of
not only the process of writing a textbook, but how our
process works.

Go Teach It

522 West First Avenue
Spokane Valley, WA 99201

Editor: Steven Denny

Publisher's Interests
Formerly known as Teacher Curriculum, this electronic publisher offers complete lesson plans and supplements for
download from its website. Its materials cover all competency
areas and grade levels, and are available in various formats.
Website: www.goteachit.com

Freelance Potential
Published many titles in 2009: 90% were by unpublished
writers and 75% were by authors who were new to the publishing house. Receives 300 queries yearly.

- **Nonfiction:** Publishes teacher curricula, grades K–12. Topics
  include computers, current events, geography, history, math,
  science, technology, social issues, literature, vocabulary, and
  reading comprehension.
- **Representative Titles:** *Jamble Scrambles* by Steve Denny
  (grades 3–6) is a collection of 10 word games related to the
  School Story curriculum. *My Side of the Mountain Complete
  Teaching Unit* by Fanny Hofer (teachers grades 7–8) includes
  a chapter-by-chapter lesson plan for this title by Jean Craig-
  head George, with discussion questions, vocabulary, chapter
  summaries, trivia questions, and true/false reading check
  questions.

Submissions and Payment
Guidelines and catalogue available at website. Potential
authors must register their interest at the website; if accepted,
a personal mentor will be assigned to work closely with
the author. Response time varies. Publication period varies.
Royalty, 10–35%.

Editor's Comments
Are you interested in making money for a curriculum you've
already written? Are you creating a curriculum that you'd like
to share? Then by all means, please contact us through our
website at the above address.

Graphia

Houghton Mifflin
222 Berkeley Street
Boston, MA 02116

Submissions: Julie Richardson

Publisher's Interests

This publisher's books speak directly to teenagers. Its catalogue is filled with fiction, nonfiction, and graphic novels about people, issues, situations, and challenges to which today's teen can relate.
Website: www.graphiabooks.com

Freelance Potential

Published 10–15 titles in 2009. Of the 10–15 titles, 2–5 were by authors who were new to the publishing house. Receives 500–600 queries, 800–1,000 unsolicited mss yearly.

- **Fiction:** Publishes young adult books, 12–18 years. Genres include contemporary, historical, and science fiction; mystery; suspense; and humor.
- **Nonfiction:** Publishes young adult books, 12–18 years. Topics include history and multicultural issues.
- **Representative Titles:** *What Your Mama Never Told You: True Stories About Sex and Love* by Tara Roberts, ed. (YA) is a collection of sexual coming-of-age memoirs from young black women designed to enlighten, inform, and sometimes warn adolescent girls. *Kid B* by Linden Dalecki (YA) is the story of a young white boy dealing with racial tension as he prepares for a cut-throat hip-hop dance competition.

Submissions and Payment

Guidelines and catalogue available at website. Send complete ms for fiction. Query with outline and sample chapters for nonfiction. Accepts hard copy. SASE. Responds in 3 months if interested. Publication period varies. Royalty; advance.

Editor's Comments

We look for authentic material that will ring true to teens. The books we choose to publish run the gamut of subjects, but all are unified in the quality of writing and all reflect the lives of teens today.

Graphic Arts Center Publishing Company

P.O. Box 10306
Portland, OR 97296-0306

Executive Editor: Tim Frew

Publisher's Interests
This company publishes national and regional titles through three imprints. It is mainly interested in Pacific Northwestern and Alaskan themed fiction, nonfiction, and photo-essay books for children and adults.
Website: www.gacpc.com

Freelance Potential
Published 20 titles (3 juvenile) in 2009: 2 were developed from unsolicited submissions, 1 was by an agented author, and 1 was a reprint/licensed property. Of the 20 titles, 3 were by authors who were new to the publishing house. Receives 120 queries, 360–480 unsolicited mss yearly.

- **Fiction:** Publishes early picture books, 0–4 years; story picture books, 4–10 years; chapter books, 5–10 years; and young adult novels, 12–18 years. Genres include contemporary and historical fiction, folklore, and suspense.
- **Nonfiction:** Publishes early picture books, 0–4 years; easy-to-read books, 4–7 years; story picture books, 4–10 years; middle-grade books, 8–12 years; and young adult books, 12–18 years. Topics include animals and natural history. Also publishes titles for adults.
- **Representative Titles:** *The Animal in Me* by Laurie Tye compares a human baby's actions to those of an animal baby. *Douggie* by Pam Flowers (5+ years) is the story of a playful puppy who grew up to be a sled-dog hero.

Submissions and Payment
Guidelines available at website. Send ms for picture books. Query with outline, table of contents, and 1–2 sample chapters for longer works. Accepts hard copy. SASE. Responds in 6 months. Publication in 2 years. Payment policy varies.

Editor's Comments
All children's books should have a theme relating to Alaska, the Pacific Northwest, or the western U.S.

Greenhaven Press

Thomson Gale
27500 Drake Road
Farmington Hills, MI 48331-3535

Administrative Assistant: Kristine Burns

Publisher's Interests

Greenhaven Press publishes book series for high school students on such themes as contemporary social issues, biography, history, geography, literature, multicultural topics, mysteries, religion, and science. It also publishes reference materials for the high school library market.
Website: www.gale.com/greenhaven

Freelance Potential

Published 189 titles in 2009: few were by unpublished writers and 10–15 were by authors who were new to the publishing house. Receives 300–600 queries yearly.

- **Nonfiction:** Publishes young adult books, 12–18 years. Topics include contemporary social issues, biography, American and world history, geography, literature, multicultural topics, mysteries, religion, and science.
- **Representative Titles:** *Biomass: Energy from Plants and Animals* by Amanda de la Garza (grades 10–12) examines the potential of this type of fuel; part of the Fueling the Future series. *Faith Healing* by Miranda Marquit (grades 10–12) presents arguments for and against the existence of this phenomenon; part of the Fact or Fiction? series. *Living Through the Civil Rights Movement* (grades 10–12) conveys what life was like during this period in American history; part of the Living Through the Cold War series.

Submissions and Payment

Query with résumé and list of publishing credits. All work is assigned. Response time varies. Publication in approximately 1 year. Flat fee.

Editor's Comments

All of our titles are created at the direction of our acquisitions editors under work-for-hire arrangements. Though we're open to working with authors who are new to us, we rarely contract with an unpublished author to create one of our titles.

Groundwood Books

110 Spadina Avenue, Suite 801
Toronto, Ontario M5V 2K4
Canada

Acquisitions Editor

Publisher's Interests
Established in 1976, Groundwood Books publishes children's books for all ages, including fiction, picture books, and nonfiction titles. Its primary publishing focus is on Canadian authors, although it does accept work from writers from other countries. Included in its catalogue are books about the First Peoples of North America, and books in Spanish.
Website: www.groundwoodbooks.com

Freelance Potential
Published 36 titles in 2009: 15 were by authors who were new to the publishing house.

- **Fiction:** Publishes early picture books, 0–4 years; easy-to-read books, 4–7 years; story picture books, 4–10 years; chapter books, 5–10 years; middle-grade books, 8–12 years; and young adult books, 12–18 years. Genres include contemporary, historical, and multicultural fiction.
- **Nonfiction:** Publishes middle-grade books, 8–12 years; and young adult books, 12–18 years. Topics include contemporary social issues, history, language arts, science, conflict study, economics, politics, and multicultural studies.
- **Representative Titles:** *It's Useful to Have a Duck* by Isol (0–3 years) tells of the many things you can do with a rubber duck, as told from both the boy's and the duck's perspectives. *A New Life* by Rukhsana Khan (8–11 years) finds two siblings from Pakistan trying to adjust to their new lives in Canada.

Submissions and Payment
Guidelines and catalogue available at website. Query with synopsis and 3 sample chapters. Accepts hard copy and simultaneous submissions if identified. SAE/IRC. Responds in 4–6 months. Publication period varies. Royalty; advance.

Editor's Comments
We are not accepting picture books at this time. Feel free to send us novel-length fiction and nonfiction projects.

Group Publishing

P.O. Box 481
Loveland, CO 80539

Contract & Copyright Administrator: Kerri Loesche

Publisher's Interests
Group Publishing's mission is "to equip churches to help children, youth, and adults grow in their relationship with Jesus." To that end, it publishes resources for Christian education and children's ministry.
Website: www.group.com

Freelance Potential
Published 40 titles in 2009: 1 was developed from an unsolicited submission and 1 was by an agented author. Of the 40 titles, 2 were by unpublished writers and 6 were by authors who were new to the publishing house. Receives 600 queries yearly.

- **Nonfiction:** Publishes Christian educational resources for all ages. Topics include children's sermons and worship ideas, Bible lessons and activities, crafts, devotions, games, plays and skits, leadership, spiritual growth, counseling, the media, current events, messages, music, retreats, and family ministry.
- **Representative Titles:** *Play-n-Worship: Play-Along Stories for Toddlers and Twos* is a multimedia kit that uses fun to connect little ones to Jesus. *Passing the Baton: Guide Your Child to Follow Jesus* provides 10 at-home activities for parents to do with their elementary-aged children. *My First 90 Days in Ministry* provides practical tips to help new youth leaders "make a splash without getting all wet."

Submissions and Payment
Guidelines available. Query with outline, 2–3 sample chapters, and sample activities. Accepts hard copy and simultaneous submissions if identified. SASE. Responds in 3–6 months. Publication period varies. Royalty, to 10%. Flat fee.

Editor's Comments
We're always looking for good writers who know kids and have the ability to write lessons that can help children grow in their relationship with Jesus.

Gryphon House

P.O. Box 207
Beltsville, MD 20704-0207

Editor-in-Chief: Kathy Charner

Publisher's Interests

Gryphon House publishes books and resources for parents and teachers of children up to age eight. Parenting books, books about children's emotional and physical development, and teacher resource books are all part of its list.
Website: www.gryphonhouse.com

Freelance Potential

Published 12 titles in 2009. Of the 12 titles, 3 were by unpublished writers and 3 were by authors who were new to the publishing house. Receives 300–400 queries yearly.

- **Nonfiction:** Publishes books for parents and teachers working with children up to age 8. Topics include art, mathematics, science, literacy, language development, teaching strategies, conflict resolution, program development, and games. Also publishes lesson plans.
- **Representative Titles:** *Educating Young Children* by M. Hohmann et al. describes indispensible strategies for effective early-childhood education. *Tasty Talk: 40 Mealtime Conversation Starters* by Beth Marshall features ideas for conversation and simple games to get children thinking, talking, reflecting, and sharing on a variety of subjects.

Submissions and Payment

Guidelines available at website. Query table of contents, introductory material, 20–40 sample pages, market analysis, and writing sample. Accepts hard copy. SASE. Responds in 3–4 months. Publication in 1–2 years. Payment policy varies.

Editor's Comments

We look for books that are developmentally appropriate for their intended age group, and based on current trends in the field. They must demonstrate that they've been solidly researched as well. Of special interest to us are books that include creative, participatory learning experiences with a common conceptual theme to tie them together.

Gumboot Books

604-980 Seymour Street
Vancouver, British Columbia V6B 1B5
Canada

Editor

Publisher's Interests
This innovative four-year-old company publishes educational books and materials for children ages four to eighteen. Its hope is to foster a sense of responsibility and respect for the planet and all who share it.
Website: www.gumbootbooks.com

Freelance Potential
Published 15 titles (10 juvenile) in 2009: 10 were developed from unsolicited submissions. Receives 300 queries yearly.

- **Fiction:** Publishes story picture books, 4–10 years; chapter books, 5–10 years; middle-grade books, 8–12 years; and young adult books, 12–18 years. Genres include adventure; contemporary, inspirational, and multicultural fiction; fantasy; and mystery.
- **Nonfiction:** Publishes story picture books, 4–10 years; chapter books, 5–10 years; middle-grade books, 8–12 years; and young adult books, 12–18 years. Topics include entertainment, multicultural issues, nature, science, and social issues.
- **Representative Titles:** *Grineida the Mad Hatter* by Mary Jo Reinhort is the story of a young hat maker who gets to show off her gifts in an upcoming play. *aRHYTHMetic* by Tiffany Stone & Kari-Lynn Winters explores basic mathematical concepts through engaging poetry.

Submissions and Payment
Guidelines available at website. Query with bio, word count, and first and last 3 pages. Accepts hard copy. SAE/IRC. Responds in 3–6 months. Publication period varies. Royalty.

Editor's Comments
With each project we use our imaginations to challenge the way people think, the way people see the world, and the way people act. At this time we are not accepting submissions for picture books. Please check our website for updates. We believe in the power of imagination.

Hachai Publishing

527 Empire Boulevard
Brooklyn, NY 11225

Editor: Devorah L. Rosenfeld

Publisher's Interests

Hachai Publishing welcomes unsolicited manuscripts to be
considered for its catalogue of Jewish-themed books for
children up to the age of 10.
Website: www.hachai.com

Freelance Potential

Published 5 titles in 2009: 4 were developed from unsolicited
submissions. Of the 5 titles, 3 were by unpublished writers
and 4 were by authors who were new to the publishing
house. Receives 240 queries, 240 unsolicited mss yearly.

- **Fiction:** Publishes early picture books, 0–4 years; easy-to-read
  books, 4–7 years; story picture books, 4–10 years; and chapter books, 5–10 years. Genres include Jewish historical fiction,
  folklore, and adventure.
- **Nonfiction:** Publishes concept books, 0–4 years; and story
  picture books, 4–10 years. Topics include the Torah, prayer,
  mitzvos, middos, and Jewish history. Also publishes biographies.
- **Representative Titles:** *I Am a Torah* by Beily Paluch (0–4
  years) is a playful action rhyme. *Dov's Mitzvah* by Risa Rotman
  (2–5 years) tells how a boy's small good deed grows to
  encompass an entire community. *More Precious Than Gold* by
  Eve-Lynn J. Gardner (7–10 years) is the story of a Jewish girl's
  experiences during the Spanish Inquisition.

Submissions and Payment

Guidelines and catalogue available at website. Query with outline and sample chapter; or send complete ms. Accepts hard
copy and email to dlr@hachai.com (no attachments). SASE.
Responds in 2–6 weeks. Publication in 18–36 months. Flat fee.

Editor's Comments

We're looking for stories that convey the traditional Jewish
experience in modern times or long ago; traditional Jewish
observances; and historical fiction that highlights devotion to
faith and the relevance of Torah in making important choices.

Harcourt Children's Books

Houghton Mifflin Harcourt
215 Park Avenue South
New York, NY 10003

Submissions Editor

Publisher's Interests

This imprint of the Houghton Mifflin Harcourt Books publishing group is well known for its engaging, creative, and well-produced children's literature. It publishes fiction for children of all ages, from birth through the young adult years, offering something for all tastes.
Website: www.hmhbooks.com

Freelance Potential

Published 150–160 titles in 2009: each was by an agented author.

- **Fiction:** Publishes concept books, toddler books, and early picture books, 0–4 years; easy-to-read books, 4–7 years; story picture books, 4–10 years; chapter books, 5–10 years; and young adult books, 12–18 years. Genres include contemporary, historical, and multicultural fiction; mystery; fantasy; and suspense. Also publishes poetry and stories about sports, nature, and the environment.
- **Representative Titles:** *Stanza* by Jill Esbaum (3–7 years) is the story of a bully named Stanza who writes poetry on the sly, but must come clean when he enters one of his poems in a contest. *King of the Screwups* by K. L. Going (YA) is a novel about a popular high school boy who learns to be truly himself when he moves in with his gay uncle after his father kicks him out.

Submissions and Payment

Agents, published authors, and members of the SCBWI only. Query. No simultaneous submissions. Accepts hard copy. SASE. Responds in 1 month. Publication in 2 years. Royalty; advance.

Editor's Comments

We regret that we cannot open the submissions process to more people, but like most major publishers, we have to limit the number and type of submissions we review.

Hard Shell Word Factory

8946 State Highway 161
Amherst Junction, WI 54407

Submissions Editor: Mary Z. Wolf

Publisher's Interests
This publisher is interested in it all—fiction and nonfiction, all genres and all subjects, for middle-grade readers and older. It publishes books in trade paperback as well as in electronic format.
Website: www.hardshell.com

Freelance Potential
Published 25–70 titles in 2009. Receives 200+ unsolicited mss yearly.

- **Fiction:** Publishes middle-grade books, 8–12 years; and young adult books, 12–18 years. Genres include romance; mystery; suspense; action; adventure; fantasy; horror; and Western, historical, mainstream, and science fiction.
- **Nonfiction:** Publishes young adult books, 12–18 years. Topics include current events, history, humor, and self-help. Also publishes biographies.
- **Representative Titles:** *Skateboard Blues* by Sydell Voeller (8–12 years) is a novel about a teen who finds herself torn between her skater friends and her father while trying to get a skateboard park built in town. *Time in a Bottle* by Karen Anzalone (YA) is a novel about a seventh-grade boy who is transported more than a century into the past, where he is faced with the choice of saving a girl from her abusive stepfather or remaining stuck in the past forever.

Submissions and Payment
Guidelines and catalogue available at website. Send complete ms with synopsis. Accepts disk submissions (Microsoft Word) and email submissions to submit@hardshell.com (Microsoft Word attachments). SASE. Responds in 3–5 weeks. Publication in 12–14 months. Royalty, 50% of net.

Editor's Comments
We don't have many restrictions on the work we accept. The best way to gauge us is by perusing our catalogue.

HarperCollins Children's Books

1350 Avenue of the Americas
New York, NY 10019

Associate Editor: Alyson Day

Publisher's Interests
Home to many of the classics of children's literature and the popular I Can Read beginning reader series, HarperCollins publishes a wide variety of fiction and nonfiction titles for children up to age 18.
Website: www.harperchildrens.com

Freelance Potential
Published 500 titles in 2009: each was by an agented author. Receives 1,000+ queries yearly.

- **Fiction:** Publishes easy-to-read books, 4–7 years old; chapter books, 5–10 years; middle-grade books, 8–12 years; and young adult books, 12–18 years. Genres include adventure; drama; humor; fantasy; folktales; mystery; horror; suspense; Westerns; and historical, contemporary, multicultural, and science fiction.
- **Nonfiction:** Publishes easy-to-read books, 4–7 years; chapter books, 5–10 years; middle-grade books, 8–12 years; and young adult books, 12–18 years. Topics include animals, science, history, geography, social studies, and biography.
- **Representative Titles:** *Fancy Nancy: Explorer Extraordinaire!* by Jane O'Connor (4–7 years) follows a girl with a penchant for fancy things and her best friend on an outdoor adventure. *The Summoning* by Kelley Armstrong (YA) tells the story of a girl who lives in a home for troubled teens that is haunted by ghosts.

Submissions and Payment
Agented authors only. Catalogue available at website. Query with résumé and clips. SASE. Responds in 2 months. Publication in 18 months. Royalty; advance.

Editor's Comments
We pride ourselves on publishing some of the highest quality children's books in the marketplace. If you feel your work is fresh and creative, we welcome your agented submission.

Hayes School Publishing Company

321 Pennwood Avenue
Pittsburgh, PA 15221

President: Clair Hayes

Publisher's Interests

This company publishes a variety of workbooks, activity books, reproducibles, and other educational resource materials to support creative teaching. Its catalogue includes products for use in kindergarten through high school classrooms.
Website: www.hayespub.com

Freelance Potential

Published 30 titles in 2009: 1 was by an author who was new to the publishing house. Receives 240–360 queries each year.

- **Nonfiction:** Publishes educational resource materials, grades K–12. Topics include language arts, multicultural studies, math, computer literacy, foreign language, social studies, science, health, creative thinking, handwriting, geography, and standardized testing.
- **Representative Titles:** *The Mastery Drills in Arithmetic* (grades 1–8) are workbooks with drills, activities, and thought problems geared to grade level goals. *Soaring to New Heights* (grades 2–4) is a reproducible book with units on character education, including sharing, honesty, friendship, kindness, and respect.

Submissions and Payment

Guidelines available. Query with outline or table of contents, 3–4 sample pages, and author bio. Accepts hard copy and simultaneous submissions if identified. SASE. Responds in 2–3 weeks. Publication period varies. Flat fee.

Editor's Comments

Most of our publications are developed and assigned by our staff, but we are open to working with teacher-writers—whether they have prior publishing experience or not. We're always interested in hearing about successful new ideas and products that will help other teachers inspire and engage their students.

Hazelden Foundation

P.O. Box 176
Center City, MN 55012-0176

Manuscript Coordinator

Publisher's Interests

The publishing arm of this nonprofit company provides real-world resources for the treatment of alcohol and drug addiction. Its titles target addiction professionals, criminal justice workers, educators, and individuals seeking treatment. Many of its books target pre-teens and teens, as well as parents who are dealing with addiction.
Website: www.hazelden.org

Freelance Potential

Published 50 titles in 2009. Receives 300 queries yearly.

- **Nonfiction:** Publishes middle-grade books, 8–12 years; and young adult books, 12–18 years. Topics include alcohol and substance abuse, health, fitness, and social issues. Also publishes titles for parents, teachers, and professionals who work with people suffering from addiction problems.
- **Representative Titles:** *A New Day, A New Life: A Guided Journal* by William Cope Moyers consists of daily inspirational and educational messages, meditations, and prayers. *The Addictive Personality* by Craig Nakken discusses the genetic factors and cultural influences that can lead to addiction; includes steps for a successful recovery.

Submissions and Payment

Guidelines and catalogue available at website. Query with outline, table of contents, 3 sample chapters, clips or writing samples, market analysis, and author credentials. Accepts hard copy. SASE. Responds in 3 months. Publication in 12–18 months. Royalty. Flat fee.

Editor's Comments

Hazelden helps people transform their lives by providing quality educational and publishing products. We're interested in fresh, new material that addresses issues relevant to substance abuse, prevention, treatment, and recovery. We do not want poetry, fiction, memoirs, or art.

HCI Books

3201 SW 15th Street
Deerfield Beach, FL 33442

Editorial Committee

Publisher's Interests

The books from Health Communications, Inc., aim to improve readers' lives and promote recovery, personal growth, and the enrichment of mind, body, and soul. Its young adult catalogue includes such topics as teen issues, health, relationships, and memoirs.

Website: www.hcibooks.com; www.ultimatehcibooks.com

Freelance Potential

Published 60 titles (7 juvenile) in 2009: 5 were developed from unsolicited submissions and 55 were by agented authors. Of the 60 titles, 5 were by unpublished writers and 10 were by authors who were new to the publishing house. Receives 480 queries yearly.

- **Nonfiction:** Publishes young adult books, 12–18 years. Topics include teen issues, health, fitness, and relationships. Also publishes self-help and parenting titles, and books for adults.
- **Representative Titles:** *Everything Sucks* by Hannah Friedman (YA) is a memoir that details the teenage years in all of their cringe-worthy absurdity. *Jon and Jayne's Guide to Getting Through School (Mostly Intact)* by Gary Rosenberg & Carol Rosenberg (YA) presents a realistic look, through stories, advice, and Web-based features, at what it takes to not only survive the school year, but also to make the most of it.

Submissions and Payment

Guidelines and catalogue available at website or with 9x12 SASE ($3 postage). Query with bio, marketing data, outline, and 2–3 sample chapters. Accepts hard copy and simultaneous submissions if identified. SASE. Responds in 3–7 months. Publication in 6–12 months. Payment policy varies.

Editor's Comments

Many—but certainly not all—of our authors are experts in their respective fields and naturally speak authoritatively on the life issue at hand.

Health Press

P.O. Box 37470
Albuquerque, NM 87176

Editor: Kathleen Frazier

Publisher's Interests

The books published by Health Press give children information about health conditions, nutrition, and safety issues. All books promote not only awareness, but tolerance and understanding of children who may seem "different" due to health issues.
Website: www.healthpress.com

Freelance Potential

Published 3 titles (2 juvenile) in 2009. Receives 500+ queries yearly.

- **Fiction:** Publishes concept books, 0–4 years; easy-to-read books, 4– 7 years; middle-grade books, 8–12 years; and young adult books, 12–18 years. Genres include humor, adventure, and contemporary fiction—all with health-related themes.
- **Nonfiction:** Publishes concept books, 0–4 years; easy-to-read books, 4–7 years; middle-grade books, 8–12 years; and young adult books, 12–18 years. Topics include general health, disabilities, medical conditions, nutrition, and grief. Also publishes books for parents.
- **Representative Titles:** *Ready, Set, Grow!* by Lynda Madaras discusses the changes that occur in girls' bodies as they get older. *Blueberry Eyes* by Monica Driscoll Beatty addresses vision issues and eye treatments, such as wearing glasses or eye patches, or undergoing eye muscle surgery.

Submissions and Payment

Guidelines and catalogue available at website. Query with synopsis, résumé, and 3 sample chapters. Accepts hard copy. SASE. Response time and publication period vary. Royalty.

Editor's Comments

Most of our books are written by medical professionals or other experts in the field. Writers should be aware that all new books are reviewed by medical experts during our review process.

Heinemann

361 Hanover Street
Portsmouth, NH 03801-3912

Acquisitions Editor

Publisher's Interests

Established in 1978 as a company that publishes works by professionals for professionals, Heinemann specializes in career development titles and educational resources for teachers and administrators of all grade levels. All curricula subjects are covered.
Website: www.heinemann.com

Freelance Potential

Published 100 titles in 2009: 10 were by agented authors. Of the 100 titles, 10 were by unpublished writers. Receives 1,200+ queries yearly.

- **Nonfiction:** Publishes educational resources and multimedia material for teachers and school administrators. Topics include math, science, social studies, art education, reading, writing, ESL, bilingual education, special and gifted education, early childhood development, school reform, curriculum development, and the creative arts.
- **Representative Titles:** *When Readers Struggle* by Gay Su Pinnell & Irene C. Fountas (teachers) is filled with specific ideas for helping children in kindergarten through grade three who are having difficulty in reading and writing. *Word Play: Building Vocabulary Across Texts and Disciplines, Grades 6–12* by Sandra R. Whitaker (teachers) provides guidelines for effective, meaningful vocabulary instruction.

Submissions and Payment

Guidelines and catalogue available at website. Query with résumé, outline, table of contents, and chapter summaries. Prefers email to proposals@heinemann.com; will accept hard copy. SASE. Responds in 6–8 weeks. Publication in 10–12 months. Payment policy varies.

Editor's Comments

We care less about your publishing history than we do about your expertise in the field of teaching.

Hendrick-Long Publishing

10635 Tower Oaks, Suite D
Houston, TX 77070

Vice President: Vilma Long

Publisher's Interests
Originally a publisher of Texas history textbooks, Hendrick-Long has expanded its scope to include books for children and young adults that celebrate the rich and lively history of Texas. Its titles include both fiction and nonfiction.
Website: www.hendricklongpublishing.com

Freelance Potential
Published 4 titles in 2009: each was developed from an unsolicited submission. Of the 4 titles, 2 were by authors who were new to the publishing house. Receives 600 queries yearly.

- **Fiction:** Publishes middle-grade books, 8–12 years. Genres include historical and regional fiction, and folklore.
- **Nonfiction:** Publishes middle-grade books, 8–12 years; and young adult books, 12–18 years. Topics include animals, natural history, geography, and folklore related to Texas and the American Southwest. Also publishes biographies.
- **Representative Titles:** *Frederic Remington, Artist of the West* by Jane Thielemann (12–18 years) is an illustrated biography of this artist's fascinating life story. *Plays & Poems from Texas History* by Billie Preston is designed as an aid for teachers using drama as a medium for better student retention of the language arts and social studies.

Submissions and Payment
Writers' guidelines available. Query with résumé, outline/synopsis, table of contents, and 1–2 sample chapters. Accepts hard copy and simultaneous submissions if identified. SASE. Responds in 6 months. Publication in 2 years. Royalty; advance.

Editor's Comments
We are always in search of a few good authors who can communicate their in-depth knowledge of the state of Texas to our audience.

Heuer Publishing LLC

211 First Avenue SE, Suite 200
Cedar Rapids, IA 52401

Editor: Geri Albrecht

Publisher's Interests

Heuer Publishing offers a variety of plays (including 10-minute plays), musicals, drama, and comedy specifically designed for the educational market and community theaters.
Website: www.hitplays.com

Freelance Potential

Published 30 titles in 2009: 15 were developed from unsolicited submissions. Of the 30 titles, 6 were by unpublished writers and 9 were by authors who were new to the publishing house. Receives 1,200 queries, 600 unsolicited mss each year.

- **Fiction:** Publishes plays, musicals, comedies, mysteries, and satire for children and young adults, 5–18 years.
- **Nonfiction:** Publishes middle-grade books, 8–12 years; and young adult books, 12–18 years. Topics include theater arts, stage production, auditions, sound effects, and theater resources for young actors.
- **Representative Titles:** *Cindergirl* by Stephen Hotchner presents a funny re-telling of the classic Cinderella tale. *No-No!* by Donna Latham, designed for classroom use, blends performing arts with English studies as double-negatives provoke laughter and learning.

Submissions and Payment

Guidelines available. Query or send complete ms with synopsis, cast list, running time, and set requirements. Accepts submissions through website. Responds in 2 months. Publication period varies. Royalty. Flat fee.

Editor's Comments

At this time, we're not reviewing theater resource texts or books. We are, however, aggressively seeking family friendly full-length plays, original fairy tales for youth theater, and short plays for high school thespian troupes. Environmental spoofs, mystery-comedies, and 10-minute plays are also of interest.

History Compass

25 Leslie Road
Auburndale, MA 02466

General Manager: Lisa Gianelly

Publisher's Interests

History Compass publishes primary source-based U.S. history books, biographies, historical fiction, and plays, each filled with original documents or personal accounts that tell the compelling stories of real moments in American history.
Website: www.historycompass.com

Freelance Potential

Published 8 titles in 2009. Of the 8 titles, 1 was by an unpublished writer and 3 were by authors who were new to the publishing house. Receives 50–60 queries yearly.

- **Fiction:** Publishes middle-grade books, 8–12 years; and young adult books, 12–18 years. Genres include historical fiction.
- **Nonfiction:** Publishes easy-to-read books, 4–7 years; chapter books, 5–10 years; middle-grade books, 8–12 years; and young adult books, 12–18 years. Topics include American history. Also publishes biographies and guidebooks for adults.
- **Representative Titles:** *Native Americans* by Pat Perrin & Arden Bowers takes a look at tribal creation myths, family life and customs, and great Native American leaders. *Daniel On the Run: Louisa, Will, and the Underground Railroad* by Claiborne Dawes (7–12 years) is the story of two children who help a slave boy on his journey along the Underground Railroad; part of the Adventures in History series.

Submissions and Payment

Guidelines and catalogue available at website. Query with résumé, outline, table of contents, market analysis, and nonfiction clips. Accepts hard copy and simultaneous submissions if identified. SASE. Responds in 3 months. Publication in 2–8 months. Royalty.

Editor's Comments

We look for interesting historical subjects, strong author credentials, solid and fresh writing, attention to detail, and energy and commitment from our authors.

Holiday House

425 Madison Avenue
New York, NY 10017

Acquisitions Editor

Publisher's Interests

Paperback and hardcover, fiction and nonfiction, books for preschoolers through young adults—this independent publisher has it all. It is interested in quality books for young people, and accepts a variety of genres and topics.
Website: www.holidayhouse.com

Freelance Potential

Published 80 titles in 2009: 3 were developed from unsolicited submissions, 15 were by agented authors, and 10 were reprint/licensed properties. Receives 8,000 queries yearly.

- **Fiction:** Publishes story picture books, 4–10 years; chapter books, 5–10 years; middle-grade books, 8–12 years; and young adult books, 12–18 years. Genres include historical and multicultural fiction, humor, mystery, and fantasy.
- **Nonfiction:** Publishes early picture books, 0–4 years; easy-to-read books, 4–7 years; and middle-grade books, 8–12 years. Topics include history, social issues, and science. Also publishes biographies.
- **Representative Titles:** *Baby Baby blah blah blah* by Jonathan Shipton (3–6 years) focuses on the list of pros and cons of having a new baby brother or sister that young Emily makes upon hearing her mother's news. *Secrets, Lies, and My Sister Kate* by Belinda Hollyer (8–12 years) is a novel about the family secrets that are revealed as a girl searches for her runaway sister and the reasons behind her sudden mood change.

Submissions and Payment

Guidelines and catalogue available at website. Query. Accepts hard copy. SASE. Responds in 2 months. Publication period varies. Royalty; advance.

Editor's Comments

Please propose only one project for us per query. Note that at this time we are focusing on literary works for middle-grade readers.

Henry Holt Books for Young Readers

175 Fifth Avenue
New York, NY 10010

Submissions Editor

Publisher's Interests

Several award-winning authors and illustrators can be found
in the catalogue of this publisher. Its picture books, chapter
books, and novels cover a wide variety of genres and target
preschool kids through young adults.
Website: www.henryholtkids.com

Freelance Potential

Published 65 titles in 2009. Receives 12,000 queries yearly.

- **Fiction:** Publishes concept books and early picture books,
  0–4 years; easy-to-read books, 4–7 years; story picture books,
  4–10 years; chapter books, 5–10 years; middle-grade books,
  8–12 years; and young adult books, 12–18 years. Genres
  include historical, multicultural, and ethnic fiction; adventure;
  drama; and fantasy. Also publishes poetry.
- **Nonfiction:** Publishes story picture books, 4–10 years; chapter
  books, 5–10 years; and middle-grade books, 8–12 years. Topics include biography, history, ethnic issues, and mythology.
- **Representative Titles:** *Don't Lick the Dog* by Wendy Wahman
  (3–8 years) shows kids the best ways to interact with an unfamiliar dog. *How Robin Saved Spring* by Debbie Ouellet (4–8 years)
  tells the story of a robin and her animal friends who try to wake
  up Sister Spring. *The Evolution of Calpurnia Tate* by Jacqueline
  Kelly (YA) is about a young girl at the turn of the twentieth century
  who develops a close bond with her cantankerous grandfather.

Submissions and Payment

Guidelines and catalogue available at website. Query.
Accepts hard copy. No SASE. Responds in 4–6 months if
interested. Publication period and payment policy vary.

Editor's Comments

We do not accept submissions for textbooks, original board
or novelty books, activity books, or instructional books.
Please don't over-package. A simple manila envelope will
protect your submission sufficiently. No original art, please.

Horizon Publishers

Cedar Fort Inc.
2373 West 700 South
Springville, UT 84663

Submissions Editors: Jennifer Fielding & Lee Nelson

Publisher's Interests

Nonfiction titles geared toward Latter-day Saints children and their parents comprise the Horizon Publishers catalogue. The focus is mainly on outdoor living, scouting, and camping, as well as activity books that teach about the Scriptures.
Website: www.cedarfort.com

Freelance Potential

Published 50 titles in 2009: 12 were by authors who were new to the publishing house. Receives 500 unsolicited mss each year.

- **Nonfiction:** Publishes activity books and educational books, 1–12 years. Topics include Latter-day Saints life, the Mormon faith, spirituality, social issues, cooking, stitchery, camping, scouting, and outdoor life. Also publishes parenting titles.
- **Representative Titles:** *Book of Mormon Activity Book— Creative Scripture Learning Experiences* by Sally Halverson (4–12 years) provides entertaining puzzles that involve children in the Scriptures. *Nobody's Better Than You, Mom* by Debbie Bowen presents a compilation of touching stories about finding the joy in motherhood.

Submissions and Payment

Guidelines and catalogue available at website. Send complete ms with résumé, outline, and submission form available at website. Accepts hard copy. SASE. Responds in 1–3 months. Publication period varies. Royalty, 10% of wholesale.

Editor's Comments

New authors are encouraged to submit their work after familiarizing themselves with our website and the books we publish. We do not publish secular material for children or teens, nor are we interested in submissions written for non-LDS readers. If we are interested in a submission, we usually respond via email unless an SASE had been provided.

Houghton Mifflin Books for Children

222 Berkeley Street
Boston, MA 02116

Submissions Coordinator

Publisher's Interests

This imprint of Houghton Mifflin Harcourt publishes a wide range of children's books, both fiction and nonfiction, of all genres and subjects. Its list contains books for toddlers, young adult fiction, and everything in between.
Website: www.hmhbooks.com

Freelance Potential

Published 60–80 titles in 2009: 1 was developed from an unsolicited submission and most were by agented authors. Receives 600 queries, 7,000 unsolicited mss yearly.

- **Fiction:** Publishes toddler books and early picture books, 0–4 years; easy-to-read books, 4–7 years; story picture books, 4–10 years; middle-grade books, 8–12 years; and young adult books, 12–18 years. Genres include historical and multicultural fiction, adventure, and humor.
- **Nonfiction:** Publishes middle-grade books, 8–12 years; and young adult books, 12–18 years. Topics include history, science, nature, and biography.
- **Representative Titles:** *The Giant Jam Sandwich* by John Vernon Lord & Janet Burroway (0–3 years) brings a town together to solve its very large wasp problem. *Extreme Scientists* by Donna M. Jackson (8–12 years) introduces readers to the scientists who work in some perilous places to better understand how our planet works; part of the Scientists in the Field series.

Submissions and Payment

Guidelines and catalogue available at website. Send complete ms with author bio for fiction. Query with synopsis, sample chapters, and author bio for nonfiction. Accepts hard copy. No SASE. Responds in 3–4 months if interested. Publication period varies. Royalty; advance.

Editor's Comments

Due to the number of submissions we receive, we will only contact you if we are interested. We will not return materials.

Humanics Learning

P.O. Box 1608
Lake Worth, FL 33460

Editor: Arthur Bly

Publisher's Interests

Children's books that focus on learning and growing are the specialty of this publisher. It also features resource materials and how-to books for teachers and parents.
Website: www.humanicspub.com

Freelance Potential

Published 20 titles in 2009: 12 were by unpublished writers and 15 were by authors who were new to the publishing house. Receives 263 queries, 105 unsolicited mss yearly.

- **Fiction:** Publishes concept books and toddler books, 0–4 years. Genres include folklore, drama, humor, and inspirational and religious fiction.
- **Nonfiction:** Publishes early picture books, 0–4 years. Also publishes activity books, biographies, how-to-books, and educational titles for teachers and parents. Topics include gifted and special education; animals; pets; crafts; hobbies; and multicultural, ethnic, and social issues.
- **Representative Titles:** *Cambio Chameleon* by Mauro Magellan is a tale of a colorful reptile and her friends. *Giggle E. Goose* by Al Newman tells how Giggle E. Goose learns that there is a time for giggling and a time for listening quietly. *Home at Last* by Mauro Magellan follows a small worm in search of a new and better home.

Submissions and Payment

Guidelines and catalogue available at website. Query or send complete ms with résumé and marketing plan. Accepts hard copy. Availability of artwork improves chance of acceptance. SASE. Response time varies. Publication in 6–9 months. Royalty; advance, $500+.

Editor's Comments

Keep in mind that our review process is a long one. Please be patient. If you would like to know the status of your manuscript, you may send us a letter.

Humanics Publishing Group

P.O. Box 1608
Lake Worth, FL 33460

Acquisitions Editor: W. Arthur Bly

Publisher's Interests

Humanics Publishing was formed to respond to the growing need for quality classroom materials that support parents as the prime educators of their children. Its catalogue includes titles on personal growth, relationships, special education, world religions, and leadership. This company also includes an imprint dedicated to New Age topics.
Website: www.humanicspub.com

Freelance Potential

Published 20 titles in 2009. Of the 20 titles, 15 were by unpublished writers and 12 were by authors who were new to the publishing house. Receives 105 unsolicited mss each year.

- **Nonfiction:** Publishes teacher resource books. Topics include science, mathematics, art, crafts, and hobbies. Also publishes parenting books.
- **Representative Titles:** *Teaching Terrific 5's and Other Children* by Lisa Bankert is designed to help teachers foster a five-year-old's growth in five developmental areas. *The Child Care Inventory* provides an assessment tool for achieving high-quality child care. *Handbook for Involving Parents in Education* by Doris K. Williams contains the history of parental education as well as an overview of intervention models.

Submissions and Payment

Guidelines and catalogue available at website. Send complete ms with résumé, synopsis, and marketing plan. A one-time, non-refundable submission fee of $50 is required with all submissions. Accepts hard copy and disk submissions (Microsoft Word or WordPerfect). SASE. Response time, publication period, and payment policy vary.

Editor's Comments

In the coming year, we are interested in receiving submissions that pertain to original thought.

Hunter House Publishers

P.O. Box 2914
Alameda, CA 94501-0914

Acquisitions Assistant: Alexi Ueltzen

Publisher's Interests
Hunter House Publishers offers "books for health, family, and community." These include self-help titles as well as resources for counselors and educators.
Website: www.hunterhouse.com

Freelance Potential
Published 15 titles (2 juvenile) in 2009. Receives 100+ queries yearly.

- **Nonfiction:** Publishes young adult books, 12–18 years. Topics include health, fitness, family, personal growth, relationships, sexuality, and violence prevention and intervention. Also publishes resources for counselors and educators, including workbooks to be used with young children.
- **Representative Titles:** *Awesome Foods for Active Kids* by Anita Bean offers recipes, menu plans, and nutritional information to ensure a healthy diet for children and young teens. *Helping Hyperactive Kids—A Sensory Integration Approach* by Lynn J. Horowitz & Cecile Rost is an accessible, practical guide to a drug-free therapy for hyperactive children.

Submissions and Payment
Guidelines and catalogue available at website. Query with résumé, overview, and chapter-by-chapter outline. Accepts hard copy, email queries to acquisitions@ hunterhouse.com, and simultaneous submissions if identified. SASE. Responds in 3–4 months. Publication in 1–3 years. Royalty.

Editor's Comments
We are always interested in reviewing manuscripts from authors whose work would provide our readers with the information necessary to affect personal improvement. We are particularly looking for additions to our Growth and Recovery Workbooks series. These workbooks are used with young children who have experienced trauma, abuse, or other critical life events.

Impact Publishers

P.O. Box 6016
Atascadero, CA 93423

Acquisitions Editor: Freeman Porter

Publisher's Interests
Impact seeks to publish "psychology you can use, from professionals you can trust." In other words, it publishes popular and professional psychology books written in everyday language by licensed therapists. These fall into the categories of personal growth, relationships, families, communities, and professional psychotherapy.
Website: www.impactpublishers.com

Freelance Potential
Published 6 titles in 2009. Receives 300–480 queries yearly.

- **Nonfiction:** Publishes middle-grade books, 8–12 years; and young adult books, 12–18 years. Also publishes books for parents and human services professionals. Topics include emotional development, self-esteem, self-expression, marriage, divorce, careers, social issues, parenting, child development and behavior, health and wellness, and practical therapy.
- **Representative Titles:** *"I Wish I Could Hold Your Hand . . ."* by Pat Palmer is a child's guide to accepting and dealing with grief and loss. *Strengthening Your Stepfamily* by Elizabeth Einstein & Linda Albert provides down-to-earth, expert help for parenting in a blended family.

Submissions and Payment
Licensed professionals only. Guidelines and catalogue available at website. Query with résumé and sample chapters. Accepts hard copy and email queries to submissions@impactpublishers.com. SASE. Responds in 1–3 months. Publication in 1 year. Royalty, 10–15%; advance.

Editor's Comments
If it's not "psychology you can use," written by a qualified professional, it won't work for us. Please include a brief curriculum vita with your proposal; we don't need your lists of publications in refereed journals and/or presentations at professional meetings—yet.

Incentive Publications

2400 Crestmoor Road, Suite 211
Nashville, TN 37215

Director of Development & Production: Jill Norris

Publisher's Interests
Offering e-books as well as those in print, Incentive Publications produces titles by educator-authors offering education research and practical classroom strategies. It focuses its publishing efforts on educational material for middle-school students, and teaching strategies for teachers of kindergarten through grade 12.
Website: www.incentivepublications.com

Freelance Potential
Published 20–30 titles in 2009. Receives 250+ queries yearly.

- **Nonfiction:** Publishes teaching strategy books for all grade levels, and reproducible student materials for grades 5–9. Topics include core curriculum subjects, art, and study skills.
- **Representative Titles:** *Getting Off On the Right Foot: A Survival Guide for New Teachers* by David Puckett shares secrets of teaching success, such as planning, working with parents, and classroom ideas. *Motivational Creative Writing* by Athy Lionikis & Lee Stevens (grades 6–8) presents 50 projects designed to take young authors through the writing process.

Submissions and Payment
Guidelines available at website. Query with table of contents, outline, and sample chapter. Accepts hard copy and simultaneous submissions if identified. SASE. Responds in 6–8 weeks. Publication period varies. Royalty. Flat fee.

Editor's Comments
Our company was founded by teachers, and we remain dedicated to educators everywhere. We are always interested in books that support teachers, help teachers motivate students, and provide continuing education for teachers. We also welcome ideas for books or materials that can be used in middle-school classrooms, either as textbooks or to supplement the textbooks already in use. Please note that we include homeschooling parents in our definition of teachers.

International Reading Association

800 Barksdale Road
P.O. Box 8139
Newark, DE 19714-8139

Book Proposals

Publisher's Interests

As one would expect from the publishing arm of the International Reading Association, this company produces books and resources that enhance the professional development of reading teachers and literacy professionals.
Website: www.reading.org

Freelance Potential

Published 40 titles in 2009. Of the 40 titles, 5 were by unpublished writers and 20 were by authors who were new to the publishing house. Receives 100 queries yearly.

- **Nonfiction:** Publishes research-based educational titles for educators at all levels, including preservice, teacher educators, literacy researchers, and policymakers. Topics include literacy programs, reading comprehension, reading research and practice, adolescent literacy, literacy coaching, differentiated literacy, learning/instruction, and content-area literacy.
- **Representative Titles:** *Practical Literacy Coaching* by Jan Miller Burkins provides a collection of tools and resources for literacy coaches. *Writing in Preschool* by Judith A. Schickedanz & Renée M. Casbergue provides a detailed picture of preschoolers' writing development and demonstrates how teachers can support students on their journey from scribble to script.

Submissions and Payment

Guidelines and catalogue available at website. Query with letter of intent, audience/market analysis, author biography, abstract, table of contents, and 1–2 sample chapters. Accepts queries via website only. Response time, publication period, and payment policy vary.

Editor's Comments

We accept only thoroughly researched and documented material. Your ideas and information should provide practical knowledge for literacy educators in the field.

InterVarsity Press

P.O. Box 1400
Downers Grove, IL 60515

Editorial Assistant: Ryan Peterson

Publisher's Interests

This publishing arm of InterVarsity Christian Fellowship pub-
lishes Christ-based books through three imprints. These
imprints specialize in general-interest books that speak to
Christian audiences, reference and resource books for bibli-
cal study and church use, and resources for church groups.
Its readership consists of college students, parents, and
Christian educators.
Website: www.ivpress.com

Freelance Potential

Published 136 titles (4 juvenile) in 2009: 2 were developed
from unsolicited submissions, 20 were by agented authors,
and 19 were reprint/licensed properties. Of the 136 titles,
20 were by unpublished writers and 31 were by authors new
to the publishing house. Receives 444 queries yearly.

- **Nonfiction:** Publishes biblically based, religious titles for educators, parents, and college students. Features informational,
  educational, how-to, and reference books.
- **Representative Titles:** *In Search of a Confident Faith* by J. P.
  Moreland & Klaus Issler provides a guide to help Christian
  educators clear away students' barriers to faith. *Becoming the
  Answer to Our Prayers* by Shane Claiborne & Jonathan Wilson-
  Hartgrove illustrates how prayer and activism must go together
  for God to change society.

Submissions and Payment

Guidelines and catalogue available at website. Query with
résumé, summary, and 2 sample chapters. Accepts hard
copy and simultaneous submissions. SASE. Responds in
3 months. Publication in 2 years. Payment policy varies.

Editor's Comments

We are currently interested in justice issues, spiritual formation, church history, theology, philosophy and ethics, and
sociology topics.

Intervisual Books

2884 Colorado Avenue
Santa Monica, CA 90404

Submissions Editor

Publisher's Interests
This imprint of Dalmatian Press focuses on fun and entertaining books for young children, and it's no coincidence
that the word "visual" figures in its name. Its catalogue features an array of pop-up, lift-the-flap, and fill-in-the-blanks
books designed to delight kids from birth through eight.
Website: www.intervisualbooks.com

Freelance Potential
Published 70 titles in 2009: 5 were developed from unso-
licited submissions and 10 were by agented authors.
Receives 1,000–2,000 unsolicited mss yearly.

- **Fiction:** Publishes early picture books, 0–4 years; and easy-to-
  read books, 4–7 years. Genres include fairly tales; humor;
  inspirational fiction; lullabies; and stories about animals,
  nature, families, weather, religion, holidays, potty time, bedtime, and school.
- **Nonfiction:** Publishes concept books and toddler books,
  0–4 years; and story picture books, 4–8 years. Topics include
  animals, vehicles, colors, numbers, letters, shapes, spelling,
  family time, and holidays.
- **Representative Titles:** *Body* by Susan Ring (8+ years) is an
  interactive guide, including pop-ups and pull-tabs, to the
  human body's anatomy and physiological processes. *When
  Pigs Fly . . . !* (3+ years) is a whimsical tale told through pop-
  ups, foil, and glitter.

Submissions and Payment
Catalogue available at website. Send complete ms with
novelty elements in dummy form or in written description.
Accepts hard copy and mock-up. SASE. Responds in 6–12
months. Publication in 1 year. Payment policy varies.

Editor's Comments
We're open to an array of subjects, but your book must have
a novelty format.

Jewish Lights

P.O. Box 237
Woodstock, VT 05091

Vice President, Editorial: Emily Wichland

Publisher's Interests

Jewish Lights publishes books and other resources designed to examine and celebrate Jewish spirituality. Its children's list includes books about Jewish holidays, traditions, folktales, and social issues. It also publishes books for adults that examine all aspects of religion, faith, and the quest for meaning in life.

Website: www.jewishlights.com

Freelance Potential

Published 25 titles in 2009. Of the 25 titles, 15 were by authors who were new to the publishing house. Receives 1,000+ queries, 400 unsolicited mss yearly.

- **Nonfiction:** Publishes toddler books, 0–4 years; easy-to-read books, 4–7 years; story picture books, 4–10 years; and young adult books, 12–18 years. Topics include religious and inspirational subjects, and self-help. Also publishes books for adults.
- **Representative Titles:** *The Adventures of Rabbi Harvey* (YA) by Steve Sheinkin uses a humorous tale of a young rabbi working in the Wild West to present a fresh look at Jewish folktales. *For Heaven's Sake* by Sandy Eisenberg Sasso (4+ years) teaches children that heaven is often found in the places you least expect it.

Submissions and Payment

Guidelines and catalogue available at website. Send complete ms for picture books. Query with résumé, table of contents, sample chapter, and marketing plan for all other material. Accepts hard copy and simultaneous submissions if identified. SASE. Responds in 4 months. Publication in 1 year. Payment policy varies.

Editor's Comments

Please be aware that at this point we plan to publish only two children's books each year. We do not publish biographies, haggadot, or poetry.

The Jewish Publication Society

2100 Arch Street, 2nd Floor
Philadelphia, PA 19103

Assistant Editor: Julia Destreich

Publisher's Interests
For more than a century, this publisher has offered genera-
tions of people books that celebrate Jewish history, culture,
and heritage. Its catalogue includes fiction and nonfiction
books for middle-grade and young adult readers. Retold
Bible stories for children also appear on its list. The Jewish
Publication Society publishes many titles for adults as well.
Website: www.jewishpub.org

Freelance Potential
Published 12 titles (4 juvenile) in 2009. Receives 500
queries yearly.

- **Fiction:** Publishes middle-grade books, 8–12 years; and young
  adult books, 12–18 years. Genres include historical and religious fiction, folklore, folktales, and graphic novels.
- **Nonfiction:** Publishes middle-grade books, 8–12 years; and
  young adult books, 12–18 years. Topics include history, multicultural and ethnic issues, and religion. Also publishes books
  for adults.
- **Representative Titles:** *The Answered Prayer* by Mishael
  Maswari Caspi & Sharlya Gold is a collection of folktales about
  Yemenite life. *Clara's Story* by Joan Adess Grossman (9+
  years) tells the true story of a young girl and her family hiding
  from the Nazis.

Submissions and Payment
Guidelines and catalogue available at website. Query with
résumé, outline/synopsis, market analysis, and author qualifications. Accepts hard copy. SASE. Responds in 6–8
months. Publication in 1–2 years. Payment policy varies.

Editor's Comments
Please note that we have detailed submission guidelines
posted at our website. We suggest that you consult them for
the latest submission information, and that you follow them
carefully in order for your query to be reviewed promptly.

JIST Publishing

7321 Shadeland Station, Suite 200
Indianapolis, IN 46256

Acquisitions Editor: Susan Pines

Publisher's Interests

JIST Publishing produces career reference books, trade books, workbooks, and career exploration/assessment materials for children in middle and high school.
Website: www.jist.com

Freelance Potential

Published 60 titles in 2009. Receives 250 queries yearly.

- **Nonfiction:** Publishes middle-grade books, 11–12 years; and young adult books, 12–18 years. Also publishes workbooks. Topics include career exploration and assessment, occupations, job retention, job searching, character education, and career development.
- **Representative Titles:** *Becoming the Best Me: 10 Career and Character Education Essentials* by Robert M. Orndorff (YA) is a workbook that helps students develop character and life skills related to careers. *Young Person's Occupational Outlook Handbook* (YA) groups related job descriptions based on interests, and offers easy-to-read, one-page overviews of each job's educational and skill requirements.

Submissions and Payment

Guidelines and catalogue available at website. Query with outline, introduction, sample chapters, résumé, and project status. Accepts hard copy and email to appropriate editor (see website). SASE. Responds in 14–16 months. Publication in 9–12 months. Royalty, 8–10%.

Editor's Comments

Please consult our detailed guidelines for more information on what we require in a query package. Prospective writers must follow our guidelines completely in order to be considered for publication. We strongly encourage writers to familiarize themselves with the type and caliber of material we offer as well. We look for work based on sound research, accuracy, and age-appropriate presentation.

Jossey-Bass

Education & Children's Books
989 Market Street
San Francisco, CA 94103

Senior Editor: Kate Bradford

Publisher's Interests
This education publisher is interested in nonfiction educational topics for children in the middle grades and high school. It also publishes a variety of teacher resources and parenting books. It has been an imprint of John Wiley & Sons, Inc., since 1999.
Website: www.wiley.com

Freelance Potential
Published 17 titles (12 juvenile) in 2009. Receives 300 queries yearly.

- **Nonfiction:** Publishes middle-grade books, 8–12 years; and young adult books, 12–18 years. Genres include animals, pets, history, nature, the environment, science, technology, and sports. Also publishes books for teachers and parents.
- **Representative Titles:** *Afterschool Around the Globe: Policy, Practices, and Youth Voice* by Jen Hilmer Capece et al., eds. draws on the variety of after-school programs across the globe to present the policies and quality standards that are working the best; part of the New Directions for Youth Development series. *All Kids Are Our Kids* by Peter L. Benson calls on entire communities to share the responsibility for making sure kids have what they need to be healthy, successful, and caring.

Submissions and Payment
Guidelines and catalogue available at website. Query with résumé, outline, sample chapter, and summary of primary market competition. Accepts hard copy and simultaneous submissions if identified. SASE. Responds in 2–3 months. Publication in 18 months. Royalty; advance.

Editor's Comments
We prefer to learn of projects in their early stages to point out potential problems and offer editorial suggestions. Do not feel you must have your manuscript completed before you query us.

JourneyForth

1700 Wade Hampton Boulevard
Greenville, SC 29614-0060

Acquisitions Editor: Nancy Lohr

Publisher's Interests

JourneyForth was created by BJU Press in 1986 to publish books for children and young adults. Its children's catalogue focuses on fiction and biographies with Christian standards. **Website: www.bjupress.com**

Freelance Potential

Published 25 titles (15 juvenile) in 2009: 10 were developed from unsolicited submissions, 1 was by an agented author, and 2 were reprint/licensed properties. Of the 25 titles, 2 were by authors who were new to the publishing house. Receives 72 queries, 480 unsolicited mss yearly.

- **Fiction:** Publishes early picture books, 0–4 years; easy-to-read books, 4–7 years; chapter books, 5–10 years; middle-grade books, 8–12 years; and young adult books, 12–18 years. Genres include historical, biblical, and Christian fiction; animal adventure; mystery; and fantasy.
- **Nonfiction:** Publishes middle-grade books, 8–12 years; and young adult books, 12–18 years. Topics include spiritual growth. Also publishes biographies.
- **Representative Titles:** *Beyond the Smoke* by Terry W. Burns follows the travels of an orphan as he creates a new life in the western wilderness. *Haiku on Your Shoe* by Eileen M. Berry (6–7 years) tells the story of how Jeremy slowly develops a friendship with a new boy in class.

Submissions and Payment

Guidelines available. Query with résumé, synopsis, and 5 sample chapters; or send complete ms. Accepts hard copy and simultaneous submissions. SASE. Responds in 3 months. Publication in 18–24 months. Royalty, negotiable.

Editor's Comments

We're interested in reviewing submissions of chapter books for beginning readers ages six to nine, and novels for tweens ages eight to twelve.

The Judaica Press

123 Ditmas Avenue
Brooklyn, NY 11218

Editor: Norman Shapiro

Publisher's Interests
The fiction and nonfiction titles in this publisher's catalogue explore and celebrate Jewish life, history, culture, and customs. It has produced board books, picture books, and young adult novels for more than 40 years.
Website: www.judaicapress.com

Freelance Potential
Published 20–25 titles in 2009. Of the 20–25 titles, 2–4 were by authors who were new to the publishing house. Receives 100 queries, 90 unsolicited mss yearly.

- **Fiction:** Publishes early picture books, 0–4 years; easy-to-read books, 4–7 years; story picture books, 4–10 years; and young adult books, 12–18 years. Genres include historical, religious, and contemporary fiction; mystery; and suspense.
- **Nonfiction:** Publishes story picture books, 4–10 years. Topics include Jewish traditions, Torah stories, the Hebrew language, crafts, and hobbies.
- **Representative Titles:** *What Do You See on Chanukah?* by Bracha Goetz is a board book that introduces the holiday's vocabulary, objects, and concepts. *Hidden Diamonds* by Eva Vogiel (YA) tells of a young girl who is reunited with her mother after the war.

Submissions and Payment
Catalogue available at website. Query with outline; or send complete ms. Accepts hard copy. Availability of artwork improves chance of acceptance. SASE. Responds in 3 months. Publication in 1 year. Royalty.

Editor's Comments
Well-written books that cover any aspect of traditional Jewish life are always welcome. Stories should enlighten, inspire, and educate our young Jewish readers and include age-appropriate language. We prefer to receive submissions that include artwork.

Judson Press

P.O. Box 851
Valley Forge, PA 19482

Editor: Rebecca Irwin-Diehl

Publisher's Interests

Judson Press is a small niche publisher specializing in Christian books for African Americans. Chapter books for middle-grade children and young adults, along with education and ministry resources, are included in its titles. All are centered around themes of the American Baptist Church.
Website: www.judsonpress.com

Freelance Potential

Published 18 titles in 2009: 6 were developed from unsolicited submissions, 2 were by agented authors, and 2 were reprint/licensed properties. Of the 18 titles, 4 were by unpublished writers and 7 were by authors who were new to the publishing house. Receives 300 queries yearly.

- **Nonfiction:** Publishes middle-grade books, 8–12 years; and young adult books, 12–18 years. Topics include the Baptist religion and history, and social issues—all with Christian African American themes.
- **Representative Titles:** *Jordan's Hair* by Ed & Sonya Spruill is about a boy who wants to change his appearance to look like everyone else. *Uncle Noah's Big Boat* by Yuki Tsurumi is a children's tale based on the story of Noah's ark.

Submissions and Payment

Guidelines and catalogue available with 9x12 SASE. Query with clips. Accepts hard copy and email to JPacquisitions@abc-usa.org. SASE. Responds in 3–6 months. Publication in 9–12 months. Royalty, 10%.

Editor's Comments

We're looking for strong writing and compelling ideas. Your query should clearly identify your audience and demonstrate a thorough knowledge of the place we hold in the industry. It should also explain how your project would suit our publishing program. Note that our guidelines are updated regularly to highlight our most wanted projects.

Just Us Books

356 Glenwood Avenue, 3rd Floor
East Orange, NJ 07017

Submissions Manager

Publisher's Interests

Just Us publishes black-interest books for children, including picture books, biographies, and chapter books. All of its titles reflect American American history and culture.
Website: www.justusbooks.com

Freelance Potential

Published 4–6 titles in 2009. Receives 1,000+ queries yearly.

- **Fiction:** Publishes concept books, 0–4 years; easy-to-read books, 4–7 years; story picture books, 4–10 years; middle-grade books, 8–12 years; and young adult books, 12–18 years. Genres include adventure; mystery; and contemporary, historical, multicultural, and ethnic fiction.
- **Nonfiction:** Publishes middle-grade books, 8–12 years. Topics include African American history, culture, and social issues. Also publishes biographies.
- **Representative Titles:** *Book of Black Heroes: From A to Z* by Wade Hudson & Valerie Wilson Wesley (7+ years) profiles African American men and women of accomplishment. *I'm Late* by Mari Evans (13–17 years) is a novel about what happens when two 14-year-old girls use their bodies to try to heal their hearts.

Submissions and Payment

Guidelines and catalogue available at website. Query with outline/synopsis and author bio. Accepts hard copy. SASE. Responds in 4–5 months. Publication period varies. Royalty.

Editor's Comments

We are currently accepting queries for young adult titles only. We are not considering picture books, poetry, activity books, or any other manuscripts at this time. Fiction manuscripts should: be targeted to readers age 13 and older; feature realistic, contemporary characters; have compelling plot lines that introduce conflict and resolution; be highly interesting and readable; and convey cultural authenticity.

Kaeden Books

P.O. Box 16190
Rocky River, OH 44116

Editor: Lisa Stenger

Publisher's Interests
Publishing high-interest, leveled books for children in preschool through grade two, Kaeden Books is focused on promoting early literacy and "Reading Recovery." Its list is created specifically for the educational market.
Website: www.kaeden.com

Freelance Potential
Published 12–16 titles in 2009: each was developed from an unsolicited submission. Receives 1,200+ mss yearly.

- **Fiction:** Publishes easy-to-read books, 4–7 years; story picture books, 4–10 years; and chapter books, 5–10 years. Genres include contemporary fiction and stories about animals.
- **Nonfiction:** Publishes easy-to-read books, 4–7 years; story picture books, 4–10 years; and chapter books, 5–10 years. Topics include animals, science, nature, nutrition, biography, careers, recreation, and social studies.
- **Representative Titles:** *We Need Trees* (Level 3) is a 33-word book that points out the food we receive from trees. *Haircuts* (Level 13) by Joe Yukish is a comical tale about two brothers who try a new barbershop. *The Pond Hockey Challenge* by Kathryn Yevchak (Level 20) is about a girl who takes on the boys in ice hockey; second in the Adventures of Sophie Bean series.

Submissions and Payment
Guidelines and catalogue available at website. Send complete ms. Accepts hard copy. SASE. Responds in 1 year if interested. Publication period varies. Royalty. Flat fee.

Editor's Comments
At this time, we have a particular need for beginning chapter books and unique nonfiction manuscripts. These should have interesting topics presented in language comprehensible to young students. They can be as minimal as 25 words for the earliest reader or as long as 2,000 words for the fluent reader. Nonfiction content should be supported with facts.

Kane Miller

A Division of EDC Publishing

P.O. Box 8515
La Jolla, CA 92038

Editorial Department

Publisher's Interests

Kane Miller publishes picture books and chapter books from other countries, and is seeking to expand its list to include works that convey American culture and communities within the U.S. It accepts fiction and nonfiction that embrace American subjects and themes.
Website: www.kanemiller.com

Freelance Potential

Published 30 titles in 2009. Receives 900 unsolicited mss each year.

- **Fiction:** Publishes concept books, toddler books, and early picture books, 0–4 years; story picture books, 4–10 years; chapter books, 5–10 years; and middle-grade books, 8–12 years. Genres include contemporary, historical, and multicultural fiction; adventure; humor; mystery; fantasy; and stories about animals.
- **Nonfiction:** Publishes early picture books, 0–4 years. Topics include animals, sports, history, and multicultural issues.
- **Representative Titles:** *Super Duck* by Jez Alborough (3–7 years) finds Duck called to save the day when his friend Frog gets carried away—literally. *Moonrunner* by Mark Thomason (9–14 years) is the story of an American boy who, while trying to adapt to his new home in Australia, finds a stallion that reminds him of his Montana home.

Submissions and Payment

Guidelines and catalogue available at website. Send complete ms. Accepts hard copy. SASE. Responds in 3–6 weeks. Publication in 1–2 years. Royalty; advance.

Editor's Comments

Although our catalogue contains mostly authors from other countries, we are actively searching for books from American authors that convey an American experience. We are interested in nonfiction on American subjects, and engaging fiction in all genres, especially those with American themes.

Kar-Ben Publishing

241 First Avenue North
Minneapolis, MN 55401

Editorial

Publisher's Interests
Children's books covering contemporary Jewish themes are the specialty of this division of Lerner Publishing Group.
Website: www.karben.com

Freelance Potential
Published 15 titles in 2009: 12 were developed from unsolicited submissions and 2 were by agented authors. Of the 15 titles, 8 were by unpublished writers and 6 were by authors who were new to the publishing house. Receives 800 unsolicited mss yearly.

- **Fiction:** Publishes Jewish-themed concept books, toddler books, and early picture books, 0–4 years; story picture books, 4–10 years; and chapter books, 5–10 years. Publishes folktales, life-cycle stories, tales from the Torah, and Jewish identity and holiday stories.
- **Nonfiction:** Publishes Jewish-themed story picture books, 4–10 years; and middle-grade books, 8–12 years. Topics include Jewish identity, traditions, holidays, and doctrine. Also publishes prayer books, activity books, and board books.
- **Representative Titles:** *A Mezuzah on the Door* by Amy Meltzer (ages 3–7) tells how this tradition helps a boy transition from his city apartment to a new home in the suburbs. *Sammy Spider's First Purim* by Sylvia A. Rouss (3–8 years) follows a spider on an adventure as he prepares for Purim.

Submissions and Payment
Guidelines available at website. Send complete ms. Accepts hard copy, email to editorial@karben.com, and simultaneous submissions if identified. SASE. Responds in 6–8 weeks. Publication period varies. Royalty, 5–8%; advance, $500–$2,000. Flat fee.

Editor's Comments
Stories that reflect the cultural diversity of today's Jewish family are of special interest to us, as are holiday stories.

Key Curriculum Press

1150 65th Street
Emeryville, CA 94608

Executive Editor: Josephine Noah

Publisher's Interests

Key Curriculum publishes student-centered, inquiry-based textbooks and supplemental materials that span the mathematics curriculum from middle school arithmetic to advanced calculus and statistics. Also included in the mix are science textbooks and professional development materials for teachers.
Website: www.keypress.com

Freelance Potential

Published 100 titles in 2009. Receives 120 queries yearly.

- **Nonfiction:** Publishes middle-grade books, 8–12 years; and young adult books, 12–18 years. Topics include mathematics and science. Also publishes books for educators, software, and supplemental teaching material for grades 6–12.
- **Representative Titles:** *Discovering Geometry* by Michael Serra (grades 8–10) is a textbook that helps students develop the ability to reason, justify, and prove geometric properties. *Engineering the Future* by the Museum of Science, Boston (grades 9–12) is a project-based curriculum that builds technological literacy and critical-reasoning skills.

Submissions and Payment

Guidelines and catalogue available at website. Query with résumé, prospectus, detailed table of contents, and 1–3 sample chapters. Accepts hard copy and simultaneous submissions if identified. SASE. Responds in 2 months. Publication period varies. Royalty, 6–10%.

Editor's Comments

When submitting your one-page proposal, please tell us what distinguishes your work from existing mathematics materials, and why you feel it is important. Please explain the prerequisite knowledge teachers and students need in order to use your materials. Describe your target audience, and give us some idea of the size of the market for your work.

Key Education Publishing

9601 Newton Avenue South
Minneapolis, MN 55431

President: Sherrill B. Flora

Publisher's Interests

Key Education publishes supplemental education materials for early childhood. Its catalogue includes books on special education, speech-language pathology, and English language learning. It is an imprint of Carson-Dellosa Publishing.
Website: www.keyeducationpublishing.com

Freelance Potential

Published 30 titles in 2009. Of the 30 titles, 4 were by unpublished writers and 2 were by authors who were new to the publishing house.

- **Nonfiction:** Publishes educational resources, preK–grade 3. Features activity books, skill-and-practice materials, instructional methodology books, learning theme books, and materials for English as a Second Language (ESL).
- **Representative Titles:** *Preschool & Kindergarten Skills* (preK) is a workbook designed to give children extra practice at home or school in the areas of letter and sight-word recognition, and number sense. *Reading for Details* by Kelly Gunzenhauser (grade 2) presents 49 fun-to-read passages designed to strengthen reading comprehension skills. *Beginning Reading* (preK–grade 1) provides lessons designed to aid in the acquisition of reading skills, along with an incentive chart.

Submissions and Payment

Guidelines and catalogue available at website. Query with table of contents or outline, sample pages, and résumé. Accepts hard copy and email submissions to sherrie@ keyeducationpublishing. SASE. Responds in 1–3 months. Publication in 9–12 months. Royalty. Flat fee.

Editor's Comments

Our editorial staff reviews proposals, but we also send some proposals to appropriate outside reviewers, thereby delaying the response time somewhat. Generally speaking, we are not interested in fiction.

KidHaven Press

Thomson Gale
27500 Drake Road
Farmington Hills, MI 48331

Administrative Coordinator: Kristine Burns

Publisher's Interests
This imprint of Thomson Gale publishes quality nonfiction books for students in elementary and middle school. Most of its titles are in series that explore history, world cultures, the sciences, and nature. They are designed to supplement classroom curricula.
Website: http://gale.cengage.com/kidhaven

Freelance Potential
Published 20–25 titles in 2009. Receives 60+ queries yearly.

- **Nonfiction:** Publishes middle-grade books, 8–12 years. Topics include animals, biography, computers, geography, health, fitness, history, multicultural issues, nature, the environment, science, technology, and social issues.
- **Representative Titles:** *Tony Hawk* by Raymond H. Miller (grades 4–8) presents a biography of the skateboard king and gives readers a peek at the attitude and effort it took to excel at the sport; part of the Stars of Sport series. *Foods of Greece* by Barbara Sheen (grades 2–6) explores the country with a blend of geography, history, culture, and, of course, food; part of the A Taste of Culture series.

Submissions and Payment
Guidelines available. Catalogue available at website. Query. Accepts hard copy. SASE. Response time and publication period vary. Flat fee.

Editor's Comments
We are always increasing the types of series we offer, and welcome writers who can make a unique contribution to those series. Most of our books are assigned on a work-for-hire basis. We look for interesting approaches to topics, and strive to produce books that convey information in an engaging manner. Query us with your qualifications to write on a certain subject or study area. If we are intrigued, we will happily contact you for further discussion.

Kids Can Press

29 Birch Avenue
Toronto, Ontario M4V 1E2
Canada

Publishing Assistant: Katy Kalmar

Publisher's Interests
The largest Canadian children's publisher, Kids Can Press
was started in 1973 by a small group of women in Toronto.
Today its list contains more than 500 titles, each designed
to develop children's literacy and a love of reading.
Website: www.kidscanpress.com

Freelance Potential
Published 32 titles in 2009. Receives 4,000 mss yearly.

- **Fiction:** Publishes toddler books, 0–4 years; easy-to-read
  books, 4–7 years; story picture books, 4–10 years; chapter
  books, 5–10 years; middle-grade books, 8–12 years; and
  young adult books, 12–18 years. Genres include fantasy, folklore, mystery, suspense, and contemporary and historical fiction. Also offers stories about animals.
- **Nonfiction:** Publishes easy-to-read books, 4–7 years; and
  middle-grade books, 8–12 years. Topics include animals,
  crafts, hobbies, nature, history, biography, and science.
- **Representative Titles:** *Big Bear Hug* by Nicholas Oldland (3–7
  years) is a contemporary fable about a bear who hugs everything in sight, until he meets up with a tree-cutting human.
  Harry Houdini by Elizabeth MacLeod (6–8 years) is a Level 3
  reader about the famous magician's life; part of the Inspiring
  Lives series. *100% Pure Fake* by Lyn Thomas (8–12 years)
  tells kids how to create such gross pranks as "Rotting Skin."

Submissions and Payment
Canadian authors only. Guidelines and catalogue available
at website. Query with synopsis and 3 chapters for fiction;
send complete ms for nonfiction. Accepts hard copy. SASE.
Responds if interested. Publication period varies. Royalty;
advance.

Editor's Comments
We do not currently accept unsolicited manuscripts from
children or teenagers, or from authors outside of Canada.

Alfred A. Knopf Books for Young Readers

Random House Children's Books
1745 Broadway, Mail Drop 9-3
New York, NY 10019

Assistant Editor: Allison Wortche

Publisher's Interests

This well-known imprint of Random House Children's Books publishes fiction titles in all genres for readers of all ages. Its list runs the gamut from silly picture books for babies to engaging romance dramas for young adult readers.
Website: www.randomhouse.com/kids

Freelance Potential

Published 75 titles in 2009. Of the 75 titles, 6 were by unpublished writers and 27 were by authors who were new to the publishing house. Receives 3,000 queries and unsolicited mss yearly.

- **Fiction:** Publishes picture books, 0–8 years; middle-grade books, 8–12 years; and young adult books, 12–18 years. Genres include historical, contemporary, and multicultural fiction.
- **Representative Titles:** *Becoming Chloe* by Catherine Ryan Hyde (14+ years) is the story of a teen who has seen too much ugliness in her young life, and the independent young man who befriends her in New York City. *The First Rule of Little Brothers* by Jill Davis (5–8 years) is an affectionate, silly-smart take on the joys, trials, and surprises of being linked to someone who will share your growing up and family experiences like no one else.

Submissions and Payment

Guidelines available at website. Send complete ms with cover letter for picture books. Query with synopsis and 25 pages of text for novels. Accepts hard copy and simultaneous submissions if identified. No electronic submissions. No SASE. Responds in 6 months if interested. Publication in 1–2 years. Royalty; advance.

Editor's Comments

While some of our titles were discovered in the slush pile, we (like many large publishers) prefer to work with agented authors. Our guidelines offer hints for obtaining an agent.

Wendy Lamb Books

Random House Children's Books
1745 Broadway
New York, NY 10019

Editor: Wendy Lamb

Publisher's Interests
Wendy Lamb Books focuses on innovative middle-grade and young adult fiction. While its list features many award-winning authors, this Random House imprint also seeks new talent and publishes many first novels.
Website: www.randomhouse.com/kids

Freelance Potential
Published 14 titles in 2009: most were by agented authors. Receives 2,400 queries yearly.

- **Fiction:** Publishes middle-grade books, 8–12 years; and young adult books, 12–18 years. Genres include contemporary, historical, and multicultural fiction; mystery; adventure; and humor.
- **Representative Titles:** *Wild Girl* by Patricia Reilly Giff (8–12 years) tells the parallel stories of a 12-year-old girl and a filly as they both begin life in a new home. *The Zippy Fix* by Graham Salisbury (7–10 years) chronicles the misadventures of a 9-year-old boy as he schemes to depose his babysitter; part of the Calvin Coconut series. *Rosie and Skate* by Beth Ann Bauman (YA) depicts the tumultuous lives of two very different teenage sisters living on the Jersey Shore.

Submissions and Payment
Guidelines and catalogue available at website. Query with 10 mss pages and list of publishing credits. Accepts hard copy. SASE for reply only. Responds in 2 months. Publication period and payment policy vary.

Editor's Comments
Please send no more than 10 pages of the manuscript with your query. Note that these pages will not be returned. Please allow some time for a response to your submission. If you haven't received a reply after six weeks or so, it's fine to inquire by regular mail. Please do not phone, email, or fax to inquire about your submission.

Learning Horizons

5301 Grant Avenue
Cleveland, OH 44125

Editorial Manager: Joanna Robinson

Publisher's Interests
Learning Horizons offers educational products designed to optimize a child's learning experience. The company produces a variety of books, activity books, games, and multimedia resources for parents, homeschoolers, and teachers. It focuses on products for preschool and elementary school students.
Website: www.learninghorizons.com

Freelance Potential
Published 20 titles in 2009. Of the 20 titles, 8 were by unpublished writers and 8 were by authors who were new to the publishing house. Receives 20–30 queries yearly.

- **Nonfiction:** Publishes story picture books, 4–10 years. Features educational informational titles. Topics include mathematics, language arts, science, social studies, holidays, nature, and the environment. Also publishes workbooks for preK–grade 1, novelty books, and board books.
- **Representative Titles:** *Reading Comprehension* (grades 4–6) is a take-along workbook that helps students increase their reading comprehension; part of the Learn on the Go workbook series. *I Am a Friend!* (3+ years) helps children understand fundamental cognitive concepts and reinforces social skills; part of the Play With Me Sesame workbook series.

Submissions and Payment
Query. No unsolicited mss. Accepts hard copy and email queries to professortrex@learninghorizons.com. SASE. Responds in 3–4 months. Publication in 18 months. Payment policy varies.

Editor's Comments
Please note that all of our products are created by professional educators and psychologists. If you have an idea for a single product or series, we'd like to hear about it. Please tell us about your professional experience as well.

Learning Resources

380 North Fairway Drive
Vernon Hills, IL 60061

Editorial Director

Publisher's Interests
Educators of children in preschool through grade six use the books, games, puzzles, activity kits, classroom manipulatives, and other curriculum-based materials offered by Learning Resources. Spanish-language (ESL and ELL) materials for literacy comprise a significant portion of this publisher's catalogue of offerings.
Website: www.learningresources.com

Freelance Potential
Published 85 titles in 2009. Of the 85 titles, 2 were by unpublished writers and 2 were by authors who were new to the publishing house. Receives 20 queries yearly.

- **Nonfiction:** Publishes educational materials, manipulatives, workbooks, games, and activity books, preK–grade 6. Topics include reading, grammar, writing, ESL, ELL, early childhood learning, geography, mathematics, measurement, sorting, nutrition and health, earth and life sciences, and Spanish. Also produces teacher resources and classroom management tools.
- **Representative Titles:** *Language Patterns & Vocabulary Themed Readers* (grades 1 and up) introduces essential vocabulary through everyday themes; includes teaching guide. *Oraciones Basicas* (grades 2 and up) focuses on basic Spanish sentences and advanced word-level skills; in English with Spanish.

Submissions and Payment
Catalogue available at website or with 9x12 SASE ($3 postage). Query with résumé and writing sample. Accepts hard copy. SASE. Responds in 6–12 weeks. Publication in 1–2 years. Flat fee.

Editor's Comments
We are interested in submissions from educators and others with a background in education. Curriculum-based materials and classroom-tested materials are especially sought.

Lee & Low Books

95 Madison Avenue
New York, NY 10016

Submissions Editor

Publisher's Interests
This award-winning publisher focuses on books that address
multicultural themes for children ages five and older. It offers
fiction and nonfiction that promote cultural awareness.
Website: www.leeandlow.com

Freelance Potential
Published 11 titles in 2009: 2–3 were developed from unsolicited submissions and 4–5 were by agented authors. Of the
11 titles, 1 was by an unpublished writer and 1 was by an
author who was new to the publishing house. Receives
1,080 unsolicited mss yearly.

- **Fiction:** Publishes story picture books, 5–10 years; and
  middle-grade books, 8–12 years. Genres include realistic,
  historical, contemporary, multicultural, and ethnic fiction.
- **Nonfiction:** Publishes story picture books, 5–10 years; and
  middle-grade books, 8–12 years. Topics include multicultural
  and ethnic issues and traditions. Also publishes biographies.
- **Representative Titles:** *The Last Black King of the Kentucky
  Derby* by Crystal Hubbard (6–11 years) is the story of Jimmy
  Winkfield, who went from a sharecropper's life to one of history's finest horsemen. *No Mush Today* by Sally Derby (4–8
  years) finds Nonie escaping her crying baby brother and mushy
  breakfasts by spending time with her grandmother, who takes
  her out into the world of grown-ups.

Submissions and Payment
Guidelines available at website. Send complete ms. Accepts
hard copy and simultaneous submissions if identified. No
SASE. Responds in 6 months if interested. Publication in
2–3 years. Royalty; advance.

Editor's Comments
We make a special effort to work with writers of color and to
encourage new voices. We will consider unsolicited manuscripts only if they abide by our submission guidelines.

Legacy Press

P.O. Box 261129
San Diego, CA 92196

Editorial Director: Andrea Christian

Publisher's Interests

Legacy specializes in Christian-themed books, activity books, and resources for children. It focuses on fiction and religious-themed books for children and pre-teens.
Website: www.rainbowpublishers.com

Freelance Potential

Published 10 titles in 2009: 8 were developed from unsolicited submissions, 1 was by an agented author, and 1 was a reprint/licensed property. Of the 10 titles, 5 were by unpublished writers and 5 were by authors who were new to the publishing house. Receives 120 queries yearly.

- **Fiction:** Publishes middle-grade books, 8–12 years. Genres include adventure, mystery, contemporary fiction, and stories about animals—all with Christian themes.
- **Nonfiction:** Publishes toddler books, 0–4 years; story picture books, 4–10 years; and chapter books, 5–10 years. Topics include the Bible, relationships, morals and values, self-esteem, prayer, holidays, cooking, crafts, and hobbies. Also publishes activity books and parenting titles.
- **Representative Titles:** *52 Games That Teach the Bible* entertains kids while teaching them Bible facts. *Instant Bible Lessons for Pre-teens: Equipped for Life* takes the lessons of the Bible and breaks them down into easy-to-understand language for pre-teens.

Submissions and Payment

Guidelines and catalogue available at website or with 9x12 SASE (2 first-class stamps). Query with table of contents and first 3 chapters. Accepts hard copy. SASE. Responds in 3 months. Publication in 6–36 months. Royalty, 8%+; advance, $500+.

Editor's Comments

We welcome any book that takes the lessons of the Bible or values of Christianity and breaks them down for children.

Lerner Publications

241 First Avenue North
Minneapolis, MN 55401

Submissions Editor

Publisher's Interests
Lerner Publications publishes high-quality nonfiction books—
many of them award-winners—for children in kindergarten
through twelfth grade. It accepts only targeted submissions
that respond to a specific subject need.
Website: www.lernerbooks.com

Freelance Potential
Published 250 titles in 2009: 5 were developed from unsolicited submissions and 50 were by agented authors. Of the
250 titles, 5 were by authors who were new to the publishing house.

- **Nonfiction:** Publishes easy-to-read books, 4–7 years; chapter
  books, 5–10 years; middle-grade books, 8–12 years; and
  young adult books, 12–18 years. Topics include ethnic and
  multicultural issues, nature, the environment, science, and
  sports. Also publishes biographies.
- **Representative Titles:** *Earth-Friendly Waste Management* by
  Charlotte Wilcox (grades 4–7) explains the environmental challenges of waste disposal, and examines new technologies
  being employed; part of the Saving Our Living Earth series.
  Vietnamese in America by Lori Coleman (grades 5–8) presents
  the struggles and triumphs of Vietnamese immigrants in America and explains how they adapted to their new country while
  holding onto their traditions; part of the In America series.

Submissions and Payment
Guidelines and catalogue available at website. No unsolicited
submissions. Accepts targeted submissions only. See website
for a list of needs aimed at specific reading levels in specific
subject areas, and for complete submission information.
Response time, publication period, and payment policy vary.

Editor's Comments
We will only look at submissions that correlate to our call for
specific subjects, as outlined at our website.

Arthur A. Levine Books

Scholastic Inc.
557 Broadway
New York, NY 10012

Publisher: Arthur A. Levine

Publisher's Interests
High-quality fiction and nonfiction for children of all ages (as well as adults) is the focus of Arthur A. Levine Books, an imprint of Scholastic Press since 1996.
Website: www.arthuralevinebooks.com

Freelance Potential
Published 15–20 titles in 2009: most were by agented authors. Receives 2,600 queries, 400 unsolicited mss yearly.

- **Fiction:** Publishes concept books, toddler books, and early picture books, 0–4 years; story picture books, 4–10 years; chapter books, 5–10 years; middle-grade books, 8–12 years; and young adult books, 12–18 years. Genres include multicultural fiction and fantasy. Also publishes poetry.
- **Nonfiction:** Publishes concept books, 0–4 years; story picture books, 4–10 years; middle-grade books, 8–12 years; and young adult books, 12–18 years. Topics include nature and animals. Also publishes biographies.
- **Representative Titles:** *Absolutely Maybe* by Lisa Yee (YA) is the story of a teen who, with two friends, heads to L.A. to find her father but ends up finding herself. *The Snowy Day* by Komako Sakai (4–10 years) presents a rabbit who finds creative ways to spend a snowy day cooped up in his house.

Submissions and Payment
Guidelines and catalogue available at website. Send complete ms for picture books. Query with synopsis and first 2 chapters for fiction; with 5 sample pages for nonfiction. Accepts hard copy. SASE. Responds to queries in 6–8 weeks, to mss in 6–8 months. Publication in 18–24 months. Payment policy varies.

Editor's Comments
We look for strong writing, authentic emotion, and ideas or perspectives we haven't seen before. We greatly enjoy working with debut authors.

Libraries Unlimited

130 Cremona Drive
Santa Barbara, CA 93117

Senior Acquisitions Editor: Barbara Ittner

Publisher's Interests

Libraries Unlimited serves the needs of the library profession through resource and professional development books for library and information science students and faculty, practicing librarians, media specialists, and teachers.
Website: www.lu.com; www.abc-clio.com

Freelance Potential

Published 100 titles in 2009: 7 were developed from unsolicited submissions. Of the 100 titles, 50 were by authors who were new to the publishing house. Receives 400+ queries yearly.

- **Nonfiction:** Publishes curriculum titles. Features bilingual books, grades K–6; and activity books, grades K–12. Also publishes bibliographies, professional reference titles, gifted education titles, and regional books. Topics include science, mathematics, social studies, whole language, and literature.
- **Representative Titles:** *Big Book of Animal Rhymes, Fingerplays, and Songs* by Elizabeth Cothen Low is filled with resources to add to any animal-themed children's story hour. *Best Books for Middle School and Junior High Readers, Grades 6–9* by Catherine Barr & John T. Gillespie serves as a reading guide and selection tool for librarians, covering more than 15,000 titles.

Submissions and Payment

Guidelines and catalogue available at website. Query with résumé, outline, sample chapter, and market analysis. Accepts hard copy. SASE. Responds in 2–3 months. Publication in 10–12 months. Royalty.

Editor's Comments

You must supply us with a current résumé along with your query, as our books are written by professionals in the library sciences. If you can share your expertise with others, we'd like to hear your ideas.

Liguori Publications

1 Liguori Drive
Liguori, MO 63057-9999

Editorial Director: Jay Staten

Publisher's Interests

This Catholic publishing house aims to effectively communicate the Word of God through print and electronic media. It provides English- and Spanish-language catechetical, pastoral, and devotional products for Catholics of all ages.
Website: www.liguori.org

Freelance Potential

Published 40 titles in 2009: several were developed from unsolicited submissions.

- **Nonfiction:** Publishes toddler books (0–4 years); easy-to-read books (4–7 years); middle-grade books (8–12 years); and young adult books, 12–18 years. Topics include prayer, catechism, Catholicism, saints, celebrations, holy days, stewardship, youth ministry, family, divorce, sexuality, chastity, abuse, and other contemporary issues. Also publishes books for parents and religious educators.
- **Representative Titles:** *My Sister Is Annoying* by Father Joe Kempf (3–5 years) offers fun yet meaningful prayers for young children. *Handbook for Today's Catholic Teen* by Jim Auer (YA) covers traditional topics such as Catholic doctrine, practices, and prayers, then tackles serious contemporary issues such as violence, the media, sex, and substance abuse.

Submissions and Payment

Guidelines and catalogue available at website. Query with outline. Accepts hard copy and email queries to manuscript_submission@liguori.org. SASE. Responds in 2–4 months. Publication in 9–18 months. Royalty.

Editor's Comments

Please submit a two- to four-page outline describing your work. A small sample of your work (such as a chapter) may be included, but please do not send the full manuscript unless we ask to see it.

Lillenas Publishing Company

2923 Troost Avenue
Kansas City, MO 64109

Drama Editor

Publisher's Interests

Lillenas Publishing produces resources and scripts for use in church and religious education programs. Its catalogue includes Christian plays, musicals, monologues, and other creative worship resources. Many of its offerings are designed to be performed or viewed by children as part of worship or Sunday school.
Website: www.lillenasdrama.com

Freelance Potential

Published 35+ titles in 2009. Of the 35+ titles, 2–3 were by authors who were new to the publishing house. Receives 30–50 unsolicited mss yearly.

- **Fiction:** Publishes full-length and one-act plays, monologues, sketches, skits, recitations, puppet plays, and dramatic exercises, all with Christian themes, for performers 6–18 years.
- **Nonfiction:** Publishes theater resource materials. Topics include stage and set design, scenery, production techniques, and drama ministry.
- **Representative Titles:** *No Limits: The Script Book* by Jeff Smith is filled with short scripts and program material for use in worship services, weekly meetings, and youth groups. *Old Testament Bible Sketches for Children* by Gillette Elvgren features 24 interactive scripts for youth and adults to perform for children.

Submissions and Payment

Guidelines available at website. Send complete ms with cast list, scene description, and prop list. Accepts hard copy. SASE. Responds in 6 months. Publication period varies. Royalty. Flat fee.

Editor's Comments

Our publications must reflect a distinctly Christian point of view, but they need not be sermonizing. Please note that we do not review submissions from January to April.

Linworth Publishing

P.O. Box 1911
Santa Barbara, CA 93116-1911

Publisher: Marlene Woo-Lun

Publisher's Interests
Now part of the Libraries Unlimited and ABC-CLIO publishing family, Linworth Publishing produces books and resources offering practical and professional development information for library professionals and media specialists.
Website: www.linworth.com

Freelance Potential
Published 12 titles in 2009. Of the 12 titles, 3 were by authors who were new to the publishing house. Receives 120 queries yearly.

- **Nonfiction:** Publishes books for school librarians, media specialists, and teachers, grades K–12. Topics include technology, school library management, information literacy, research skills, library promotion, reading motivation, and grammar.
- **Representative Titles:** *Redefining Literacy 2.0* by David F. Warlick explains what literacy means in this modern age, and provides a new model for literacy based on today's quick-moving, multimedia technology. *Thematic Inquiry Through Fiction and Nonfiction, PreK to Grade 6* by Colleen MacDonell presents everything librarians need to teach sound library lessons, including fiction and nonfiction book lists.

Submissions and Payment
Guidelines and catalogue available at website. Query with résumé, outline, table of contents, sample chapter, and market analysis. Accepts hard copy, disk submissions, and email queries to linworth@linworthpublishing.com. SASE. Responds in 1 week. Publication in 6 months. Royalty.

Editor's Comments
When sending us your résumé, please also include descriptions of other books you have written. We accept proposals from established professionals in the fields of library science, school or library administration, and media and technology specialists.

Lion Children's Books

Wilkinson House
Jordan Hill Road
Oxford 0X2 8DR
United Kingdom

Editorial Administrator: Kate Leech

Publisher's Interests

This imprint of Lion Hudson publishes books that are designed to take Christian values into the general marketplace. It offers books for children of all ages, from birth through age 18, that either reflect Christian values or are inspired by a Christian worldview.
Website: www.lionhudson.com

Freelance Potential

Published 45 titles in 2009: 3 were developed from unsolicited submissions, 2 were by agented authors, and 1 was a reprint/licensed property. Receives 960 queries yearly.

- **Fiction:** Publishes early picture books, concept books, and toddler books, 0–4 years; chapter books, 5–10 years; and young adult books, 12–18 years. Genres include fairy tales, religious and inspirational fiction, and adventure.
- **Nonfiction:** Publishes toddler books and early picture books, 0–4 years; easy-to-read books, 4–7 years; story picture books, 4–10 years; middle-grade books, 8–12 years; and young adult books, 12–18 years. Topics include religion, current events, history, nature, social issues, health, and fitness.
- **Representative Titles:** *The Lion Book of Prayers to Read and Know* by Sophie Piper is a collection of simple and sincere prayers to encourage a young child in faith and goodness. *Bedtime Stories for Little Angels* by Sarah J. Dodd (3–5 years) presents an engaging and entertaining collection of virtuous stories inspired by the parables.

Submissions and Payment

Guidelines available. Catalogue available at website. Query with résumé. Accepts hard copy. SAE/IRC. Responds in 3 months. Publication period and payment policy vary.

Editor's Comments

Books that promote good Christian values and encourage children to live caring lives will be of interest to us.

Little, Brown and Company Books for Young Readers

237 Park Avenue
New York, NY 10017

Publisher: Megan Tingley

Publisher's Interests
This publisher, now a division of Hachette Book Group, has been publishing books for children since 1926. It publishes picture books and hardcover and paperback fiction, as well as a limited number of nonfiction titles for middle-grade and young adult readers.
Website: www.lb-kids.com; www.lb-teens.com

Freelance Potential
Published 150 titles in 2009: each was by an agented author.

- **Fiction:** Publishes toddler books, 0–4 years; picture books, 4–8 years; easy-to-read books, 4–7 years; chapter books, 5–10 years; and young adult books, 12–18 years. Genres include fantasy, contemporary, and multicultural fiction. Also publishes stories about the holidays.
- **Nonfiction:** Publishes titles with trade market potential. Topics include multicultural issues, history, self-help, and sports.
- **Representative Titles:** *Baby Giggles* by Rachael Hale (0–3 years) explores the wide range of emotions that every child experiences, from silly to sad, from grumpy to glad. *The Postcard* by Tony Abbott (10+ years) follows two teens as they embark on an adventure to uncover extraordinary family secrets, starting with the clue of an old, yellowed postcard.

Submissions and Payment
Accepts submissions from agented authors only. Accepts hard copy. SASE. Responds in 2–3 months. Publication period varies. Royalty; advance.

Editor's Comments
As with most major publishing houses, we do not accept unsolicited submissions. Please be aware that they will be returned unopened or recycled. We consider proposals sent through literary agents only. We look for creative, high-quality books with engaging characters and stories.

Little Simon

Simon & Schuster Children's Publishing Division
1230 Avenue of the Americas
New York, NY 10020

Editorial Department

Publisher's Interests
This imprint of Simon & Schuster has "little" in its name for a reason. It publishes books designed for the little hands of little children. Novelty and board books are the mainstays of this company, which features pop-ups and other devices designed to keep little minds interested.
Website: http://kids.simonandschuster.com

Freelance Potential
Published 65 titles in 2009: 20 were by agented authors and 15 were reprint/licensed properties. Receives 200 queries each year.

- **Fiction:** Publishes concept books and toddler books, 0–4 years. Features stories about animals, holidays, trucks and automobiles, families, and the weather. Also publishes board books, 0–4 years; and pop-up books, 4–8 years.
- **Representative Titles:** *Journey to the Moon* by Lucio & Meera Santoro (3+ years) is a pop-up book that takes readers on a journey under the sea, into the sky, across the valleys, and up to the moon. *Over the River* by Derek Anderson (4–8 years) is a board book that puts a humorous twist on the classic "traveling to grandmother's house" Thanksgiving tale. *Night Night, Baby* by David McPhail is a board book that brings classic lullabies to life as the illustrations encourage parent/baby sharing and singing at bedtime.

Submissions and Payment
Query. Accepts queries through literary agents only. Accepts hard copy. SASE. Responds in 6 months. Publication in 2 years. Royalty; advance. Flat fee.

Editor's Comments
We accept only the highest quality in storytelling, for we believe our young audience deserves nothing but the best. Due to the overwhelming volume of submissions we have received, we now accept queries from literary agents only.

Little Tiger Press

1 The Coda Centre
189 Munster Road
London SW6 6AW
United Kingdom

Submissions Editor: Laura Roberts

Publisher's Interests

Little Tiger Press publishes picture books and novelty books for children up to the age of seven. An imprint of Magi Publications, its catalogue features bold, colorful books with creatively written stories.
Website: www.littletigerpress.com

Freelance Potential

Published 65 titles (64 juvenile) in 2009: 15 were by agented authors. Of the 65 titles, 2 were by unpublished writers. Receives 3,000 unsolicited mss yearly.

- **Fiction:** Publishes concept books and early picture books, 0–4 years; and story picture books, 3–7 years. Genres include contemporary and classic fiction. Also publishes board books.
- **Representative Titles:** *Sylvia and Bird* by Catherine Rayner (4–7 years) is a touching story about an unlikely friendship between a lonely dragon and a chirpy bird. *Gruff the Grump* by Steve Smallman (3–7 years) is the story of a grumpy bear and how his life is changed by a small rabbit. *I've Finished!* by Victoria Roberts & Lee Wildish (2+ years) follows Mo through a week in which he is determined to learn how to use the toilet by himself.

Submissions and Payment

Guidelines available at website. Send complete ms with brief cover letter. Accepts hard copy. Material is not returned. Responds via email in 3 months. Publication period and payment policy vary.

Editor's Comments

Manuscripts should be no longer than 750 words. We are open to cozy, emotional, quirky, and humorous stories on any child-relevant topic. We are proud of our reputation for developing and supporting new talent, and welcome the opportunity to review creative work. Please remember to include your email address in your cover letter.

Living Ink Books

AMG Publishers
6815 Shallowford Road
Chattanooga, TN 37421

Managing Editor: Rick Steele

Publisher's Interests
This imprint of AMG Publishers focuses on biblically oriented nonfiction books as well as contemporary and fantasy fiction for readers ages eight and older. The titles on its fiction list blend Christian and biblical themes into their story lines.
Website: www.amgpublishers.com

Freelance Potential
Published 25 titles (4 juvenile) in 2009. Of the 25 titles, 3 were by unpublished writers and 4 were by authors who were new to the publishing house. Receives 2,500 queries each year.

- **Fiction:** Publishes middle-grade books, 8–12 years; and young adult books, 12–18 years. Genres include fantasy fiction with Christian themes.
- **Nonfiction:** Publishes Christian-oriented books and Bible reference books for parents, educators, and others. Topics include Bible study, family issues, relationships, and parenting.
- **Representative Titles:** *The Ark, the Reed, & the Fire Cloud* by Jenny L. Cote (8–12 years) is an adventure- and mystery-filled story of a dog who becomes the leader of all the animals of the ark as they journey toward Noah. *The Bones of Makaidos* by Bryan Davis is a fantasy tale of good versus evil, dragon slayers, and the people of Second Eden; part of the Oracles of Fire series.

Submissions and Payment
Guidelines and catalogue available at website. Query with synopsis and author bio. Accepts hard copy and email queries to ricks@amgpublishers.com. SASE. Response time and publication period vary. Royalty; advance.

Editor's Comments
With the exception of our middle-grade and young adult fantasy fiction titles, we do not publish general fiction or children's books.

Llewellyn Publishing

2143 Wooddale Drive
Woodbury, MN 55125-2989

Publisher: Bill Krause

Publisher's Interests

Information about mind, body, and spirit, as well as the para-normal, are within the realm of Llewellyn Publishing. Its young adult list includes both fantasy fiction and nonfiction titles. 2% self-, subsidy-, co-venture, or co-op published material.
Website: www.llewellyn.com

Freelance Potential

Published 140 titles in 2009: 20 were developed from unsolicited submissions, 100 were by agented authors, and 4 were reprint/licensed properties. Of the 140 titles, 15 were by unpublished writers and 12 were by authors who were new to the publishing house. Receives 600 queries, 1,200 unsolicited mss yearly.

- **Fiction:** Publishes middle-grade books, 8–12 years; and young adult books, 12–18 years. Genres include mystery, fantasy, science fiction, and suspense.
- **Nonfiction:** Publishes young adult books, 12–18 years. Topics include astrology, Wicca, magic, shamanism, tarot cards, herbalism, alternative health, religion, and spirituality.
- **Representative Titles:** *Vamped* by Lucienne Diver (YA) relates the perks and pitfalls of being a high school girl turned vampire. *Initiation* by Susan Fine (YA) tells of a middle-class Latino boy trying to survive ninth grade at a brutal prep school. *Goddess Signs* by Angelica Danton helps young women tap into their own goddess power.

Submissions and Payment

Guidelines and catalogue available at website. Query with 3 sample chapters; or send complete ms with table of contents and author bio. Accepts hard copy. SASE. Responds in 2–6 months. Publication in 1–2 years. Royalty, 10%.

Editor's Comments

We accept submissions directly from authors (including first-time authors), as well as from literary agents.

Lobster Press

1620 Sherbrooke Street West, Suites C&D
Montreal, Quebec H3H 1C9
Canada

Assistant Editor: Meghan Nolan

Publisher's Interests
A mix of high-quality fiction and nonfiction books for children, tweens, teens, and their families can be found in the Lobster Press catalogue.
Website: www.lobsterpress.com

Freelance Potential
Published 23 titles in 2009. Of the 23 titles, 2 were by unpublished writers and 4 were by authors who were new to the publishing house. Receives 2,000 queries yearly.

- **Fiction:** Publishes toddler books, 2–4 years; story picture books, 4–10 years; middle-grade books, 8–12 years; and young adult books, 12–18 years. Genres include contemporary fiction, fantasy, and humor.
- **Nonfiction:** Publishes early picture books, 2–4 years; story picture books, 4–10 years; middle-grade books, 8–12 years; and young adult books, 12–18 years. Topics include history, science, nature, health, sports, travel, and social issues.
- **Representative Titles:** *Penelope and the Humongous Burp* by Sheri Radford (3–7 years) relates the consequences of gulping a few glasses of grape soda too quickly. *I Don't Want to Go* by Addie Meyer Sanders (1–3 years) shares a little boy's experiences when he tries new things with his grandparents.

Submissions and Payment
Canadian authors only. Guidelines and catalogue available at website. Query with résumé and synopsis. Accepts email queries to LobsterPressSubmissions@gmail.com. Responds if interested. Publication period varies. Royalty, 5–10%.

Editor's Comments
We seek original literary fiction for young adults, mystery and horror fiction for ages nine to twelve, and nonfiction books or children's reference books for all ages. We review queries from Canadian authors only. Please visit our website for the most current submission information.

James Lorimer & Company

317 Adelaide Street West, Suite 1002
Toronto, Ontario M5V 1P9
Canada

Children's Book Editor: Faye Smailes

Publisher's Interests
Canadian-themed fiction and nonfiction are available from
this publisher, which works with Canadian authors only.
Website: www.lorimer.ca

Freelance Potential
Published 25 titles (17 juvenile) in 2009: 3 were developed
from unsolicited submissions and 1 was a reprint/licensed
property. Of the 25 titles, 2 were by unpublished writers and
4 were by authors who were new to the publishing house.
Receives 240 queries, 120 unsolicited mss yearly.

- **Fiction:** Publishes easy-to-read books, 4–7 years; chapter
  books, 5–10 years; middle-grade books, 8–12 years; and
  young adult books, 12–18 years. Genres include contemporary, realistic, historical, and sports-themed fiction; mystery;
  suspense; adventure; and humor.
- **Nonfiction:** Publishes easy-to-read books, 4–7 years; middle-
  grade books, 8–12 years; and young adult books, 12–18
  years. Topics include multicultural subjects, nature, sports,
  and contemporary social issues.
- **Representative Titles:** *Anna's Pet* by Margaret Atwood &
  Joyce Barkhouse follows a young city girl's exploration of the
  Canadian countryside; part of the Kids in Canada series.
  Storm Child by Brenda Bellingham is a historical novel about
  a young girl, part Scottish and part First Nation, struggling to
  understand who she is in the 1830s Canadian West.

Submissions and Payment
Canadian authors only. Guidelines available. Prefers query
with outline; will accept complete ms. Accepts hard copy
and simultaneous submissions if identified. SASE. Responds
in 3–4 months. Publication period varies. Royalty; advance.

Editor's Comments
Well-written, Canada-based tales featuring believable characters and situations are welcome here.

Lucent Books

Thomson Gale
27500 Drake Road
Farmington Hills, MI 48331-3535

Administrative Assistant: Kristine Burns

Publisher's Interests
This imprint of Thomson Gale publishes educational nonfiction for students in the middle grades and high school. Like its sister company Greenhaven Press, Lucent Books offers numerous series covering wide-ranging topics in social studies, geography, health, science, and sports.
Website: www.gale.cengage.com/lucent

Freelance Potential
Published 110 titles in 2009. Of the 110 titles, 3 were by unpublished writers and 10 were by authors who were new to the publishing house. Receives 100 queries yearly.

- **Nonfiction:** Publishes middle-grade books, 8–12 years; and young adult books, 12–18 years. Topics include contemporary social issues, biography, history, geography, health, science, and sports.
- **Representative Titles:** *Queen Latifah* by Judy Galens (grades 7–10) profiles the life and career of the singer/actress; part of the People in the News series. *Art in Glass* by Phyllis Emert (grades 7–10) explores the roots, influences, and key components of this style of art; part of the Eye On Art series. *The Holocaust* by Sean Sheehan (grades 4–8) explains the causes and effects of this key event in history; part of the How Did It Happen? series.

Submissions and Payment
Query with résumé and list of publishing credits. All work is assigned. Response time varies. Publication in 1 year. Flat fee.

Editor's Comments
We strive to offer students valuable tools for conducting research and sharpening critical thinking skills. All of our titles tackle complex ideas in a manner that is coherent and relevant to our young readers, while maintaining the depth and objectivity demanded by a more mature audience.

MacAdam/Cage

155 Sansome Street, Suite 550
San Francisco, CA 94104

Manuscript Submissions

Publisher's Interests

MacAdam/Cage publishes literary fiction and high-quality narrative nonfiction for children ages four to young adult. With no subject or genre boundaries, it chooses manuscripts based solely on quality and interest. Although not currently reading children's submissions, it does accept titles for adults that may have crossover appeal for young adults.
Website: www.macadamcage.com

Freelance Potential

Published 30 titles in 2009. Of the 30 titles, 18 were by authors who were new to the publishing house. Receives 6,000 queries yearly.

- **Fiction:** Publishes easy-to-read books, 4–10 years; and young adult novels, 12–18 years. Genres include literary fiction.
- **Nonfiction:** Publishes young adult books, 12–18 years. Features narrative nonfiction on a variety of subjects.
- **Representative Titles:** *Dream City* by Brendan Short is a novel set in Depression-era Chicago that features a young boy's obsession with comic book heroes, and his lifelong attempt to both recapture and escape his childhood. *The Little Book of the Sea* by Lorenz Schröter is a fun and informative book of ocean trivia and nautical facts.

Submissions and Payment

Guidelines and catalogue available at website or with SASE. Query with author biography, synopsis, and sample chapters (30 pages maximum); or send complete ms. Accepts hard copy. No SASE. Responds in 4–5 months if interested. Publication period and payment policy vary.

Editor's Comments

We're not currently reading children's books or young adult submissions. The guidelines posted at our website will announce any changes to this policy. Prospective authors are advised to peruse our catalogue before submitting.

Mage Publishers

1032 29th Street NW
Washington, DC 20007

Submissions Editor: Amin Sepehri

Publisher's Interests
"Bridging the East and West," Mage Publishers is an independent publisher that features high-quality, English-language books about Persian culture. Its titles focus on cuisine, music, gardens, art, and history. It is currently expanding its children's line to include legends, folktales, and historical and cultural books.
Website: www.mage.com

Freelance Potential
Published 4–5 titles in 2009. Of the 4–5 titles, 1 was by an author who was new to the publishing house. Receives 50 queries, 25 unsolicited mss yearly.

- **Fiction:** Publishes children's tales and legends about Persia.
- **Nonfiction:** Publishes books on Persian literature, culture, history, and life. Also publishes books for adults on Persian cooking, architecture, music, history, poetry, and literature.
- **Representative Titles:** *The Heavenly Rose Garden* by Abbas Qoli Aqa Bakikhanov offers an in-depth look at the Caucasus during the eighteenth and nineteenth centuries. *Letter From Tabriz* by Edward G. Browne presents the letters sent to the author by Iranian constitutionalist leaders during the Russian occupation in the early 1900s.

Submissions and Payment
Guidelines and catalogue available at website. Query or send complete ms with brief biographical statement. Accepts hard copy. SASE. Responds in 1–3 months. Publication in 9–15 months. Royalty; advance.

Editor's Comments
Our goal is to bring readers outside of Iran and around the globe the best quality books of Persian arts, culture, and history. If you have something that fits the bill, please contact us. Remember, only books relating to Persian culture will be considered by our editors.

Magination Press

750 First Street NE
Washington, DC 20002-4242

Acquisitions Editor

Publisher's Interests
This imprint of the American Psychological Association publishes a variety of books for children, each with the goal of helping kids and their caregivers through the psychologically challenging issues of young life.
Website: www.maginationpress.com

Freelance Potential
Published 9 titles in 2009: 4 were developed from unsolicited submissions. Of the 9 titles, 2 were by unpublished writers and 4 were by authors who were new to the publishing house. Receives 700+ unsolicited mss yearly.

- **Fiction:** Publishes picture books and easy-to-read books, 4–8 years; and story picture books, 8–12 years. Stories address psychological concerns.
- **Nonfiction:** Publishes story picture books, 4–8 years; middle-grade books, 8–12 years; and young adult books, 12–18 years. Topics include divorce, ADHD/ADD, learning disabilities, depression, death, anxieties, self-esteem, and family matters. Also publishes workbooks.
- **Representative Titles:** *Nobody's Perfect* by Ellen Flanagan Burns (8–12 years) tells the story of a girl who is secretly afraid to be something other than perfect. *Little Tree* by Joyce C. Mills (4–8 years) targets children who have experienced life-challenging illnesses or accidents with a story about a tree that has lost some of its branches in a storm.

Submissions and Payment
Guidelines available at website. Send complete ms with résumé, synopsis, and market analysis. Accepts hard copy. SASE. Responds in 2–6 months. Publication in 2–3 years. Royalty.

Editor's Comments
All books must include comprehensive coping and resolution suggestions, not a single answer (however clever).

Master Books

P.O. Box 726
Green Forest, AR 72638

Assistant Editor: Craig Froman

Publisher's Interests

Master Books, an imprint of New Leaf Publishing Group, publishes Christian-themed nonfiction books for children under age 12. Its list includes books that are appropriate for Sunday school lessons or homeschooling.
Website: www.masterbooks.net

Freelance Potential

Published 20–25 titles (15 juvenile) in 2009: 3–4 were developed from unsolicited submissions, 2–3 were by agented authors, and 1–2 were reprint/licensed properties. Of the 20–25 titles, 3 were by unpublished writers and 8 were by authors who were new to the publishing house. Receives 1,200 queries yearly.

- **Nonfiction:** Publishes story picture books, 4–10 years; and middle-grade books, 8–12 years. Topics include science, technology, and animals. Also publishes homeschooling materials with Christian themes.
- **Representative Titles:** *The Answers Book for Kids* by Ken Ham (6–10 years) provides compact, easy-to-understand answers to children's tough faith questions about topics such as dinosaurs, creation, and Christian life. *Global Warming and the Creator's Plan* by Jay A. Auxt and Dr. William M. Curtis III makes the argument that the theories of man-induced global warming are unfounded, and that environmental changes are all part of God's plan.

Submissions and Payment

Guidelines and catalogue available at website. Query using author proposal form at website. Accepts hard copy and email to submissions@newleafpress.net. SASE. Responds in 3–4 months. Publication in 1 year. Royalty.

Editor's Comments

Books for the homeschool market, especially those serving grades one through eight, are among our current needs.

Margaret K. McElderry Books

Simon & Schuster Children's Publishing Division
1230 Avenue of the Americas
New York, NY 10020

Submissions Editor

Publisher's Interests
This publisher is interested in picture books, middle readers, and young adult books—fiction and nonfiction—in unlimited styles and subject matter. It also publishes books of poetry for young readers.
Website: http://kids.simonandschuster.com

Freelance Potential
Published 35 titles in 2009: 1 was developed from an unsolicited submission, 30 were by agented authors, and 4 were reprint/licensed properties. Receives 3,000 queries yearly.

- **Fiction:** Publishes early picture books, 0–4 years; story picture books, 4–10 years; chapter books, 5–10 years; and young adult books, 12–18 years. Genres include contemporary and historical fiction, folklore, fantasy, and humor. Also publishes poetry books.
- **Nonfiction:** Publishes story picture books, 4–10 years; middle-grade books, 8–12 years; and young adult books, 12–18 years. Topics include sports and nature.
- **Representative Titles:** *Alistair and Kip's Great Adventure* by John Segal (3–6 years) is a picture book about a cat and a beagle who build a boat and set a course for adventure. *Uncle Pirate* by Douglas Rees (7–10 years) is a lively story about what every boy wants—a pirate for an uncle.

Submissions and Payment
Agented authors only. Guidelines available. Query with résumé and outline/synopsis; include first 3 chapters for novels. Accepts hard copy. SASE. Responds in 1–2 months. Publication in 2–4 years. Royalty; advance.

Editor's Comments
Please note that we do not publish activity books, religious books, or textbooks. We are interested in a variety of subjects and genres for young children through young adults, as long as creative storylines and engaging writing exist.

Meadowbrook Press

5455 Smetana Drive
Minnetonka, MN 55343

Submissions Editor

Publisher's Interests

This publishing house focuses its attention on babies and youngsters, producing books for preschool-age children and older kids, as well as books for adults on kid-related topics. It also publishes poetry for children.
Website: www.meadowbrookpress.com

Freelance Potential

Published 10 titles in 2009. Receives 100 queries yearly.

- **Nonfiction:** Publishes concept books, 0–4 years; and middle-grade books, 8–12 years. Topics include toilet training, school, party games, and crafts. Also publishes nursery rhymes and activity books, as well as titles on pregnancy, childbirth, parenting, breastfeeding, and child care.
- **Representative Titles:** *What I Did on My Summer Vacation* by Bruce Lansky is a collection of more than 40 funny poems about summer vacation. *Grandma Knows Best, But No One Ever Listens!* by Mary McBride provides humorous (but real) advice for grandmothers who have been stuck with babysitting on how to scheme, lie, cheat, and threaten in order to be thought of as sweet and darling.

Submissions and Payment

Guidelines and catalogue available at website. Query. Accepts hard copy and simultaneous submissions if identified. No SASE. Responds only if interested. Publication in 2 years. Royalty; advance.

Editor's Comments

Although we have in the past, we do not currently publish children's fiction. We are also not currently accepting humor, adult fiction and poetry, picture books for children, travel titles, or scholarly or literary work. We do still accept children's poetry. Please refer to the submissions guidelines at our website for information on our current needs before sending us your work.

Medallion Press

1020 Cedar Avenue, Suite 216
St. Charles, IL 60174

Acquisitions Editor: Jessica Vicich

Publisher's Interests
Medallion Press is dedicated to quality. Its catalogue includes fiction and nonfiction for young adults and adults—titles that run the gamut of genres and subject matter.
Website: www.medallionpress.com

Freelance Potential
Published 32 titles in 2009. Of the 32 titles, 5–10 were by authors who were new to the publishing house. Receives 500+ queries yearly.

- **Fiction:** Publishes young adult books, 12–18 years. Genres include mainstream, contemporary, historical, and science fiction; fantasy; adventure; mystery; thriller; suspense; romance; and horror. Also publishes books for adults.
- **Representative Titles:** *The Secret of Shabaz* by Jennifer Macaire (YA) is a fantasy novel about a unicorn who comes out of retirement to fight the evil Dark Lord, and unearths some truths about his young friend's magical heritage. *The Cardinal's Heir* by Jaki Demarest is a novel of fantasy and mystery as a powerful French Cardinal's niece shape-shifts her way through an investigation of her uncle's murder.

Submissions and Payment
Guidelines and catalogue available at website. Query with publishing credits, 2- to 5-page synopsis, and first 3 chapters. Accepts hard copy, email queries to submissions@medallionpress.com, and simultaneous submissions if identified. SASE. Responds in 6–8 months. Publication in 2–3 years. Royalty; advance.

Editor's Comments
We believe that every book is a work of art. We nurture our books every step of the way—from concept to cover. Please note that we have specific submissions guidelines we ask all authors to follow. Failure to do so will result in your submissions packet being recycled.

Meriwether Publishing Ltd.

885 Elkton Drive
Colorado Springs, CO 80907

Associate Editor: Arthur L. Zapel

Publisher's Interests

Since its founding in 1967, Meriwether has been publishing "how-to" books for acting students of all ages, professional performers, and acting teachers. It also produces collections of plays, monologues, and children's theater pieces.
Website: www.meriwether.com

Freelance Potential

Published 12 titles (6 juvenile) in 2009: 6 were developed from unsolicited submissions. Of the 12 titles, 1 was by an unpublished writer and 3 were by new authors. Receives 250 queries, 100 unsolicited mss yearly.

- **Fiction:** Publishes middle-grade books, 8–12 years; and young adult books, 12–18 years. Genres include drama, comedy, and musicals; one-act plays; monologues; dialogues; and folktales.
- **Nonfiction:** Publishes middle-grade books, 8–12 years; and young adult books, 12–18 years. Topics include acting, directing, auditioning, improvisation, public speaking, interpersonal communication, debate, mime, clowning, storytelling, costuming, stage lighting, and sound effects.
- **Representative Titles:** *Comedy Scenes for Student Actors* (YA) by Laurie Allen is a collection of 31 real-life, juvenile comedy scenes for kids to perform. *Hey, Girlfriend* (YA) by Kimberly McCormick presents 75 monologues—some funny, some dramatic—that deal with the dilemmas that teenage girls face every day at school, at home, and in society.

Submissions and Payment

Guidelines available at website. Query with outline and sample chapter for books. Send complete ms for plays. Accepts hard copy and simultaneous submissions. SASE. Responds in 4–6 weeks. Publication in 6 months. Royalty. Flat fee.

Editor's Comments

For children's theater, we are interested in plays that can be performed in a classroom setting.

Milkweed Editions

1011 Washington Avenue South, Suite 300
Minneapolis, MN 55415

Editors

Publisher's Interests
Founded in 1979, this nonprofit literary press publishes novels for readers ages 8 through 13. For adults, it features literary fiction and nonfiction about the natural world, and poetry. **Website: www.milkweed.org**

Freelance Potential
Published 16 titles (4 juvenile) in 2009: 4 were developed from unsolicited submissions, 5 were by agented authors, and 6 were reprint/licensed properties. Receives 1,200 queries, 1,200 unsolicited mss yearly.

- **Fiction:** Publishes middle-grade books, 8–13 years. Genres include historical, multicultural, and ethnic fiction; and stories about nature. Also publishes poetry.
- **Representative Titles:** *Border Crossing* by Jessica Lee Anderson (8–13 years) is a novel about a mixed-race young man who struggles with his schizophrenia, his alcoholic mother, and his town's growing anti-immigrant stance. *Floramel and Esteban* by Emilie Buchwald (8–13 years) finds a lonely and curious cow befriending a cattle egret and learning all about the world outside her pasture.

Submissions and Payment
Guidelines available at website. Query with outline, sample chapter, and writing samples; or send complete ms. Accepts hard copy and simultaneous submissions if identified. SASE. Responds to queries in 1 month, to mss in 1–6 months. Publication in 2 years. Royalty, 6% of retail; advance, varies.

Editor's Comments
We are happy to accept unsolicited submissions from authors of all backgrounds, whether they have been previously published or not. In return, we ask that you familiarize yourself with our list so that you do not waste time submitting work that is beyond our publishing scope. Please note we do not publish picture books or children's nonfiction.

Millbrook Press

241 First Avenue North
Minneapolis, MN 55401

Submissions

Publisher's Interests
Millbrook Press, an imprint of Lerner Publishing Group, publishes nonfiction books on science, math, social studies, and language arts subjects. Its books are targeted for classroom and home use by children in preschool through high school.
Website: www.lernerbooks.com

Freelance Potential
Published 60 titles in 2009.

- **Nonfiction:** Publishes concept books and toddler books, 0–4 years; middle-grade books, 8–12 years; and young adult books, 12–18 years. Topics include the arts, sports, social studies, history, math, science, nature, the environment, and crafts. Also publishes biographies.
- **Representative Titles:** *Tsunami: Helping Each Other* by Ann Morris (8–12 years) presents the experiences of a family living in Thailand before, during, and after the tragic tsunami. *Long Ball* by Mark Stewart (10–18 years) is a detailed look at professional baseball's longest, shortest, strangest, and most famous home run hits. *20 Hungry Piggies* by Trudy Harris (grades 2–3) combines a funny story about hungry pigs and mathematics to introduce number concepts; part of the Math Is Fun! series.

Submissions and Payment
Guidelines and catalogue available at website. Accepts targeted submissions only. See website for a list of needs at specific reading levels and in specific subject areas.

Editor's Comments
We are not accepting unsolicited manuscripts or queries at this time. We do, however, accept submissions in response to our calls for material—that is, proposals that match our specific needs at the moment. Please visit our website, which is updated frequently with information about the subject areas for which we are accepting.

Mirrorstone Books

Wizards of the Coast
P.O. Box 707
Renton, WA 98057-0707

Submissions Editor

Publisher's Interests

Mirrorstone publishes only fantasy fiction books for children and teens based on the lore of the Dungeons & Dragons fantasy game, which was created by Mirrorstone's parent company, Wizards of the Coast. Its new books will be part of its existing collection of fantasy fiction series.
Website: www.mirrorstonebooks.com

Freelance Potential

Published 10 titles in 2009: 5 were by agented authors. Of the 10 titles, 1 was by an unpublished writer and 1 was by an author who was new to the publishing house. Receives 360 queries yearly.

- **Fiction:** Publishes story picture books, 4–10 years; chapter books, 5–10 years; middle-grade novels, 8–12 years; and young adult books, 12–18 years. Genres include medieval, mystical, heroic, epic, and light fantasy fiction.
- **Representative Titles:** *Brass Dragon Codex* by R. D. Henham involves a reluctant alliance between a baby brass dragon and a gnome who must protect a secret invention from knights; part of the Dragon Codex series. *Flames in the City* by Candice Ransom finds the Time Spies going back to the War of 1812 to rescue George Washington's portrait before the British burn Washington, DC, to the ground; part of the Time Spies series.

Submissions and Payment

Guidelines and catalogue available at website. Send writing samples for assignment consideration. Accepts hard copy. SASE. Responds in 4 months. Publication in 1 year. Payment policy varies.

Editor's Comments

Though we no longer consider series proposals or stand-alone manuscripts, we are always looking for talented freelancers who are willing to write our series on a work-for-hire basis. Send writing samples if you wish to be considered.

Mitchell Lane Publishers

P.O. Box 196
Hockessin, DE 19707

President: Barbara Mitchell

Publisher's Interests

Mitchell Lane specializes in children's and young adult non-fiction titles that appeal to even the most reluctant readers. Its catalogue includes everything from biographies of Allen Iverson, Shirley Temple, and Nancy Pelosi to profiles in Greek mythology and American history, to book series on gardening and the environment.
Website: www.mitchelllane.com

Freelance Potential

Published 85 titles in 2009. Of the 85 titles, 1 was by an unpublished writer and 3 were by authors who were new to the publishing house. Receives 300 queries yearly.

- **Nonfiction:** Publishes chapter books, 5–10 years; middle-grade books, 8–12 years; and young adult books, 12–18 years. Topics include animals, natural disasters, biography, sports, mythology, art, history, poets, playwrights, science, music, health and fitness, and multicultural topics.
- **Representative Titles:** *Amelia Earhart* by Amie Jane Leavitt (grades 2–3) offers an easy-to-read narrative about the life of Amelia Earhart; part of the What's So Great About . . . ? series. *Polar Bears on the Hudson Bay* by Dan Leathers (grades 1–4) explains why polar bears are at risk and what scientists are doing about it; part of the On the Verge of Extinction series.

Submissions and Payment

Guidelines and catalogue available at website. Work-for-hire only. Query with unedited writing sample, résumé, and publishing credits. Flat fee.

Editor's Comments

All of our publications fit into a series format. Because we operate on a work-for-hire basis, we will not respond unless we have a suitable assignment for you. Please note that we are interested in seeing nonfiction writing samples only.

Mondo Publishing

980 Avenue of the Americas
New York, NY 10018

Editorial Director

Publisher's Interests

Mondo Publishing is interested in books, both fiction and nonfiction, that increase literacy and comprehension while instilling in students a love of reading. It publishes high-quality, research-based literary materials, and offers professional development for literacy teachers. Its offerings target readers in kindergarten through grade five.
Website: www.mondopub.com

Freelance Potential

Published 30 titles in 2009.

- **Fiction:** Publishes easy-to-read books, 4–7 years; story picture books, 4–10 years; chapter books, 5–10 years; and middle-grade books, 8–12 years. Genres include contemporary, historical, and science fiction; fantasy; mystery; folktales; adventure; and humor.
- **Nonfiction:** Publishes early picture books, 0–4 years; story picture books, 4–10 years; and young adult books, 12–18 years. Topics include science, nature, animals, the environment, language arts, history, music, crafts, and hobbies.
- **Representative Titles:** *A Lion for Michael* by Uri Orlev (5–9 years) follows a young boy's adventures with a ferocious lion that has jumped off his T-shirt. *Blueberry Mouse* by Alice Low (3–7 years) is a humorous tale of a mouse who lives in blueberry pie, and nibbles away at it until it starts to collapse.

Submissions and Payment

Query. Accepts hard copy. SASE. Response time varies. Publication in 1–3 years. Royalty.

Editor's Comments

Our books for children are designed to help readers along the path of literacy. They should be research-based literacy tools, intended to be used as classroom aids. Many of our books are in series form, and we accept proposals for additions to those series.

Moose Enterprise

684 Walls Road
Sault Ste. Marie, Ontario P6A 5K6
Canada

Owner/Publisher: Richard Mousseau

Publisher's Interests
This small publisher produces children's and young adult novels, short stories, and nonfiction in a range of genres and topics. It also publishes titles for adults. 1% self-, subsidy-, co-venture, or co-op published material.
Website: www.moosehidebooks.com

Freelance Potential
Published 7 titles (5 juvenile) in 2009: each was developed from an unsolicited submission. Of the 7 titles, 2 were by unpublished writers and 4 were by authors who were new to the publishing house. Receives 600 queries yearly.

- **Fiction:** Publishes story picture books, 4–10 years; chapter books, 5–10 years; middle-grade books, 8–12 years; and young adult books, 12–18 years. Genres include adventure, drama, fantasy, historical and science fiction, humor, horror, mystery, suspense, and Westerns.
- **Nonfiction:** Publishes middle-grade books, 8–12 years; and young adult books, 12–18 years. Topics include local, Canadian, and military history. Also publishes biographies.
- **Representative Titles:** *An Oak Rocking Chair* by Richard E. Mousseau (5–12 years) tells a loving story of the endurance and longevity of a family and the oak rocking chair that has been passed down through generations. *Memories of Korah Township in History 1776–1964* by Clint Moore (10+ years) tells the history one Sault Ste. Marie township.

Submissions and Payment
Guidelines and catalogue available at website. Query with 2–3 sample chapters, brief author bio, and publishing credits. Accepts hard copy. SAE/IRC. Responds in 1 month. Publication in 1 year. Royalty, 10–30%.

Editor's Comments
We specialize in working with both emerging and experienced authors to bring their works to their full potential.

Morgan Reynolds

620 South Elm Street, Suite 387
Greensboro, NC 27406

Submissions: Sharon F. Doorasamy

Publisher's Interests

For more than 15 years, Morgan Reynolds has been publishing high-quality nonfiction for its young adult readership. The titles in its catalogue focus on historical figures and the major events from the worlds of literature, sports, science, the arts, and social studies.
Website: www.morganreynolds.com

Freelance Potential

Published 50 titles in 2009: 3 were developed from unsolicited submissions. Of the 50 titles, 3 were by authors who were new to the publishing house. Receives 180 queries, 60 unsolicited mss yearly.

- **Nonfiction:** Publishes young adult books, 12–18 years. Topics include history, music, science, business, feminism, and world events. Also publishes biographies of notable figures in those subject areas.
- **Representative Titles:** *Reggae Poet: The Story of Bob Marley* by Calvin Craig Miller (YA) is the life story of reggae master Bob Marley; part of the Modern Music Masters series. *The Firing on Fort Sumpter: A Splintered Nation Goes to War* by Nancy Colbert (YA) presents the story of the opening battle of the U.S. Civil War.

Submissions and Payment

Guidelines and catalogue available at website. Published authors, query with outline and sample chapter; unpublished authors, send complete ms. Accepts hard copy and simultaneous submissions if identified. SASE. Responds to queries in 1 month, to mss in 1–3 months. Publication in 12–18 months. Payment policy varies.

Editor's Comments

We like to bring history alive for our readers and help them understand the people who had an impact on the world. We like books with lively, but factual, text.

Mott Media

1130 Fenway Circle
Fenton, MI 48430

Editorial Contact: Joyce Bohn

Publisher's Interests

Christian parents who homeschool their children are the target audience for the books from Mott Media. It publishes "classic" curriculum materials that feature yesterday's values for today's child, as well as books that support the homeschooling parent.
Website: www.mottmedia.com

Freelance Potential

Published 10 titles in 2009. Of the 10 titles, each was by an author new to the publishing house. Receives 3 queries yearly.

- **Fiction:** Publishes chapter books, 5–10 years; middle-grade books, 8–12 years; and young adult books, 12–18 years. Genres include contemporary and historical fiction, adventure, and mystery.
- **Nonfiction:** Publishes chapter books, 5–10 years; middle-grade books, 8–12 years; and young adult books, 12–18 years. Topics include animals, history, humor, language arts, grammar, spelling, phonics, religion, and biography. Also publishes books for adults.
- **Representative Titles:** *The Cabin and the Ice Palace* by Ruth Beechick (grades 5–12) provides a subtle message of creation and heaven through the story of children enjoying life in a sub-arctic paradise. *Navigating Through Homeschooling Waters* by Lori Coeman (parents) gives parents the information they need to chart their homeschooling course.

Submissions and Payment

Catalogue available at website. Query with outline and sample chapter; or send complete ms. Accepts hard copy and simultaneous submissions. SASE. Responds in 1–2 months. Publication in 6 months. Royalty; advance. Flat fee.

Editor's Comments

We look for books that have not been stripped of Christian values and biblical principles.

Mountain Press Publishing Company

P.O. Box 2399
Missoula, MT 59806-2399

Editor: Beth Parker

Publisher's Interests
Mountain Press seeks to engage its young readers in the world around them through nonfiction titles on geology, natural history, earth science, and Western U.S. history. Its catalog includes field guides to plants, birds, and other wildlife.
Website: www.mountain-press.com

Freelance Potential
Published 12 titles (5 juvenile) in 2009: 9 were developed from unsolicited submissions. Receives 120 queries yearly.

- **Nonfiction:** Publishes easy-to-read books, 4–7 years; story picture books, 4–10 years; chapter books, 5–10 years; middle-grade books, 8–12 years; and young adult books, 12–18 years. Topics include natural history, geology, earth science, and Western U.S. history.
- **Representative Titles:** *You Can Be a Nature Detective* by Peggy Kochanoff (5+ years) teaches children how to solve such mysteries as which animal left tracks in the snow, and which butterfly a caterpillar will turn into. *I'm a Medicine Woman Too!* by Jesse Wolf Hardin (3–12 years) provides a lesson in herbs and healing, as well as compassion.

Submissions and Payment
Guidelines available at website. Query with table of contents, bibliography, and 2 sample chapters. Accepts hard copy. SASE. Responds in 2 months. Publication in 1–2 years. Royalty.

Editor's Comments
We accept only well-written, responsibly researched manuscripts. Your book must be both informative and engaging to the reader, written in lively, lucid prose. The topic must have broad, long-term appeal. The sources you rely on must be thoroughly documented and not infringe on any existing copyrights. You are responsible for supplying all photographs, maps, and other graphics.

Napoleon & Company

178 Willowdale Avenue, Suite 201
Toronto, Ontario M2N 4Y8
Canada

Submissions Editor: Allister Thompson

Publisher's Interests

All of the books published by Napoleon & Company are written by authors based in Canada, and they feature Canadian themes. Its catalogue includes fiction, biographies, and educational resources for young adults.
Website: www.napoleonandcompany.com

Freelance Potential

Published 14 titles (5 juvenile) in 2009: 6 were developed from unsolicited submissions and 7 were by agented authors. Of the 14 titles, 3 were by unpublished writers and 7 were by authors who were new to the publishing house. Receives 240 queries, 120 unsolicited mss yearly.

- **Fiction:** Publishes chapter books, 5–10 years; middle-grade books, 8–12 years; and young adult novels, 12–18 years. Genres include adventure, drama, humor, mystery, and historical and contemporary fiction.
- **Nonfiction:** Publishes young adult books, 12–18 years. Features biographies and educational resources.
- **Representative Titles:** *Trail of Secrets* by Brenda Chapman (12–18 years) follows Jennifer through her senior year in high school as she deals with a new move, a long distance relationship, and her best friend's secrets; part of the Jennifer Bannon Mystery series. *The Gargoyle in My Yard* by Phillippa Dowding (9–12 years) tells a humorous tale of the havoc caused by a 400-year-old gargoyle and how the family tries to get rid of it.

Submissions and Payment

Canadian authors only. Guidelines available at website. Query or send complete ms. Accepts hard copy. SASE. Responds in 1 year. Publication in 2 years. Royalty; advance.

Editor's Comments

Please note that we're not accepting picture books at this time, and that our authors must be based in Canada.

National Council of Teachers of English

The Books Program
1111 West Kenyon Road
Urbana, IL 61801-1096

Senior Editor: Bonny Graham

Publisher's Interests
Books that help language arts and English teachers—from elementary school through college—teach more effectively and develop their careers are the focus of this publisher.
Website: www.ncte.org

Freelance Potential
Published 11 titles in 2009: Of the 11 titles, 2 were by unpublished writers and 8 were by authors who were new to the publishing house. Receives 50 queries yearly.

- **Nonfiction:** Publishes books for English and language arts teachers. Topics include reading, writing, grammar, literature, poetry, rhetoric, censorship, media studies, technology, research, classroom practices, student assessment, and professional issues.
- **Representative Titles:** *Wondrous Words* by Katie Wood Ray explains the theoretical basis of how young students learn to write from their reading. *Talking in Class* by Thomas M. McCann et al. explains how to develop skills that promote authentic discussion in the English language arts classroom.

Submissions and Payment
Guidelines available at website. Query with cover letter, project rationale, table of contents, chapter summaries, 2–3 sample chapters, bibliography, and résumé. Accepts queries through www.editorialmanager.com/nctebp/. Response time varies. Publication in 18 months. Royalty.

Editor's Comments
We consider our writers to be a community of professionals who have served and shaped the profession through our research, teaching, and scholarship. We seek proposals that represent the rich diversity of the profession, provide practical solutions, and offer effective teaching methods. In your query, please tell us the current status of your manuscript.

National Geographic Society

Children's Books
1145 17th Street NW
Washington, DC 20036-4688

Associate Editor: Priyanka Lamichhane

Publisher's Interests
As one would expect from the literary arm of the National Geographic Society, this publisher produces nonfiction books that introduce children ages 4 to 18 to the wonders of nature, fascinating historical events, and interesting people around the globe.
Website: www.nationalgeographic.com/books

Freelance Potential
Published 91 titles in 2009: 89 were by agented authors and 2 were reprint/licensed properties. Of the 91 titles, 3 were by authors who were new to the publishing house. Receives 240 queries yearly.

- **Nonfiction:** Publishes easy-to-read books, 4–7 years; story picture books, 4–10 years; chapter books, 5–10 years; middle-grade books, 8–12 years; and young adult books, 12–18 years. Topics include life, earth, and general science; American and world cultures and history; animals; multicultural issues; and geography. Also publishes biographies.
- **Representative Titles:** *What Did One Elephant Say to the Other?* by Becky Baines (5–8 years) teaches readers about elephants, habitats, and communication. *Muckrakers* by Ann Bausum (10+ years) follows a generation of dedicated journalists who forced responsible changes in industry and politics at the beginning of the twentieth century.

Submissions and Payment
Query with outline and sample chapter. No unsolicited mss. Accepts hard copy. SASE. Responds in 3–4 months. Publication period varies. Flat fee.

Editor's Comments
Our biggest need right now is for books serving ages 7 through 14. We're looking for science, social studies, and history books; atlases; picture books; memoirs; biographies; and reference books.

Naturegraph Publishers

P.O. Box 1047
Happy Camp, CA 96039

Owner: Barbara Brown

Publisher's Interests
Naturegraph strives to publish books on nature and Native American history that increase the reader's understanding and appreciation for these topics. 5% self-, subsidy-, co-venture, or co-op published material.
Website: www.naturegraph.com

Freelance Potential
Published 2 titles in 2009: each was developed from an unsolicited submission. Of the 2 titles, 1 was by an unpublished writer. Receives 360 queries yearly.

- **Fiction:** Publishes middle-grade books, 8–12 years; and young adult books, 12–18 years. Features books that pertain to Native American folklore.
- **Nonfiction:** Publishes middle-grade books, 8–12 years; and young adult books, 12–18 years. Topics include Native American wildlife, birds, the environment, crafts, hiking, backpacking, outdoor skills, rocks and minerals, marine life, and natural history.
- **Representative Titles:** *Animals of the Western Rangelands* by Ernest Elms provides intimate portrayals of the day-to-day lives of eagles, owls, jackrabbits, wolves, and wild horses, and their struggles to survive and thrive. *The Hoop of Peace* by Jan Havnen-Finley (YA) tells about the Lakota hoop dance and Kevin Locke, one of the few modern hoop dancers who travels around the world to spread his peace message.

Submissions and Payment
Guidelines available at website. Query with outline and 1–2 sample chapters. Accepts hard copy and email queries to nature@sisqtel.net. SASE. Response time and publication period vary. Royalty.

Editor's Comments
We do not accept poetry or books for very young children. Contact us only if your writing fits our publishing niches.

Neal-Schuman Publishers

100 William Street, Suite 2004
New York, NY 10038

Director of Publishing: Charles T. Harmon

Publisher's Interests
This company prides itself on producing authoritative books that help school librarians develop curriculum, promote literacy, and teach information science.
Website: www.neal-schuman.com

Freelance Potential
Published 36 titles in 2009: 10 were developed from unsolicited submissions. Of the 36 titles, 26 were by unpublished writers and 31 were by authors who were new to the publishing house. Receives 300 queries yearly.

- **Nonfiction:** Publishes resource materials for school media specialists and librarians. Topics include curriculum support, the Internet, technology, literacy skills, reading programs, collection development, reference needs, staff development, management, and communications.
- **Representative Titles:** *Baby Rhyming Time* by Linda L. Ernst is full of activities that stimulate infants' and toddlers' cognitive, physical, and emotional growth. *Libraries Designed for Kids* by Nolan Lushington tells how to create special places in the library that promote and encourage curiosity, learning, and reading.

Submissions and Payment
Guidelines and catalogue available at website. Query with résumé, outline, and sample chapter. Prefers email queries to charles@neal-schuman.com; will accept hard copy. SASE. Responds in 2 weeks. Publication in 10–12 months. Royalty.

Editor's Comments
Some successful proposals run to all of ten pages or so; others are much longer. We prefer to receive an entire sample chapter, but six to ten sample pages usually suffice. These should be representative of the book's theme (sample introductions are not as helpful as samples drawn from the proposal's body).

New Canaan Publishing Company

P.O. Box 752
New Canaan, CT 06840

Editor

Publisher's Interests

The focus of this independent publishing house is to produce books that bolster traditional values. In addition to its
fiction and nonfiction children's books, it also publishes
humor and books with Christian themes for adults.
Website: www.newcanaanpublishing.com

Freelance Potential

Published 3 titles in 2009. Of the 3 titles, 2 were by unpublished writers and each was by an author new to the publishing house. Receives 750 queries and unsolicited mss yearly.

- **Fiction:** Publishes chapter books, 5–10 years; middle-grade
  books, 8–12 years; and young adult books, 12–18 years. Genres include historical fiction. Also publishes stories with strong
  moral and Christian themes.
- **Nonfiction:** Publishes chapter books, 5–10 years; middle-
  grade books, 8–12 years; and young adult books, 12–18
  years. Topics include teen and pre-teen issues, Christianity,
  and life in a military family. Also publishes devotionals.
- **Representative Titles:** *Levi Dust* by Steven J. Givens (8–11
  years) is a tale of historical adventure as young twins embark on
  a journey in nineteenth-century St. Louis. *The Drummer Boy* by
  Sharron Hilbrecht (9+ years) tells the story of Col. George
  Rogers Clark and some of the bravest battles of the Revolutionary War, told through the eyes of Clark's young drummer.

Submissions and Payment

Guidelines and catalogue available at website. Query with
résumé, synopsis, 2 sample chapters, and market analysis;
or send complete ms. Accepts hard copy. SASE. Responds in
10–12 months. Publication period and payment policy vary.

Editor's Comments

We now accept only the following types of submissions:
books for children of military families; books for ages 8
through 18 that have Christian themes; and historical fiction.

New Harbinger Publications

5674 Shattuck Avenue
Oakland, CA 94609

Acquisitions Manager: Tesilya Hanauer

Publisher's Interests

New Harbinger publishes scientifically sound self-help books
that deal with a range of topics in psychology, health, and
personal growth. It publishes titles on parenting, childcare,
family relationships, and alternative families. It also publishes
books for professionals in the psychology field.
Website: www.newharbinger.com

Freelance Potential

Published 50 titles (7 juvenile) in 2009: 30 were developed
from unsolicited submissions, 20 were by agented authors,
and 5 were reprint/licensed properties. Of the 50 titles, 38
were by unpublished writers and 30 were by authors who were
new to the publishing house. Receives 600 queries yearly.

- **Nonfiction:** Publishes therapeutic workbooks for children and
  young adults. Topics include communication, divorce, adoption, pregnancy, ADHD, autism, sensory processing disorder,
  depression, social anxiety, eating disorders, self-injury, and
  self-control. Also publishes parenting titles.
- **Representative Titles:** *The Relaxation and Stress Reduction
  Workbook for Kids* by Lawrence E. Shapiro & Robin K.
  Sprague is for psychology professionals to use with their
  clients who are going through stressful situations. *It's Time to
  Sit Still in Your Own Chair* by Lawrence E. Shapiro introduces
  a new game parents can use to help little ones learn to sit still
  anytime, anywhere.

Submissions and Payment

Guidelines and catalogue available at website. Query with
table of contents and 1–3 chapters. Accepts hard copy and
email to proposals@newharbinger.com. SASE. Responds in
4–6 weeks. Publication in 1 year. Royalty; advance. Flat fee.

Editor's Comments

We have outlined four editorial principles that all books
should follow. You will find them posted at our website.

New Hope Publishers

P.O. Box 12065
Birmingham, AL 35201-2065

Manuscript Submissions

Publisher's Interests

New Hope has established itself as a publisher of titles that are relevant to the current issues of Christian living. It focuses its efforts on Christ-centered children's books; books about faith-building; Bible studies and religious education resources; and books on the many topics of interest to women and families.
Website: www.newhopepublishers.com

Freelance Potential

Published 26 titles in 2009: 13 were by agented authors.

- **Fiction:** Publishes story picture books, 4–10 years; chapter books, 5–10 years; middle-grade books, 8–12 years; and young adult books, 12–18 years. Genres include inspirational fiction.
- **Nonfiction:** Publishes inspirational and spiritual books for men, women, families, and religious education teachers. Topics include spiritual growth, women's issues, parenting, prayer, relationships, mission life, Christian living, and Bible study.
- **Representative Titles:** *Baby Boot Camp* by Rebecca Ingram Powell presents 42 daily devotionals that help steer new moms through the first six weeks of motherhood. *Families on a Mission* by Angie Quantrell offers creative projects that help parents involve their preschoolers in ministry activities designed for little hands.

Submissions and Payment

Catalogue available at website. No unsolicited submissions. Post proposal at christianmanuscriptsubmissions.com. Response time and publication period vary. Royalty. Flat fee.

Editor's Comments

Don't send us your manuscript or query—we do not accept unsolicited submissions. If you have an idea for a book that might fit well with our list, please post it through the Christian manuscript submission service and we will review it.

New Horizon Press

34 Church Street
Liberty Corner, NJ 07938

Submissions: JoAnne Thomas

Publisher's Interests
"Gripping, emotionally driven books about real people caught in extraordinary circumstances" best describes the adult nonfiction published by New Horizon Press. Topics covered include true crime, social issues, and self-help. This publisher does not offer fiction, poetry, plays, memoirs, or biographies.
Website: www.newhorizonpressbooks.com

Freelance Potential
Published 16 titles in 2009: 5 were developed from unsolicited submissions and 11 were by agented authors. Receives 720 queries yearly.

- **Nonfiction:** Publishes titles for adults. Topics include crime and justice, medical drama, women's rights, health, the environment, self-help, and recovery.
- **Representative Titles:** *When the Fairy Tale Fails* by Susan Indenbaum debunks the "happily ever after" myth and helps women of all ages seek fulfillment and create complete satisfaction in their lives. *Thrill Killers* by Raymond Pingitore & Paul Lonardo is a true crime story of the senseless murder of an innocent couple and the detectives who fought to bring the killers to justice.

Submissions and Payment
Guidelines and catalogue available at website. Query with résumé, outline, and 2 sample chapters. Accepts hard copy and email to jct@newhorizonpressbooks.com. SASE. Response time varies. Publication period and payment policy vary.

Editor's Comments
True crime with an underlying social issue and a hero fighting back is one of our specialties. We also seek proposals that cover hard-hitting issues with news impact. Please note that we are willing to work with first-time authors.

New Leaf Press

P.O. Box 726
Green Forest, AR 72638

Assistant Editor: Craig Froman

Publisher's Interests
The children's books published by New Leaf Press, targeting ages 4 through 18, teach Bible lessons or invoke Christian values. The company publishes nonfiction titles that answer kids' tough questions about life and God, reinforce Christian values, and tackle the issue of creationism for all ages.
Website: www.nlpg.com

Freelance Potential
Published 20–25 titles (10–15 juvenile) in 2009. Of the 20–25 titles, 4 were by unpublished writers and 10 were by authors who were new to the publishing house. Receives 1,200 queries yearly.

- **Nonfiction:** Publishes easy-to-read books, 4–7 years; story picture books, 4–10 years; and young adult books, 12–18 years. Topics include the Bible, Christian living, history, current events, and social issues.
- **Representative Titles:** *101 Favorite Bible Stories* by Ura Miller presents timeless stories from the Bible, retold in a way that brings them alive for young readers. *Nine Things Teens Should Know & Parents Are Afraid to Talk About* by Joe White & Nicholas Comninellis (YA) provides a handbook for dealing with the issues of adolescence.

Submissions and Payment
Guidelines and catalogue available at website. Query with table of contents, synopsis, sample chapter, and proposal form from website. Accepts hard copy and simultaneous submissions if identified. SASE. Responds in 3 months. Publication in 12–18 months. Royalty, 10% of net.

Editor's Comments
Please keep in mind that we do not publish fiction, personal stories, or poetry. We are interested in books for the home-school market that help young readers understand the Bible and learn to live Christian lives.

New Society Publishers

P.O. Box 189
Gabriola Island, British Columbia V0R 1X0
Canada

Editor: Ingrid Witvoet

Publisher's Interests
This progressive publishing company specializes in books for activists—specifically, books that contribute to building an ecologically sustainable and just society. It also publishes books on parenting and education.
Website: www.newsociety.com

Freelance Potential
Published 30 titles in 2009. Of the 30 titles, 18 were by unpublished writers and 22 were by authors who were new to the publishing house. Receives 300 queries yearly.

* **Nonfiction:** Publishes young adult books, 12–18 years. Topics include education, the environment, conflict resolution, social responsibility, and democratic behavior in young people. Also publishes parenting titles.
* **Representative Titles:** *The Green Teen* by Jenn Savedge (YA) combines eco-friendly tips, interviews with "green teens," and ideas for organizing and communicating environmental change. *Parenting for a Peaceful World* by Robin Grille (parents) looks at how child-rearing customs have shaped societies, and explains how safeguarding children's emotional development is the key to creating a more peaceful, harmonious, and sustainable world.

Submissions and Payment
Guidelines and catalogue available at website. Query with résumé, synopsis, table of contents, and sample chapter. Accepts hard copy. SAE/IRC. Responds in 2–3 months. Publication in 1 year. Payment policy varies.

Editor's Comments
We look for solutions-oriented material that allows readers to participate in creating a sustainable economy and environment. We do not publish books that merely catalogue what is wrong in the world; we publish books that show that we can take control of our lives and change the way things are.

Nimbus Publishing

3731 Mackintosh Street
P.O. Box 9166
Halifax, Nova Scotia B3K 5A5
Canada

Senior Editor: Patrick Murphy

Publisher's Interests

Children's books that focus on Atlantic Canada are the specialty of Nimbus Publishing.
Website: www.nimbus.ns.ca

Freelance Potential

Published 36 titles (13 juvenile) in 2009: 10 were developed from unsolicited submissions and 1 was by an agented author. Of the 36 titles, 10 were by unpublished writers and 15 were by authors who were new to the publishing house. Receives 300 queries yearly.

- **Fiction:** Publishes story picture books, 4–10 years; chapter books, 5–10 years; middle-grade books, 8–10 years; and young adult books, 12–18 years. Genres include adventure; folklore; and regional, historical, and multicultural fiction.
- **Nonfiction:** Publishes toddler books, 0–4 years; easy-to-read books, 4–7 years; story picture books, 4–10 years; and middle-grade books, 8–12 years. Topics include Atlantic Canada's geography, history, and environment.
- **Representative Titles:** *Acadian Star* by Helene Boudreau (8–12 years) offers a young girl's perspective on the Acadian Deportation. *The Terrible, Horrible, Smelly Pirate* by Carrie Muller & Jacqueline Halsey (3–6 years) follows the adventures of Pirate Sydney and his parrot Polly around Halifax Harbour.

Submissions and Payment

Guidelines available at website. Query with synopsis, author bio, detailed table of contents, and sample chapter. Accepts hard copy and simultaneous submissions if identified. Material is not returned. Responds if interested. Publication in 1–2 years. Royalty; advance. Flat fee.

Editor's Comments

Currently, we're not accepting unsolicited nonfiction manuscripts. Send queries only. All material must reflect or speak to Atlantic Canada's people, places, history, or culture.

NL Associates

P.O. Box 1199
Hightstown, NJ 08520

President: Nathan Levy

Publisher's Interests
The "NL" is for "Nathan Levy," whose *Stories with Holes* collection serves as the cornerstone of this publishing house. Its catalogue is full of various activity books for use at home and at school, all meant to stimulate critical thinking in children while making learning fun.
Website: www.storieswithholes.com

Freelance Potential
Published 1 title in 2009. Receives 20 queries, 50 unsolicited mss yearly.

- **Nonfiction:** Publishes educational materials and activity books for grades K–12. Topics include reading, writing, creativity, social studies, math, science, and critical thinking. Also publishes books about classroom management and special education for teachers.
- **Representative Titles:** *101 Things Everyone Should Know About Science* by Dia L. Michels & Nathan Levy (7+ years) uses a Q&A format to cover key concepts in biology, chemistry, physics, earth science, and general science. *Write, From the Beginning* by Amy Burke & Nathan Levy (grades K–6) provides more than 100 activities to stimulate written expression. *More Ready-to-Tell Tales from Around the World* by David Holt & Bill Mooney (grades 3–12) offers not just stories, but performance tips and cultural background as well.

Submissions and Payment
Query or send complete ms. Accepts hard copy. SASE. Response time, publication period, and payment policy vary.

Editor's Comments
We publish books for people who like to stretch their minds, or to help others do the same. Our goal is to keep children intellectually challenged in both the classroom and the home. Therefore, we welcome submissions in all subject areas and for all ages.

North Country Books

220 Lafayette Street
Utica, NY 13502

Publisher: Rob Igoe, Jr.

Publisher's Interests
This publisher is interested in books about New York State, specifically the region's history, wildlife, folklore, and people. Its children's catalogue includes both fiction and nonfiction that educate young readers about the region.
Website: www.northcountrybooks.com

Freelance Potential
Published 8 titles (2 juvenile) in 2009: 3 were developed from unsolicited submissions and 1 was by an agented author. Of the 8 titles, 2 were by unpublished writers and 4 were by new authors. Receives 36 unsolicited mss yearly.

- **Fiction:** Publishes early picture books, 0–4 years; story picture books, 4–10 years; and chapter books, 5–10 years. Themes include the folklore, history, and wildlife of New York State.
- **Nonfiction:** Publishes early picture books, 0–4 years; easy-to-read books, 4–7 years; and middle-grade books, 8–12 years. Topics include New York history, ecology, geology, cuisine, travel, recreation, art, and Native American culture. Also publishes biographies and books for adults.
- **Representative Titles:** *Adirondack ABC's* by Joyce Burgess Snavlin helps young children learn the alphabet while gaining an appreciation for the wild side of the Adirondacks. *Erie Canal Cousins* by Dorothy Stacy follows a family as they travel from Albany to Utica on the Erie Canal.

Submissions and Payment
Guidelines and catalogue available at website or via email to ncbooks@verizon.net. Send complete ms with synopsis, table of contents, and market analysis. Accepts hard copy. SASE. Responds in 1–2 months. Publication in 2–5 years. Royalty.

Editor's Comments
Please note that we are not interested in poetry collections or books about other areas of the country.

North-South Books

350 Seventh Avenue, Suite 1400
New York, NY 10001

Submissions Editor

Publisher's Interests
Creating books that enthrall, entertain, and sometimes even educate children is the focus of this publisher, the English-language imprint of the Swiss publisher NordSüd. It publishes titles for children ages 10 and under on a variety of subjects and in many genres.
Website: www.northsouth.com

Freelance Potential
Published 40 titles in 2009: each was by an agented author.

- **Fiction:** Publishes concept books, toddler books, and early picture books, 0–4 years; easy-to-read books, 4–7 years; story picture books, 4–10 years; and chapter books, 5–10 years. Genres include multicultural and contemporary fiction, adventure, drama, fairy tales, folklore, fantasy, humor, and stories about nature and the environment. Also publishes board books and novelty books.
- **Nonfiction:** Publishes early picture books, 0–4 years. Topics include animals, hobbies, crafts, humor, nature, religion, science, technology, social issues, sports, and multicultural and ethnic issues.
- **Representative Titles:** *I Have a Little Problem, Said the Bear* by Heinz Janisch (3–8 years) is the story a bear with a problem and lots of people offering suggestions without listening to what the problem actually is. *Little Polar Bear Finds a Friend* by Hans de Beer (1–4 years) is the story of a little bear bound for the zoo who finds a friend in a very unlikely place.

Submissions and Payment
Agented authors only. Publication period and payment policy vary.

Editor's Comments
You must have your agent represent your book for you. Our motto has always been "quality, not quantity." We are proud of our reputation for bringing our readers authors from various countries and cultures.

O Books

The Bothy, Deershot Lodge
Park Lane, Ropley
Hampshire SO24 0BE
United Kingdom

Editor: John Hunt

Publisher's Interests

O Books embraces all spiritual topics, from Christianity and astrology to goddess worship and mysticism. It publishes fiction and nonfiction on spirituality, philosophy, psychology, self-help, and women's studies.
Website: www.o-books.net

Freelance Potential

Published 100 titles (5 juvenile) in 2009: 50 were developed from unsolicited submissions and 20 were by agented authors. Of the 100 titles, 40 were by unpublished writers and 60 were by new authors. Receives 6,000 queries yearly.

- **Fiction:** Publishes easy-to-read books, 4–7 years; story picture books, 4–10 years; chapter books, 5–10 years; middle-grade books, 8–12 years; and young adult books, 12–18 years. Also publishes books for adults. Genres include religious and spiritual fiction.
- **Nonfiction:** Publishes story picture books, 4–10 years; chapter books, 5–10 years; middle-grade books, 8–12 years; and young adult books, 12–18 years. Also publishes books for adults. Topics include spirituality, religion, meditation, prayer, and astrology.
- **Representative Titles:** *Baby Star Signs* by Chrissie Blaze provides parents with an astrological guide to better understanding their children. *Q is for Question* by Tiffany Poirier uses playful verse to guide children to discover their own beliefs.

Submissions and Payment

Guidelines and catalogue available at website. Query with sample chapters. Accepts email queries to john.hunt@ o-books.net (Microsoft Word attachments). Response time varies. Publication in 18 months. Royalty. Flat fee.

Editor's Comments

Approximately half of our new authors are coming from North America.

OnStage Publishing

190 Lime Quarry Road, Suite 106J
Madison, AL 35758

Senior Editor: Dianne Hamilton

Publisher's Interests
Chapter books, middle-grade novels, and young adult titles
are the focus of this small publishing company. Topics
include drama, fantasy, mystery, history, and science fiction.
Website: www.onstagepublishing.com

Freelance Potential
Published 2 titles in 2009: both were developed from unsolicited submissions. Receives 500 queries, 2,000 unsolicited
mss yearly.

- **Fiction:** Publishes chapter books, 5–10 years; middle-grade
  books, 8–12 years; and young adult books, 12–18 years.
  Genres include adventure; drama; fantasy; horror; mystery;
  suspense; and contemporary, historical, humorous, and
  science fiction.
- **Representative Titles:** *The Secret of Crybaby Hollow* by
  Darren J. Butler features a sixth-grade girl who gets caught
  up in a search for a missing friend and a missing shipment of
  Confederate gold in her small Alabama town; part of the
  Abbie, Girl Spy series. *Spies* by Mary Ann Taylor is the story
  of a group of kids who try to outwit German spies during
  World War II.

Submissions and Payment
Guidelines and catalogue available at website. Query with
3 sample chapters and plot summary for mss longer than
100 pages. Send complete ms for shorter works. Accepts
hard copy, email to onstage123@knology.net (no attachments), and simultaneous submissions if identified. SASE for
response only; mss are not returned. Responds in 4–6
months. Publication in 1–2 years. Royalty; advance.

Editor's Comments
Our current book needs include topics that are of interest to
boys, adventure stories, and mysteries. We do not publish
picture books, short stories, or poetry at this time

Ooligan Press

Portland State University
P.O. Box 751
Portland, OR 97207

Acquisitions Committee

Publisher's Interests

As a general trade press, Ooligan seeks to publish works of
literary, cultural, and social value. It is especially interested
in historical fiction for young adults, and gives preference to
Pacific Northwestern topics and authors.
Website: www.ooliganpress.pdx.edu

Freelance Potential

Published 4–5 titles (1–2 juvenile) in 2009: 4 were developed from unsolicited submissions and 1 was by an agented
author. Receives 600 queries and unsolicited mss yearly.

- **Fiction:** Publishes young adult books, 12–18 years. Genres
  include historical and regional fiction. Also publishes collections of poetry.
- **Nonfiction:** Publishes young adult books, 12–18 years. Topics
  include the Pacific Northwest, writing, editing, publishing, and
  book arts. Also publishes translations of foreign works.
- **Representative Titles:** *A Heart for Any Fate* by Linda Crew
  (YA) is a historical novel that follows a family of pioneers on
  their treacherous journey from Missouri to Oregon in 1845.
  Oregon at Work by Tom Fuller & Art Ayre uses personal stories and photos to document typical jobs during three distinct
  eras in Oregon's history.

Submissions and Payment

Guidelines available at website. Query with outline/synopsis
and brief author bio; or send complete ms. Prefers hard
copy; will accept email queries to ooliganacquisitions@
pdx.edu (no attachments). SASE. Responds in 2–3 months.
Publication period varies. Royalty.

Editor's Comments

We are particularly interested in local nonfiction and regional
fiction, as well as new or rediscovered works with a Pacific
Northwest connection. Collections of poetry from local poets
are especially valuable to us.

Orca Book Publishers

P.O. Box 5626, Station B
Victoria, British Columbia V8R 6S4
Canada

Publisher: Andrew Wooldridge

Publisher's Interests
This publisher is interested in high-quality fiction from Canadian authors. It accepts everything from picture books to teen novels. It also publishes a small number of nonfiction titles on nature subjects.
Website: www.orcabook.com

Freelance Potential
Published 60 titles in 2009: 30 were developed from unsolicited submissions, 30 were by agented authors, and 1 was a reprint/licensed property. Of the 60 titles, 12 were by unpublished writers and 35 were by new authors. Receives 2,000 queries, 500 unsolicited mss yearly.

- **Fiction:** Publishes toddler books and early picture books, 0–4 years; easy-to-read books, 4–7 years; story picture books, 4–10 years; chapter books, 5–10 years; middle-grade books, 8–12 years; and young adult books, 12–18 years. Genres include regional, historical, and contemporary fiction; mystery; adventure; and stories about sports.
- **Nonfiction:** Publishes middle-grade books, 8–12 years. Topics include nature and history.
- **Representative Titles:** *Buttercup's Lovely Day* by Carolyn Beck (4–8 years) describes a typical day on the farm. *Tabloidology* by Chris McMahen (9–12 years) finds an unlikely duo trying to liven up the school's boring newspaper.

Submissions and Payment
Canadian authors only. Guidelines and catalogue available at website. Query with 2–3 sample chapters for novels. Send complete ms for picture books. Accepts hard copy. SASE. Responds in 2–3 months. Publication in 18–24 months. Royalty, 10% split; advance.

Editor's Comments
Current needs include graphic novels and nonfiction for middle-grade readers, and contemporary young adult fiction.

Orchard Books

Scholastic Books
557 Broadway
New York, NY 10012-3999

Editorial Assistant: Michael Joosten

Publisher's Interests

Orchard Books' catalogue features a large selection of children's books for all age groups. An imprint of Scholastic, its mission is helping children around the world to read and learn with titles that educate, entertain, and motivate.
Website: www.scholastic.com

Freelance Potential

Published 20 titles in 2009: each was by an agented author. Receives 360–600 queries yearly.

- **Fiction:** Publishes concept books, toddler books, and early picture books, 0–4 years; easy-to-read books, 4–7 years; story picture books, 4–10 years; chapter books, 5–10 years; middle-grade books, 8–12 years; and young adult books, 12–18 years. Genres include historical, contemporary, and multicultural fiction; fairy tales; folktales; fantasy; and humor. Also publishes stories about sports, animals, and nature.
- **Representative Titles:** *Stone Bench in an Empty Park* by Paul B. Janeczko (grades 3–6) is a book of poetry accompanied by black and white images of city living. *Dazzle's New Friend* by Olivia Moss (4+ years) tells how Dazzle the butterfly tries to help a hedgehog in trouble even though his prickly spines could tear her wings; part of the Butterfly Meadow series.

Submissions and Payment

Query. No unsolicited mss. Accepts hard copy. SASE. Responds in 3 months. Publication period varies. Royalty; advance.

Editor's Comments

Our focus in the coming year will be on books for young children, moving away from books for young adults. We receive a large number of queries each year, so think of your query as an opportunity to make an impression and capture our interest. Don't think of it as a form to fill out; a query should be as individual as the book it describes.

Our Sunday Visitor

200 Noll Plaza
Huntington, IN 46750

Acquisitions Editor

Publisher's Interests

Our Sunday Visitor is a Catholic, nonprofit publisher of books, tapes, software, and educational products promoting Catholic history and perspectives. Its juvenile list features books that help children and young adults navigate life as good Catholics. Parenting titles are also offered, as well as books for use in religious education programs.
Website: www.osv.com

Freelance Potential

Published 50 titles (5 juvenile) in 2009. Of the 50 titles, 6 were by authors who were new to the publishing house. Receives 1,300 queries yearly.

- **Nonfiction:** Publishes concept books, 0–4 years; story picture books, 4–10 years; chapter books, 5–10 years; middle-grade books, 8–12 years; and young adult books, 12–18 years. Topics include family issues, parish life, church heritage, and the lives of the saints.
- **Representative Titles:** *Blessings Every Day* (2–5 years) presents daily devotions paired with easy-to-read Bible verses to introduce children to Scripture. *Kelly's Family and Friends* by Joan Ensor Plum & Paul S. Plum is an activity book for use in religious education classrooms designed to reinforce Christian attitudes and the lessons learned throughout the year.

Submissions and Payment

Guidelines and catalogue available at website. Query with résumé and sample chapter. Accepts hard copy and simultaneous submissions if identified. SASE. Responds in 2–3 months. Publication in 1+ years. Royalty; advance. Flat fee.

Editor's Comments

We are particularly interested in books that provide Catholic guidance for families; that serve the parish through religious education topics; and that offer information on preparing children to receive the sacraments.

The Overmountain Press

P.O. Box 1261
Johnson City, TN 37605

Submissions

Publisher's Interests

This publisher specializes in books about the American Appalachian region—its history, its traditions, and its people. For children, it publishes both fiction and nonfiction titles about these regions.
Website: www.overmountainpress.com

Freelance Potential

Published 10 titles (2 juvenile) in 2009. Of the 10 titles, 2 were by authors who were new to the publishing house. Receives 500 queries yearly.

- **Fiction:** Publishes early picture books, 0–4 years; middle-grade books, 8–12 years; and young adult books, 12–18 years. Genres include folklore, folktales, mystery, and regional fiction—all pertaining to the Appalachian region.
- **Nonfiction:** Publishes story picture books, 4–10 years; and chapter books, 5–10 years. Topics include southern Appalachia, regional history, and cultural issues of the region.
- **Representative Titles:** *Appalachian ABCs* by Francie Hall features each letter of the alphabet representing life along the Appalachian Trail. *Appalachian Scrapbook* by Pauline Cheek presents information about the culture and heritage of the Southern Highlands.

Submissions and Payment

Guidelines and catalogue available at website or with 6x9 SASE ($.85 postage). Query with résumé and sample chapters. Accepts hard copy. SASE. Responds in 3–6 months. Publication in 18 months. Royalty, 15%.

Editor's Comments

Your manuscript must have a strong regional flavor in order to be considered. Unlike most publishers, we prefer to have copies of the illustrations at the time we review your text or proposal. If you need an illustrator, we have a list of artists with whom we have worked.

Richard C. Owen Publishers

P.O. Box 585
Katonah, NY 10536

Director of Children's Books: Richard C. Owen

Publisher's Interests

Richard C. Owens publishes fiction and nonfiction for young learners—books for children ages five to ten who are just beginning to learn to read. It also publishes a number of professional books on literacy education for teachers and administrators.

Website: www.rcowen.com

Freelance Potential

Published 2 titles in 2009. Of the 2 titles, both were by authors who were new to the publishing house. Receives 1,000 unsolicited mss yearly.

- **Fiction:** Publishes story picture books, 4–10 years; easy-to-read books, 5–8 years; and chapter books, 5–10 years. Genres include contemporary fiction, mystery, humor, and folktales. Also publishes stories about animals and nature; and books with social, ethnic, and multicultural themes.
- **Nonfiction:** Publishes story picture books, 4–10 years; and easy-to-read books, 5–8 years. Topics include current events, geography, music, science, nature, and the environment. Also publishes professional books and resources for teachers.
- **Representative Titles:** *Little Panda* (grades K–1) is the story of a hungry little panda that discovers that lots of tasty treats are not always the best things to eat. *Nightwalk* (grades K–1) tells of the many things that a young girl and her mother encounter while walking to the store.

Submissions and Payment

Guidelines available at website. Send complete ms. Accepts hard copy and simultaneous submissions if identified. SASE. Responds in 3–6 months. Publication period and payment policy vary.

Editor's Comments

We produce many of our books in Spanish as well, so we welcome bilingual authors with education experience.

Pacific Educational Press

6365 Biological Sciences Road
Faculty of Education
University of British Columbia
Vancouver, British Columbia V6T 1Z4
Canada

Director: Catherine Edwards

Publisher's Interests
Pacific Education Press publishes teacher education text-books and professional resource books for practicing teachers in all curriculum areas. It also publishes children's fiction for use in middle and high school language arts, social studies, and multicultural programs.
Website: www.pep.educ.ubc.ca

Freelance Potential
Published 4 titles in 2009. Of the 4 titles, 2 were by unpublished writers and 2 were by authors who were new to the publishing house. Receives 60–120 queries yearly.

- **Nonfiction:** Publishes middle-grade books, 8–12 years; and young adult books, 12–18 years. Also publishes books for teachers, grades K–12. Topics include math, language arts, science, social studies, multicultural education, and critical thinking.
- **Representative Titles:** *Teaching to Wonder: Responding to Poetry in the Secondary Classroom* by Carl Leggo provides teaching strategies to engage young readers in the often-intimidating genre of poetry. *The Reluctant Deckhand* by Jan Padgett (8–11 years) is a novel about a girl forced to spend the summer on her family's fishing boat; includes an animated film and teacher's guide.

Submissions and Payment
Guidelines available. Query with résumé, outline, and 2 sample chapters. Accepts hard copy and simultaneous submissions if identified. SAE/IRC. Responds in 4–6 months. Publication in 18–24 months. Royalty, 10% of net.

Editor's Comments
We are interested in all areas of professional education and resource material for teachers, including First Nations education for Canadian teachers. Although we are a Canadian university press we welcome authors from any country, as long as they have something to offer educators.

Pacific Press Publishing Association

P.O. Box 5353
Nampa, ID 83653

Acquisitions Editor: Tim Lale

Publisher's Interests

As the publishing house of the Seventh-day Adventist Church, Pacific Press provides Bible-based books, historical books, and picture books for children that encourage a strong and healthy relationship with God.
Website: www.pacificpress.com

Freelance Potential

Published 30 titles (20 juvenile) in 2009: 1 was developed from an unsolicited submission. Of the 30 titles, 1 was by an author who was new to the publishing house. Receives 60 queries yearly.

- **Fiction:** Publishes early picture books, 0–4 years; easy-to-read books, 4–7 years; story picture books, 4–10 years; chapter books, 5–10 years; and middle-grade books, 8–12 years. Genres include adventure, mystery, and suspense—all with Christian themes.
- **Nonfiction:** Publishes easy-to-read books, 4–7 years; chapter books, 5–10 years; and middle-grade books, 8–12 years. Topics include children, animals, and Seventh-day Adventist beliefs.
- **Representative Titles:** *I Miss Grandpa* by Karen Holford tells a story of love and loss to help children deal with the death of a loved one. *Beanie the Horse That Wasn't a Horse* by Heather Grovet (6–10 years) is a humorous story about learning to love and appreciate differences.

Submissions and Payment

Guidelines and catalogue available at website. Query. Accepts hard copy and email queries to booksubmissions@ pacificpress.com. SASE. Responds in 3 weeks. Publication in 6–12 months. Royalty, 6–12%, to $1,500.

Editor's Comments

The most successful proposals are well written, with a unique or interesting topic that grabs our attention. All books must deal with distinctively Adventist beliefs.

P & R Publishing

P.O. Box 817
Phillipsburg, NJ 08865

Editorial Director: Marvin Padgett

Publisher's Interests

P & R is interested in fiction and nonfiction that promote Christian living and a better understanding of the Bible's teachings. Its catalogue includes titles on Bible study, church and youth resources, Christian living, and books for children ages eight and older.
Website: www.prpbooks.com

Freelance Potential

Published 40 titles (3 juvenile) in 2009: 1 was by an agented author. Of the 40 titles, 2 were by authors who were new to the publishing house. Receives 400 queries yearly.

- **Fiction:** Publishes middle-grade books, 8–12 years; and young adult books, 12–18 years. Genres include inspirational and religious fiction, and fantasy.
- **Nonfiction:** Publishes middle-grade books, 8–12 years; and young adult books, 12–18 years. Topics include Christian living, counseling, theology, apologetics, Christian issues and ethics, and women's issues. Also publishes study aids.
- **Representative Titles:** *Beyond the Summerland* by L. B. Graham is a fantasy based in part on prophecy from the book of Isaiah; part of the Blinding of the Blade series. *King Without a Shadow* by R. C. Sproul is the story of a young boy's questions about shadows and how they lead a king to seek out the only King without a shadow—God.

Submissions and Payment

Guidelines available at website. Query with outline and 2 sample chapters. Accepts queries through electronic proposal form at website only. Responds in 1–3 months. Publication period varies. Royalty.

Editor's Comments

We accept fiction for children, as well as books for religious education teachers on preparing youngsters for the sacraments and for living godly lives.

Parenting Press

P.O. Box 75267
Seattle, WA 98175-0267

Acquisitions: Carolyn J. Threadgill

Publisher's Interests
The goal of Parenting Press is to offer useful books that teach practical life skills to children and the people who care for them.
Website: www.parentingpress.com

Freelance Potential
Published 6 titles (1 juvenile) in 2009: 2 were developed from unsolicited submissions. Of the 6 titles, 2 were by authors who were new to the publishing house. Receives 804 queries yearly.

- **Nonfiction:** Publishes concept books, 2–8 years. Also publishes books for adults. Topics include parenting, child development, problem-solving, handling emotions, abuse prevention, parent desertion, sleep issues, toilet training, safety, and guiding children to independence and responsibility.
- **Representative Titles:** *What About Me? 12 Ways to Get Your Parents' Attention (Without Hitting Your Sister)* by Eileen Kennedy-Moore (3–8 years) shows children the best way to get noticed. *Why Don't You Understand?* by Susie Leonard Weller (parents) demystifies new brain research to explain how four thinking styles affect family communication.

Submissions and Payment
Guidelines and catalogue available at website. Query with outline, table of contents, introduction, and 2 sample chapters. Accepts hard copy. SASE. Responds in 1 month. Publication in 18–24 months. Royalty, 4–8% of net; advance, negotiable.

Editor's Comments
We're looking for books that are nonjudgmental in attitude, useful to people with many different value systems, and full of options rather than "shoulds." The best books are short and easily understood, and present material in a fresh way. All of our titles are field-tested prior to publication by a variety of people in a variety of settings.

Parkway Publishers

P.O. Box 3678
Boone, NC 28607

President: Rao Aluri

Publisher's Interests

Parkway Publishers, an imprint of John F. Blair, is interested in books about western North Carolina history, people, and tourism. All of its titles pertain to this region, or to Appalachia in general.
Website: www.parkwaypublishers.com

Freelance Potential

Published 6 titles (1 juvenile) in 2009: each was developed from an unsolicited submission. Of the 6 titles, 2 were by unpublished writers and 4 were by authors who were new to the publishing house. Receives 24 unsolicited mss yearly.

- **Fiction:** Publishes story picture books, 4–10 years; chapter books, 5–10 years; and young adult books, 12–18 years. Genres include regional and historical fiction, folklore, mystery, and adventure.
- **Nonfiction:** Publishes story picture books, 4–10 years; chapter books, 5–10 years; and young adult books, 12–18 years. Topics include regional history, culture, and the environment. Also publishes biographies and memoirs of regional personalities.
- **Representative Titles:** *My Father's Beast* by Gail E. Haley is a picture book about addiction, told from the viewpoint of a child. *The Bridge Crew* by Sam Shumate is a memoir of growing up in the Blue Ridge Mountains during the 1940s and '50s.

Submissions and Payment

Guidelines and catalogue available at website. Send complete ms. Accepts hard copy. SASE. Responds in 2–6 months. Publication in 6–12 months. Royalty, 10%.

Editor's Comments

We are seeking more manuscripts along the lines of Gail E. Haley's *Mountain Jack Tales*, as well as children's fiction and nonfiction in general. Please remember that we publish only books related to the western North Carolina region—its history, its geography, and its people.

Pauline Books & Media

50 St. Pauls Avenue
Boston, MA 02130–3491

Children's Editors: Christina Wegendt, FSP, & Diane Lynch

Publisher's Interests
Children's books relevant to Catholic teachings and practices are the mainstay of this publishing house.
Website: www.pauline.org

Freelance Potential
Published 21 titles (19 juvenile) in 2009: 3 were developed from unsolicited submissions and 2 were reprint/licensed properties. Of the 21 titles, 1 was by an unpublished writer and 1 was by a new author. Receives 360+ queries yearly.

- **Fiction:** Publishes toddler books and early picture books, 0–4 years; story picture books, 4–8 years; easy-to-read books, 7–9 years; and middle-grade books, 8–12 years. Features books that relate Christian faith and values.
- **Nonfiction:** Publishes toddler books, 0–4 years; chapter books, 5–10 years; and middle-grade books, 8–12 years. Topics include religious education, church holidays, prayer, faith, spirituality, saints, and sacraments. Also publishes religious coloring and activity books.
- **Representative Titles:** *God Made Wonderful Me* by Genny Monchamp (0–4 years) encourages young readers to discover the many parts of their body that God created. *Joseph from Germany* by Claire Jordan Mohan follows Joseph Ratzinger's childhood in Bavaria to his election as Pope Benedict XVI.

Submissions and Payment
Guidelines available at website. Query with outline/synopsis and 2 sample chapters. Send complete ms for board books and picture books only. Accepts hard copy and email to editorial@paulinemedia.com. SASE. Responds in 3 months. Publication in 2–3 years. Royalty, 5–10% of net; advance, $200–$500.

Editor's Comments
We seek manuscripts that reflect a positive worldview, good moral values, and respect for all people.

Paulist Press

997 Macarthur Boulevard
Mahwah, NJ 07430

Managing Editor: Paul McMahon

Publisher's Interests

Paulist Press publishes ecumenical theology, Roman Catholic studies, and books on Scripture, church history, and faith. It also publishes a small number of Catholic-themed children's stories, prayer books, and activity books.
Website: www.paulistpress.com

Freelance Potential

Published 92 titles (12 juvenile) in 2009: 9 were developed from unsolicited submissions, 9 were by agented authors, and 2 were reprint/licensed properties. Of the 92 titles, 46 were by unpublished writers and 46 were by authors who were new to the publishing house. Receives 900 unsolicited mss yearly.

- **Nonfiction:** Publishes easy-to-read books, 4–7 years; story picture books, 4–10 years; middle-grade books, 8–12 years; and young adult books, 12–18 years. Topics include blessings; prayers; saints; modern heroes; Bible stories; and Catholic traditions, holidays, and doctrine. Also publishes biographies.
- **Representative Titles:** *Dorothy Day: Champion of the Poor* by Elaine Murray Stone (9+ years) is a biography of the social activist and founder of the Catholic Worker movement. *Jesus Loves Me Pre-School Activity Book* by Jennifer Galvin (3–6 years) features biblically-based activities built around the song, "Jesus Loves Me."

Submissions and Payment

Guidelines available at website. Send complete ms with résumé. Accepts hard copy. SASE. Responds in 6–8 weeks. Publication in 2–3 years. Royalty, 8%; advance, $500.

Editor's Comments

We're interested in all books that bring a Christian or Catholic message to children, particularly biographies of saints, books about the sacraments, and works appropriate for religious education curricula.

Paws IV Books

119 South Main Street, Suite 400
Seattle, WA 98104

Acquisitions Editor: Susan Roxborough

Publisher's Interests
This publisher is the children's imprint of Sasquatch Books—
a western regional publisher of books from the Pacific Northwest, Alaska, and California. Paws IV Books publishes fiction
and nonfiction embracing Alaskan themes for children up to
age eight.
Website: www.sasquatchbooks.com

Freelance Potential
Published 2 titles in 2009. Receives 600 queries, 540 unsolicited mss yearly.

- **Fiction:** Publishes concept books, toddler books, and early
  picture books, 0–4 years; and easy-to-read books, 4–7 years.
  Features stories about animals, nature, and the environment—
  all with Alaskan themes.
- **Nonfiction:** Publishes concept books, toddler books, and early
  picture books, 0–4 years; and easy-to-read books, 4–7 years.
  Topics include Alaskan history, culture, natural history, the
  environment, and wildlife.
- **Representative Titles:** *Alaska ABC Book* by Charlene Kreeger
  (3+ years) uses goats, glaciers, ice worms, igloos, and zero
  temperatures to teach children the ABCs of Alaska. *Alaska's
  12 Days of Summer* by Pat Chamberlin-Calamar presents the
  many splendors of an Alaskan summer in the style of *The 12
  Days of Christmas*, ending with a black bear in a spruce tree.

Submissions and Payment
Guidelines available at website. Query or send complete ms
with résumé and clips. Accepts hard copy. SASE. Responds
in 2–4 months. Publication in 1–3 months. Publication period
varies. Royalty; advance.

Editor's Comments
Your book should be three things: designed to educate
readers about Alaska or embrace an Alaskan theme; geared
toward toddlers or young readers; and original.

Peachtree Publishers

1700 Chattahoochee Avenue
Atlanta, GA 30318-2112

Submissions Editor: Helen Harriss

Publisher's Interests
Peachtree Publishers is interested in high-quality literary fiction and nonfiction for both the children's and young adult markets. It seeks books that are powerful, affecting, and fun.
Website: www.peachtree-online.com

Freelance Potential
Published 23 titles (22 juvenile) in 2009: 1 was developed from an unsolicited submission and 4 were reprint/licensed properties. Of the 23 titles, 3 were by authors who were new to the publishing house. Receives 18,000 mss yearly.

- **Fiction:** Publishes early picture books, 0–4 years; easy-to-read books, 4–7 years; story picture books, 4–10 years; chapter books, 5–10 years; middle-grade books, 8–12 years; and young adult books, 12–18 years. Genres include regional, historical, and multicultural fiction.
- **Nonfiction:** Publishes early picture books, 0–4 years; story picture books, 4–10 years; and middle-grade books, 8–12 years. Topics include nature, the outdoors, travel, and recreation.
- **Representative Titles:** *Keep On! The Story of Matthew Henson* by Deborah Hopkinson (6–10 years) is the little-known story of the black man who was part of the first expedition to the North Pole in 1909. *Larabee* by Kevin Luthardt (2–6 years) is a fun story about a postman's dog who helps deliver the mail, but yearns to get a letter himself.

Submissions and Payment
Guidelines and catalogue available at website. Send complete ms for picture books. Send complete ms or table of contents and 3 sample chapters for other works. Accepts hard copy. SASE. Responds in 6–9 months. Publication period and payment policy vary.

Editor's Comments
We do not publish science fiction, fantasy, short stories, or reference/text books.

Pelican Publishing Company

1000 Burmaster Street
Gretna, LA 70053

Editorial Department

Publisher's Interests
Books for children and adults about the people, history, architecture, food, and culture of Louisiana and its neighbors are the focus of this publisher.
Website: www.pelicanpub.com

Freelance Potential
Published 98 titles (28 juvenile) in 2009: 70 were developed from unsolicited submissions and 4 were by agented authors. Of the 98 titles, 16 were by unpublished writers and 32 were by authors who were new to the publishing house. Receives 3,600 queries, 7,800 unsolicited mss yearly.

- **Fiction:** Publishes easy-to-read books, 4–7 years; middle-grade books, 8–12 years; and young adult books, 12–18 years. Genres include historical, regional, and multicultural fiction.
- **Nonfiction:** Publishes easy-to-read books, 4–7 years; and middle-grade books, 8–12 years. Topics include regional history, food, people, and culture; and multicultural issues.
- **Representative Titles:** *Toby Belfer Learns About Heroes and Martyrs* by Gloria Teles Pushker & Mel Tarman (8–12 years) follows a fifth-grader to Israel, where she learns about Righteous Gentiles; part of the Toby Belfer series. *I Spy in the Texas Sky* by Deborah Ousley Kadair (5–8 years) is a colorful rhyming book that teaches about Texas state symbols.

Submissions and Payment
Guidelines available. Catalogue available at website. Send complete ms for easy-to-read books only. Query with synopsis for all others. Accepts hard copy. No simultaneous submissions. SASE. Responds in 3 months. Publication in 9–18 months. Royalty.

Editor's Comments
Of particular interest to us right now are nonfiction manuscripts for children ages five through eight, especially biography, history, and science titles.

Pembroke Publishers

538 Hood Road
Markham, Ontario L3R 3K9
Canada

Submissions Editor: Mary Macchiusi

Publisher's Interests
This publisher is interested in educational nonfiction for teachers, librarians, and parents, as well as some books for classroom use. Its books for parents and professionals focus on classroom management, teaching strategies, language arts, and learning.
Website: www.pembrokepublishers.com

Freelance Potential
Published 10–20 titles in 2009. Of the 10–20 titles, 1 was by an author who was new to the publishing house. Receives 50 queries yearly.

- **Nonfiction:** Publishes chapter books, 5–10 years; and middle-grade books, 8–12 years. Topics include history, science, writing, and notable Canadians. Also publishes titles for educators about reading, writing, literacy learning, drama, the arts, school leadership, discipline, and working with parents.
- **Representative Titles:** *Text Me a Strategy* by Kathy Paterson offers teachers practical tools that promote student learning and personal growth in our fast-paced information age. *The Picture Book Experience* by Larry Swartz describes how experiencing and responding to picture books can lead readers to new understandings; provides tips and activities for using picture books in the classroom.

Submissions and Payment
Guidelines available. Query with résumé, outline, and sample chapter. Accepts hard copy and simultaneous submissions if identified. SAE/IRC. Responds in 1 month. Publication in 6–24 months. Royalty.

Editor's Comments
While some of our books are specific to Canada, the majority are about teaching strategies and school issues that are faced by teachers everywhere. Promoting effective learning is our goal.

Perigee Books

Penguin Group USA, Inc.
375 Hudson Street
New York, NY 10014

Publisher: John Duff

Publisher's Interests

A publisher of self-help and how-to books for teens and adults, this Penguin imprint is especially focused on parenting titles. It is currently in the process of expanding its list of popular reference books.
Website: www.penguin.com

Freelance Potential

Published 60 titles in 2009: 4 were developed from unsolicited submissions and 56 were by agented authors.
Receives 300–400 queries yearly.

- **Nonfiction:** Publishes young adult books, 12–18 years. Topics include sexuality, fitness, business, health, hobbies, and recreation. Also publishes parenting and childcare titles, and reference books for adults.
- **Representative Titles:** *I Love the New Baby at Our House. . . Most of the Time* by Leslie Kimmelman (parents) is an illustrated and interactive journal for helping children express their feelings about a new sibling. *Wacky Baby Knits* by Alison Jenkins is a colorful and quirky collection of knitting projects to outfit baby. *Help—My Kid Is Driving Me Crazy* by David Swanson (parents) describes 17 ways kids manipulate their parents, and offers advice for dealing with such tactics.

Submissions and Payment

Guidelines and catalogue available at website. Query. Accepts hard copy. SASE. Responds in 4–6 weeks. Publication in 18 months. Royalty; advance.

Editor's Comments

The preferred and standard method for having manuscripts considered for publication by a major publisher is to submit them through an established literary agent. Due to the high volume of manuscripts received, most Penguin Group USA imprints do not normally accept unsolicited submissions. However, at this time we are reviewing queries.

Peter Pauper Press

202 Mamaroneck Avenue, Suite 400
White Plains, NY 10601

Children's Editor: Mara Conlon

Publisher's Interests
This specialty publisher focuses on gift books—humorous, helpful, or touching books, many of which are packaged specifically for gift-giving and special occasions. Its children's list is filled with activity and novelty books, journals, puzzle books, and story books.
Website: www.peterpauper.com

Freelance Potential
Published 23 titles (7 juvenile) in 2009: 2 were developed from unsolicited submissions and 2 were reprint/licensed properties. Of the 23 titles, 1 was by an unpublished writer and 7 were by authors who were new to the publishing house. Receives 192 queries, 600 unsolicited mss yearly.

- **Fiction:** Publishes story picture books, 4–10 years. Genres include humor, fantasy, and adventure. Also offers story-based activity books, 5–11 years.
- **Nonfiction:** Publishes activity books, 3–13 years. Topics include animals, the environment, science, math, and humor.
- **Representative Titles:** *Brainiac's Gross-Out Activity Book* by Ruth Cullen (8–12 years) presents appealing and educational games, puzzles, facts, and jokes related to various bodily functions. *Who R U? Quiz Book* by Suzanne Beilenson is filled with tween- and teen-targeted quizzes and interpretive answer keys regarding readers' BFFs, boyfriends, and other *Cosmo*-for-tweens subjects.

Submissions and Payment
Guidelines available. Query with cover letter, outline, 2 sample chapters, and credentials; or send complete ms. Accepts hard copy. SASE. Responds in 3+ months. Publication period varies. Flat fee.

Editor's Comments
Please send us your marketing, novelty, or gift tie-in ideas along with your submission.

Philomel Books

Penguin Group USA, Inc.
345 Hudson Street
New York, NY 10014

Editorial Assistant

Publisher's Interests
With a name that means "love of learning," Philomel has a
reputation for high-quality books for children of all ages that
appeal to parents as much as to the readers they target. Its
children's list includes both fiction and nonfiction titles on a
variety of subjects.
Website: www.penguingroup.com

Freelance Potential
Published 40–50 titles (25 juvenile) in 2009: 3 were developed from unsolicited submissions and 44 were by agented
authors. Receives 600 queries yearly.

- **Fiction:** Publishes early picture books, 0–4 years; story picture
  books, 4–10 years; chapter books, 5–10 years; middle-grade
  books, 8–12 years; and young adult books, 12–18 years. Genres include fantasy and contemporary, historical, multicultural,
  and science fiction. Also publishes poetry.
- **Nonfiction:** Publishes story picture books, 4–10 years; and
  young adult books, 12–18 years. Publishes biographies and
  first-person narratives.
- **Representative Titles:** *Make Your Mark, Franklin Roosevelt* by
  Judith St. George (5+ years) reveals the turning point for the
  young man who would grow up to become one of America's
  most beloved presidents. *Magpie Gabbard and the Quest for
  the Buried Moon* by Sally M. Keehn (10+ years) presents an
  original Appalachian tall tale about a young mountain girl's
  fantastic adventures.

Submissions and Payment
Guidelines available. Query with outline/synopsis. Accepts
hard copy. SASE. Responds if interested. Publication in
1–2 years. Royalty.

Editor's Comments
We have no formula for accepting proposals; we simply
jump at the ones that present us with something special.

Phoenix Learning Resources

910 Church Street
Honesdale, PA 18431

Submissions

Publisher's Interests

This educational publisher produces skill-based and basal and supplemental materials for use in the primary grades through adult education. Its books and resources focus on the fields of language arts, reading, mathematics, social studies, science, and study skills, as well as special education, ESL/ELL, and adult education.

Website: www.phoenixlearningresources.com

Freelance Potential

Published 43 titles in 2009. Receives 25 queries yearly.

- **Nonfiction:** Publishes textbooks and educational materials for preK–grade 12 and beyond. Also publishes books for special education and for gifted students, materials for use with ESL students, reference books, and biographies. Topics include language skills, integrated language arts, reading comprehension, math, study skills, and social studies.
- **Representative Titles:** *The Atlas of Natural Disasters* by Jeff Groman educates students about the wonders of the natural world as it explains avalanches, earthquakes, hurricanes, volcanos, wildfires, and storms. *Science Simplified* provides hands-on science experiments and activities with lessons on plants, animals, the environment, and chemistry. *How to Be a Recycling Hero* reinforces social skills while expanding students' understanding of the world around them.

Submissions and Payment

Guidelines available. Catalogue available at website. Query with résumé. Accepts hard copy and simultaneous submissions if identified. SASE. Responds in 1–4 weeks. Publication in 1–15 months. Royalty. Flat fee.

Editor's Comments

We are interested in any proposal that not only helps teachers, but that makes lessons fun for students. Authors must have educational or professional experience in their subjects.

Pick-a-WooWoo Publishers

P.O. Box 178
Nannup 6275
Western Australia

Editor: Athie Chambers

Publisher's Interests
This niche publisher of spiritual books for children ages 3 to
17 seeks to nourish young minds, bodies, and spirits. While
it is primarily a trade publisher, Pick-a-WooWoo also enters
into four joint-publishing ventures each year.
Website: www.pickawoowoo.com

Freelance Potential
Published 9 titles in 2009: 7 were developed from unsolicited
submissions. Receives 180–240 queries, 360–480 unsolicited
mss yearly.

- **Fiction:** Publishes easy-to-read books, 4–7 years; story picture
  books, 4–10 years; middle-grade books, 8–12 years; and
  young adult books, 12–18 years. Genres include fairy tales,
  fantasy, and contemporary fiction.
- **Nonfiction:** Publishes easy-to-read books, 4–7 years; story picture books, 4–10 years; middle-grade books, 8–12 years; and
  young adult books, 12–18 years. Topics include spirituality,
  nature, and the environment.
- **Representative Titles:** *Frolicking with the Fairies* by Julie-Ann
  Harper (3–9 years) introduces children to different kinds of
  fairies. *Bliss* by Dorreya Wood (3–9 years) tells the story of an
  enlightened little butterfly that happily spreads light and wonder wherever she goes.

Submissions and Payment
Guidelines available. Query or send complete ms. Accepts
disk submissions with hard copy. SAE/IRC. Response time,
publication period, and payment policy vary.

Editor's Comments
We work closely with the authors and artists who wish to
produce books that enlighten little souls. Please check our
website to see when our submissions page is open, keeping
in mind that we are a small company and only able to print
a limited number of titles each year.

Picture Window Books

7825 Telegraph Road
Bloomington, MN 55438

Editor: Krista Monyhan

Publisher's Interests
Picture Window Books offers books designed specifically
with the reluctant or struggling reader in mind. Its titles span
kindergarten through high school levels.
Website: www.picturewindowbooks.com

Freelance Potential
Published 215 titles in 2009: 3 were developed from unsolicited submissions. Of the 215 titles, 10 were by authors
who were new to the publishing house. Receives 40 queries
each year.

- **Fiction:** Publishes young adult books, 12–18 years. Genres
  include realistic and science fiction, adventure, fantasy, horror, mystery, and humor. Also offers fiction collections and
  accelerated reader titles, grades 3–9.
- **Nonfiction:** Publishes story picture books, grades K–4. Topics
  include nature, science, and ecology.
- **Representative Titles:** *Happy Birthday, Gus!* by Jacklyn
  Williams (grades K–3) is an interactive story in which Gus's
  mom sends him to karate camp, where Gus and his friend
  Bean encounter a bully. *Chicken Little* by Christianne C. Jones
  (grades K–3) is a retelling of the classic story about how a
  falling acorn leads Chicken Little to believe that the sky is
  falling. *Dirt: The Scoop on Soil* by Natalie M. Rosinsky (grades
  K–4) discusses the importance of soil and the many forms of
  life that it supports.

Submissions and Payment
Guidelines available at website. Query with synopsis and
first 3 chapters. Prefers email queries to author.sub@
stonearchbooks.com; will accept hard copy. SASE. Response
time, publication period, and payment policy vary.

Editor's Comments
We're looking for writers who can engage young readers with
wholesome, bright, and fun fiction.

Pilgrim Press

700 Prospect Avenue East
Cleveland, OH 44115-1100

Editorial Director: Kim Sadler

Publisher's Interests

Pilgrim Press is the publishing imprint of the United Church of Christ. It offers books for church scholars, students, laypersons, and church professionals. Its catalogue includes books on religious education and family topics.
Website: www.thepilgrimpress.com

Freelance Potential

Published 40 titles in 2009: 23 were developed from unsolicited submissions and 1 was by an agented author. Of the 40 titles, 1 was by an unpublished writer and 12 were by authors who were new to the publishing house. Receives 200+ queries yearly.

- **Nonfiction:** Publishes educational titles of interest to religious educators, clergy, parents, and caregivers. Also publishes informational titles on religion, social issues, and multicultural and ethnic subjects.
- **Representative Titles:** *Show Me a Picture: 30 Children's Sermons Using Visual Aids* by Phyllis Vos Wezeman & Anna L. Liechty provides sermons to use when preaching to children from kindergarten through upper-elementary school. *9 Ways to Bring Out the Best in You and Your Child* by Maggie Reign is all about raising children who are full of spirit and life, and teaching them to be caring human beings.

Submissions and Payment

Guidelines and catalogue available at website. Query via form at website. Responds in 9–12 months. Flat fee for work-for-hire projects.

Editor's Comments

We do not publish fiction of any kind, including children's fiction. In order to get our interest, your proposal must have compelling and unique features, and quality of content. You as an author must also have sufficient credentials and experience to write on a given topic.

Pineapple Press

P.O. Box 3889
Sarasota, FL 34230

Executive Editor: June Cussen

Publisher's Interests
Pineapple Press publishes mainly nonfiction books about the history, people, culture, and environment of Florida, intended for Florida students. Its small fiction list includes stories set in Florida.
Website: www.pineapplepress.com

Freelance Potential
Published 18 titles (5 juvenile) in 2009: 14 were developed from unsolicited submissions. Of the 18 titles, 1was by an unpublished writer and 8 were by authors who were new to the publishing house. Receives 1,200 queries yearly.

- **Fiction:** Publishes story picture books, 4–10 years; chapter books, 5–10 years; middle-grade books, 8–12 years; and young adult books, 12–18 years. Genres include folklore, mystery, science fiction, and historical fiction related to Florida.
- **Nonfiction:** Publishes easy-to-read books, 4–7 years; story picture books, 4–10 years; and middle-grade books, 8–12 years. Topics include the history, sports, wildlife, nature, and environment of Florida.
- **Representative Titles:** *Those Magical Manatees* by Jan Lee Wicker (5–9 years) presents interesting facts about Florida's manatees. *Kidnapped in Key West* by Edwina Raffa & Annelle Rigsby (8–12 years) is a daring adventure tale set on Flagler's Over-Sea Railroad.

Submissions and Payment
Guidelines available at website. Query with clips, synopsis, and sample chapters for fiction. Query with table of contents and sample chapters for nonfiction. Accepts hard copy and simultaneous submissions if identified. SASE. Responds in 2 months. Publication in 12–18 months. Royalty.

Editor's Comments
If your query is rejected, you will receive a form letter so that we may devote more time to reviewing submissions.

Pioneer Drama Service

P.O. Box 4267
Englewood, CO 80155-4267

Submissions Editor: Lori Conary

Publisher's Interests
Pioneer Drama publishes scripts that are designed to be produced by children's theater companies or used in classrooms. It accepts dramas, musicals, skits, and monologues for elementary through high school audiences. It also publishes resource books about play production.
Website: www.pioneerdrama.com

Freelance Potential
Published 40 titles in 2009: 10–20 were developed from unsolicited submissions. Of the 40 titles, 8 were by unpublished writers and 10 were by new authors. Receives 200 queries, 250 unsolicited mss yearly.

- **Fiction:** Publishes play scripts, 4–18 years. Genres include comedy, mystery, fantasy, adventure, folktales, and musicals.
- **Nonfiction:** Publishes theatrical textbooks and resources for children's and school theaters.
- **Representative Titles:** *The Mysterious Case of the Missing Ring* by Janie Downey Maxwell is a mystery surrounding the queen's missing ring, and the eccentric group of characters who join in the search for it. *Wooing Wed Widing Hood* by Charlie Lovett puts a comedic spin on the old Red fairy tale by adding two sisters and a couple of crazy princes.

Submissions and Payment
Guidelines and catalogue available at website. Prefers query; will accept ms with synopsis, cast list and breakdown, running time, set design, prop list, and proof of production. Accepts hard copy, email submissions to submissions@pioneerdrama.com, and simultaneous submissions if identified. SASE. Responds in 4–6 months. Publication period varies. Royalty.

Editor's Comments
Our current need is for large-cast comedies with more female than male roles, suitable for family audiences.

Pipers' Ash Ltd.

Church Road, Christian Malford
Chippenham, Wiltshire SN15 4BW
United Kingdom

Manuscript Evaluation Desk

Publisher's Interests

Pipers' Ash Ltd. publishes New ChapBooks, which run about one-third the length of an average novel; but, the company states, must be three times better to compete. It accepts chapbooks in a variety of genres and on many topics for children and for young adults.

Website: www.supamasu.com

Freelance Potential

Published 15 titles (2 juvenile) in 2009: 10 were developed from unsolicited submissions. Of the 15 titles, 10 were by unpublished writers and 10 were by authors who were new to the publishing house. Receives 9,000 queries yearly.

- **Fiction:** Publishes chapbooks, 5–10 years; middle-grade books, 8–12 years; and young adult books, 12–18 years. Genres include short stories, mystery, science fiction, and contemporary and historical fiction.
- **Nonfiction:** Publishes young adult books, 12–18 years. Topics include animals, crafts, hobbies, sports, and history. Also publishes biographies and poetry.
- **Representative Titles:** *Free-Wheeler* by Shay Wilson features a girl who doesn't let her wheelchair get in the way of fun with her friends. *The Cockatoos of Kelly's Place* by Prue Mason is a series of stories about an Australian farming family.

Submissions and Payment

Guidelines available at website. Query with brief proposal (to 25 words). Accepts email queries to pipersash@ supamasu.com. Response time and publication period vary. Royalty, 10%.

Editor's Comments

We love to discover exciting new authors with talent and potential. We prefer true-to-life children's stories that take readers into unknown situations to enable them to better cope with difficulties they face in the real world.

Pitspopany Press

40 East 78th Street, Suite 16D
New York, NY 10021

Publisher

Publisher's Interests

Pitspopany Press specializes in children's books with Jewish themes. Its fiction and nonfiction titles are designed to be visually appealing, educational, and entertaining.
Website: www.pitspopany.com

Freelance Potential

Published 12 titles in 2009. Receives 60 unsolicited mss each year.

- **Fiction:** Publishes toddler books and early picture books, 0–4 years; easy-to-read books, 4–7 years; story picture books, 4–10 years; chapter books, 5–10 years; middle-grade books, 8–12 years; and young adult books, 12–18 years. Genres include Jewish-themed historical, multicultural, and religious fiction; mystery; adventure; and humor.
- **Nonfiction:** Publishes easy-to-read books, 4–7 years; story picture books, 4–10 years; middle-grade books, 8–12 years; and young adult books, 12–18 years. Topics include religion, history, sports, fitness, and multicultural and ethnic issues— all relating to Israel, Judaism, or Jewish life.
- **Representative Titles:** *Mr. Mentch* by The Mamas (3–6 years) is about a man who is searching for his special talent to share at a Chanukah contest. *A Mitzvah for Zelda* by Susan Wigden (3–6 years) tells the story of a woman who makes a perfect yarmulke, until she loses her ability to knit.

Submissions and Payment

Guidelines and catalogue available at website. Send complete ms. Accepts hard copy and email submissions to pitspop@netvision.net.il. SASE. Responds in 3 months. Publication in 4–6 months. Royalty; advance.

Editor's Comments

We are always looking for series books and prefer that stories include both boy and girl characters. All of our titles are respectful of mainstream Jewish viewpoints and beliefs.

Platypus Media

725 8th Street SE
Washington, DC 20003

President: Dia L. Michels

Publisher's Interests
Platypus Media is an independent publisher interested in books that help support family life through education, positive images and role models, and entertainment. Its catalogue features titles that are geared toward children, parents, teachers, and parenting professionals.
Website: www.platypusmedia.com

Freelance Potential
Published 4 titles in 2009: 2 were by agented authors. Receives 180 queries, 24 unsolicited mss yearly.

- **Fiction:** Publishes concept books, 0–4 years; and middle-grade books, 8–12 years. Themes include families, family diversity, and animals.
- **Nonfiction:** Publishes concept books, toddler books, and early picture books, 0–4 years; easy-to-read books, 4–7 years; story picture books, 4–10 years; chapter books, 5–10 years; middle-grade books, 8–12 years; and young adult books, 12–18 years. Topics include family issues, science, and math. Also publishes parenting titles.
- **Representative Titles:** *If My Mom Were a Platypus* by Dia L. Michels (8–12 years) shows the many human family rituals that are echoed in the world of mammals. *Sleeping with Your Baby* by James J. McKenna (parents) is a guide to sleeping safely with an infant.

Submissions and Payment
Guidelines available at website. Query or send complete ms with brief author biography and marketing analysis. Accepts hard copy and simultaneous submissions if identified. SASE. Response time varies. Publication in 9–12 months. Royalty. Flat fee.

Editor's Comments
We encourage books dealing with ethnic and cultural diversity, and the relationships that contribute to close-knit families.

Players Press

P.O. Box 1132
Studio City, CA 91614

Business Manager: David Cole

Publisher's Interests
Players Press publishes performing arts books and scripts for use both in the classroom and in the theater.
Website: www.ppeps.com

Freelance Potential
Published 90 titles (35 juvenile) in 2009: 2 were reprint/licensed properties. Of the 90 titles, 2 were by unpublished writers and 6 were by authors who were new to the publishing house. Receives 6,000–12,000 queries yearly.

- **Fiction:** Publishes full-length and one-act plays for children, 4–18 years. Genres include drama, comedy, musicals, and fairy tales. Also publishes monologues.
- **Nonfiction:** Publishes toddler books and early picture books, 0–4 years; easy-to-read books, 4–7 years; chapter books, 5–10 years; middle-grade books, 8–12 years; and young adult books, 12–18 years. Also publishes guides for educators. Topics include auditioning, theater arts, film, television, music, costume design, stage management, set construction, and theater history.
- **Representative Titles:** *Cinderella vs. the Step-Family* by Dana Proulx-Willis is a comical courtroom play. *Curse of the Tomb Raiders* by William Hezlep (YA) follows two teens as they confront modern-day tomb raiders in Egypt; part of the Travelers series. *Movement Games* (teachers) is a collection of warm-ups for the classroom and theater.

Submissions and Payment
Guidelines available. Query with table of contents and outline for books; with production flyer and program, score and CD (for musicals), and reviews for scripts. Accepts hard copy. SASE. Responds in 3–12 months. Publication in 3–24 months. Royalty, 10%; advance.

Editor's Comments
No manuscript will be considered unless it has been produced. Please see our guidelines for details.

Playwrights Canada Press

215 Spadina Avenue, Suite 230
Toronto, Ontario M5T 2C7
Canada

Editorial Coordinator

Publisher's Interests

This drama publisher accepts plays written by Canadian playwrights. Its catalogue includes plays of all genres and for all ages, including some specifically for children's audiences and/or children's theater groups. It also publishes books about the craft of play production.

Website: www.playwrightscanada.com

Freelance Potential

Published 35 titles (2 juvenile) in 2009: 1 was developed from an unsolicited submission. Receives 10–15 queries each year.

- **Fiction:** Publishes dramatic plays for elementary, middle school, and high school students.
- **Nonfiction:** Publishes books about acting and play production, and theater resources for drama teachers.
- **Representative Titles:** *The Nutmeg Princess* by Richardo Keens-Douglas is a play about the adventures of two characters living on magical Caribbean island. *Plays for Young People* by Charles Way presents three short plays for young actors; one about overcoming odds, one a contemporary version of *The Tempest*, and one about ethnic war.

Submissions and Payment

Canadian authors only. Guidelines and catalogue available at website. Query with synopsis and first-production information, including cast and crew. Accepts hard copy and simultaneous submissions if identified. SASE. Responds in 6–12 months. Publication in 5 months. Royalty.

Editor's Comments

Please note that we only accept plays from Canadian citizens or landed immigrants who have had a play produced in the last 10 years. We occasionally participate in drama festivals or anthologies, and will send out a call for specific material. Check our website and submission guidelines for news.

Plexus Publishing

143 Old Marlton Pike
Medford, NJ 08055

Editor-in-Chief: John B. Bryans

Publisher's Interests
Calling itself the "Gateway to the Garden State," Plexus Publishing specializes in books spotlighting New Jersey and the surrounding region. Topics covered include history, travel and tourism, science, and nature. It publishes regional fiction as well as nonfiction.
Website: www.plexuspublishing.com

Freelance Potential
Published 4 titles in 2009: 1 was developed from an unsolicited submission. Of the 4 titles, 1 was by an unpublished writer and 2 were by authors who were new to the publishing house. Receives 150–300 queries yearly.

- **Fiction:** Genres include mystery, adventure, folklore, and contemporary and historical fiction—all with New Jersey settings.
- **Nonfiction:** Publishes regional field guides, reference books, and biographies. Topics include New Jersey's history, natural resources, Pine Barrens, seashore, wildlife, recreation, tourism, and travel.
- **Representative Titles:** *A Pine Barrens Odyssey* by Howard P. Boyd chronicles a year of seasonal changes in the region. *Down Barnegat Bay* by Robert Jahn is an illustrated maritime history of the Jersey Shore's Age of Sail. *Cape Mayhem* by Jane Kelly follows a woman investigating a mystery on Cape May during the off-season.

Submissions and Payment
Guidelines available. Catalogue available at website. Query with synopsis and table of contents. Accepts hard copy. SASE. Responds in 2 months. Publication in 10 months. Royalty, 12%.

Editor's Comments
Our emphasis is on South Jersey (including the greater Philadelphia area), Atlantic City, the Jersey Shore, and the Pine Barrens.

Polychrome Publishing Corporation

4509 North Francisco Avenue
Chicago, IL 60625-3808

Editorial Department

Publisher's Interests

Polychrome Publishing Corporation publishes domestic multicultural fiction and nonfiction children's books for kids of all ages. Its books feature characters of all races and ethnicities, with themes of racial, ethnic, and cultural diversity and tolerance.
Website: www.polychromebooks.com

Freelance Potential

Plans to resume publishing (1 or more titles) in 2010. Receives 500 unsolicited mss yearly.

- **Fiction:** Publishes toddler books and early picture books, 0–4 years; story picture books, 4–10 years; chapter books, 5–10 years; middle-grade books, 8–12 years; and young adult books, 12–18 years. Genres include contemporary, historical, and multicultural fiction.
- **Nonfiction:** Publishes books about Asian American culture for families and educators.
- **Representative Titles:** *The Lobster and the Sea* by Esther Chiu (grades 1–4) is the reassuring story of a child reconciling her American values with her grandfather's Asian roots as he approaches the end of his life. *One Small Girl* by Jennifer L. Chan (preK–grade 2) is the whimsical story of a mischievous girl who finds entertainment in fooling grown-ups.

Submissions and Payment

Guidelines and catalogue available at website. Send complete ms with author bio. Accepts hard copy and simultaneous submissions if identified. SASE. Responds in 3–6 months. Publication in 1–2 years. Royalty; advance.

Editor's Comments

Although many of our stories are about Asian Americans, we welcome books featuring African Americans, Hispanics, Latinos, or Native Americans. We are interested in these cultures' American experience, not books set in foreign countries.

Portage & Main Press

100-318 McDermot Avenue
Winnipeg, Manitoba R3A OA2
Canada

Editor: Catherine Gerbasi

Publisher's Interests
Quality educational resources for teachers are the focus of
this publisher. Its goal is to provide educators with practical
material, based on solid theory and research, that helps
educators make real changes in their classrooms and in the
lives of their students.
Website: www.portageandmainpress.com

Freelance Potential
Published 10–15 titles in 2009.

- **Nonfiction:** Publishes educational resource books for teachers, grades K–12. Topics include assessment, continual learning, ESL, visual literacy, reading, spelling, writing, safe
  schools, social studies, mathematics, and science.
- **Representative Titles:** *How Do You Say Hello to a Ghost?* by
  Marlene & Robert McCracken (4–6 years) is used in kindergarten classes as learn-to-read material. *Guided Writing
  Instruction* by Shelley S. Petersen (teachers, grades 4–7) provides classroom-tested teaching and assessment tools and
  ideas for teaching informational and narrative writing.

Submissions and Payment
Guidelines and catalogue available at website or with 9x12
SAE/IRC ($.50 Canadian postage). Query with table of con-
tents and sample chapter; or send complete ms. Accepts
hard copy and disk submissions. SAE/IRC. Responds in
1–2 months. Publication in 6 months. Royalty, 8–12%.

Editor's Comments
We do not publish books outside of the educational realm,
student writing, unrevised dissertations, or personal journals. Most of our writers are master educators themselves
who are dedicated to the success of all learners. Before submitting a proposal, we invite you to become familiar with our
books and authors. Our book proposal form, found at our
website, will guide you through the submission process.

PowerKids Press

29 East 21st Street
New York, NY 10010

Editorial Director: Rachel O'Conner

Publisher's Interests

An imprint of Rosen Publishing Group, PowerKids Press presents a wide range of educational subjects for children in preschool through grade six. Its catalogue includes books for all curriculum areas, marketed for use in classrooms and libraries.
Website: www.powerkidspress.com

Freelance Potential

Published 200 titles in 2009. Of the 200 titles, 15 were by unpublished writers and 15 were by authors who were new to the publishing house. Receives 500 queries yearly.

- **Nonfiction:** Publishes educational materials, preK–grade 8. Topics include art, social studies, science, geography, health, fitness, sports, math, Native Americans, ancient history, natural history, politics and government, and multicultural and ethnic issues. Also publishes biographies and titles for special education and bilingual programs.
- **Representative Titles:** *Australia* by Wendy Vierow (grades 3–5) is filled with fascinating facts about this continent and its coral reef; part of the Altas of the Seven Continents series. *Learning About Integrity From the Life of Eleanor Roosevelt* by Nancy Ellwood (grades 2–5) presents the story of Mrs. Roosevelt and her many causes; part of the Character Building Book series.

Submissions and Payment

Guidelines available. Catalogue available at website. Query with outline and sample chapter. Accepts hard copy and simultaneous submissions if identified. SASE. Responds in 3 months. Publication in 9–18 months. Flat fee.

Editor's Comments

We expect all books to be thoroughly researched and factually accurate. At the same time, they should be appealing to their intended audience, encouraging them to read and learn.

Mathew Price Ltd.

5013 Golden Circle
Denton, TX 76208

Publisher: Mathew Price

Publisher's Interests
Well-established at home in the United Kingdom, Mathew
Price has recently launched a stateside publishing house. It
looks for captivating picture books and early readers that
draw children in and "educate through delight."
Website: www.mathewprice.com

Freelance Potential
Published 30 titles in 2009.

- **Fiction:** Publishes early picture books, 0–4 years; easy-to-read
  books, 4–7 years; and story picture books, 4–10 years. Also
  publishes board books, novelty books, and bilingual titles.
  Features stories about animals, sports, cars, families, and
  holidays.
- **Nonfiction:** Publishes early picture books, 0–4 years; easy-to-
  read books, 4–7 years; and story picture books, 4–10 years.
  Also publishes board books, novelty books, and bilingual titles.
  Topics include nature, animals, vehicles, the alphabet, and
  early math.
- **Representative Titles:** *Animal Stories for Bedtime* by Georgie
  Adams (1–4 years) is a collection of short, funny tales; part of
  the Join-In Stories series. *Nature Hide & Seek: Oceans* by
  John Norris Wood (5–8 years) is packed with information
  about the creatures who live in the sea; part of the Nature
  Hide & Seek series.

Submissions and Payment
Send complete ms. Accepts email submissions to mathewp@
mathewprice.com. Response time varies. Publication in 18
months. Royalty.

Editor's Comments
Using beautiful artwork, stimulating ideas, and a sense of
play, our books gather the child into the learning process,
heightening interaction and turning reading into a thrilling
process of discovery.

Prometheus Books

59 John Glenn Drive
Amherst, NY 14228-2119

Editor-in-Chief: Steven L. Mitchell

Publisher's Interests

This publisher specializes in thoughtful and authoritative nonfiction on a variety of topics for the educational, professional, scientific, and popular/consumer markets. Its children's list includes books on moral and emotional issues, as well as science and sex education books.
Website: www.prometheusbooks.com

Freelance Potential

Published 100 titles in 2009: 15–20 were developed from unsolicited submissions. Receives 300 queries, 400 unsolicited mss yearly.

* **Nonfiction:** Publishes easy-to-read books, 4–7 years; and middle-grade books, 8–12 years. Topics include social issues, health, sexuality, religion, politics, critical thinking, and decision-making.
* **Representative Titles:** *It's Up to You . . . What Do You Do?* by Sandra McLeod Humphrey (6+ years) presents contemporary anecdotes of children making choices in the face of challenging situations, and provides opportunities for readers to contemplate their own actions. *Girls Are Girls, and Boys Are Boys* by Sol Gordon (8–12 years) explains the physical and reproductive differences between the sexes, while emphasizing that sex plays no part in careers or other interests.

Submissions and Payment

Guidelines and catalogue available at website. Query or send complete ms with résumé and bibliography. Accepts hard copy and simultaneous submissions if identified. SASE. Responds in 2–3 months. Publication in 12–18 months. Payment policy varies.

Editor's Comments

We accept submissions from both authors and literary agents. We ask, however, that you follow the guidelines at our website, as that expedites the review process.

Pruett Publishing Company

P.O. Box 2140
Boulder, CO 80306-2140

Editor: James Pruett

Publisher's Interests
Books about the Rocky Mountain region of the U.S. are the signature of this publisher. It offers a variety of nonfiction books, textbooks, and activity books on the history, environment, and outdoor recreation of the region. 5% self-, subsidy-, co-venture, or co-op published material.
Website: www.pruettpublishing.com

Freelance Potential
Published 5 titles in 2009: 1 was developed from an unsolicited submission. Receives 180 queries, 144 unsolicited mss yearly.

- **Nonfiction:** Publishes middle-grade books, 8–12 years; and young adult books, 12–18 years. Topics include biography, health, fitness, history, multicultural issues, nature, and the environment—all related to the Rocky Mountain West. Also publishes coloring and activity books for younger children.
- **Representative Titles:** *Discover Colorado* by Matthew Downey & Ty Bliss (grades 3–4) traces the state's history from the time of the Paleo Indians through the building of the Denver International Airport. *Color the Wild Rockies* by Mary Pruett (4–8 years) provides brief descriptions of the animals and flowers of the Rocky Mountains along with pictures that children can color.

Submissions and Payment
Guidelines and catalogue available at website. Query with résumé, outline, sample chapters, and market analysis; or send complete ms. Accepts hard copy and simultaneous submissions if identified. SASE. Responds to queries in 2 weeks, to mss in 1–2 months. Publication period varies. Royalty, 10–15%.

Editor's Comments
We are interested in any idea that will bring the culture and history of the Rocky Mountains alive for young readers.

Prufrock Press

5926 Balcones Drive, Suite 220
Austin, TX 78731

Submissions Editor

Publisher's Interests
Gifted students in kindergarten through grade 12 are the
focus of this educational publisher. It is interested in nonfiction books on teaching, parenting, and supporting these
advanced learners.
Website: www.prufrock.com

Freelance Potential
Published 30–35 titles (2 juvenile) in 2009. Of the 30–35
titles, 10–12 were by authors new to the publishing house.

- **Nonfiction:** Publishes supplemental classroom materials for
  gifted and advanced learners, grades K–12. Topics include
  math, science, social studies, language arts, thinking skills,
  problem-solving, research, and presentation skills. Also publishes books for teachers and parents of gifted children.
  Topics include differentiated instruction; teaching strategies;
  independent study; identifying, parenting, and counseling
  gifted children; and enrichment.
- **Representative Titles:** *Blind Justice: Courtroom Simulations
  for the Classroom* by Michael S. Hoey brings four of the most
  controversial court cases in American history into the classroom with guidelines for creating mock trials. *Detective Club:
  Mysteries for Young Thinkers* by Judy Leimbach & Sharon Eck-
  ert (grades 2–4) lets readers work along with the young detectives to solve six different mysteries.

Submissions and Payment
Guidelines and catalogue available at website. Query with
table of contents; or send complete ms. Accepts hard copy.
SASE. Responds in 2–4 months. Publication period varies.
Royalty; advance.

Editor's Comments
We are aggressively seeking quality materials that support
the education of gifted and advanced learners. We include a
detailed description of our current needs at our website.

Puffin Books

Penguin Group USA, Inc.
345 Hudson Street, 15th Floor
New York, NY 10014

Manuscript Submissions

Publisher's Interests

Puffin Books and its three children's imprints publish a com-
mercially successful mix of classic children's stories and new
titles. Its mix includes fiction and nonfiction for the very
young through young adults.
Website: www.penguin.com/youngreaders

Freelance Potential

Published 200 titles in 2009. Receives 500+ queries yearly.

- **Fiction:** Publishes early picture books, 0–4 years; easy-to-read
  books, 4–7 years; story picture books, 4–10 years; chapter
  books, 5–10 years; middle-grade books, 8–12 years; and
  young adult books, 12–18 years. Genres include historical,
  contemporary, and science fiction; mystery; adventure; and
  romance. Also publishes novelty books, 0–4 years.
- **Nonfiction:** Publishes story picture books, 4–10 years; and
  middle-grade books, 8–12 years. Topics include social issues
  and science.
- **Representative Titles:** *Roar of a Snore* by Marsha Diane
  Arnold (3–5 years) follows Jack as he searches bedrooms and
  barnyard to discover whose snoring is keeping him awake.
  Americans Who Tell the Truth by Robert Shetterly (9–11 years)
  portrays 50 citizens whose freedom of speech challenged the
  status quo. *Yours Till Niagara Falls, Abby* by Jane O'Connor
  finds Abby facing summer camp without her best friend.

Submissions and Payment

Guidelines available. Query with outline/synopsis. Accepts
hard copy. SASE. Responds in 4–5 months. Publication in
12–18 months. Royalty, 2–6%.

Editor's Comments

We are fans of any book that will be devoured by young
readers, or that will cause a young child to fall in love with
books. A good story, great writing, and original thought are
elements that we require in every book we publish.

G. P. Putnam's Sons

345 Hudson Street
New York, NY 10014

Manuscript Editor

Publisher's Interests
This popular children's publisher, an imprint of Penguin
Young Readers Group, is interested in fiction and nonfiction
for children in preschool through high school.
Website: www.penguin.com

Freelance Potential
Published 56 titles in 2009: 1 was developed from an unsolicited submission, 36 were by agented authors, and 5 were
reprint/licensed properties. Of the 56 titles, 5 were by
unpublished writers and 19 were by new authors. Receives
1,500 queries, 7,200 unsolicited mss yearly.

- **Fiction:** Publishes toddler books and early picture books,
  0–4 years; story picture books, 4–10 years; chapter books,
  5–10 years; middle-grade books, 8–12 years; and young adult
  books, 12–18 years. Genres include contemporary and multicultural fiction.
- **Nonfiction:** Publishes early picture books, 0–4 years; story
  picture books, 4–10 years; chapter books, 5–10 years; and
  middle-grade books, 8–12 years.
- **Representative Titles:** *Pouch!* by David Ezra Stein (3–5 years)
  features a young kangaroo who is excitedly exploring his new
  world. *Black Angels* by Linda Beatrice Brown (12+ years) is a
  novel featuring three orphans who must depend on each other
  in order to survive on their own during the Civil War.

Submissions and Payment
Guidelines available. Query with synopsis and 3 sample
chapters. Send ms for picture books. Accepts hard copy and
simultaneous submissions. No SASE. Responds in 4 months
if interested. Publication period varies. Royalty; advance.

Editor's Comments
If sending us a query, please provide a plot description,
genre, the intended reader age group, and your publishing
credits, if any.

Quest Books

306 West Geneva Road
P.O. Box 270
Wheaton, IL 60187

Assistant Editor: Idarmis Rodriguez

Publisher's Interests
Quest Books is the publishing house of the Theosophical
Society in America. Its books are compatible with the organization's purpose, which is to promote fellowship among
all people and to encourage the study of religion, science,
and philosophy.
Website: www.questbooks.net

Freelance Potential
Published 10 titles in 2009: 3 were developed from unsolicited submissions, 3 were by agented authors, and 1 was a
reprint/licensed property. Of the 10 titles, 2 were by unpublished writers and 8 were by authors who were new to the
publishing house. Receives 450 queries, 210–330 unsolicited mss yearly.

- **Nonfiction:** Publishes self-help books. Topics include healing,
  spirituality, philosophy, theosophy, religion, meditation, spiritual ecology, transpersonal psychology, new science, holistic
  health, mysticism, mythology, and ancient wisdom.
- **Representative Titles:** *The Templars and the Grail* by Karen
  Ralls is a true tale of the medieval Templar Knights once
  believed to guard the Holy Grail. *Visual Journaling* by Barbara
  Ganim & Susan Fox presents a 6-week course on journaling
  with images.

Submissions and Payment
Guidelines and catalogue available at website. Query with
author biography, table of contents, introduction, and
sample chapter; or send complete ms. Prefers email to
submissions@questbooks.net (no attachments); will accept
hard copy. SASE. Responds in 4–6 weeks. Publication period
varies. Royalty; advance.

Editor's Comments
We are committed to publishing books of intelligence, read-
ability, and insight for the contemporary spiritual seeker.

Rainbow Publishers

P.O. Box 261129
San Diego, CA 92196

Submissions: Daniel Miley

Publisher's Interests

This Christian publisher offers books and reproducible resources that help religious education teachers lead kids ages 2 through 12 to a stronger relationship with Jesus Christ. Its catalogue includes age-appropriate books on Bible-teaching and resources for turning volunteers into successful teachers. Many of its materials are reproducible for use in classrooms.
Website: www.rainbowpublishers.com

Freelance Potential

Published 16 titles in 2009. Receives 100 queries yearly.

- **Fiction:** Publishes middle-grade books, 8–12 years. Genres include inspirational and religious fiction.
- **Nonfiction:** Publishes Christian education resource materials, preK–grade 6. Topics include the Bible, religion, crafts, and hobbies. Also offers titles in series, 8+ years; and activity books, 2–12 years.
- **Representative Titles:** *Favorite Bible Children* (2–3 years) includes a variety of games, crafts, and Bible memory verses that help put very young children on the path to a strong relationship with God. *Bible Stories About Jesus* (4–5 years) presents activities that bring Bible stories to life and teach children about Jesus' time on Earth.

Submissions and Payment

Guidelines and catalogue available at website or with 9x12 SASE (2 first-class stamps). Query with résumé, table of contents, 2–5 sample chapters, and market analysis. Accepts hard copy and simultaneous submissions if identified. SASE. Responds in 2–8 weeks. Publication in 1–3 years. Flat fee.

Editor's Comments

We are interested classroom ideas that will help dedicated Sunday school teachers and other religious educators creatively teach the Bible. When submitting, please tell us about your religious teaching experience.

Random House Children's Books

1745 Broadway
New York, NY 10019

Submissions Editor

Publisher's Interests

Random House is widely known for its quality books, both fiction and nonfiction. The same holds true for its Children's Books division. It accepts fiction and nonfiction projects in all subject areas and genres for children in preschool through young adulthood. It considers work only from authors already aligned with an agent.
Website: www.randomhouse.com

Freelance Potential

Published 350 titles in 2009: each was by an agented author. Receives 1,200 queries yearly.

- **Fiction:** Publishes concept books, toddler books, and early picture books, 0–4 years; easy-to-read books, 4–7 years; story picture books, 4–10 years; chapter books, 5–10 years; middle-grade books, 8–12 years; and young adult books, 12–18 years. Genres include contemporary, historical, inspirational, multicultural, and science fiction; adventure; drama; horror; humor; mystery and suspense; fairy tales; romance; and stories about animals, nature, and the environment.
- **Nonfiction:** Publishes easy-to-read books, 4–7 years; story picture books, 4–10 years; chapter books, 5–10 years; and middle-grade books, 8–12 years. Topics include animals, history, nature, the environment, adventure, and humor. Also publishes biographies.
- **Representative Titles:** *The Yellow Tutu* by Kirsten Bramsen (4–7 years) is the story of a yellow tutu and the imagination of the girl who owns it. *Looking for Marco Polo* by Alan Armstrong (8–12 years) finds a boy retracing Marco Polo's travels.

Submissions and Payment

Query through agent only. Accepts hard copy. SASE. Responds in 1 month. Publication in 18 months. Payment policy varies.

Editor's Comments

Please note that we do not consider unsolicited manuscripts or queries from authors without agent representation.

Raven Productions Inc.

P.O. Box 188
Ely, MN 55731

Editor: Johnna Hyde

Publisher's Interests

With a mission to encourage readers to enjoy and protect
the natural world, Raven Productions publishes books about
children and adults in natural settings.
Website: www.ravenwords.com

Freelance Potential

Published 4 titles (3 juvenile) in 2009: 3 were developed
from unsolicited submissions and 1 was a reprint/licensed
property. Of the 4 titles, 2 were by unpublished writers and
each was by an author who was new to the publishing
house. Receives 24 queries, 240 unsolicited mss yearly.

- **Fiction:** Publishes early picture books, 0–4 years; story picture
  books, 4–10 years; chapter books, 5–10 years; middle-grade
  books, 8–12 years; and young adult books, 12–18 years.
  Genres include regional, historical, multicultural, and ethnic
  fiction; folklore; and books about nature and sports.
- **Nonfiction:** Publishes easy-to-read books, 4–7 years; story
  picture books, 4–10 years; middle-grade books, 8–12 years;
  and young adult books, 12–18 years. Also publishes books for
  adults. Topics include animals, nature, science, technology,
  biography, history, sports, and regional subjects.
- **Representative Titles:** *Lucy's Hero* by Karen Shragg (5–10
  years) is a story based on an environmentally concerned
  senator. *I Saw a Moose Today* by Anne Stewart (3–10 years)
  educates children about various animals and their habitats.

Submissions and Payment

Guidelines available at website. Query with clips for adult
books. Send ms for children's books. Accepts hard copy and
disk submissions (Microsoft Word). SASE. Responds in 8–12
months. Publication in 3–5 years. Royalty, 10–15% of net.

Editor's Comments

We will not accept books with anthropomorphic animals,
except those in folktales, myths, or legends.

Raven Tree Press

1400 Miller Parkway
McHenry, IL 60050

Submissions

Publisher's Interests
With the intention of fostering multicultural awareness and language development, Raven Tree Press publishes picture books in both English and Spanish. It looks for family-oriented storylines with universal appeal for elementary-aged children. It does not publish reference books, religious topics, nonfiction, or activity books.
Website: www.raventreepress.com

Freelance Potential
Published 15 titles in 2009: 2 were by agented authors. Of the 15 titles, 3 were by unpublished writers and 10 were by authors who were new to the publishing house. Receives 500 unsolicited mss yearly.

- **Fiction:** Publishes early picture books, 0–4 years; easy-to-read books, 4–7 years; and story picture books, 4–10 years. Themes include conflict resolution, family values, and multicultural and ethnic issues.
- **Representative Titles:** *Where Does It Go?/¿Donde va?* by Cheryl Christian (0–4 years) introduces babies to language and concepts; part of the Star Bright Lift-the-Flap Books series. *I Wish I Was Tall Like Willie/Quisiera ser tan alto como Willie* by Kathryn Heling & Deborah Hembrook (4–7 years) is the story of a boy who goes to elaborate lengths to be taller; part of the I Wish . . . series.

Submissions and Payment
Guidelines and catalogue available at website. Send complete ms with synopsis, author bio, and publishing credits. Accepts hard copy and email to raven@raventreepress.com. SASE. Responds in 1–2 months. Publication period varies. Royalty; advance.

Editor's Comments
Always check our website for updates to our writers' guidelines before submitting. Remember, we do *not* accept queries.

Rayve Productions

P.O. Box 726
Windsor, CA 95492

Editor: Barbara Ray

Publisher's Interests

Rayve publishes adult self-help and nonfiction informational books on a variety of subjects. Its children's catalogue is filled with creative fiction designed to instill a love of reading in children, and a nonfiction list that appeals to the many interests of kids and young adults. It also publishes books on parenting issues.
Website: www.rayveproductions.com

Freelance Potential

Published 5 titles (1 juvenile) in 2009: 1 was developed from an unsolicited submission. Of the 5 titles, 1 was by a new author. Receives 100+ queries, 75 unsolicited mss yearly.

- **Fiction:** Publishes easy-to-read books, 4–7 years; story picture books, 4–10 years; and chapter books, 5–10 years. Genres include contemporary, historical, multicultural, and ethnic fiction; folktales; and adventure.
- **Nonfiction:** Publishes chapter books, 5–10 years; middle-grade books, 8–12 years; and young adult books, 12–18 years. Topics include history and biography. Also publishes educational and multicultural titles for teachers and parents.
- **Representative Titles:** *Buffalo Jones: The Man Who Saved America's Bison* by Carol A. Winn (10–14 years) is the true story of the man who risked his life to rescue baby buffalos. *When Molly Was in the Hospital* by Debbie Duncan (3–12 years) targets siblings of sick children with a tale of Molly's hospitalization.

Submissions and Payment

Guidelines and catalogue available at website. Query for adult books. Send complete ms for children's books. Accepts hard copy. SASE. Responds in 6 weeks. Publication in 1 year. Royalty, 10%; advance, varies.

Editor's Comments

We are currently interested in career-related titles for adults, but would hate to miss a terrific children's book manuscript.

Razorbill

Penguin Group USA, Inc.
345 Hudson Street, 15th Floor
New York, NY 10014

Editorial Assistant

Publisher's Interests

Razorbill, an imprint of Penguin Young Readers Group, offers middle-grade and young adult books. It publishes trade paperback fiction and nonfiction.
Website: www.razorbillbooks.com

Freelance Potential

Published 35–40 titles in 2009. Receives 500 queries yearly.

- **Fiction:** Publishes middle-grade books, 8–12 years; and young adult books, 12–18 years. Genres include contemporary and science fiction, mystery, suspense, and fantasy.
- **Nonfiction:** Publishes middle-grade books, 8–12 years; and young adult books, 12–18 years. Topics include adventure and pop culture.
- **Representative Titles:** *Pretty Little Devils* by Nancy Holder (12+ years) finds Hazel befriended by the evil and popular girls of her high school, until she finds out that popularity can come with a deadly price. *Beautiful Americans* by Lucy Silag (14+ years) is the story of four American teens in Paris, and the scandal that leads one girl to disappear. *The Boy in the Dress* by David Walliams (9+ years) is a humorous tale of a boy with a flare for fashion who must fight for the respect of his father.

Submissions and Payment

Query. Accepts hard copy. SASE. Response time and publication period vary. Advance.

Editor's Comments

We pride ourselves on publishing the kinds of books that middle-grade readers and young adults *want* to read. It is sometimes a difficult feat to get these readers to choose books over their social lives, but we produce the kinds of books that touch them, that speak to them, and that entertain them. We look for unique stories and high-interest nonfiction subjects that captivate readers ages 8 to 18.

Reagent Press Books for Young Readers

P.O. Box 362
East Olympia, WA 98540-0362

Submissions: Jeannie Kim

Publisher's Interests
This new imprint has been carved from the greater Reagent Press catalogue and focuses on science fiction and fantasy for children ages four through twelve.
Website: www.reagentpress.com

Freelance Potential
Published 15–20 titles in 2009: 7 were by agented authors. Receives 1,200–1,500 queries yearly.

- **Fiction:** Publishes easy-to-read books, 4–7 years; story picture books, 4–10 years; chapter books, 5–10 years; and middle-grade books, 8–12 years. Genres include contemporary and science fiction; fantasy; mystery; suspense; adventure; fairy tales; and stories about insects and nature.
- **Nonfiction:** Publishes easy-to-read books, 4–7 years; story picture books, 4–10 years; chapter books, 5–10 years; and middle-grade books, 8–12 years. Topics include animals, sports, and multicultural and ethnic subjects.
- **Representative Titles:** *The Bugville Critters Compete in the BIG Spelling Bee* by Robert Stanek (3–8 years) tells how Lass, a young bug, copes with stage fright; part of the Bugville Critters series. *How Mother Nature Flowered the Fields of Earth and Mars* by Tom Schwartz (7–11 years) is a collection of stories about how our natural world works.

Submissions and Payment
Guidelines and catalogue available at website. Query with synopsis and author bio. Accepts email to reagentpress@aol.com. Responds in 1–6 months if interested. Publication period varies. Royalty; advance.

Editor's Comments
Our review policy for queries is this: every query reviewed and carefully considered, every time. If your idea meets our guidelines and is a work we're interested in, we'll respond to your query. We do not otherwise respond to queries.

Red Deer Press

195 Allstode Parkway
Markham, Ontario L3R 4T8
Canada

Children's Editor: Peter Carver

Publisher's Interests

The mandate of Red Deer Press is to publish books by, about, or of interest to Canadians, with special emphasis on the Prairie West. It publishes juvenile and young adult fiction, nonfiction, and picture books, and titles for adults.
Website: www.reddeerpress.com

Freelance Potential

Published 18 titles (10 juvenile) in 2009: 2 were by unpublished writers and 4 were by authors who were new to the publishing house. Receives 2,000+ unsolicited mss yearly.

- **Fiction:** Publishes story picture books, 4–10 years; middle-grade books, 8–12 years; and young adult books, 12–18 years. Genres include regional, contemporary, and ethnic fiction; adventure; fantasy; mystery; suspense; and drama.
- **Nonfiction:** Publishes activity books, field guides, and biographies, 4–18 years. Topics include Canadian nature, wildlife, First Nations, history, and personalities.
- **Representative Titles:** *Long Powwow Nights* by David Bouchard & Pam Aleekuk uses poetic verses to narrate the story of a mother's dedication to her roots and her efforts to impress upon her children the importance of culture and identity. *Egghead* by Caroline Pignat (12+ years) is the story of three teens who must each decide how to play their role in a bullying scenario.

Submissions and Payment

Guidelines available at http://fitzhenry.ca/red_deer_submission_guide.aspx. Send complete ms for picture books and YA fiction; query with synopsis and sample chapters for all others. Accepts hard copy. SAE/IRC. Responds in 4–6 months. Publication in 2–3 years. Royalty.

Editor's Comments

We are especially committed to developing talent from the prairie region.

Redleaf Press

10 Yorkton Court
St. Paul, MN 55117

Editor-in-Chief: David Heath

Publisher's Interests

Redleaf Press is a nonprofit publisher of curriculum, management, and business resources for early childhood professionals. It seeks to improve the lives of children by strengthening and supporting the teachers and families who care for them.
Website: www.redleafpress.org

Freelance Potential

Published 25 titles in 2009: 5 were developed from unsolicited submissions and 10 were by authors who were new to the publishing house. Receives 200+ queries yearly.

- **Nonfiction:** Publishes curriculum, management, and business resources for early childhood professionals. Topics include math, science, language, literacy, cultural diversity, music, movement, health, safety, nutrition, child development, special needs, and teacher training and assessment.
- **Representative Titles:** *Medical Emergencies in Early Childhood Settings* is a quick-reference guide to the crucial steps of treating a child's injury; part of the Redleaf Quick Guide series. *Everyday Early Learning* by Jeff A. Johnson shows ways to turn ordinary household items into toys while also teaching skills in literacy, math, and science.

Submissions and Payment

Guidelines and catalogue available at website. Query with résumé, outline, table of contents, and sample chapters. Accepts email queries to acquisitions@redleafpress.org. Responds in 6 weeks. Publication in 18–24 months. Payment policy varies.

Editor's Comments

Our titles represent a broad range of topics designed to assist teachers in providing a stimulating, child-centered curriculum. The material you submit must be age- and audience-appropriate, based on sound theory and research in child development, and take cultural differences into account.

Resource Publications

160 East Virginia Street, Suite 290
San Jose, CA 95112

Acquisitions Editor: William Burns

Publisher's Interests

Professional resource materials and books for Christian worship and religious education are the focus of this privately owned publishing house. It works with both new and previously published authors and is not affiliated with a particular church or denomination. 5% self-, subsidy-, co-venture, or co-op published material.
Website: www.rpinet.com

Freelance Potential

Published 6 titles in 2009: 2 were developed from unsolicited submissions. Of the 6 titles, 2 were by unpublished writers and 2 were by authors who were new to the publishing house. Receives 60–96 queries yearly.

- **Fiction:** Publishes young adult books, 12–18 years. Genres include religious and spiritual fiction.
- **Nonfiction:** Publishes middle-grade books, 8–12 years; and young adult books, 12–18 years. Topics include prayer, religion, catechism, faith, meditations, the sacraments, and spirituality. Also publishes books on prayer and personal growth.
- **Representative Titles:** *Developing Children's Liturgy* by Gail Fabbro offers step-by-step instruction for creating a children's liturgy. *Experiences for Exploring God's Word* by Steve Mason & Sandy Rigsby is an interactive Scripture guide for young teens.

Submissions and Payment

Guidelines and catalogue available at website. Query with clips. Accepts hard copy and email queries to editor@rpinet.com. SASE. Responds in 6–8 weeks. Publication in 9–18 months. Royalty, 8% of net.

Editor's Comments

We are always looking for new and innovative ideas in worship, ministry, and catechism while supporting the vision of the Second Vatican Council. We welcome your queries.

River City Publishing

1719 Mulberry Street
Montgomery, AL 36106

Editor: Jim Gilbert

Publisher's Interests

Most of River City Publishing's books are written by authors
from the American South and focus on the region's history
and culture. While its list includes children's books, the publisher is currently closed to submissions of children's and
young adult titles.
Website: www.rivercitypublishing.com

Freelance Potential

Published 6 titles in 2009: 2 were developed from unsolicited
submissions. Of the 6 titles, 5 were by unpublished writers
and 2 were by authors who were new to the publishing
house. Receives 3,000 queries, 1,500 unsolicited mss yearly.

- **Fiction:** Publishes early picture books, 0–4 years; story picture
  books, 4–10 years; and middle-grade books, 9–12 years. Genres include regional, historical, and multicultural fiction; folklore; and humor. Also publishes literary fiction for adults.
- **Nonfiction:** Publishes narrative nonfiction for adults. Topics
  include travel, history, and biography related to the South.
- **Representative Titles:** *It Was Big, It Was Scary, It Was . . .* by
  Diana Aubut & Leslie Nordness (4–8 years) tells how an elf
  helps a young boy to overcome his fears. *Cochula's Journey*
  by Virginia Pounds Brown (9–12 years) is the fictional account
  of an Indian girl who travels with DeSoto.

Submissions and Payment

Guidelines and catalogue available at website. Query or send
complete ms. Accepts hard copy and email queries only to
jgilbert@rivercitypublishing.com (no attachments). SASE.
Responds in 3–9 months. Publication period varies. Royalty;
advance, $1,000–$5,000.

Editor's Comments

Due to our publishing schedule and reading backlog, we do
occasionally, if briefly, close to submissions. Please be
patient. You may check our website for updates.

Rocky River Publishers

P.O. Box 1679
Shepherdstown, WV 25443

Acquisitions Editor

Publisher's Interests

Since 1987, Rocky River has published books that feature creative approaches to helping children deal with the problems they may face from infancy onward. It publishes books for children as well as for parents, teachers, and counselors. Topics covered include such issues as self-esteem, substance abuse prevention, peer pressure, stress, and a variety of other contemporary pressures.

Website: www.rockyriver.com

Freelance Potential

Published several titles in 2009. Receives 240 queries, 720 unsolicited mss yearly.

- **Fiction:** Publishes toddler books, 0–4 years; easy-to-read books, 4–7 years; story picture books, 4–10 years; and young adult books, 12–18 years. Genres include contemporary, inspirational, and educational fiction.
- **Nonfiction:** Publishes middle-grade books, 8–12 years; and young adult books, 12–18 years. Topics include drug education, self-esteem, stress, youth safety, abuse, health, disabilities, and addiction. Also publishes parenting resources.
- **Representative Titles:** *Henrietta* by Wayne Walker uses a panicky ostrich to teach children that it is better to face their fears than pretend that problems don't exist. *Mac's Choice* by Debra Wert (7–10 years) prepares young children to deal with the issues surrounding drug use; includes a workbook that allows children to further discuss this topic.

Submissions and Payment

Guidelines and catalogue available at website. Query or send complete ms. Accepts hard copy. SASE. Response time and publication period vary. Royalty; advance. Flat fee.

Editor's Comments

The books we publish are not only helpful and educational, but also interesting and creative.

Ronsdale Press

3350 West 21st Avenue
Vancouver, British Columbia V6S 1G7
Canada

Director: Ronald B. Hatch

Publisher's Interests
This literary publishing house presents fiction, biographies, history, and children's literature from Canadian authors. It specializes in titles with Canadian themes, locations, and topics.
Website: www.ronsdalepress.com

Freelance Potential
Published 13 titles (3 juvenile) in 2009: 8 were developed from unsolicited submissions and 1 was by an agented author. Of the 13 titles, 2 were by unpublished writers and 3 were by authors who were new to the publishing house. Receives 300 queries, 1,200 unsolicited mss yearly.

- **Fiction:** Publishes middle-grade books, 8–12 years; and young adult books, 12–18 years. Genres include Canadian historical fiction. Also publishes books for adults.
- **Nonfiction:** Publishes titles for adults on politics, economics, regional history, and language. Also publishes biographies and autobiographies.
- **Representative Titles:** *Tragic Links* by Cathy Beveridge (10+ years) takes a time-traveling girl back into the midst of two of Canada's historic disasters. *Submarine Outlaw* by Philip Roy (10+ years) features a Newfoundland boy who builds a submarine that he sails around the Canadian Maritimes, resulting in high-speed chases, rescues, and treasure hunts.

Submissions and Payment
Canadian authors only. Guidelines available at website. Query with sample chapter; or send complete ms. Accepts hard copy. SASE. Responds in 1–2 months. Publication in 1 year. Royalty, 10%.

Editor's Comments
For our children's collection, we look for titles for readers ages 8 to 15. We are especially interested in young adult historical novels. We no longer publish picture books.

The Rosen Publishing Group

29 East 21st Street
New York, NY 10010

Editorial Director, YA Division: Iris Rosoff

Publisher's Interests

A family-owned educational publisher since 1950, The Rosen Publishing Group specializes in guidance books and curriculum-based, high-interest nonfiction books for children ages 8 to 18.

Website: www.rosenpublishing.com

Freelance Potential

Published 200 titles in 2009. Of the 200 titles, 20 were by unpublished writers and 20 were by authors who were new to the publishing house. Receives 75 queries yearly.

- **Nonfiction:** Publishes middle-grade books, 8–12 years; and young adult books, 12–18 years. Topics include history, health, science, the arts, safety, guidance, careers, and contemporary social issues.
- **Representative Titles:** *Cool Careers Without College for People Who Love to Build Things* by Joy Paige (grades 7–12) outlines 12 careers—including salary ranges and future prospects—that involve constructing or creating, but do not require a college degree; part of the Cool Careers Without College series. *Deacon Jones* by Karen Donnelly (grades 5–8) profiles the great L.A. Rams defensive end; part of the Football Hall of Famers series.

Submissions and Payment

Catalogue available at website. All work is assigned. Query with résumé. Accepts email queries to irisr@rosen.com. Responds in 3 months. Publication in 9 months. Flat fee.

Editor's Comments

Please note that we do not accept unsolicited submissions. All of our books are assigned on a work-for-hire basis. We are always interested in adding talented writers to our list, so send us your résumé listing the fields in which you have expertise. If you have a specific book or series idea, let us hear it—we might assign it to you.

Royal Fireworks Press

41 First Avenue
P.O. Box 399
Unionville, NY 10988

Submissions: William Neumann

Publisher's Interests
Books for gifted students and homeschoolers are available
from this publisher, which has a complete line of books for
an advanced curriculum on all subjects, but is especially
strong in language arts. It also produces books for teachers,
administrators, and parents on teaching gifted students.
Website: www.rfwp.com

Freelance Potential
Published 100 titles in 2009. Of the 100 titles, 50 were by
new authors. Receives 300 unsolicited mss yearly.

- **Fiction:** Publishes chapter books, 5–10 years; middle-grade
  books, 8–12 years; and young adult books, 12–18 years.
  Genres include contemporary, historical, Western, and science
  fiction; folklore; adventure; and mystery.
- **Nonfiction:** Publishes chapter books, 5–10 years; middle-
  grade books, 8–12 years; and young adult books, 12–18
  years. Topics include creative problem solving, logic, strategy,
  memory enhancement, guidance, leadership, science, math,
  social studies, history, philosophy, the arts, and language arts.
  Also publishes books on the education of gifted children.
- **Representative Titles:** *Smuggler's Nest* by Patti W. Hillenius
  (grades 3–5) is the story of a young Mexican boy who gets
  caught up in a bird smuggling ring. *Girls, Women, and Giftedness* by Julie Ellis & John Willinsky, eds. is a collection of
  studies and essays about teaching gifted females.

Submissions and Payment
Guidelines and catalogue available at website. Send complete ms; include synopsis for fiction. Accepts hard copy. No
simultaneous submissions. SASE. Responds in 1 month.
Publication in 8 months. Royalty.

Editor's Comments
We want books for serious young students who can take a
subject matter deeper than most.

RP Books

P.O. Box 362
East Olympia, WA 98540-0362

Associate Publisher: Thomas Green

Publisher's Interests
This publisher's books fall into a variety of categories, with the majority being science fiction/fantasy books for children, young adults, and adults. RP Books also produces a number of nonfiction reference books.
Website: www.reagentpress.com

Freelance Potential
Published 100–130 titles (80 juvenile) in 2009: 20 were developed from unsolicited submissions and 40 were by agented authors. Of the 100–130 titles, 10 were by unpublished writers and 20 were by authors who were new to the publishing house. Receives 3,600–6,000 queries yearly.

- **Fiction:** Publishes story picture books, 4–10 years; chapter books, 5–10 years; middle-grade books, 8–12 years; and young adult books, 12–18 years. Genres include contemporary and science fiction, fantasy, mystery, adventure, and stories about insects and nature.
- **Nonfiction:** Publishes reference books, 5–10 years. Topics include writing, business, computers, and history. Also publishes classroom resources for teachers.
- **Representative Titles:** *Arianna Kelt and the Wizards of Skyhall* by J. R. King (9+ years) relates the sometimes humorous adventures of a reformed thief in a land of wizards. *Journey Beyond the Beyond* by Robert Stanek (9+ years) follows Ray as he faces coming-of-age tests that challenge his will, his mind, and his very self; part of the Magic Lands series.

Submissions and Payment
Guidelines available at website. Query with synopsis and author bio. Accepts email to reagentpress@aol.com. Responds in 1–6 months. Publication period varies. Royalty; advance.

Editor's Comments
When querying, please give us your thoughts on how your book could be marketed.

Running Press Kids

2300 Chestnut Street, Suite 200
Philadelphia, PA 19103-4399

Assistant to the Editorial Director

Publisher's Interests

This imprint of Running Press publishes innovative nonfiction and fiction for children up to age 12. Its list includes books that are accompanied by games and activities.
Website: www.runningpress.com

Freelance Potential

Published 50 titles in 2009. Of the 50 titles, 5 were by unpublished writers and 2 were by authors who were new to the publishing house. Receives 800 queries, 700 mss yearly.

- **Fiction:** Publishes story picture books, 4–10 years; chapter books, 5–10 years; middle-grade books, 8–12 years; and young adult books, 12–18 years. Genres include contemporary and historical fiction, folklore, fairy tales, adventure, and suspense.
- **Nonfiction:** Publishes concept books, toddler books, and early picture books, 0–4 years; and easy-to-read books, 4–7 years. Topics include geography, holidays, science, and arts and crafts. Also publishes biographies, activity kits, discovery books, and parenting titles.
- **Representative Titles:** *Say a Little Prayer* by Dionne Warwick et al. is a picture book that uses the story of a girl singing in front of an audience as encouragement for kids to find their talent and embrace it. *Dream Machines* by Mark Rogalski is a picture book that brings readers along on Dream Machines, a collection of vehicles that can go anywhere.

Submissions and Payment

Guidelines and catalogue available at website. Send complete ms for picture books. Query with outline, table of contents, and synopsis for other material. Accepts hard copy. SASE. Responds in 2–3 months. Publication in 1–2 years. Advance.

Editor's Comments

We are interested in interactive nonfiction, concept books, and beginning reading projects. At this time, we are not publishing novels or fiction longer than picture-book length.

St. Anthony Messenger Press

28 West Liberty Street
Cincinnati, OH 45202

Editorial Director: Lisa Biedenbach

Publisher's Interests

St. Anthony Messenger Press seeks to spread the word of Jesus Christ in the style of St. Francis and St. Anthony, and supports the ministry and charities of the Franciscan Friars of St. John the Baptist Province. Through its print and electronic media, this publisher endeavors to evangelize, inspire, and inform those who search for God and seek a richer Catholic life.

Website: www.americancatholic.org

Freelance Potential

Published 19 titles in 2009. Of the 19 titles, 4 were by unpublished writers and 7 were by authors who were new to the publishing house. Receives 200 queries yearly.

• **Nonfiction:** Publishes books for parents, ministers, and religious education teachers. Topics include Christian living, personal growth, faith, the sacraments, Scripture, prayer, spirituality, the saints, marriage, family, and parenting.
• **Representative Titles:** *Bringing Home the Gospel* by Judith Dunlap (parents) is a weekly journal for Catholic parents that helps them apply the Word of God to daily life. *When Your Spouse Isn't Catholic* by Carol Gastelum is a practical resource for living with and loving your spouse faithfully. *When Your Child Becomes Catholic* by Rita Burns Senseman (parents) answers frequently asked questions about the Christian initiation of children.

Submissions and Payment

Guidelines and catalogue available at website. Query with outline. Accepts hard copy. SASE. Responds in 2–3 months. Publication in 1–2 years. Royalty, 10%; advance, $1,000.

Editor's Comments

We seek manuscripts that educate and inspire adult Catholic Christians, that identify trends surfacing in the Catholic world, and that help Catholics better understand their faith.

Saint Mary's Press

702 Terrace Heights
Winona, MN 55987-1318

Submissions Coordinator: Linda Waldo

Publisher's Interests

St. Mary's Press publishes a range of textbooks, teaching manuals, and resource materials for religious educators, youth ministers, and parents of adolescents and teens. Spirituality resources for teens themselves are also included.
Website: www.smp.org

Freelance Potential

Published 26 titles (16 juvenile) in 2009: 2 were developed from unsolicited submissions. Of the 26 titles, 3 were by authors who were new to the publishing house. Receives 360 queries yearly.

- **Nonfiction:** Publishes middle-grade books, 8–12 years; and young adult books, 12–18 years. Topics include spirituality, Christianity, and the Catholic faith. Also publishes titles for adults who teach or minister to youth.
- **Representative Titles:** *Growing in Christian Morality* by Julia Ahlers et al. offers a Christian vision for the difficult questions teens face by highlighting various stories, cases, and quotes. *I'm Glad You Asked* by Fr. Mark R. Pierce (YA) presents clear and clever answers to the most commonly asked questions about the Bible.

Submissions and Payment

Guidelines available at website. Query with synopsis, table of contents, introduction, sample chapter, author bio, and list of publishing credits. Accepts hard copy, email to submissions@smp.org, and simultaneous submissions if identified. SASE. Responds in 2 months. Publication in 12–18 months. Royalty, 10%.

Editor's Comments

Keep in mind that we are looking for material that is new, significant, or unique, and in touch with the needs of our audiences. We do not publish personal memoirs, fiction, or books of poetry.

Salina Bookshelf

3120 North Caden Court, Suite 4
Flagstaff, AZ 86004

Editor: LaFrenda Frank

Publisher's Interests
Since 1994, this independent publisher has been producing Navajo-related picture books and textbooks (as well as reference books for adults) in both Navajo and English.
Website: www.salinabookshelf.com

Freelance Potential
Published 10 titles in 2009: 5 were developed from unsolicited submissions and 3 were reprint/licensed properties. Of the 10 titles, 2 were by unpublished writers and 6 were by authors who were new to the publishing house. Receives 120–144 unsolicited mss yearly.

- **Fiction:** Publishes toddler books and early picture books, 0–4 years; easy-to-read books, 4–7 years; story picture books, 4–10 years; chapter books, 5–10 years; middle-grade books, 8–12 years; and young adult books, 12–18 years. Genres include folklore, folktales, multicultural and ethnic fiction, and stories about nature and the environment. Also publishes bilingual Navajo/English books, 4–7 years.
- **Nonfiction:** Publishes middle-grade books, 8–12 years; and young adult books, 12–18 years. Topics include Navajo history and culture. Also publishes biographies.
- **Representative Titles:** *Bidii* by Marjorie W. Thomas is a humorous story of a greedy boy who loves showing off until he learns a valuable lesson in humility. *Father's Boots* by Baje Whitethorne, Sr., is a touching story about three brothers who gain an appreciation of their culture through stories.

Submissions and Payment
Guidelines available. Send complete ms. Accepts hard copy. SASE. Responds in 3 weeks. Publication in 1 year. Royalty, varies; advance, varies.

Editor's Comments
Your book must deal with the Navajo people, their language, or their culture.

Samhain Publishing

577 Mulberry Street, Suite 1520
Macon, GA 31201

Executive Editor: Angela James

Publisher's Interests

Samhain Publishing is interested in adult and young adult titles in all genres of romance fiction, including fantasy, celtic, and science fiction (with romantic elements). It publishes mainly books for adults, many of which appeal to young adult readers. While most of its books are digital, it does produce a selection for the print market.
Website: www.samhainpublishing.com

Freelance Potential

Published 50 titles (2–3 juvenile) in 2009. Receives 240–360 queries yearly.

- **Fiction:** Publishes young adult novels, 12–18 years. Genres include contemporary fiction, romance, fantasy, urban fantasy, and science fiction.
- **Representative Titles:** *Life on the Move* by Megan Reilly (YA) is the story of a teen girl who lives life on the move with her father, until she lands in a town that she doesn't want to leave. *Wiccan Cool* by Traci Hall (YA) is a novel about a teen girl who has learned to balance her normal life with her psychic abilities, until she meets a boy and a ghost that threaten to upend that balance.

Submissions and Payment

Guidelines and catalogue available at website. Query with 2- to 5-page synopsis and 3+ sample chapters. Accepts email queries to editor@samhainpublishing.com (Microsoft Word or RTF attachments) and simultaneous submissions if identified. Responds in 3–4 months. Publication period varies. Royalty, 30–40% of retail.

Editor's Comments

We are currently refocusing our efforts on romance, erotica, fantasy, and science fiction. For the time being, we're not accepting other genres or young adult titles. Please check our website for updates.

Sandlapper Publishing

P.O. Box 730
Orangeburg, SC 29116

Managing Editor: Amanda Gallman

Publisher's Interests
Sandlapper Publishing—an independent, regional publisher—specializes in books about South Carolina's history, culture, and natural resources.
Website: www.sandlapperpublishing.com

Freelance Potential
Published 4–6 titles (3 juvenile) in 2009. Receives 150 queries each year.

- **Nonfiction:** Publishes easy-to-read books, 4–7 years; story picture books, 4–10 years; chapter books, 5–10 years; middle-grade books, 8–12 years; and young adult books, 12–18 years. Topics include South Carolina history, flora, fauna, travel, culture, literature, and cooking.
- **Representative Titles:** *The Mystery of Edisto Island* by Idella Bodie (10+ years) relates the adventures of four vacationing youngsters who try to help an old fisherman. *A Turtle Named Caretta* by Ruth "Booie" Chappell teaches children about the delicate life cycle of the endangered loggerhead turtle. *A Living Mascot* by Rhonda S. Edwards describes the family of bald eagles that lives in harmony with the children of Eagle Nest Elementary School in North Charleston.

Submissions and Payment
Guidelines and catalogue available at website. Query with outline, résumé, and writing samples. Accepts hard copy and email queries to agallman@sandlapperpublishing.com. SASE. Responds in 2 months. Publication in 2 years. Royalty, 15% of net.

Editor's Comments
We strive to produce quality books that are promoted individually and marketed throughout the region. To this end, we prefer that content cover the entire state of South Carolina, rather than concentrating on one particular area. We will consider works previously published, but please query first.

Sasquatch Books

119 South Main Street, Suite 400
Seattle, WA 98104

Acquisitions Editor: Terence Meikel

Publisher's Interests

Sasquatch produces "regional books without boundaries," and specializes in fiction and nonfiction titles about the Pacific Northwest and Alaska. Its children's list includes fiction for readers up to age seven, and nonfiction for young children and young adults.

Website: www.sasquatchbooks.com

Freelance Potential

Published 42 titles (7 juvenile) in 2009: 2 were developed from unsolicited submissions and 6 were by agented authors. Of the 42 titles, 10 were by unpublished writers. Receives 3,000 queries, 2,700 unsolicited mss yearly.

- **Fiction:** Publishes concept books, toddler books, and early picture books, 0–4 years; and easy-to-read books, 4–7 years. Genres include regional historical, multicultural, and ethnic fiction, and stories about animals and nature.
- **Nonfiction:** Publishes concept books, toddler books, and early picture books, 0–4 years; easy-to-read books, 4–7 years; and young adult books, 12–18 years. Also publishes cookbooks, gardening books, travel books, and books on photography for adults. Topics include the Pacific Northwest and Canada.
- **Representative Titles:** *Larry Gets Lost in San Francisco* by John Skewes follows a curious dog as he wanders through all the landmarks of the City by the Bay. *Lootas: Little Wave Eater* by Clare Hodgson Meeker presents the true story of an orphaned sea otter that was adopted by the Seattle Aquarium.

Submissions and Payment

Guidelines and catalogue available at website. Query or send complete ms. Accepts hard copy. SASE. Responds in 1–3 months. Publication period and payment policy vary.

Editor's Comments

We accept manuscripts and proposals from authors as well as agents. All work must have a regional theme or subject.

Scarecrow Press

4501 Forbes Boulevard, Suite 200
Lanham, MD 20706

Acquisitions Editor

Publisher's Interests
Part of the Rowman & Littlefield Publishing Group, Scarecrow Press publishes reference tools to help librarians in serving young readers, as well as scholarly, professional, and academic reference books on a variety of subjects.
Website: www.scarecrowpress.com

Freelance Potential
Published 180 titles in 2009: 115 were developed from unsolicited submissions and 9 were by agented authors. Receives 1,200 queries, 240 unsolicited mss yearly.

- **Nonfiction:** Publishes handbooks, reference tools, bibliographies, historical dictionaries, library science monographs, and other scholarly and professional works. Topics include the humanities, history, geography, religion, social and multicultural issues, ancient civilizations, music, and science.
- **Representative Titles:** *Body Image and Appearance: The Ultimate Teen Guide* by Kathlyn Gay addresses the preoccupation teens have with body image, and provides them with a healthy way to think about themselves; part of the It Happened to Me series. *The ABCs of Running a School Library* by Terri L. Lyons provides a broad overview of running a school library, targeting teacher-librarians who are teachers first.

Submissions and Payment
Guidelines and catalogue available at website. Query with résumé, table of contents, and sample chapter; or send ms. Accepts hard copy and email to ekurdyla@scarecrowpress.com (Microsoft Word attachments). SASE. Responds in 3–5 months. Publication in 6–12 months. Royalty, 8–12.5%.

Editor's Comments
We require an extensive C.V. from all prospective writers listing professional experience and previous publication experience, if applicable. Please also include a tentative title for your manuscript.

Scholastic Children's Books

Euston House
24 Eversholt Street
London NW1 1DB
United Kingdom

Editorial Department

Publisher's Interests

Creative, high-quality children's fiction and nonfiction comprise the catalogue of this well-known publisher. It produces books for children of all ages, in all genres, and on a variety of topics.
Website: www.scholastic.co.uk

Freelance Potential

Published 200 titles in 2009: most were by agented authors. Receives 350–400 queries yearly.

- **Fiction:** Publishes concept books, toddler books, and early picture books, 0–4 years; easy-to-read books, 4–7 years; story picture books, 4–10 years; chapter books, 5–10 years; middle-grade books, 8–12 years; and young adult books, 12–18 years. Genres include contemporary and historical fiction, adventure, drama, and fantasy.
- **Nonfiction:** Publishes chapter books, 5–10 years. Topics include geography, history, math, and sports.
- **Representative Titles:** *Ruthless Romans* by Terry Deary presents the history of the Roman Empire with enough gore and "nasty" facts to appeal to any young reader; part of the Horrible Histories series. *Harry and Hopper* by Margaret Wild has a boy learning about the shock of grief and the sustaining power of love after his beloved dog dies.

Submissions and Payment

Guidelines and catalogue available at website. Query with synopsis and 3 sample chapters. Accepts hard copy. SAE/IRC. Response time, publication period, and payment policy vary.

Editor's Comments

Unfortunately, we are not able to receive any submission sent via email or on disk. Though you do not need an agent to have your work considered by us, having one does give you a leg up.

Scholastic Inc./Trade Paperback Division

557 Broadway
New York, NY 10012

Group Publisher: Suzanne Murphy

Publisher's Interests

The Trade Paperback Division, an imprint of Scholastic Trade, is mainly concerned with high-quality and creative fiction in all genres for young readers. It also publishes a number of nonfiction titles on nature, hobbies, and sports. It does not accept unsolicited submissions, preferring instead to work solely with literary agents.

Website: www.scholastic.com

Freelance Potential

Published 600 titles in 2009: each was by an agented author. Receives 250 queries, 150 unsolicited mss yearly.

- **Fiction:** Publishes chapter books, 5–10 years; middle-grade books, 8–12 years; and young adult books, 12–18 years. Genres include contemporary and science fiction, fantasy, adventure, and romance. Also publishes scary stories and stories about sports, animals, and friendship.
- **Nonfiction:** Publishes books for children of all ages. Topics include animals, science, nature, and multicultural issues.
- **Representative Titles:** *The Bride of Frankenstein Doesn't Bake Cookies* by Debbie Dadey & Marcia Thornton Jones (7–10 years) has school kids wondering about the identity of the new snack bar lady; part of the Adventures of the Bailey School Kids series. *Along Came Spider* by James Preller (9–12 years) is a story of two friends who find their friendship tested when they get to fifth grade, when peer opinions matter.

Submissions and Payment

Accepts submissions through literary agents and from previous Scholastic authors only. SASE. Response time, publication period, and payment policy vary.

Editor's Comments

We publish a variety of books for young readers—books that instill a love of reading at an important age. If your book can do that, have your agent contact us.

Scholastic Press

557 Broadway
New York, NY 10012

Senior Editor: Jennifer Rees

Publisher's Interests

An imprint of Scholastic Inc. since 1920, this publisher is interested in picture books for young children—both fiction and nonfiction—as well as nonfiction and novels for older children and young adults.
Website: www.scholastic.com

Freelance Potential

Published 40–50 titles in 2009. Receives 3,000 queries each year.

- **Fiction:** Publishes toddler books and early picture books, 0–4 years; story picture books, 4–10 years; chapter books, 5–10 years; middle-grade books, 8–12 years; and young adult books, 12–18 years. Genres include contemporary and science fiction, adventure, fantasy, humor, and mystery.
- **Nonfiction:** Publishes story picture books, 4–10 years; chapter books, 5–10 years; middle-grade books, 8–12 years; and young adult books, 12–18 years. Topics include humor, history, nature, the environment, and multicultural subjects. Also publishes biographies.
- **Representative Titles:** *Chasing Lincoln's Killer* by James Swanson (grade 7) tells the story of the pursuit and capture of John Wilkes Booth and his accomplices. *Always in Trouble* by Corinne Demas (preK–grade 3) is the story of a dog who always seems to get in trouble, and the dog trainer who teaches him everything a dog needs to know.

Submissions and Payment

Writers' guidelines available. Query. Accepts hard copy. SASE. Responds in 2–3 weeks. Publication in 1–2 years. Royalty; advance.

Editor's Comments

Due to the overwhelming volume of submissions we receive, we will only accept queries from agented authors, or writers with whom we have previously worked.

Scholastic Professional Books

524 Broadway
New York, NY 10012-3999

Editorial Director: Virginia Dooley

Publisher's Interests

This publisher offers "resources for every teacher to reach every child." Its catalogue is filled with books on the latest research and best practices that address the challenges facing educators today.

Website: www.scholastic.com/professional

Freelance Potential

Published 120 titles in 2009: 10 were developed from unsolicited submissions and 1 was by an agented author. Of the 120 titles, 70 were by unpublished writers and 50 were by new authors. Receives 900 queries yearly.

- **Nonfiction:** Publishes books for educators, preK–grade 8. Topics include teaching strategies, curriculum development, assessment, evaluation, cooperative learning, and classroom management. Also offers cross-curriculum and literature-based materials for teaching reading, language arts, literature, mathematics, science, social studies, and art.
- **Representative Titles:** *RTI: Assessments & Remediation for K–2* by Dr. Brenda M. Weaver provides an assessment system that enables teachers to screen students and monitor their progress in reading and writing all year long. *Teaching Teens and Reaping Results in a Wi-Fi, Hip-Hop, Where-Has-All-the-Sanity-Gone World* by Alan Sitomer (teachers, grades 6–12) offers strategies for preparing teens for a world filled with technologies and challenges that don't yet exist.

Submissions and Payment

Guidelines and catalogue available at website. Query with synopsis, table of contents, sample chapter, and biography. Accepts hard copy. SASE. Responds in 2 months. Publication period and payment policy vary.

Editor's Comments

We welcome submissions from all educators who can offer helpful, insightful, and inspiring ideas.

Science, Naturally!

725 8th Street SE
Washington, DC 20003

President: Dia L. Michels

Publisher's Interests

Science, Naturally! publishes nonfiction books on science topics. It specializes in books that break down scientific and math concepts into fun, easy-to-understand language and activities for children from preschool to high school.
Website: www.sciencenaturally.com

Freelance Potential

Published 3 titles in 2009: each was by an agented author. Receives 60 queries yearly.

- **Nonfiction:** Publishes concept books and early picture books, 0–4 years; easy-to-read books, 4–7 years; story picture books, 4–10 years; chapter books, 5–10 years; middle-grade books, 8–12 years; and young adult books, 12–18 years. Topics include science and mathematics.
- **Representative Titles:** *101 Things Everyone Should Know About Science* by Dia Michels & Nathan Levy (all ages) uses a question-and-answer format to show how science has an impact on everyday life. *65 Short Mysteries You Solve with Math* by Eric Yoder & Natalie Yoder (all ages) presents short mysteries that require the use of math skills to be solved; part of the One-Minute Mysteries series.

Submissions and Payment

Guidelines and catalogue available at website. Query. Accepts hard copy and simultaneous submissions if identified. SASE. Response time varies. Publication in 9–12 months. Royalty. Flat fee.

Editor's Comments

We believe in "teaching the science of everyday life." We are interested in books that make science or math enjoyable and accessible to both children and adults. Please note that we put an emphasis on fun—we're interested only in books that can entertain young readers and teach them without lecturing.

Scobre Press Corporation

2255 Calle Clara
La Jolla, CA 92037

Editor: Scott Blumenthal

Publisher's Interests

Founded in 1999 by a pair of college students who had grown up without a love of reading, Scobre Press publishes educational books designed to truly interest young people. Each title is available on two reading levels, which allows students of varying abilities to participate in the same lesson. **Website: www.scobre.com**

Freelance Potential

Published 6 titles in 2009. Of the 6 titles, 2 were by unpublished writers and 4 were by authors who were new to the publishing house. Receives 10–15 queries yearly.

- **Fiction:** Publishes middle-grade books, 8–12 years; and young adult books, 12–18 years. Features stories about sports, dance, and music.
- **Nonfiction:** Publishes middle-grade books, 8–12 years; and young adult books, 12–18 years. Topics include sports, dance, music, and video games. Also publishes teacher resources.
- **Representative Titles:** *Safe at Home* by Paula Bott (grades 3–6) is the story of a young Latina girl who suddenly loses her mother, but eventually finds herself through softball. *The Highest Stand* by Tonie Campbell (grades 4–7) takes an in-depth look at the 110-meter hurdles through the eyes of an Olympic athlete. *Future Stars of America 2* by Ron Berman (grade 5) profiles nine kids who are pursuing their extreme sports dreams.

Submissions and Payment

Guidelines available via email to info@scobre.com. Query. Accepts hard copy and email queries to info@scobre.com. SASE. Responds in 1 week. Publication in 6 months. Royalty, 12%.

Editor's Comments

Don't underestimate your audience, and remember that you are competing with TV, text messaging, the Internet, and the Xbox for their attention.

Seal Press

1700 Fourth Street
Berkeley, CA 94710

Senior Editor: Brooke Warner

Publisher's Interests

Dedicated to the real issues and challenges that comprise
womanhood, Seal Press publishes books that provide an
edgy, honest, and sometimes funny perspective on issues
that affect women and mothers. It also publishes books for
the emerging woman in young adult female readers.
Website: www.sealpress.com

Freelance Potential

Published 25 titles in 2009: 1–2 were developed from unsolicited submissions. Receives 600 queries yearly.

- **Nonfiction:** Publishes young adult books, 12–18 years. Topics
  include health, sexuality, abuse, politics, travel, and other
  women's issues. Also publishes parenting titles.
- **Representative Titles:** *Conquering Eating Disorders: How
  Family Communication Heals* by Sue Cooper & Peggy Norton
  helps teens coping with anorexia and their parents gain communication skills to support the healing process. *Choosing
  You* by Alexandra Soiseth is a humorous and touching memoir
  about one woman's journey to have a baby on her own. *Deliver
  This!* by Marisa Cohen provides an overview of the birthing
  options available to women in the U.S., from home births to
  birthing centers and C-sections in hospitals.

Submissions and Payment

Guidelines and catalogue available at website. Query with
outline, sample chapter, and author bio. Accepts hard copy.
SASE. Responds in 6–8 weeks. Publication period and payment policy vary.

Editor's Comments

There is no subject affecting women that we do not consider,
whether it be transgender identification, workplace politics
(especially regarding maternity leave), lesbian relationships,
or parenting issues. We're always open to queries that offer a
women's perspective, especially on motherhood.

Second Story Press

20 Maud Street, Suite 401
Toronto, Ontario M5V 2M5
Canada

Editorial Manager

Publisher's Interests
This small, feminist press offers fiction and nonfiction that deals with issues affecting girls and women. It focuses on the work of Canadian authors.
Website: www.secondstorypress.ca

Freelance Potential
Published 13 titles (10 juvenile) in 2009. Of the 13 titles, 4 were by unpublished writers and 9 were by authors who were new to the publishing house. Receives 240 queries, 240 unsolicited mss yearly.

- **Fiction:** Publishes story picture books, 4–10 years; chapter books, 5–10 years; middle-grade books, 8–12 years; and young adult books, 12–18 years. Genres include mystery and historical, contemporary, and multicultural fiction.
- **Nonfiction:** Publishes middle-grade books, 8–12 years; and young adult books, 12–18 years. Topics include history, nature, the environment, contemporary social issues, family life, and ethics. Also publishes parenting titles.
- **Representative Titles:** *The Diary of Laura's Twin* by Kathy Kacer (9+ years) is the story of a modern-day Jewish girl who becomes caught up in the story of a girl imprisoned during the Holocaust. *Reconcilable Differences* by Cate Cocher (all ages) shows how families can stay together despite divorce.

Submissions and Payment
Preference given to Canadian authors. Guidelines available at website. Prefers query with outline and sample chapters; will accept complete ms. Accepts hard copy. SAE/IRC. Responds in 4–6 months. Publication period varies. Royalty; advance.

Editor's Comments
We're currently most interested in receiving submissions of strong First Nations fiction. We are always seeking fiction and nonfiction that features female characters and issues, but we're not interested in traditional romances.

Seedling Publications

520 East Bainbridge
Elizabethtown, PA 17022

Managing Editor: Megan Bergonzi

Publisher's Interests

As hinted at in its name, Seedling Publications produces books designed to plant the seed of literacy in its young readers. Part of the Continental Press educational publishing family, Seedling publishes early literacy materials and books for children in preschool through grade two. It also publishes story collections for under-performing readers in the upper grades, and books for parents and teachers.
Website: www.continentalpress.com

Freelance Potential

Published 6 titles in 2009: each was developed from an unsolicited submission. Receives 300 unsolicited mss yearly.

- **Fiction:** Publishes easy-to-read books, 4–7 years. Genres include fairy tales, adventure, and humor. Also publishes stories about sports and nature.
- **Nonfiction:** Publishes easy-to-read books, 4–7 years. Topics include nature, science, technology, mathematics, animals, and multicultural subjects.
- **Representative Titles:** *Barnaby Bullfrog* (preK–grade 2) is the story of a bored bullfrog who leaves his pond to see the world. *Help Your Child Learn to Read* guides parents through the process and language of reading instruction; includes activities for reinforcing classroom experiences.

Submissions and Payment

Guidelines and catalogue available at website. Send complete ms. Accepts hard copy and simultaneous submissions if identified. SASE. Responds in 6 months. Publication in 1 year. Payment policy varies.

Editor's Comments

Manuscript length should be a minimum of 25 words and a maximum of 300 words. Nonfiction manuscripts should be presented in language appropriate for the student to read independently. We do not accept manuscripts in rhyme.

Servant Books

P.O. Box 7015
Ann Arbor, MI 48107

Editorial Director: Cynthia Cavnar

Publisher's Interests
This imprint of St. Anthony Messenger Press shares its parent company's Franciscan mission of helping Catholics live in accordance with the Gospel of Jesus Christ. It executes this mission through books on a wide variety of topics, from the lives of the saints to living a Christian life today. Its list includes books for young adults, parents, and teachers.
Website: www.servantbooks.org

Freelance Potential
Published 14 titles in 2009: 1 was a reprint/licensed property. Of the 14 titles, 2 were by unpublished writers and 5 were by authors who were new to the publishing house. Receives 150 queries yearly.

- **Nonfiction:** Publishes young adult books, 12–18 years. Also publishes books for parents and teachers. Topics include Christian living, the sacraments, Scripture, prayer, spirituality, popular apologetics, church teaching, Mary, the saints, charismatic renewal, marriage, family life, and popular psychology.
- **Representative Titles:** *God, Help Me* by Jim Beckman (YA) provides guidance on how to grow in prayer. *If You Really Loved Me* by Jason Avert (YA) answers 100 questions on dating, relationships, and sexual purity. *Adoption: Choosing It, Living It, Loving It* by Dr. Ray Guarendi (parents) tries to dispel unsettling misperceptions about adoption, encourage adoption, and guide adoptive parents to a more relaxed, rewarding family life for all.

Submissions and Payment
Guidelines available at website. Query with outline. Accepts hard copy. SASE. Responds in 2–3 months. Publication in 1–2 years. Royalty, 10%; advance, $1,000.

Editor's Comments
Our readers are parents, young adults, priests, directors of religious education, catechists, and teachers.

Shen's Books

1547 Palos Verdes Mall, #291
Walnut Creek, CA 94597

Owner: Renee Ting

Publisher's Interests
Shen's Books publishes fiction and nonfiction titles that emphasize cultural diversity and tolerance, with a focus on introducing children to the cultures of Asia.
Website: www.shens.com

Freelance Potential
Published 2 titles in 2009: both were developed from unsolicited submissions. Of the 2 titles, 1 was by an unpublished writer and 1 was by an author who was new to the publishing house. Receives 600 unsolicited mss yearly.

- **Fiction:** Publishes story picture books, 4–10 years. Genres include fairy tales, folklore, and historical and multicultural fiction about Asia and its people.
- **Nonfiction:** Publishes story picture books, 4–10 years. Topics include world cultures and immigrants.
- **Representative Titles:** *Cora Cooks Pancit* by Dorina K. Lazo Gilmore (4–8 years) finds little Cora finally getting a chance to help her mother make dinner, and to hear stories of her Filipino heritage while stirring. *The Day the Dragon Danced* by Kay Haugaard (4–8 years) tells of a culturally diverse community coming together to make a dragon dance in the Chinese New Year parade.

Submissions and Payment
Guidelines available at website. Send complete ms with author biography and publishing history. Accepts hard copy and simultaneous submissions if identified. SASE. Responds in 6–12 months. Publication in 18–24 months. Payment policy varies.

Editor's Comments
Currently, we're considering picture books of fewer than 2,500 words only. Stories must reflect the culture of an Asian country or Asian Americans. Stories involving multiple ethnicities are acceptable, but one culture must be Asian.

Silver Moon Press

381 Park Avenue South, Suite 1121
New York, NY 10016

Submissions Editor

Publisher's Interests

Silver Moon Press brings America's past alive for children through its historical fiction and biographies. It also covers other academic areas—such as science, math, and test preparation—as well as multicultural issues.
Website: www.silvermoonpress.com

Freelance Potential

Published 2 titles in 2009. Receives 50–150 queries yearly.

- **Fiction:** Publishes chapter books, 5–10 years; and middle-grade books, 8–12 years. Genres include historical and multicultural fiction.
- **Nonfiction:** Publishes workbooks, test preparation materials, and biographies for grades 2–8. Topics include math, science, language arts, poetry, composition, social studies, history, primary sources, and note-taking.
- **Representative Titles:** *Ride for Freedom* by Judy Hominick & Jeanne Spreier (9–12 years) is the story of Sybil Ludington, a 16-year-old girl who alerted troops to a British invasion during the Revolutionary War; part of the Heroes to Remember series. *Faraway Families* (4–8 years) is a collection of stories about how children are affected when their families are separated; part of the Family Ties series.

Submissions and Payment

Guidelines available at website. Query with résumé, table of contents, and first chapter. Accepts hard copy and simultaneous submissions if identified. SASE. Responds in 6 months. Publication period and payment policy vary.

Editor's Comments

Your query letter should present a synopsis of your work and also describe your research sources and methods. Please include approximate word count.

Simon & Schuster Books for Young Readers

Simon & Schuster Children's Publishing Division
1230 Avenue of the Americas
New York, NY 10020

Submissions Editor

Publisher's Interests

Books in a variety of genres and on a variety of subjects can be found in this catalogue. The imprint of Simon & Schuster publishes high-quality, engaging fiction and nonfiction for children and young adults.
Website: http://kids.simonandschuster.com

Freelance Potential

Published 90 titles in 2009: 60 were by agented authors. Receives 10,000 queries yearly.

- **Fiction:** Publishes toddler books and early picture books, 0–4 years; easy-to-read books, 4–7 years; story picture books, 4–10 years; chapter books, 5–10 years; middle-grade books, 8–12 years; and young adult books, 12–18 years. Genres include contemporary, historical, and multicultural fiction; mystery; fantasy; folklore; and fairy tales.
- **Nonfiction:** Publishes story picture books, 4–10 years; middle-grade books, 8–12 years; and young adult books, 12–18 years. Topics include social issues, science, nature, math, and history. Also publishes anthologies and biographies.
- **Representative Titles:** *Suspicion* by Kate Brian (14+ years) is the continuing story of Reed Brennan, this time finding her leaving the stigma and trauma of her private school behind for an exclusive island home; part of Private series. *Robot Zot!* by Jon Scieszka (3–7 years) is the story of a quixotic robot determined to conquer the earth, until he is stymied by the appliances of the suburban kitchen into which he has landed.

Submissions and Payment

Guidelines available. Catalogue available at website. Query with outline/synopsis. Accepts hard copy. SASE. Responds in 2 months. Publication in 2–4 years. Royalty; advance.

Editor's Comments

While we don't demand it, we recommend that you have an agent represent you and your work.

Simon Pulse

Simon & Schuster Children's Publishing Division
1230 Avenue of the Americas
New York, NY 10020

Submissions Editor

Publisher's Interests
This imprint of Simon & Schuster keeps its finger on the pulse of the literary tastes of modern young adults, offering quality contemporary fiction and nonfiction.
Website: http://kids.simonandschuster.com

Freelance Potential
Published 100 titles in 2009. Of the 100 titles, 10 were by authors who were new to the publishing house.

- **Fiction:** Publishes young adult books, 12–18 years. Genres include contemporary, inspirational, ethnic, and multicultural fiction; mystery; suspense; fantasy; drama; and horror.
- **Nonfiction:** Publishes young adult books, 12–18 years. Topics include age-appropriate social issues.
- **Representative Titles:** *The Social Climber's Guide to High School* by Robyn Schneider (YA) is a tongue-in-chic guide to not just surviving high school, but charming one's way to the top. *Bloom* by Elizabeth Scott (YA) is a novel about the choices one girl must make when the new boy in school has her re-thinking the plans she is making with her conservative boyfriend. *The Straight Road to Kylie* by Nico Medina (YA) is a humorous story of a gay boy who finds himself at a cross-roads: pretend to be straight to be popular, or go back to his old life.

Submissions and Payment
Guidelines available. Query with outline and author biography. Accepts hard copy. SASE. Response time, publication period, and payment policy vary.

Editor's Comments
We publish books that high school students want to read. We do not shy away from contemporary subjects such as teenage sexuality, drug use, or adolescent anxiety, as long as they are explored in an authentic manner that will resonate with our readers.

Skinner House Books

25 Beacon Street
Boston, MA 02108

Administrator: Betsy Martin

Publisher's Interests
Skinner House publishes books that teach Unitarian Universalist principles to children. It seeks proposals on a broad range of topics, including how to nurture tolerance in our children, and how to talk to children about spiritual subjects.
Website: www.uua.org/skinner

Freelance Potential
Published 12 titles (1 juvenile) in 2009: 6 were developed from unsolicited submissions. Of the 12 titles, 4 were by unpublished writers and 5 were by authors who were new to the publishing house. Receives 180 queries yearly.

- **Fiction:** Publishes toddler books and early picture books, 0–4 years; easy-to-read books, 4–7 years; story picture books, 4–10 years; middle-grade books, 8–12 years; and young adult books, 12–18 years. Genres include stories about nature.
- **Nonfiction:** Publishes toddler books and early picture books, 0–4 years; easy-to-read books, 4–7 years; story picture books, 4–10 years; middle-grade books, 8–12 years; and young adult books, 12–18 years. Topics include spirituality; religion; biography; history; nature; diversity; tolerance; peace; activism; grief; conflict; and multicultural, ethnic, and social issues.
- **Representative Titles:** *Come Sing a Song with Me* by Melodie Feather, ed. presents child-friendly arrangements of 25 traditional UU songs, along with explanations of each. *Earth Day* by Gary Kowalski (3+ years) is a picture book that celebrates the wonders of nature from A to Z.

Submissions and Payment
Guidelines and catalogue available at website. Query. Accepts hard copy and simultaneous submissions if identified. SASE. Responds in 1 month. Publication in 1 year. Royalty, 8%.

Editor's Comments
We welcome submissions of collected stories for children with spiritual, social, or environmental themes.

Small Horizons

34 Church Street
Liberty Corner, NJ 07938

Acquisitions Editor: P. Patty

Publisher's Interests
This imprint of New Horizon Press publishes children's books that build self-esteem while dealing with difficult issues. Also included are books for parents and teachers.
Website: www.newhorizonpressbooks.com

Freelance Potential
Published 2 titles in 2009. Receives 192+ queries yearly.

- **Fiction:** Publishes story picture books, 4–10 years. Themes include coping with anger, anxiety, divorce, grief, and violence; understanding ADHD; and fostering tolerance.
- **Nonfiction:** Publishes easy-to-read books, 4–7 years; and story picture books, 4–10 years. Also publishes parenting books and books for adults who work with children. Topics include coping with anger, anxiety, divorce, grief, and violence; hyperactive and aggressive children; tolerance; and services.
- **Representative Titles:** *Tommy and the T-Tops* by Frederick Alimonti with Ann M. Tedesco (4–9 years) tells of a herd of Triceratops who learn about the importance of character over appearance when they encounter an unfamiliar and strange-looking family of dinosaurs. *Jessica's Two Families* by Lynne Hugo (4–9 years) teaches children how to cope with blended households.

Submissions and Payment
Guidelines and catalogue available at website. Query with résumé, outline, 2 sample chapters, and market comparison. Accepts hard copy and email queries to nhp@newhorizonpressbooks.com. Availability of artwork improves chance of acceptance. SASE. Responds in 3 months. Publication period varies. Royalty, 7.5% of net; advance.

Editor's Comments
We look for topics that help children deal with anger, grief, violence, and anxiety.

Smith and Kraus

177 Lyme Road
Hanover, NH 03755

Editor: Marisa Kraus

Publisher's Interests

Since 1990, Smith and Kraus has published books for the theater community. Its list runs the gamut from plays and monologues for classroom or school use to books about the art of acting and how to teach it.
Website: www.smithandkraus.com

Freelance Potential

Published 35 titles (10 juvenile) in 2009. Of the 35 titles, 17 were by authors who were new to the publishing house. Receives 100 queries yearly.

- **Fiction:** Publishes collections of plays, scenes, and monologues, grades K–12. Also publishes anthologies, translations, and collections of works by contemporary playwrights.
- **Nonfiction:** Publishes instructional books for teachers, grades K–12. Topics include theater history, stage production, Shakespeare, movement, and dramatizing literature.
- **Representative Titles:** *Shakespeare With Children: Six Scripts for Young Players* by Elizabeth Weinstein (8–13 years) presents six adaptations of the Bard's plays that are designed for middle-grade students' understanding and enjoyment. *My First Scene Book: Acting Out, Acting Up, Acting Right* by Kristen Dabrowski (5–9 years) presents 51 short scenes for young actors to try, and offers tips and discussion questions to bring out the actor in every reader.

Submissions and Payment

Guidelines and catalogue available at website. Query with synopsis, reviews, writing sample, and production information (for plays). Accepts hard copy, email to sandk@sover.net, and simultaneous submissions if identified. SASE. Responds in 1–2 months. Publication in 1 year. Royalty; advance. Flat fee.

Editor's Comments

We'll consider any proposal that instills in readers a better understanding of and love for the theater.

Soho Press

853 Broadway
New York, NY 10003

Editor: Katie Herman

Publisher's Interests

Soho Press publishes primarily literary fiction in a variety of genres, with a large portion of its list leaning toward mystery and suspense. It also publishes narrative nonfiction, including biographies and cultural historical accounts. Though intended for adults, many of its books appeal to young adult readers.

Website: www.sohopress.com

Freelance Potential

Published 55 titles in 2009: 6 were developed from unsolicited submissions and 49 were by agented authors. Of the 55 titles, 9 were by unpublished writers and 33 were by authors who were new to the publishing house. Receives 1,800 queries yearly.

- **Fiction:** Publishes literary fiction and mystery series with foreign or exotic settings.
- **Nonfiction:** Publishes autobiographies, biographies, and historical and cultural accounts.
- **Representative Titles:** *Murder in the Latin Quarter* by Cara Black has a half-French, half-American female detective investigating murders tied to Haitian politics on the Left Bank of Paris; part of the Aimee Leduc mystery series. *Zoo Station* by David Downing is a historical novel set in Berlin on the eve of World War II.

Submissions and Payment

Guidelines and catalogue available at website. Query with first 3 chapters, outline, and publishing credits. Accepts hard copy. SASE. Responds in 3 months. Publication in 9+ months. Royalty; advance.

Editor's Comments

Though eager to accept a wide range of literary fiction, we are generally unenthusiastic about publishing formula fiction short story collections, stock romances, and "quick reads."

Soundprints

353 Main Avenue
Norwalk, CT 06851

Editor: Jamie McCune

Publisher's Interests
Publishing "top quality products that are both educational and fun" is the focus of this award-winning publisher of books for children.
Website: www.soundprints.com

Freelance Potential
Published 25 titles in 2009: 1 was developed from an unsolicited submission and 6 were reprint/licensed properties. Of the 25 titles, 1 was by an author who was new to the publishing house. Receives 360 queries, 360 unsolicited mss yearly.

- **Fiction:** Publishes easy-to-read books, 3–7 years; story picture books, 0–10 years; and middle-grade books, 8–12 years. Genres include fantasy and inspirational fiction. Also publishes board books.
- **Nonfiction:** Publishes easy-to-read books, 4–7 years; story picture books, 4–10 years; and middle-grade books, 8–12 years. Topics include animals, history, nature, and the environment. Also publishes educational books.
- **Representative Titles:** *Alphabet Earth* by Barbie Heit Schwaeber (grades K–2) is a rhyming alphabet book that explores jungles, deserts, and volcanoes; includes a read-along CD. *First Look at Farm Animals* by Laura Gates Galvin (18 months–5 years) uses felt art and photography to teach young children about farm animals; part of the First Look series.

Submissions and Payment
Guidelines available. Query or send complete ms. Accepts hard copy. SASE. Response time varies. Publication in 1–2 years. Payment policy varies.

Editor's Comments
We look for books that communicate information about their subjects through an exciting storyline, while also being based solidly on fact and supported by careful research.

Sourcebooks

1935 Brookdale Road, Suite 139
Naperville, IL 60563

Editorial Submissions

Publisher's Interests

Sourcebooks publishes a multitude of self-help and how-to books on parenting and women's issues, and produces children's novels, poetry, and nonfiction through its Sourcebooks Jabberwocky imprint.
Website: www.sourcebooks.com

Freelance Potential

Published 300 titles (40 juvenile) in 2009: 50 were developed from unsolicited submissions and 200 were by agented authors. Receives 3,000 unsolicited mss yearly.

- **Fiction:** Publishes early picture books, 0–4 years; chapter books, 5–10 years; and middle-grade books, 8–12 years. Genres include poetry, contemporary fiction, fantasy, and classics.
- **Nonfiction:** Publishes toddler books, 0–4 years; and middle-grade books, 8–12 years. Topics include sign language, forensic science, and teen rights. Also publishes adult titles on pregnancy, childbirth, parenting, potty training, special needs, and gifted education.
- **Representative Titles:** *Cinnabar and the Island of Shadows* by J. H. Sweet & Holly Sierra follows Cinnabar and her friends as they travel by elf magic to a secret island to try to locate the lost shadows; part of the Fairy Chronicles series. *Fairy Foals* by Suzanah is the story of a woman who chronicles the magical tiny horse with butterfly wings she finds in her garden.

Submissions and Payment

Guidelines and catalogue available at website. Query with résumé, synopsis, table of contents, 2 sample chapters, and market analysis. Accepts hard copy and simultaneous submissions if identified. SASE. Responds in 4–6 months. Publication in 1 year. Royalty, 6–15%.

Editor's Comments

We are known for our strong publicity and marketing efforts on behalf of our authors.

The Speech Bin

3155 Northwoods Parkway
Norcross, GA 30071

Catalogue Director: Tobi Isaacs

Publisher's Interests

This company publishes books and other resources for working with people who have speech, language, and hearing disorders. Its books are written for speech professionals as well
as parents and caregivers, and many are geared toward children and young adults with speech issues.
Website: www.speechbin.com

Freelance Potential

Published 7 titles (5 juvenile) in 2009: each was developed
from an unsolicited submission. Receives 500 queries yearly.

- **Nonfiction:** Publishes concept books and early picture books,
  0–4 years; story picture books, 4–10 years; and middle-grade
  books, 8–12 years. Topics include autism, stuttering, articula-
  tion, phonology, language skills, sensory-motor skills, and cleft
  palate. Also publishes treatment manuals and workbooks for
  communication disorders.
- **Representative Titles:** *Straight Speech: How to Deal With
  Those Pesky Lateral Lisps* by Jane Folk provides an effective,
  easy-to-use program for dealing with lateral lisps. *Speaking,
  Listening & Understanding: Games for Young Children* by
  Catherine Delamain & Jill Spring is a collection of graded
  games and activities that are specifically designed to foster the
  speaking, listening, and understanding skills of children ages
  five to seven.

Submissions and Payment

Guidelines and catalogue available at website. Query with
résumé and outline. Accepts hard copy and email queries to
tisaacs@sportime.com. SASE. Responds in 1–2 months. Publication in 1–2 years. Royalty.

Editor's Comments

We are open to any book proposal that will help professionals
or families increase their knowledge of and effectiveness in
dealing with speech disorders.

Square One Publishers

115 Herricks Road
Garden City, NY 11040

Publisher: Rudy Shur

Publisher's Interests

"An independent publishing company with big ideas,"
Square One Publishers features a wide selection of adult
nonfiction titles on topics that pertain to parenting and child
development. Its authors are typically among the leaders in
their respective fields.
Website: www.squareonepublishers.com

Freelance Potential

Published 15 titles in 2009: 10 were developed from unsolicited submissions. Of the 15 titles, 8 were by unpublished
writers and 5 were by authors who were new to the publishing house. Receives 1,200 queries yearly.

- **Nonfiction:** Publishes self-help and how-to books for adults.
  Topics include pregnancy, childbirth, infant care, discipline,
  potty training, children with special needs, sports, and early
  childhood learning.
- **Representative Titles:** *And Then We Went Fishing* by Dirk
  Benedict is an autobiographical story of two events that had
  an enormous impact on the author's life. *Enough, Inigo,
  Enough* by Janet Dorman is designed for use by young children who are being taught to read at home by their parents.

Submissions and Payment

Guidelines available at website. Query with synopsis, target
audience, table of contents, and author bio. Accepts hard
copy. SASE. Responds in 4–6 weeks. Publication period
varies. Royalty.

Editor's Comments

Our books provide information that is designed to meet the
needs of specific audiences. We are currently interested in
receiving proposals on health, alternative health, parenting,
gambling, and personal finance. We want books that offer a
fresh and/or different point of view by authors who truly
know their topic.

Standard Publishing

8805 Governors Hill Drive, Suite 400
Cincinnati, OH 45249

Editorial Director, Children's Products: Ruth Frederick

Publisher's Interests
Standard Publishing produces true-to-the-Bible resources meant to inspire, educate, and motivate Christians. Its children's catalogue includes fiction and nonfiction resources for use in children's ministries.
Website: www.standardpub.com

Freelance Potential
Published 110 titles (10 juvenile) in 2009: 10 were developed from unsolicited submissions and 6 were by agented authors. Of the 110 titles, 10 were by new authors. Receives 200 queries, 300 unsolicited mss yearly.

- **Fiction:** Publishes board books, 0–4 years; story picture books, 4–10 years; and middle-grade books, 8–12 years. Genres include Christian fiction and stories of the Bible.
- **Nonfiction:** Publishes board books, concept books, and early picture books, 0–4 years; and middle-grade books, 8–12 years. Topics include religion, faith, Christianity, and Christian values. Also publishes devotionals.
- **Representative Titles:** *The House in the Middle of Town* by Crystal Bowman (3–7 years) finds neighbors and friends of all ages coming together to lovingly help someone in need. *365 Trivia Twist Devotions* by Betsy Schmitt & David Veerman (8–12 years) contains daily devotions that are based on a historical happening, intriguing invention, or offbeat holiday.

Submissions and Payment
Guidelines available at website. Query with outline and 1–2 sample chapters. Send ms for picture books. Accepts hard copy, email to ministrytochildren@standardpub.com, and simultaneous submissions if identified. SASE. Responds in 4–5 months. Publication in 18 months. Royalty. Flat fee.

Editor's Comments
We are not interested in books that are specifically denominational, nor do we want fiction or poetry.

Star Bright Books

30-19 48th Avenue
Long Island City, NY 11101

Submissions

Publisher's Interests

Star Bright is interested in books with multicultural perspectives. Its titles range from picture books to young adult novels; all feature multiethnic, multicultural, or otherwise diverse characters, settings, and themes. Many of its books are bilingual.
Website: www.starbrightbooks.com

Freelance Potential

Published 20 titles in 2009. Of the 20 titles, 10 were by authors who were new to the publishing house. Receives 360–480 queries, 240–360 unsolicited mss yearly.

- **Fiction:** Publishes concept books, toddler books, and early picture books, 0–4 years; easy-to-read books, 4–7 years; story picture books, 4–10 years; chapter books, 5–10 years; middle-grade books, 8–12 years; and young adult books, 12–18 years. Genres include contemporary, multicultural, and educational fiction. Also publishes board books.
- **Representative Titles:** *Opposites/Opostos* by Brian Wildsmith (0–4 years) is a board book in both Portuguese and English that uses all sorts of animals to teach the concept of opposites. *Brothers and Sisters* by Laura Dwight (4–8 years) presents a number of sibling groups in which at least one member has a disability, yet they all play, fight, and help each other—just like all brothers and sisters.

Submissions and Payment

Guidelines available. Catalogue available at website. Query or send complete ms. Accepts hard copy. SASE. Responds in 6 months. Publication period varies. Royalty; advance.

Editor's Comments

We want all children to be able to see themselves reflected in a book, therefore we are open to any story that embraces diversity, whether it be racial, cultural, or physical. Please note that we are interested in fiction only.

Stemmer House Publishers

4 White Brook Road
Gilsum, NH 03448

Editor: Dave Eisenstadter

Publisher's Interests

Stemmer House offers classic children's stories as well as a growing list by new authors. Its list includes children's fiction along with nonfiction titles, especially those about nature and science.
Website: www.stemmer.com

Freelance Potential

Published 7 titles (4 juvenile) in 2009: 3 were developed from unsolicited submissions. Of the 7 titles, 2 were by unpublished writers and 2 were by authors who were new to the publishing house. Receives 240 queries, 300 mss yearly.

- **Fiction:** Publishes story picture books, 4–10 years. Genres include contemporary, historical, and multicultural fiction.
- **Nonfiction:** Publishes story picture books, 4–10 years; easy-to-read books, 4–7 years; chapter books, 5–10 years; middle-grade books, 8–12 years; and young adult books, 12–18 years. Topics include nature, science, natural history, art, music, and geography. Also publishes biographies, cookbooks, design books, and gardening books for adults.
- **Representative Titles:** *I Hear the Wind* by Greg Budig is a story about what happens when a child's imagination greets the wind. *DesertAlphabet Encyclopedia* by Sylvester Allred presents interesting facts about the plants and animals that live in the driest and harshest habitat on earth.

Submissions and Payment

Guidelines and catalogue available with 9x12 SASE ($.77 postage). Send ms for picture books. Query with outline/synopsis and 2 sample chapters for longer works. Accepts hard copy and simultaneous submissions. SASE. Responds in 2 weeks. Publication in 1–3 years. Royalty; advance.

Editor's Comments

We pride ourselves on our careful evaluation of submissions, so please be patient waiting for a response.

Sterling Publishing Company

387 Park Avenue South
New York, NY 10016-8810

Editorial Director, Children's Publishing: Frances Gilbert

Publisher's Interests
The children's list of Sterling Publishing includes picture books for young children and nonfiction for readers up to age 16. The nonfiction topics it accepts are activity-based subjects, with a few dealing with history and biography.
Website: www.sterlingpublishing.com/kids

Freelance Potential
Published 160 titles in 2009: 10 were developed from unsolicited submissions, 25 were by agented authors, and 25 were reprint/licensed properties. Receives 1,500 queries and unsolicited mss yearly.

- **Fiction:** Publishes toddler books and early picture books, 0–4 years; easy-to-read books, 4–7 years; and story picture books, 4–10 years. Genres include fairy tales, fantasy, ghost stories, contemporary fiction, and stories about animals.
- **Nonfiction:** Publishes toddler books and early picture books, 0–4 years; easy-to-read books, 4–7 years; middle-grade books, 8–12 years; and young adult books, 12–18 years. Topics include routines, colors, sounds, shapes, numbers, animals, nature, science, biography, holidays, seasons, cooking, crafts, activities, and games.
- **Representative Titles:** *Just Like Me* by Adam Relf (4–6 years) invites kids to help an armadillo search for his cousins. *Cartooning: The Ultimate Character Design Book* by Chris Hart (10–18 years) shows kids how to draw original characters.

Submissions and Payment
Guidelines available at website. Query with outline, sample chapter, and publishing credits. Send mss for picture books. Accepts hard copy and simultaneous submissions. SASE. Response time varies. Publication in 1 year. Royalty; advance.

Editor's Comments
Please note that we do not publish fictional character books or novels. No electronic submissions, please.

Stone Arch Books

7825 Telegraph Road
Bloomington, MN 55438

Editor: Krista Monyhan

Publisher's Interests

Stone Arch Books offers "safe" graphic novels that capture the interest of reluctant readers, while helping to develop vocabulary, fluency, and comprehension. Titles are categorized into more than a dozen different series.
Website: www.stonearchbooks.com

Freelance Potential

Published 215 titles in 2009: 3 were developed from unsolicited submissions. Of the 215 titles, 5 were by unpublished writers and 10 were by authors who were new to the publishing house. Receives 40 queries yearly.

- **Fiction:** Publishes fiction collections and accelerated reader titles, grades 3–9; and young adult books, 12–18 years. Genres include realistic and historical fiction, adventure, fantasy, horror, science fiction, mystery, sports, and humor.
- **Representative Titles:** *Freedom Songs* by Trina Robbins (grades 3-6) is a graphic novel about a young slave whose only hope of freedom is to travel the Underground Railroad; part of the Graphic Flash series. *The Creeping Bookends* by Michael Dahl (grades 3-8) is a hi-lo novel about a young boy who is accidentally locked inside a library with a pair of lizard bookends that come to life; part of the Zone Books series.

Submissions and Payment

Guidelines available at website. Query with synopsis and first 3 chapters. Prefers email queries to author.sub@ stonearchbooks.com; will accept hard copy. SASE. Response time, publication period, and payment policy vary.

Editor's Comments

We strive to present culturally and ethnically diverse characters as positive role models to our readers, as well as themes aligned with character education curriculum. Writers are encouraged to familiarize themselves with our catalogue to determine if their work fits our program.

Storytellers Ink Publishing Co.

P.O. Box 33398
Seattle, WA 98133-0398

Editor-in-Chief: Quinn Currie

Publisher's Interests

Storytellers Ink has a mission to help teach children to love reading through its appealing books about animals, the environment, and the people of the world. Its books target children in preschool through middle school.
Website: www.storytellers-ink.com

Freelance Potential

Published 3 titles in 2009. Receives 120 unsolicited mss each year.

- **Fiction:** Publishes story picture books, 2–10 years; and middle-grade books, 8–12 years. Genres include adventure, folktales, fantasy, and multicultural and ethnic fiction. Also publishes stories about animals, nature, and the environment.
- **Nonfiction:** Publishes story picture books, 2–10 years; and middle-grade books, 8–12 years. Topics include animals, nature, the environment, and social issues. Also publishes biographies and bilingual titles.
- **Representative Titles:** *If a Seahorse Wore a Saddle* by Mary Jane Flynn (preK) is a rhyming story that uses a high-spirited seahorse to teach children to be kind to others. *Cousin Charlie the Crow* by Marshall Houts (grade 6) is the true story of a young farm boy in the 1950s who rescues an orphaned crow, then enjoys its antics until it shows its need to return to the wild.

Submissions and Payment

Guidelines available. Catalogue available at website. Send complete ms. Accepts hard copy and simultaneous submissions if identified. SASE. Response time, publication period, and payment policy vary.

Editor's Comments

We will like your book if it is well written. We will like your book even better if the story helps children become more caring and understanding of the world around them.

Tanglewood Press

688 Hollowbrook Court
Terre Haute, IN 47803

Acquisitions Editor

Publisher's Interests
This publisher, which brought us *The Kissing Hand*, produces an array of fiction books for children of all ages. Its list includes everything from picture books for young children to tender coming-of-age stories for young adults. It puts an emphasis on books that young readers *want* to read.
Website: www.tanglewoodbooks.com

Freelance Potential
Published 3 titles in 2009. Receives 1,500 queries yearly.

- **Fiction:** Publishes early picture books, 0–4 years; story picture books, 4–8 years; middle-grade books, 8–12 years; and young adult books, 12–18 years. Genres include adventure, historical fiction, mystery, and humor.
- **Representative Titles:** *The Tiptoe Guide to Tracking Fairies* by Ammi-Joan Paquette (4–8 years) invites children to have a backyard adventure searching for fairies, while also learning about nature. *My Brother the Dog* by Kim Williams Justesen (8–12 years) brings readers along as teenaged Mattie tries to choose between a budding romance, a best friend, and a little brother who needs her. *Chester Raccoon and the Acorn Full of Memories* by Audrey Penn (3–8 years) uses animals mourning the loss of a friend to help young children understand death.

Submissions and Payment
Guidelines available at website. Query with 3–5 sample chapters. Accepts hard copy. SASE. Responds in 6–12 months. Publication in 2–3 years. Royalty, 6% of retail.

Editor's Comments
We have a tremendous amount of backlogged submissions that we are trying to get through. Therefore, it may take even longer to respond than our stated goal above. That said, we are always looking for great stories that children or teens would love to absorb. Competition is fierce, so you may want to use this time to sharpen what you've written.

Teacher Created Resources

6421 Industry Way
Westminster, CA 92683

Editor-in-Chief: Ina M. Levin

Publisher's Interests

The educational materials produced by this publisher are teacher-generated and classroom-tested. Its catalogue is filled with a variety of resources—including reference books, lesson planners, workbooks, and games—for preschool through eighth grade.
Website: www.teachercreated.com

Freelance Potential

Published 70 titles in 2009: 4–6 were developed from unsolicited submissions. Of the 70 titles, 2 were by unpublished writers and 3 were by authors who were new to the publishing house.

- **Nonfiction:** Publishes workbooks and activity books, preK–grade 8. Topics include art, geography, history, social studies, science, mathematics, reading, phonics, spelling, writing, language arts, and technology. Also publishes teacher resource materials on student testing, multiple intelligences, assessment, and classroom management.
- **Representative Titles:** *Weather* (grades 2–5) offers introductory weather-related activities for students; part of the Super Science Activities series. *Nonfiction Strategies* (grades 1–3, 4–8) contains lessons that give students practice in how to read, write, discuss, research, remember, and listen to information from nonfiction sources.

Submissions and Payment

Guidelines and catalogue available at website. Query with synopsis, table of contents, and 10–12 manuscript pages. Accepts hard copy. SASE. Responds in 3–6 months. Publication in 3–12 months. Flat fee.

Editor's Comments

We encourage projects that deal with technology as it applies to classroom research, and critical thinking at the elementary level. All material must be standards-based.

Teaching & Learning Company

1204 Buchanan Street
P.O. Box 10
Carthage, IL 62321

Vice President, Production: Jill Day

Publisher's Interests

Teaching & Learning publishes a variety of education resources designed to make teaching and learning easier. Its products and teacher resource books cover all the basic curriculum areas, and reflect the cultural and ethnic diversity of today's classrooms.

Website: www.teachinglearning.com

Freelance Potential

Published 30–35 titles in 2009: 25–30 were developed from unsolicited submissions. Of the 30–35 titles, 3 were by unpublished writers and 6 were by authors who were new to the publishing house. Receives 1,200 unsolicited mss yearly.

- **Nonfiction:** Publishes educational teacher resource materials, preK–grade 8. Topics include language arts, social studies, current events, biographies, mathematics, computers, science, nature, the environment, animals, holidays, arts and crafts, hobbies, multicultural and ethnic issues, and responsibility.
- **Representative Titles:** *100 Little Language Lessons* by Margaret Brinton (grades 1–4) is a collection of language skill-building activities, including a pre-test, definition match, writing practice, and critical thinking exercises. *101 Science Activities for Emerging Einsteins* by Tracey Ann Coveart (grades 3–6) is filled with simple yet fun science experiments and activities to help students discover for themselves how the world works.

Submissions and Payment

Guidelines available. Send complete ms. Accepts hard copy and Macintosh disk submissions (Quark Xpress or Microsoft Word documents). SASE. Responds in 6–9 months. Publication in 1–3 years. Royalty.

Editor's Comments

Please keep in mind when preparing your material that our market is diverse and culturally rich.

TEACH Services, Inc.

254 Donovan Road
Brushton, NY 12916

Editor: Timothy Hullquist

Publisher's Interests

TEACH Services is an independent organization owned by
Seventh-day Adventists. It publishes nonfiction titles about
health, education, and religion for the retail and wholesale
markets. 20% self-, subsidy-, co-venture, or co-op published
material.
Website: www.teachservices.com

Freelance Potential

Published 60–80 titles (15 juvenile) in 2009: 65 were developed from unsolicited submissions. Receives 240 queries
each year.

- **Nonfiction:** Publishes easy-to-read books, 4–7 years; chapter
  books, 5–10 years; middle-grade books, 8–12 years; and
  young adult books, 12–18 years. Topics include Bible study,
  church doctrine and history, prayer, youth and children's ministry, health, education, and spiritual growth. Also publishes
  biographies, ministerial resources, and titles for adults.
- **Representative Titles:** *Dinosaurs on the Ark* by David Larsen
  addresses the issue of Creationism and evolution from scientific and biblical perspectives. *Tommy & Sara's Country
  Adventures* by Lanette Richard features young siblings who
  visit their grandparents' North Dakota home, depicting life on
  a farm, family togetherness, and how God works in our lives.

Submissions and Payment

Guidelines and catalogue available at website. Query with
outline. Accepts hard copy and simultaneous submissions
if identified. SASE. Responds in 2–3 weeks. Publication in
4–6 months. Royalty, 10%; advance.

Editor's Comments

Though we are not supported nor endorsed by the Seventh-
day Adventist church, we publish only books that embrace
its values and teachings. We do not publish fiction, fantasy,
or material that's contrary to Seventh-day Adventist doctrine.

Texas Tech University Press

P.O. Box 41037
Lubbock, TX 79409-1037

Editor-in-Chief: Judith Keeling

Publisher's Interests
This publisher offers fiction for middle-grade readers and young adults, and some nonfiction adult titles that appeal to young adult readers. Most of the books in these areas focus on the Great Plains and the American West.
Website: www.ttup.ttu.edu

Freelance Potential
Published 80–100 titles in 2009. Receives 200–250 queries each year.

- **Fiction:** Publishes middle-grade books, 8–12 years; and young adult books, 12–18 years. Genres include regional and historical fiction, and folkore. Also publishes novels for adults.
- **Nonfiction:** Publishes books for adults. Topics include the natural sciences, history, and natural history of the Great Plains and American Southwest; costume and textile history; and Southeast Asia. Also publishes American Southwest regional biographies and memoirs.
- **Representative Titles:** *In My Father's House: A Memoir of Polygamy* by Dorothy Allred Solomon is the memoir of a daughter of a plural marriage in Utah that reveals the fear, secrecy, and faith that ruled her young life. *Aurora Crossing: A Novel of the Nez Perces* by Karl H. Schlesier is a historical coming-of-age novel about a Native American youngster who struggles to find his place in a clash of cultures.

Submissions and Payment
Guidelines and catalogue available at website. Query with brief author bio, outline, table of contents, introduction, and 2 sample chapters. Accepts hard copy. SASE. Responds in 2 months. Publication in 1 year. Royalty, 10%.

Editor's Comments
Although all must pass a rigorous review in terms of substance, many of our titles address a general readership. They should not be too deeply entrenched in theory, analysis, or jargon.

Theytus Books

Green Mountain Road, Lot 45
RR 2, Site 50, Comp. 8
Penticton, British Columbia V2A 6J7
Canada

Submissions: Anita Large

Publisher's Interests
Theytus Books is a First Nation-owned publisher of indigenous Canadian voices. It publishes books for children, young adults, and adults that embrace indigenous culture, history, and perspectives. It works with Aboriginal authors only.
Website: www.theytus.com

Freelance Potential
Published 10 titles (6 juvenile) in 2009. Of the 10 titles, 1–2 were by unpublished writers and 3 were by authors who were new to the publishing house. Receives 20 queries, 30–60 unsolicited mss yearly.

- **Fiction:** Publishes story picture books, 4–10 years; and young adult books, 12–18 years. Genres include contemporary, historical, and literary fiction; adventure; drama; and humor. Also publishes poetry and anthologies.
- **Nonfiction:** Publishes young adult books, 12–18. Also publishes books for adults. Topics include social history and policy relating to Aboriginal issues. Also publishes humor.
- **Representative Titles:** *Jenneli's Dance* by Elizabeth Denny (6–11 years) instills a sense of pride in the Métis culture through a story about a young girl learning and performing the Métis Red-River jig. *Neekna and Chemai* by Jeannette Armstrong presents a story of two little girls growing up in the Okanagan Valley long before the coming of the white man.

Submissions and Payment
Canadian Aboriginal authors only. Guidelines and catalogue available at website. Query with synopsis, 4 sample chapters, and author bio. Send complete ms for story picture books and poetry. Accepts hard copy. SASE. Responds in 6–8 months. Publication in 1–2 years. Royalty, 10%.

Editor's Comments
We believe our mission to be documenting indigenous cultures and publishing their voices.

Third World Press

7822 South Dobson
P.O. Box 19730
Chicago, IL 60619

Assistant to the Publisher

Publisher's Interests
Third World Press publishes literature that focuses on issues, themes, and critiques related to an African American readership. It accepts fiction and nonfiction that celebrates African American culture for children of all ages.
Website: www.thirdworldpressinc.com

Freelance Potential
Published 12 titles in 2009. Receives 400 unsolicited mss each year.

- **Fiction:** Publishes concept books, toddler books, and early picture books, 0–4 years: easy-to-read books, 4–7 years; story picture books, 4–10 years; chapter books, 5–10 years; middle-grade books, 8–12 years; and young adult books, 12–18 years. Features stories about African, African American, and Caribbean life; and the Diaspora.
- **Nonfiction:** Publishes easy-to-read books, 4–7 years; story picture books, 4–10 years; chapter books, 5–10 years; middle-grade books, 8–12 years; and young adult books, 12–18 years. Topics include African history and culture, and multicultural issues.
- **Representative Titles:** *Afrocentric Self Inventory and Discovery Workbook for African American Youth* by Useni Perkins (12–15 years) introduces black youth to the basics of African-centered cultural issues. *Free! Great Escapes from Slavery on the Underground Railroad* by Lorene Cary presents real accounts of the people who sought liberation from slavery.

Submissions and Payment
Guidelines available at website. Send complete ms in July only with synopsis, marketing plan, and copy of publisher's guidelines. Accepts hard copy and simultaneous submissions. SASE. Response time varies. Publication in 1 year. Royalty.

Editor's Comments
Failure to adhere to our submission guidelines will result in the elimination of your manuscript.

Thomas Nelson Children's Books and Education

P.O. Box 141000
501 Nelson Place
Nashville, TN 37214

Acquisitions Editor

Publisher's Interests
Christian books and Bibles for children up to age 14 are the mainstay of this publisher. It looks for entertaining and exciting books that are consistent with the teachings of the Bible while expanding and nurturing the imaginations of young readers.
Website: www.thomasnelson.com

Freelance Potential
Published 36 titles in 2009: 2 were reprint/licensed properties. Receives 120 queries yearly.

- **Fiction:** Publishes story picture books, 4–10 years; and middle-grade books, 8–12 years. Publishes religious fiction.
- **Nonfiction:** Publishes concept books, 0–4 years; story picture books, 4–10 years; and middle-grade books, 8–12 years. Also publishes Bible storybooks.
- **Representative Titles:** *How Noah Knew What to Do* by Karen Ann Moore teaches children to trust in God and not to be afraid to try something new. *Isle of Swords* by Wayne Thomas Batson tells the story of a young boy who finds himself alone and injured on a deserted island. *My Little Girl* by John MacArthur is about a young girl, her dad, and their blood-hound who set off on some adventures.

Submissions and Payment
Guidelines and catalogue available at website. Accepts submissions through literary agents only. Royalty; advance.

Editor's Comments
Our award-winning books do more than simply entertain; they spark children's imaginations and encourage a love of reading and learning. We seek books that contain innovative, entertaining, and educational messages. Please review our website and catalogue to see the types of books we publish. No unsolicited submissions; we will only work with agented authors.

Charles C. Thomas, Publisher Ltd.

2600 South First Street
Springfield, IL 62707

Editor: Michael P. Thomas

Publisher's Interests

Charles C. Thomas has been producing specialty titles and textbooks in the biomedical sciences since 1927. Its list also includes titles for teachers and professionals on education, the behavioral sciences, speech-language, and rehabilitation.
Website: www.ccthomas.com

Freelance Potential

Published 60 titles in 2009: each was developed from an unsolicited submission. Receives 600 queries and unsolicited mss yearly.

- **Nonfiction:** Publishes titles for educators, preK–grade 12. Topics include early childhood, elementary, and higher education; reading; research and statistics; physical education and sports; special education; the learning disabled; teaching the blind and visually impaired; gifted and talented education; and speech and language pathology. Also offers parenting titles and professional development books for individuals in the criminal justice field.
- **Representative Titles:** *Play with Them: Theraplay Groups in the Classroom* by Phyllis B. Rubin & Jeanine Tregay guides teachers and other professionals in helping children develop self-confidence and a sense of security. *Straight Talk on Stuttering* by Lloyd M. Hulit offers basic information about this disorder and discusses new therapy approaches.

Submissions and Payment

Guidelines and catalogue available at website. Query or send complete ms with résumé. Accepts disk submissions with hard copy. SASE. Responds in 1 week. Publication in 6–8 months. Royalty.

Editor's Comments

We always give prompt and careful consideration to freelance submissions. Please visit our website for detailed information about our submission requirements.

Thompson Educational Publishing

20 Ripley Avenue
Toronto, Ontario M6S 3N9
Canada

Publisher: Keith Thompson

Publisher's Interests

This is a publisher specializing in undergraduate textbooks for the social sciences and humanities, and professional development books for teachers. It also publishes single-author scholarly research and a small number of books geared toward the middle-grade student. It is particularly interested in books that feature Canadian perspectives.
Website: www.thompsonbooks.com

Freelance Potential

Published 8–10 titles in 2009: 1–2 were by unpublished writers. Receives 20 queries yearly.

- **Nonfiction:** Publishes middle-grade books, 8–12 years. Also publishes textbooks and single-author monographs for use in undergraduate education, as well as books for educators. Topics include social studies, sociology, social work, economics, communication, native studies, labor studies, and sports.
- **Representative Titles:** *The Art of Evaluation: A Resource for Educators and Trainers* by Tara Fenwick & Jim Parsons is a practical introduction to learner evaluation in the various contexts of adult education. *Sports Ethics: Concepts and Cases in Sport and Recreation* by David Cruise Malloy et al. provides an analytical framework to enable readers to explore and understand many of the ethical issues and controversies in sports.

Submissions and Payment

Guidelines and catalogue available at website. Query. Accepts email queries to publisher@thompsonbooks.com. Response time, publication period, and payment policy vary.

Editor's Comments

In order to be considered, a book proposal should aim to meet the content requirements of particular college and university courses. Please consult our guidelines for complete submission information.

Tilbury House, Publishers

103 Brunswick Avenue
Gardiner, ME 04345

Associate Editor: Karen Fisk

Publisher's Interests
Tilbury House publishes children's books that help young
people build character, appreciate cultural diversity, understand social issues, and explore their natural world. Many of
its books feature children as their own problem-solvers.
Website: www.tilburyhouse.com

Freelance Potential
Published 4 titles in 2009: 2 were developed from unsolicited
submissions. Of the 4 titles, 1 was by an unpublished writer
and 2 were by authors who were new to the publishing
house. Receives 960–1,200 unsolicited mss yearly.

- **Fiction:** Publishes story picture books, 4–10 years; and middle-
  grade books, 8–12 years. Genres include realistic and multicultural fiction, and stories about nature and the environment.
- **Nonfiction:** Publishes middle-grade books, 8–12 years. Topics
  include nature, social studies, and multicultural and ethnic
  issues.
- **Representative Titles:** *Always My Brother* by Jean Reagan
  (grades 3–6) is a realistic story of a young girl who gradually
  understands that memories of her late brother continue to
  make him part of her life and family. *Bear-ly There* by Rebekah
  Raye (grades 3–6) has a neighborhood in a tizzy when a bear
  keeps showing up in the backyards, until a child figures out the
  best way to keep the bear in the woods, where he is safe.

Submissions and Payment
Guidelines and catalogue available at website. Send complete manuscript. Accepts hard copy and email submissions
to karen@tilburyhouse.com. SASE. Responds in 1 month.
Publication in 1 year. Royalty; advance, negotiable.

Editor's Comments
We're specifically looking for titles on nonpoint source pollu-
tion, global warming, and building community. Books that
could be used in classroom settings are preferred.

TokyoPop

5900 Wilshire Boulevard, Suite 2000
Los Angeles, CA 90036

Editor

Publisher's Interests

TokyoPop uses the Japanese graphic art of manga as a base
for its graphic novels and children's and young adult fiction. It
publishes manga-inspired fiction in all genres, all designed to
entice children and teens to read and enjoy storytelling from a
new perspective. All of its books have a strong visual compo-
nent, but fiction authors need not be artists.
Website: www.tokyopop.com

Freelance Potential

Published 175 titles in 2009: 18 were developed from unsolicited submissions. Of the 175 titles, 158 were by unpublished writers and 88 were by authors who were new to the
publishing house. Receives 200+ queries and unsolicited
mss yearly.

- **Fiction:** Publishes chapter books, 5–10 years; middle-grade
  books, 8–12 years; and young adult books, 12–18 years. Genres include contemporary, historical, multicultural, Western,
  and science fiction; adventure; drama; fairy tales; fantasy; folktales; horror; humor; mystery; suspense; and romance.
- **Representative Titles:** *+Anima Volume 1* tells the tale of
  beings who possess animal-like powers and walk among
  humans in an alternate universe. *Hack//G.U. Volume 1* is a
  story about a massively-multiplayer online game—played by
  more than 12 million across the globe—that goes awry.

Submissions and Payment

Guidelines and catalogue available at website. Query with
outline; or send complete ms with résumé. Accepts hard
copy and CD submissions (Microsoft Word). SASE. Responds
to queries in 6–12 months, to mss in 3–6 months. Publication in 1–2 years. Royalty; advance.

Editor's Comments

When submitting your work, please include the submission
release agreement found at our website.

Tor Books

Tom Doherty Associates
175 Fifth Avenue
New York, NY 10010

Senior Editor, Children's/YA: Susan Chang

Publisher's Interests

Tor Books publishes science fiction and fantasy novels for adults, but many books find a readership among young adults. For younger readers, it publishes under its Starscape middle-grade and Tor Teen young adult imprints. The latter two publish a mix of commercial and literary fiction, including science fiction, fantasy, paranormal romance, horror, mysteries, and books that combine the genres.
Website: www.tor-forge.com

Freelance Potential

Published 30 titles in 2009: 22 were by agented authors and 10 were reprint/licensed properties. Of the 30 titles, 3 were by unpublished writers and 3 were by authors who were new to the publishing house.

- **Fiction:** Publishes middle-grade books, 8–10 years; and young adult books, 12–18 years. Genres include fantasy and science fiction. Also publishes fiction titles for adults.
- **Representative Titles:** *The Dragon's Lair* by Elizabeth Haydon (10+ years) is another installment in the fantasy adventures of young Ven, this one involving two warring kingdoms and the lair of an angry dragon. *The Battle of the Red Hot Pepper Weenies* by David Lubar (10+ years) is a collection of 35 warped and creepy tales involving the Weenies.

Submissions and Payment

Guidelines and catalogue available at website. Send synopsis and first 3 chapters. Do not send query letter. Accepts hard copy. SASE. Responds in 4–6 months. Publication in 18–24 months. Royalty; advance.

Editor's Comments

Most of our writers have agents. This is not a requirement; however, if you do not have an agent, we ask that you follow the detailed submission guidelines for unagented authors posted at our website.

Toy Box Productions

Division of CRT, Custom Products, Inc.
7532 Hickory Hills Court
Whites Creek, TN 37189

President: Cheryl J. Hutchinson

Publisher's Interests

Toy Box produces educational and entertaining read-along and audio-interactive storybooks for children. Each book has an accompanying CD to help strengthen reading skills, memorization, and timing coordination. The majority of its products deal with Bible stories or historical and social events.
Website: www.crttoybox.com

Freelance Potential

Published 3 titles in 2009: each was by an agented author. Of the 3 titles, 1 was by an unpublished writer and 1 was by an author who was new to the publishing house. Receives 1–2 queries yearly.

- **Fiction:** Publishes story picture books, 4–10 years; and chapter books, 5–10 years. Genres include historical, Western, multicultural, ethnic, and religious fiction.
- **Nonfiction:** Publishes story picture books, 4–10 years; and middle-grade books, 8–12 years. Topics include history, religion, and multicultural and ethnic issues.
- **Representative Titles:** *Lions, Lions Everywhere* by Joe Loesch follows a friendly family of lions as they tell the biblical story of Daniel. *Rosa Parks: Not Giving In* by James Collins introduces children to the story of Rosa Parks and how her actions in 1955 changed America forever.

Submissions and Payment

Catalogue available at website. All work is assigned. Query with résumé and clips. Accepts hard copy. SASE. Response time, publication period, and payment policy vary.

Editor's Comments

We believe in the power of "edu-tainment," and are always ready to consider talented writers and artists who can help us in that mission. If we like what you send us, we may give you an assignment.

Tradewind Books Ltd.

202-1807 Maritime Mews
Vancouver, British Columbia V6H 3W7
Canada

Submissions Editor: R. David Stephens

Publisher's Interests
Tradewind Books has been publishing books for young people since 1996. The home of many award-winning authors
and illustrators, its multicultural stories are designed to
spark young imaginations.
Website: www.tradewindbooks.com

Freelance Potential
Published 7 titles (5 juvenile) in 2009: 1 was developed
from an unsolicited submission and 1 was by an agented
author. Of the 7 titles, 1 was by an unpublished writer and
2 were by authors who were new to the publishing house.
Receives 900 queries, 600 unsolicited mss yearly.

- **Fiction:** Publishes early picture books, 0–4 years; easy-to-read
  books, 4–7 years; chapter books, 5–10 years; middle-grade
  books, 8–12 years; and young adult books, 12–18 years.
  Genres include multicultural and ethnic fiction, folklore, and
  stories about animals. Also publishes poetry.
- **Representative Titles:** *The Doomsday Mask* by Simon Rose
  follows two children as they try to prevent an ancient ceremo-
  nial mask from falling into the wrong hands and causing catastrophe. *Broken* by Alyxandra Harvey-Fitzhenry presents its
  young heroine as a modern-day Cinderella, but with an eerie
  and dangerous power.

Submissions and Payment
Guidelines available at website. Query with résumé and
sample chapter. Send complete ms for picture books only.
Accepts hard copy. SAE/IRC. Responds in 3 months. Publication in 3 years. Royalty; advance.

Editor's Comments
Please note that we're looking for more chapter books this
year. In order to reduce the number of misdirected manuscripts we receive, all submissions must include a detailed
indication that you have read at least three of our books.

Tricycle Press

P.O. Box 7123
Berkeley, CA 94707

Submissions: Nicole Geiger

Publisher's Interests

This imprint of Crown Publishing Group—a division of Random House—publishes fiction and nonfiction for children in preschool through high school.
Website: www.tricyclepress.com

Freelance Potential

Published 30 titles in 2009: 8 were by agented authors and 2 were reprint/licensed properties. Of the 30 titles, 3 were by unpublished writers and 7 were by new authors. Receives 480 queries, 3,600–4,800 unsolicited mss yearly.

- **Fiction:** Publishes concept books, toddler books, and early picture books, 0–4 years; story picture books, 4–10 years; and middle-grade books, 8–12 years. Publishes contemporary and humorous fiction, stories that teach tolerance, character education books, and nature stories.
- **Nonfiction:** Publishes concept books, toddler books, and early picture books, 0–4 years; story picture books, 4–10 years; and middle-grade books, 8–12 years. Also publishes board books. Topics include gardening, cooking, math, and real-life issues.
- **Representative Titles:** *Busy Chickens* by John Schindel (0–4 years) is a picture book featuring all sorts of chickens and roosters doing what they do best. *A Curious Collection of Cats* by Betsy Franco features more than 30 visual poems capturing the quirky ways of cats.

Submissions and Payment

Guidelines and catalogue available at website or with 9x12 SASE. Query with 2–3 sample chapters. Send complete ms for picture books. Accepts hard copy and simultaneous submissions if identified. SASE. Responds in 2–6 months. Publication period varies. Royalty; advance.

Editor's Comments

Please understand that due to the volume we receive, we may not be able to personally respond to your submission.

Turtle Books

866 United Nations Plaza, Suite 525
New York, NY 10017

Publisher: John Whitman

Publisher's Interests
This small press exclusively publishes story picture books,
each one with both an English and a Spanish edition. It also
produces lesson plans and DVDs to accompany each title.
As Turtle Bay's list is very selective, stories must have a
strong cultural message in order to be considered.
Website: www.turtlebooks.com

Freelance Potential
Published 5 titles in 2009: 3 were developed from unsolicited
submissions and 2 were by agented authors. Receives 1,200–
2,400 unsolicited mss yearly.

- **Fiction:** Publishes story picture books, 4–10 years. Genres
  include multicultural, ethnic, historical, contemporary, Western, and regional fiction; and folklore.
- **Representative Titles:** *The Crab Man* by Patricia E. Van West
  (4–10 years) is the story of a young Jamaican boy who must
  choose between earning money and treating animals compas-
  sionately. *Finding Daddy* by Jo & Josephine Harper (4–10 years)
  tells of a strong girl in Depression-era America who discovers a
  special talent that can help her impoverished family. *Alphabet
  Fiesta* by Anne Miranda (4–10 years) tells a story using English
  and Spanish words beginning with the same letter.

Submissions and Payment
Catalogue available at website. Send complete ms. Accepts
hard copy. SASE. Response time varies. Publication in 1 year.
Royalty; advance.

Editor's Comments
We are a very small, independent publishing house with a
specific niche: story picture books that illuminate a particular culture or socioeconomic issue, thus broadening a child's
view of the world. Since these books contain relatively brief
text, we will read only complete manuscripts. Please do not
send us a query.

Tuttle Publishing

364 Innovation Drive
North Clarendon, VT 05759

Associate Editor: William Notte

Publisher's Interests

Western readers interested in Asian culture—whether it be folklore, food, or feng shui—find much to their liking in the catalogue of Tuttle Publishing. Its Monsoon Books imprint brings Asian stories and language to life for children.
Website: www.tuttlepublishing.com

Freelance Potential

Published 120 titles (24 juvenile) in 2009: 96 were developed from unsolicited submissions, 6 were by agented authors, and 6 were reprint/licensed properties. Of the 120 titles, 78 were by unpublished writers and 96 were by authors who were new to the publishing house. Receives 120 queries yearly.

- **Fiction:** Publishes early picture books, 0–4 years; story picture books, 4–10 years; chapter books, 5–10 years; and young adult books, 12–18 years. Genres include folklore, mystery, suspense, and historical and ethnic fiction.
- **Nonfiction:** Publishes early picture books, 0–4 years; easy-to-read books, 4–7 years; story picture books, 4–10 years; chapter books, 5–10 years; middle-grade books, 8–12 years; and young adult books, 12–18 years. Topics include martial arts, culture, history, religion, art, crafts, games, and languages.
- **Representative Titles:** *Monkey Magic: The Curse of Mukada* by Grant S. Clark is a novel about an 11-year-old girl who breaks a spell that has been plaguing orangutans in Borneo. *Japanese Celebrations: Cherry Blossoms, Lanterns and Stars!* by Betty Reynolds introduces these to kids through colorful illustrations.

Submissions and Payment

Guidelines and catalogue available at website. Query with outline/synopsis. Accepts hard copy. SASE. Responds in 1–2 months. Publication in 18 months. Royalty; advance.

Editor's Comments

We seek collections of Asian folktales, language titles, martial arts instructional books, and children's Asian cookbooks.

Twenty-First Century Books

241 First Avenue North
Minneapolis, MN 55401

Submissions Editor: Jennifer Zimian

Publisher's Interests
This publisher, a division of Lerner Books, produces high-interest nonfiction books for students in middle school and high school. It does not publish textbooks. Rather, its books about science, politics, social studies, history, and contemporary issues are designed to augment classroom lessons. It does not accept unsolicited submissions. Instead, it calls for targeted solicitations at specific reading levels and in specific areas.
Website: www.lernerbooks.com

Freelance Potential
Published 100+ titles in 2009. Receives 100 queries yearly.

- **Nonfiction:** Publishes middle-grade books, 8–12 years; and young adult books, 12–18 years. Topics include science, technology, health, medicine, history, social studies, contemporary issues, language arts, government, politics, and sports. Also publishes biographies and multicultural titles.
- **Representative Titles:** *Flappers and the New American Woman: Perceptions of Women from 1918 through the 1920s* by Catherine Gourley (13–18 years) looks at the social influences and popular images that shaped how America saw women; part of the Images and Issues of Women in the Twentieth Century series. *Meth: America's Drug Epidemic* by Elaine Landau (12–18 years) presents the legal, social, and physical perils of the drug.

Submissions and Payment
No unsolicited submissions. See website for submission details. Publication period and payment policy vary.

Editor's Comments
Our books may be nonfiction, but they are definitely not dry textbooks. Our books are intended to engage and enthrall our readers. We occasionally list targeted solicitations in national newsletters, such as the SCBWI *Bulletin*.

Twilight Times Books

P.O. Box 3340
Kingsport, TN 37664

Submissions: Ardy Scott

Publisher's Interests

Starting out as an e-publisher and expanding to print publishing in 2004, Twilight Times Books features compelling literary fiction and nonfiction for young adults and adults. Its catalogue includes science and historical fiction, mystery, New Age, fantasy, humor, and how-to titles.
Website: http://twilighttimesbooks.com

Freelance Potential

Published 12–14 titles (3 juvenile) in 2009. Of the 12–14 titles, 3 were by unpublished writers and 6 were by authors who were new to the publishing house. Receives 1,200 queries yearly.

- **Fiction:** Publishes young adult books, 12–18 years. Genres include historical, literary, and science fiction; mystery; suspense; realism; and stories about magic realism and New Age subjects.
- **Representative Titles:** *Dragon's Moon* by Bent Lorentzen is the story of a young dragon who discovers that his disability may be the key weapon against an antagonist. *The Dog Who Thought He Was a Cat* by Darrell Bain features a dog who goes on a search for his identity.

Submissions and Payment

Guidelines and catalogue available at website. Query with synopsis, first chapter, brief author bio, and marketing plan. Accepts email queries to publisher@twilighttimesbooks.com (no attachments); "ttbooks" or "ttb" must appear in subject line. Responds in 1–2 months. Publication period varies. Royalty.

Editor's Comments

We are dedicated to enhancing the prospects of getting great literary, New Age, and science fiction books into the hands of readers. We look for exemplary literary works that transcend genres and/or are beautifully written.

Tyndale House Publishers

351 Executive Drive
Carol Stream, IL 60188

Acquisitions Director, Children & Family:
Katara Washington Patton

Publisher's Interests
This ecumenical publisher is interested in fiction and nonfiction that embraces Christian values and lessons. It publishes fiction with Christian messages for children under age 12, and nonfiction titles for all ages that teach about Jesus, the Bible, and Christianity.
Website: www.tyndale.com

Freelance Potential
Published 15 titles in 2009: each was by an agented author. Receives 240 queries yearly.

- **Fiction:** Publishes toddler books, 0–4 years; story picture books, 4–10 years; middle-grade books, 8–12 years. Features fiction on general interest topics written from a Christian perspective.
- **Nonfiction:** Publishes toddler books and early picture books, 0–4 years; easy-to-read books, 4–7 years: story picture books, 4–10 years; middle-grade books, 8–12 years; and young adult books, 12–18 years. Features books about the Christian faith. Also publishes parenting books.
- **Representative Titles:** *My Pajama Bible* by Andy Holmes, ed. (0–4 years) presents 30 well-known Bible stories from the Old and New Testaments written in a way that captures the imaginations of toddlers. *Wait Until Then* by Randy Alcorn uses a story about Nathan and his beloved grandfather to teach children about heaven, following Jesus, and waiting until we see lost loved ones again.

Submissions and Payment
Accepts work from agented authors, Tyndale authors, and authors introduced through other publishers only. Publication period varies. Royalty; advance. Flat fee.

Editor's Comments
Although some of our nonfiction books are for young adults or parents, most focus on the 12 and under market.

Upstart Books

401 South Wright Street
Janesville, WI 53547

Editor: Kelly Loughman

Publisher's Interests

Library promotional materials and reading incentives are available from Upstart, a division of Highsmith, Inc. It publishes books for library professionals and teachers, and books designed to teach information-seeking skills to children from preschool through high school.
Website: www.upstartbooks.com

Freelance Potential

Published 20 titles in 2009: 5 were developed from unsolicited submissions. Of the 20 titles, 5 were by authors who were new to the publishing house. Receives 80–100 queries, 80–100 unsolicited mss yearly.

- **Fiction:** Publishes story picture books, 4–10 years; and chapter books, 5–10 years. Features stories that teach library skills.
- **Nonfiction:** Publishes elementary and middle-grade books, 6–12 years. Topics include library and research skills. Also publishes books for librarians and teachers on story times, reading activities, and literature.
- **Representative Titles:** *"R" Is for Research* by Toni Buzzeo (4–10 years) is a picture book that introduces basic research concepts. *Goldie Socks and the Three Libearians* by Jackie Mims Hopkins (4–10 years) presents a fractured fairy tale about a girl who makes herself at home at a cottage filled with storybooks and owned by three "libearians."

Submissions and Payment

Guidelines and catalogue available at website. Query with outline or sample chapters for mss longer than 100 pages. Send complete ms for shorter works. Accepts hard copy and simultaneous submissions. SASE. Responds in 2 months. Publication period varies. Royalty, 10–12%; advance.

Editor's Comments

Any project that lets kids have fun while learning the value of their library will interest us.

URJ Press

633 Third Avenue
New York, NY 10017

Editor-in-Chief: Michael H. Goldberg

Publisher's Interests
URJ Press, a division of the Union for Reform Judaism, publishes a variety of fiction and nonfiction books for children, parents, and teachers that reinforce the history, traditions, and values of Judaism.
Website: www.urjbooksandmusic.com

Freelance Potential
Published 25 titles (12 juvenile) in 2009: 3 were developed from unsolicited submissions. Of the 25 titles, 8 were by unpublished writers and 4 were by authors who were new to the publishing house. Receives 100 queries, 300 unsolicited mss yearly.

- **Fiction:** Publishes early picture books, 0–4 years; story picture books, 4–10 years; and young adult books, 12–18 years. Genres include religious and historical fiction, and stories based in Judaism.
- **Nonfiction:** Publishes toddler books and early picture books, 0–4 years. Also publishes textbooks and educational resource materials for grades K–12. Topics include Jewish history and holidays, the Holocaust, and the Hebrew language.
- **Representative Titles:** *Shavua Tov!* by Michelle Shapiro Abraham introduces young children to the Havdalah blessings and rituals. *The Mystery of the Coins* by Chaya M. Burstein (grades 4–6) offers a suspenseful tale about a collection of coins that leads readers on a chase through Jewish history.

Submissions and Payment
Guidelines available. Query with résumé, outline, and 2 sample chapters. Send complete ms for picture books. Accepts hard copy and email to press@urj.org. SASE. Response time and publication period vary. Royalty; advance.

Editor's Comments
We are also interested in program guides, songbooks, and CD projects.

UXL

27500 Drake Road
Farmington Hills, MI 48331-3535

Editorial: Jim Person

Publisher's Interests

UXL makes comprehensive reference books for middle and high school students. Its list includes encyclopedias, biographies, almanacs, chronologies, and primary source volumes.
Website: www.gale.cengage.com

Freelance Potential

Published 20 titles in 2009.

- **Nonfiction:** Publishes young adult books, 12–18 years. Topics include science, medicine, history, social studies, current events, multicultural issues, the arts, sports, and careers. Also publishes curriculum-based reference titles, encyclopedias, and biographies.
- **Representative Titles:** *UXL Encyclopedia of Diseases and Disorders* is a five-volume set containing more than 200 entries on medical conditions. *UXL Encyclopedia of U.S. History* by Sonia Benson explores the timeline of America, including its founders, key historical figures, wars, events, economy, culture, and politics. *Outlaws, Mobsters, & Crooks* details the nation's most notorious criminals, from the Old West to the age of the Internet.

Submissions and Payment

Most work is assigned. Guidelines and catalogue available at website. Query with résumé and writing samples. Accepts hard copy, simultaneous submissions if identified, and queries submitted through website. SASE. Accepts some unsolicited material, but mostly assigns on a work-for-hire basis. Response time and publication period vary. Flat fee.

Editor's Comments

Regardless of subject matter, all of our books are written in an easy-to-understand format that appeals to students at a variety of reading levels. We prefer to assign topics, but are occasionally drawn to an idea or query that offers something new and intriguing.

Viking Children's Books

Penguin Group USA, Inc.
345 Hudson Street
New York, NY 10014

Editorial Assistant: Leila Sales

Publisher's Interests

This imprint of the Penguin Young Readers Group publishes hardcover literary fiction and nonfiction for children. It prefers to work with agented authors.
Website: www.us.penguin.com

Freelance Potential

Published 57 titles in 2009: 1 was developed from an unsolicited submission, 40 were by agented authors, and 2 were reprint/licensed properties. Of the 57 titles, 6 were by unpublished writers and 18 were by authors who were new to the publishing house. Receives 1,200 queries, 1,200 unsolicited mss yearly.

- **Fiction:** Publishes early picture books, 0–4 years; easy-to-read books, 4–7 years; story picture books, 4–10 years; chapter books, 5–10 years; middle-grade books, 8–12 years; and young adult books, 12–18 years. Genres include adventure; mystery; and contemporary, multicultural, and science fiction.
- **Nonfiction:** Publishes middle-grade books, 8–12 years; and young adult books, 12–18 years. Topics include animals, geography, history, sports, science. Also publishes biographies.
- **Representative Titles:** *Wintergirls* by Laurie Halse Anderson (YA) chronicles two friends' descent into the powerful vortex of anorexia. *Moon Rabbit* by Natalie Russell (3–5 years) is the story of a little rabbit who longs for a friend.

Submissions and Payment

Catalogue available at website. Agented authors preferred. Query or send ms. Accepts hard copy. Does not guarantee return of materials. Responds in 4 months if interested. Publication period varies. Royalty, 2–10%; advance. Flat fee.

Editor's Comments

We regret that we cannot respond personally to each submission, but rest assured that we do make every effort to consider each and every one we receive.

Walch Education

40 Walch Drive
Portland, ME 04103

Submissions: Susan Graham

Publisher's Interests
Middle school, high school and adult education are the core markets targeted by this publisher. Education and resource materials in mathematics, science, social studies, language arts, and special education are among its offerings.
Website: www.walch.com

Freelance Potential
Published 50 titles in 2009: 2 were developed from unsolicited submissions. Of the 50 titles, 45 were by unpublished writers and 5 were by authors who were new to the publishing house. Receives 24 queries yearly.

- **Nonfiction:** Publishes middle-grade and high school education books. Topics include reading, writing, vocabulary, grammar, geometry, algebra, critical thinking, world history, social science, chemistry, physics, money management, careers, and special education. Also offers resource materials for teachers.
- **Representative Titles:** *Shakespeare Made Easy: An Illustrated Approach* by Muriel J. Morris (grades 7–9) introduces 12 widely read Shakespearean plays in comic strip formats. *25 Low-Cost Biology Investigations* by Joel Beller (grades 8–10) explores botany, physiology, human biology, and ecology through 25 classroom-proven labs.

Submissions and Payment
Guidelines available at website. Query with résumé, learning objectives, table of contents, sample chapter, and supporting material. Accepts hard copy and email submissions to ideas@walch.com. SASE. Responds in 4–6 months. Publication period varies. Royalty. Flat fee.

Editor's Comments
If you are an educator with an idea that will engage learners, we'd love to hear from you. We welcome submissions in all core subject areas. Be sure to include a market analysis and description of your target audience in your query package.

Walker & Company

175 Fifth Avenue, 8th Floor
New York, NY 10011

Submissions

Publisher's Interests
Established in 1961, Walker & Company takes pride in its
commitment to finding and fostering new voices in children's literature. It publishes three lists per year, each consisting of approximately 10 picture books and four to five
middle-grade and/or young adult works.
Website: www.walkeryoungreaders.com

Freelance Potential
Published 45 titles in 2009. Receives 8,000 queries, 5,000
unsolicited mss yearly.

- **Fiction:** Publishes toddler books, 0–4 years; story picture
  books, 4–10 years; middle-grade books, 8–12 years; and
  young adult books, 12–18 years. Genres include historical and
  contemporary fiction.
- **Nonfiction:** Publishes concept books, 0–4 years; story picture
  books, 4–10 years; middle-grade books, 8–12 years; and
  young adult books, 12–18 years. Topics include history, biography, and social issues.
- **Representative Titles:** *Abigail Iris: The One and Only* by Lisa
  Glatt & Suzanne Greenberg follows a girl who wishes she
  could be an only child on a trip without her siblings. *Breath-
  less* by Jessica Warman (YA) is a semi-autobiographical novel
  about a teen girl and her schizophrenic brother's hold on her.

Submissions and Payment
Guidelines and catalogue available at website. Query with
outline/synopsis and 3–5 chapters. Send complete ms for
picture books only. Accepts hard copy and simultaneous
submissions if identified. SASE. Responds in 5 months. Publication in 18–24 months. Royalty; advance.

Editor's Comments
Because of our dedication to new talent, we accept unsolicited manuscripts and manuscripts from authors without
agents. However, please be sure to follow our guidelines.

Warner Press

1201 East Fifth Street
P.O. Box 2499
Anderson, IN 46016

Acquisitions Editor: Robin Fogle

Publisher's Interests
What began in 1881 as the publishing house of the Church of God Reformation Movement has grown into a publisher of church resources, children's products, and religious gifts. Its publications now target a wide Christian audience.
Website: www.warnerpress.org

Freelance Potential
Published 3 titles (2 juvenile) in 2009. Receives 120 queries each year.

- **Fiction:** Publishes easy-to-read books, 4–7 years; and story picture books, 4–10 years. Genres include religious history and stories with biblical themes.
- **Nonfiction:** Publishes puzzle and activity books, 8–10 years. Topics include the Bible, religion, and Christianity. Also publishes reference books for parents and teachers.
- **Representative Titles:** *The Adventures of 10 Gallon Sam and the Perilous Mine* by Chris Miller & Alan Miller is an adventure based on the Bible story of Samson; part of the Heroes of Promise series. *God's Amazing Book* by Kathleen Ruckman (4–7 years) presents an introduction to the Bible and the many amazing stories it contains.

Submissions and Payment
Guidelines and catalogue available at website. Query with synopsis and publishing credits for picture books. Send complete ms with illustration ideas for activity books. Accepts email queries to rfogle@warnerpress.org. Responds in 3–6 months. Publication in 12–18 months. Flat fee.

Editor's Comments
Please be aware that we publish only a small number of picture books each year, and we usually publish authors with whom we have previously worked. We are, however, open to considering queries from freelancers who are new to us.

WaterBrook Multnomah Publishing Group

12265 Oracle Boulevard, Suite 200
Colorado Springs, CO 80921

Submissions Editor

Publisher's Interests

The goal of this evangelical division of Random House is to provide a deep well of spiritual refreshment with books that are relevant to the unique needs of today's Christian. It publishes parenting and family titles as well as inspirational books for children and youth.

Website: www.randomhouse.com/waterbrook

Freelance Potential

Published 65–70 titles in 2009: most were by agented authors. Receives 500 queries yearly.

- **Fiction:** Publishes story picture books, 4–10 years; and young adult books, 12–18 years. Genres include religious, inspirational, and contemporary fiction; and fantasy.
- **Nonfiction:** Publishes young adult books, 12–18 years. Topics include religion, Christianity, and personal faith. Also publishes parenting titles.
- **Representative Titles:** *God Loves Me More Than That* by Dandi Daley Mackall is a picture book that imparts its message of God's love through lively rhymes. *Sir Dalton and the Shadow Heart* by Chuck Black is an allegorical tale of a knight-in-training, whose waning devotion to the king brings on attacks by an evil warrior. *For Young Men Only* by Jeff Feldhahn & Eric Rice (YA) gives teen boys the inside scoop on their favorite subject: teen girls.

Submissions and Payment

Catalogue available at website. Accepts queries through literary agents only. Responds in 6–10 weeks. Publication in 1 year. Royalty; advance.

Editor's Comments

Our books are filled with unforgettable characters that will captivate children's attention while enriching their souls with godly principles. We look for life-changing messages that will teach the love of God with truths that will last a lifetime.

Watson-Guptill Publications

Random House
770 Broadway
New York, NY 10003

Senior Acquisitions Editor: Julie Mazur

Publisher's Interests
This imprint of Random House and Crown Publishing Group publishes books with artistic themes for readers in the middle grades and high school. Its catalogue is filled with titles on art techniques, graphic artistry, architecture, film, design, music, and the world of entertainment. Most of its books have a "how-to" element that instructs readers in creating the art form in which they are interested.
Website: www.watsonguptill.com

Freelance Potential
Published 77 titles in 2009: 25 were by agented authors.

- **Nonfiction:** Publishes middle-grade books, 8–12 years; and young adult books, 12–18 years. Topics include fine arts, drawing, painting, sculpture, cartooning, animation, graphic design, crafts, dramatic arts, music, photography, makeup artistry, architecture, and interior design.
- **Representative Titles:** *Xtreme Art* by Christopher Hart provides readers with a crash course in character drawing, including the popular manga characters. *The Hip Handbag Kit: Funky Handbags to Make and Wear* by Sherri Haab presents instructions for making totes, purses, and bags out of a variety of commonly found materials. *Get Animated!* by Tim Maloney is an illustrated guide to creating great animation on a home computer.

Submissions and Payment
Guidelines and catalogue available at website. Query with table of contents, sample chapter, author bio, and market analysis. Accepts hard copy. SASE. Response time and publication period vary. Royalty; advance.

Editor's Comments
We're interested in books that can help readers advance in their chosen crafts. Authors should be able to provide step-by-step guidelines throughout their books.

Wayne State University Press

The Leonard N. Simons Building
4809 Woodward Avenue
Detroit, MI 48201-1309

Acquisitions Editors: Kathryn Wildfong & Annie Martin

Publisher's Interests

This mid-size university press publishes a variety of scholarly and general interest titles for adults and students, including books on child development and children's literature. It publishes books for young readers in its Great Lakes series, which specializes in books of regional interest and importance to Michigan and the Great Lakes region.
Website: http://wsupress.wayne.edu

Freelance Potential

Published 35 titles in 2009: 2 were by agented authors and 2 were reprint/licensed properties. Receives 200 queries each year.

- **Nonfiction:** Publishes early picture books, 0–4 years; and middle-grade books, 8–12 years. Topics include the art, architecture, and culture of the Michigan region; the history of the Upper Peninsula and the Great Lakes; and historical Detroit personalities. Also publishes child development titles.
- **Representative Titles:** *Who's Jim Hines?* by Jean Alicia Elster (8–12 years) presents the history and realities of racism in Depression-era Detroit through the eyes of a 12-year-old African American boy. *Under Fire* by Elizabeth Goodenough & Andrea Immel, eds. explores the representation of war and its after-effects in children's books and documentary films.

Submissions and Payment

Guidelines and catalogue available at website. Query with résumé, outline, table of contents, and sample chapters. Accepts hard copy and email queries to k.wildfong@ wayne.edu. SASE. Responds in 4–6 weeks. Publication in 15 months. Royalty, 6–7.5%.

Editor's Comments

Some book series have their own submission guidelines, so it's a good idea to read our website thoroughly before submitting your material.

Weigl Publishers

350 Fifth Avenue, Suite 3304
PMB 6G
New York, NY 10118-0069

Managing Editor: Heather Hudak

Publisher's Interests
Since 1992, Weigl has been creating educational books at all
grade levels for school library and classroom use. It produces books in series that cover a multitude of subjects,
including language arts, science, history, and social studies.
Website: www.weigl.com

Freelance Potential
Published 80 titles in 2009. Of the 80 titles, 5 were by
authors who were new to the publishing house.

- **Nonfiction:** Publishes chapter books, 5–10 years; middle-grade
  books, 8–12 years; and young adult books, 12–18 years. Topics include global cultures, social and environmental issues,
  plant and animal life, biography, sports, and real-life stories.
- **Representative Titles:** *For the Love of Biking* by Rennay
  Craats (grades 4 and up) gives readers an exciting glimpse
  into the world of biking, from the type of equipment used to
  the techniques of successful BMX racers and mountain bikers;
  part of the For the Love of Sports series. *Beatrix Potter* by
  Jennifer Hurtig (grades 5 and up) presents the life of the well-
  known children's author and some interesting stories behind
  her books; part of the My Favorite Writer series.

Submissions and Payment
Catalogue available at website. All work is done on a work-
for-hire basis. Send résumé only. No queries or unsolicited
mss. Accepts hard copy and email to linda@weigl.com.
SASE. Responds in 6–12 months. Publication in 2 years.
Flat fee.

Editor's Comments
Most of our projects are designed in-house and assigned to
writers. Send us your résumé, publishing history, and subject area of expertise to be included on our list of go-to
writers. We like to work with writers who have experience in
the educational book market.

Weiser Books

500 Third Street, Suite 230
San Francisco, CA 94107

Acquisitions Editor: Pat Bryce

Publisher's Interests

This imprint of Red Wheel/Weiser publishes self-described "esoteric" books about such topics as magic, Wicca, tarot, astrology, and Kabbalah. While it does not have a separate children's list, many of its titles are likely to be of interest to young adult readers.
Website: www.weiserbooks.com

Freelance Potential

Published 50 titles in 2009: 10 were developed from unsolicited submissions and 30 were by agented authors.
Receives 720 queries yearly.

- **Nonfiction:** Publishes self-help, inspirational, and informational books. Topics include magic, Wicca, tarot, astrology, Kabbalah, the occult, and metaphysics.
- **Representative Titles:** *Friends on a Rotten Day* by Hazel Dixon-Cooper describes the astrology of friendships; part of the Rotten Day series. *The Weiser Concise Guide to Practical Astrology* by Priscilla Costello introduces the reader to the basic principles of modern astrology. *The Essential Laws of Fearless Living* by Guy Finley contains 40 essays that encourage readers to lighten their loads of fear and suffering, and enlighten their days.

Submissions and Payment

Guidelines and catalogue available at website. Query with résumé, outline, table of contents, and 3 chapters. Accepts hard copy and simultaneous submissions if identified. SASE. Responds in 3 months. Publication in 18 months. Royalty; advance.

Editor's Comments

Send copies of your material only—keep the original for your records. Please note that we can't use international postage coupons; Canadian and any other foreign submissions must include U.S. postage.

Whitecap Books Ltd.

351 Lynn Avenue
North Vancouver, British Columbia V7J 2C4
Canada

Editor: Taryn Boyd

Publisher's Interests

The children's books on this Canadian publisher's list all have a common theme: nature and wildlife. It has a soft spot for stories and nonfiction centering on its homeland. **Website: www.whitecap.ca**

Freelance Potential

Published 43 titles (6 juvenile) in 2009: 2 were developed from unsolicited submissions and 3 were by agented authors. Receives 300 queries yearly.

- **Fiction:** Publishes easy-to-read books, 4–7 years; middle-grade books, 8–12 years; and young adult books, 12–18 years. Genres include contemporary fiction, adventure, fantasy, folklore, and stories about animals, nature, and the environment.
- **Nonfiction:** Publishes easy-to-read books, 4–7 years; and story picture books, 4–10 years. Topics include animals, natural history, science, the environment, and regional subjects.
- **Representative Titles:** *Investigate Australia* by Margaret McPhee describes the culture, wildlife, topography, and geography of this continent; part of the Investigate series. *Animals Eat the Weirdest Things* by Diane Swanson is a buffet of disgusting animal delights, from book-eating slugs to toenail-chewing rats.

Submissions and Payment

Guidelines available. Prefers query with outline; will accept complete ms. Accepts hard copy and simultaneous submissions if identified. SAE/IRC. Responds in 2–4 months. Publication in 18 months. Royalty; advance. Flat fee.

Editor's Comments

Although some publishing houses refuse to accept unagented submissions, Whitecap Books is not one of them. We read every submission that is sent to us, and we take pride in discovering new voices and in publishing previously unpublished authors.

White Mane Kids

White Mane Publishing Company
73 West Burd Street
P.O. Box 708
Shippensburg, PA 17257

Acquisitions Department

Publisher's Interests
The children's division of White Mane Publishing Company offers history-based novels for middle-grade and young adult readers. Each book contains accurate historical information, packaged within a compelling story. The majority of its titles deal with America's Civil War. 30% self-, subsidy-, co-venture, or co-op published material.
Website: www.whitemane.com

Freelance Potential
Published 3 titles in 2009: 1 was developed from an unsolicited submission. Receives 100 queries yearly.

- **Fiction:** Publishes middle-grade books, 8–14 years; and young adult books, 12–18 years. Genres include historical fiction.
- **Representative Titles:** *Discoveries in the Shriver Family Attic* by Kajsa C. Cook finds the Shriver family returning to their abandoned home and discovering what happened there during the Battle of Gettysburg. *Hayfoot, Strawfoot: The Bucktail Recruits* by William P. Robertson & David Rimer tells the Civil War story of two boys who find themselves together in one of the Union's most famous regiments.

Submissions and Payment
Guidelines and proposal submission form available. Query via proposal form only with market analysis and brief author biography. Accepts hard copy. SASE. Responds in 3–6 months. Publication in 12–18 months. Royalty, 7–10%.

Editor's Comments
We look for books that draw young readers in with their exciting situations and interesting characters, while teaching them about a period in America's history. All books must be historically accurate, as they are marketed with additional educational resources for classroom use. In your query, please state the historical relevance and educational benefits of your work.

Albert Whitman & Company

6340 Oakton Street
Morton Grove, IL 60053-2723

Editor-in-Chief: Kathleen Tucker

Publisher's Interests
A publisher of "good books for children" since 1919, Albert
Whitman accepts picture books, novels, and nonfiction titles
for children ages 2 through 12. Its Concept Book series
addresses children who are dealing with challenging life situations such as grief, illness, family strife, or bullying.
Website: www.albertwhitman.com

Freelance Potential
Published 30 titles in 2009. Receives 300 queries, 4,500
unsolicited mss yearly.

- **Fiction:** Publishes early picture books, 0–4 years; chapter
  books, 5–10 years; middle-grade books, 8–12 years; and
  young adult books, 12–18 years. Genres include historical
  fiction, humor, and mystery.
- **Nonfiction:** Publishes early picture books, 0–4 years; chapter
  books, 5–10 years; and middle-grade books, 8–12 years. Topics include social, multicultural, ethnic, and family issues; history; and biography.
- **Representative Titles:** *The No-Good Do-Good Pirates* by Jim
  Kraft (5–8 years) follows a scurvy gang of pirates as they
  search for a good deed to do. *The Saddest Time* by Norma
  Simon (grades 1–4) focuses on the emotions children feel
  when death touches someone close to them.

Submissions and Payment
Guidelines and catalogue available at website. Query with
3 sample chapters. Send complete ms for picture books
only. Accepts hard copy and simultaneous submissions if
identified. SASE. Responds to queries in 6 weeks, to mss in
3–4 months. Publication in 18–24 months. Royalty; advance.

Editor's Comments
If five or more months pass without a response from us,
writers may inquire about the status of their submissions by
contacting us through the mail.

The Wild Rose Press

P.O. Box 708
Adams Basin, NY 14410

Editor-in-Chief: Rhonda Penders

Publisher's Interests
Romance is the key element in all the titles published by
Wild Rose Press. Its fiction books, many of which are part of
popular series, are geared to young adults.
Website: www.thewildrosepress.com

Freelance Potential
Published 100 titles (10–12 juvenile) in 2009: 98 were
developed from unsolicited submissions and 2 were by
agented authors. Of the 100 titles, 33 were by unpublished
writers and 33 were by authors who were new to the publishing house. Receives 1,800 queries yearly.

- **Fiction:** Publishes young adult books, 12–18 years. Features
  14 subgenres of romance, from suspense to inspirational-
  themed romances.
- **Representative Titles:** *Moonlight Dancer* by Mona Ingram
  (12–18 years) follows the romance of two teens as they
  grapple with the appearance of a strange ghostly figure. *Seek
  Ye First My Heart* by Kimberlee Mendoza (12–18 years) tells
  the story of a young girl's quest to avenge a wrong while
  learning some very important lessons; part of the Russell
  Family series.

Submissions and Payment
Guidelines and catalogue available at website. Query with
synopsis. No unsolicited mss. Prefers email queries to
queryus@thewildrosepress.com (include "TWRP Ms Submission" in the subject line; no attachments); will accept hard
copy. SASE. No simultaneous submissions. Response time
and publication period vary. Royalty.

Editor's Comments
We publish romance and sub-genres of romance only, so
love is an essential element in all of our titles. For more
information on how we define romance, please refer to
our website.

Windward Publishing

8075 215th Street West
Lakeville, MN 55044

President: Alan E. Krysan

Publisher's Interests
Windward, an imprint of Finney Company, covers the topics
of natural history and science, outdoor recreation, and children's literature.
Website: www.finneyco.com

Freelance Potential
Published 4–5 titles (2–3 juvenile) in 2009: 4 were developed from unsolicited submissions. Of the 4–5 titles, 3 were
by unpublished writers and 3 were by authors who were new
to the publishing house. Receives 180–240 queries, 180–
240 unsolicited mss yearly.

- **Fiction:** Publishes easy-to-read books, 4–7 years; and story
  picture books, 4–10 years. Genres include books about nature
  and the natural world.
- **Nonfiction:** Publishes easy-to-read books, 4–7 years; story
  picture books, 4–10 years; chapter books, 5–10 years; middle-
  grade books, 8–12 years; and young adult books, 12–18
  years. Topics include space, seashells and sea life, nature,
  flowers, birds, reptiles, amphibians, and fishing.
- **Representative Titles:** *Wild Beach* by Marion Coste (5+ years)
  follows a girl and her dog as they explore the beach before
  the sunbathers gather. *Through Endangered Eyes* by Rachel
  Allen Dillon (all ages) uses paintings and poetry to educate
  readers about endangered creatures.

Submissions and Payment
Guidelines available at website. Query with overview, table
of contents, and up to 3 chapters; or send complete ms.
Accepts hard copy and simultaneous submissions. Artwork
improves chance of acceptance. SASE. Responds in 10–12
weeks. Publication in 6–8 months. Royalty, 10% of net.

Editor's Comments
Although primarily a nonfiction publisher, we occasionally
accept fiction books with educational value.

Woodbine House

6510 Bells Mill Road
Bethesda, MD 20817

Acquisitions Editor: Nancy Gray Paul

Publisher's Interests
Woodbine House publishes books for and about children with disabilities, as well as for their parents and the professionals who work with them.
Website: www.woodbinehouse.com

Freelance Potential
Published 10 titles (3 juvenile) in 2009: 5 were developed from unsolicited submissions and 2 were by agented authors. Receives 300 queries, 300 unsolicited mss yearly.

- **Fiction:** Publishes concept books, 0–4 years; story picture books, 2–10 years; and chapter books, 8–18 years. Offers stories for and about children with developmental disabilities.
- **Nonfiction:** Publishes guides and reference books for parents and professionals. Topics include autism spectrum disorders, Down syndrome, Tourette syndrome, executive dysfunction, and other developmental disabilities.
- **Representative Titles:** *Kids Like Me . . . Learn ABCs* by Laura Ronay (0–6 years) is an alphabet board book featuring children with Down syndrome; part of the Kids Like Me . . . series. *Fasten Your Seatbelt* by Brian Skotko & Susan P. Levine (grades 6–12) is a crash course on Down syndrome for siblings.

Submissions and Payment
Guidelines available. Send complete ms for picture books only. Query with résumé, outline, and sample chapters for other work. Accepts hard copy and simultaneous submissions if identified. SASE. Responds in 3 months. Publication in 1 year. Payment policy varies.

Editor's Comments
We publish very few children's books; therefore, it is unlikely that we will publish more than one book on the same topic. We prefer stories with a narrative drive or plot (conflict/resolution) rather than "what it's like to have" or "a day in the life" stories.

Workman Publishing

225 Varick Street
New York, NY 10014

Editorial Assistant: Natalie Rinn

Publisher's Interests

This independent company has been "publishing books, calendars, and big ideas for over 40 years." Included in its extensive catalogue are fun, educational books and nonfiction for children, as well as several popular pregnancy and parenting titles.

Website: www.workman.com

Freelance Potential

Published 40 titles (7 juvenile) in 2009: 7 were by agented authors. Receives 1,000 queries, 360+ unsolicited mss yearly.

- **Fiction:** Publishes toddler books, 0–4 years. Also publishes board books and novelty books.
- **Nonfiction:** Publishes concept books and toddler books, 0–4 years; middle-grade books, 8–12 years; and young adult books, 12–18 years. Topics include science, nature, humor, hobbies, and crafts. Also publishes pregnancy and parenting titles.
- **Representative Titles:** *Good Egg* by Barney Saltzberg (0–4 years) is an interactive board book with flaps and pull-tabs that enables the egg to do tricks. *The Zoo's Shoes* by Lynn Brunelle (0–4 years) is die-cut in the shape and size of a child's sneaker and features four sets of colorful laces to provide a hands-on guide along with a fun story.

Submissions and Payment

Guidelines and catalogue available at website. Query with sample chapters and outline/synopsis; or send complete ms. Accepts hard copy. SASE. Responds in 3 months. Publication period varies. Royalty; advance.

Editor's Comments

We look for strong writing, an original approach, and intelligence in concept and execution. Our review process may take up to several months. If there is an important reason for us to contact you sooner, please let us know that reason in your cover letter.

YouthLight

P.O. Box 115
Chapin, SC 29036

Submissions Editor: Susan Bowman

Publisher's Interests

YouthLight is an educational support company that publishes kindergarten- through twelfth grade-level books on social skills and dealing with social issues and pressures. It also publishes books for educators and counselors.
Website: www.youthlightbooks.com

Freelance Potential

Published 16 titles (4 juvenile) in 2009; each was developed from an unsolicited submission. Of the 16 titles, 3 were by unpublished writers and 6 were by authors who were new to the publishing house. Receives 60–120 unsolicited mss yearly.

- **Fiction:** Publishes easy-to-read books, 4–7 years; story picture books, 4–10 years; middle-grade books, 8–12 years; and young adult novels, 12–18 years. Genres include multicultural fiction and stories about children dealing with social pressures.
- **Nonfiction:** Publishes easy-to-read books, 4–7 years; story picture books, 4–10 years; middle-grade books, 8–12 years; and young adult books, 12–18 years. Topics include self-help and social issues. Also publishes titles for adults.
- **Representative Titles:** *Words Are Not for Hurting* by Elizabeth Verdick (preK–grade 3) teaches children to think before they speak. *My Secret Bully* by Trudy Ludwig (grades K–6) is an inspirational story about a girl who is being bullied and learns how to cope, survive, and thrive.

Submissions and Payment

Guidelines and catalogue available at website. Query for nonfiction. Send complete ms with table of contents for fiction. Accepts disk submissions and email to sbowman@youthlightbooks.com. SASE. Responds in 1–3 weeks. Publication in 6 months. Royalty, 10%.

Editor's Comments

At this time, we're not looking for books about grief, obesity, anger management, character education, or academics.

Zephyr Press

814 North Franklin Street
Chicago, IL 60610

Acquisitions: Jerome Pohler

Publisher's Interests
Zephyr Press targets "inspired educators" with books on such topics as gifted students, special needs, crafts, critical thinking, and every academic subject across the kindergarten through grade 12 curricula.
Website: www.zephyrpress.com

Freelance Potential
Published 6 titles in 2009. Receives 250+ queries yearly.

- **Nonfiction:** Publishes educational titles for use in grades K–12. Topics include art, brain-compatible learning, counseling, critical thinking, cultural studies, history, gifted and talented education, math, engineering, multiple intelligence and differentiation, music, drama, dance, professional development, reading, writing, science, social and emotional development, Spanish, technology, new media, and testing.
- **Representative Titles:** *Amazing Kitchen Chemistry Projects You Can Build Yourself* by Cynthia Light Brown (grades 4–7) describes several at-home experiments. *Language Is Served* by Cheryl Miller Thurston (grades 7 and up) offers games, writing prompts, and other language arts activities on the topic of food. *Understanding Sam* by Clarabelle van Niekerk & Liezl Venter (grades K–2) helps readers learn to communicate better with children who have Asperger Syndrome.

Submissions and Payment
Guidelines and catalogue available. Query with completed submissions packet from guidelines. Accepts hard copy. Availability of artwork improves chance of acceptance. SASE. Responds in 3–6 months. Publication in 1–2 years. Royalty, 7.5–10%.

Editor's Comments
Classroom-tested strategies accompanied by hands-on activities are of great interest to us—especially those illustrated with appropriate photos or artwork.

Zumaya Publications

3209 South Interstate 35, #1086
Austin, TX 78741-6905

Executive Editor: Elizabeth K. Burton

Publisher's Interests
This publisher of both print and e-books offers high-quality
fiction for middle-grade and young adult readers in a range
of genres, including fantasy, romance, horror, and historical
and science fiction.
Website: www.zumayapublications.com

Freelance Potential
Published 36 titles (5–6 juvenile) in 2009: 20 were developed from unsolicited submissions. Of the 36 titles, 6 were
by unpublished writers and 8 were by authors who were new
to the publishing house. Receives 840 queries yearly.

- **Fiction:** Publishes chapter books, 5–10 years; middle-grade
  books, 8–12 years; and young adult books, 12–18 years. Genres include adventure; fantasy; folklore; folktales; romance;
  Western; fantasy; horror; and historical, mainstream, seasonal,
  and science fiction.
- **Representative Titles:** *Quilt As Desired* by Arlene Sachitano
  is a mystery that features a woman racing to determine how
  her vandalized quilting studio is connected to a friend's murder. *Spencer the Adventurer and The Castle of Bran* tells the
  sequel story of Spencer venturing into a haunted Romanian
  castle to save his sister.

Submissions and Payment
Guidelines and catalogue available at website. Query with
synopsis. Accepts email submissions to acquisitions@
zumayapublications.com (Microsoft Word or RTF attachments). Responds in 1–3 months. Publication period varies.
Royalty, 20% for print; 50% for e-books.

Editor's Comments
We are actively seeking quality books for a broad age range,
especially chapter books for ages 8 to 12. Please take the
time to thoroughly read our submissions guidelines, which
you can find at our website.

Additional Listings

We have selected the following publishers to offer you additional marketing opportunities. Most of these publishers have special submissions requirements or they purchase a limited number of juvenile titles each year.

For published authors, we include information about houses that produce reprints of previously published works. For writers who are proficient in foreign languages, we list publishers of foreign-language material. You will also find publishers that accept résumés only; who work with agented authors; or who usually accept unsolicited submissions, but due to a backlog, are not accepting material at this time.

As you survey these listings, you may find that a small regional press is a more appropriate market for your submission than a large publisher. Also, if you are involved in education or are a specialist in a certain field, consider sending your résumé to one of the educational publishers—you may have the qualifications they are looking for.

Publishers who usually accept unsolicited submissions but were not accepting unsolicited material at our press time are designated with an **X**.

Be sure to contact the publisher before submitting material to determine the current submissions policy.

As you review the listings that follow, use the Publisher's Interests section as your guide to the particular focus of each house.

Abbeville Family

137 Varick Street, 5th Floor
New York, NY 10013

Editor: Susan Costello

Publisher's Interests
Formerly called Abbeville Kids, this division of Abbeville Press offers highly illustrated fiction and nonfiction for children of all ages, as well as parenting guides. 50% self-, subsidy-, co-venture, or co-op published material.
Website: www.abbeville.com

Freelance Potential
Published 10–12 titles in 2009. Of the 10–12 titles, 4 were by authors who were new to the publishing house. Receives 600 queries yearly.
Submissions and Payment: Guidelines and catalogue available at website. Query with author bio. Accepts hard copy. SASE. Responds in 5 weeks. Publication in 18–24 months. Royalty; advance. Flat fee.

Abingdon Press

201 Eighth Avenue South
P.O. Box 801
Nashville, TN 37203

Manuscript Submissions

Publisher's Interests
This religious publisher, an imprint of the United Methodist Publishing House, is devoted to meeting the spiritual needs of children and adults. It publishes religious education resources, materials for music ministries, and other print and nonprint material. Active members of the church work on assignment. 50% co-op published material.
Website: www.abingdonpress.com

Freelance Potential
Published 10 titles in 2009. Receives 600 queries yearly.
Submissions and Payment: Guidelines available. Query with outline and 1–2 sample chapters. Accepts hard copy. SASE. No simultaneous submissions. Responds in 2 months. Publication in 2 years. Royalty.

Academic Therapy Publications

20 Commercial Boulevard
Novato, CA 94949

Acquisitions Editor

Publisher's Interests
Since its inception in 1965, Academic Therapy Publications has extended its range of special education assessments and supplementary materials to include publications that can be used by classroom teachers, speech-language pathologists, occupational therapists, ESL teachers, and parents. It is interested in titles that address reading and writing challenges; memory and cognition; decision-making; speech and language; and math.
Website: www.academictherapy.com

Freelance Potential
Published 10–20 titles in 2009.
Submissions and Payment: Query with synopsis and author bio. Accepts hard copy. SASE. Response time varies. Publication period varies. Flat fee.

Accord Publishing

1404 Larimer Street, Suite 200
Denver, CO 80202

Submissions Editor

Publisher's Interests
An imprint of Andrews McMeel Publishing, Accord Publishing produces board, picture, and story picture books that feature eye-popping illustrations and interactive elements such as tactile pads, animotion technology, pop-ups, and mirrors. It also publishes calendars, humor, and novelty books.
Website: www.accordpublishing.com

Freelance Potential
Published 20 titles (17 juvenile) in 2009: each was by an author who was new to the publishing house. Receives 72–144 queries, 120+ unsolicited mss yearly.
Submissions and Payment: Guidelines available at website. Query or send complete ms. Accepts hard copy. SASE. Response time, publication period, and payment policy vary.

Adasi Publishing

6 Dover Point Road, Suite B
Dover, NH 03820

Office Manager: Parvaneh Ghavami

Publisher's Interests
Pronounced like "Odyssey," Adasi publishes intellectual and educational books on science and the history of science for teachers and adults. It offers science classics—such as translations of Galileo's works—as well as new science titles. It is interested in physics and math, and books that delve into the history of science.
Website: www.adasi.com

Freelance Potential
Published 1 title in 2009. Receives 12 queries yearly.
Submissions and Payment: Guidelines available at website. Query. Accepts hard copy and email queries to info@adasi.com. SASE. Responds in 1 month. Publication in 6 months. Royalty, 5% (negotiable).

Aladdin Mix

Simon & Schuster Children's Publishing Division
1230 Avenue of the Americas, 4th Floor
New York, NY 10020

Submissions Editor

Publisher's Interests
Encouraging kids to read and have fun at the same time is the mission of Aladdin Mix, an imprint of Simon & Schuster. It publishes a wide variety of books for children ages 9 to 13. The titles are both kid-friendly and valued by teachers and parents. Many best-selling and acclaimed titles can be found in the catalogue.
Website: www.simonsays.com

Freelance Potential
Published 10 titles in 2009.
Submissions and Payment: Writers' guidelines available. Query with outline and biography. No unsolicited mss. Accepts hard copy. SASE. Response time, publication period, and payment policy vary.

The Alternate Press

P.O. Box 112
Niagara Falls, NY 14304-0112

Submissions Editor

Publisher's Interests
This imprint of Life Media specializes in positive, adult nonfiction about natural parenting, alternative education, homeschooling, green business, and environmental lifestyles. Its books focus on "how-to" rather than on philosophy.
Website: www.lifemedia.ca/altpress

Freelance Potential
Published 5 titles in 2009.
Submissions and Payment: Guidelines and catalogue available at website. Query with synopsis, 25 sample pages, and author bio. Accepts hard copy, email queries to altpress@lifemedia.ca (Microsoft Word attachments), and simultaneous submissions if identified. SASE. Responds in 2 months. Publication period and payment policy vary.

Ambassador International

427 Wade Hampton Boulevard
Greenville, SC 29609

Publisher: Samuel Lowry

Publisher's Interests
This Christian publisher produces fiction and nonfiction titles on a variety of devotional and Christ-based topics, some that may be of interest to young adults and parents. 50% self-, subsidy-, co-venture, or co-op published material.
Website: www.emeraldhouse.com

Freelance Potential
Published 30 titles in 2009: 14 were developed from unsolicited submissions and 6 were by agented authors. Receives 480 queries yearly.
Submissions and Payment: Guidelines and catalogue available at website. Query. Accepts hard copy and email queries to publisher@emeraldhouse.com. SASE. Responds in 6 weeks. Publication in 1 year. Royalty, 5–15%; advance, $250–$1,000.

American Girl Publications

8400 Fairway Place
Middleton, WI 53562

Submissions Editor

Publisher's Interests
American Girl celebrates girls ages seven through thirteen by
publishing age-appropriate books that foster individuality,
intellectual curiosity, and imagination. Historically accurate
nonfiction only is considered.
Website: www.americangirl.com

Freelance Potential
Published 30–40 titles in 2009. Receives 150 queries, 350
unsolicited mss yearly.
Submissions and Payment: Guidelines and catalogue avail-
able at website. Prefers query; will accept complete ms.
Accepts hard copy and simultaneous submissions if identified.
SASE. Responds in 3–4 months. Publication period and pay-
ment policy vary.

Anova Books

10 Southcombe Street
London W14 0RA
England

Submissions

Publisher's Interests
This publisher offers both fiction and nonfiction books for
children and young adults. Its fiction titles cover a wide range
of genres, from fairy tales to adventure stories. Topics such
as animals, nature, and the environment are explored on its
nonfiction list.
Website: www.anovabooks.com

Freelance Potential
Published 175 titles in 2009. Receives 200 queries yearly.
Submissions and Payment: Guidelines and catalogue available at website. Query with synopsis. Accepts hard copy and
email queries to appropriate editor; list of editors and email
addresses available at website. SAE/IRC. Responds in 2
months. Publication in 15 months. Royalty; advance. Flat fee.

Association for Childhood Education International

17904 Georgia Avenue, Suite 215
Olney, MD 20832-2277

Director, Editorial Department: Anne Bauer

Publisher's Interests
The Association for Childhood Education International is a
nonprofit organization that supports the professional development of educators of young children. It publishes books on
a variety of curriculum subjects, parenting, health and safety,
literacy, early childhood development, and special education.
Website: www.acei.org

Freelance Potential
Published 2–3 titles in 2009. Receives 120 unsolicited mss
each year.
Submissions and Payment: Guidelines available at website.
Send complete ms. Accepts hard copy and disk submissions
(ASCII or Microsoft Word). SASE. Responds in 2 weeks.
Publication in 1–3 years. No payment.

August House

3500 Piedmont Road NE
Altanta, GA 30305

Editorial Department

Publisher's Interests
August House is an award-winning multimedia publisher of picture books and children's fiction for ages 10 and younger;
folktale anthologies; and resource books on the subject of
storytelling. It looks for family-friendly stories that support
emerging readers, encourage the development of good character, and promote cross-cultural understanding.
Website: www.augusthouse.com

Freelance Potential
Published 20–40 titles in 2009.
Submissions and Payment: Guidelines and catalogue available at website. Query or send ms. Accepts hard copy and
simultaneous submissions. SASE. Responds in 5 months if
interested. Publication period and payment policy vary.

A/V Concepts Corporation

30 Montauk Boulevard
Oakdale, NY 11769

Editor: Janice Cobas

Publisher's Interests
This publisher specializes in research-based learning material
for students in preschool through high school. It offers
books, videos, and computer software in many subjects. It is
currently focusing on environmental and conservation topics.
Website: www.edconpublishing.com

Freelance Potential
Published 10 titles (5 juvenile) in 2009. Of the 10 titles, 3
were by unpublished writers. Receives 120 queries yearly.
Submissions and Payment: Guidelines available with 9x12
SASE ($1.75 postage). Catalogue available at website. Query
with résumé and clips or writing samples. Accepts hard copy.
SASE. Responds in 1 month. Publication in 6 months. Flat fee,
$300–$1,000.

Avocet Press

19 Paul Court
Pearl River, NY 10965-1539

Editor: Sally Williams

Publisher's Interests
"Fiction with an attitude" is how this independent publisher
describes the books it seeks to publish. Historical fiction and
mysteries, as well as other genres, can be found in its catalogue. It does not publish romances or science fiction, and it
is not accepting poetry submissions at this time.
Website: www.avocetpress.com

Freelance Potential
Published 4 titles in 2009. Of the 4 titles, 1 was by an unpublished writer and 2 were by authors who were new to the publishing house. Receives 600 queries yearly.
Submissions and Payment: Guidelines available at website.
Query. Accepts hard copy. SASE. Response time and publication period vary. Royalty; advance.

Azro Press

1704 Llano Street B
PMB 342
Santa Fe, NM 87505

Publisher: Gae Eisenhardt

Publisher's Interests
Azro Press publishes picture books and easy readers for children up to age 14. It is currently focusing on the work of authors living in the American Southwest. It is currently closed to submissions.
Website: www.azropress.com

Freelance Potential
Published 2 titles in 2009. Of the 2 titles, 1 was by an unpublished writer and 1 was by an author who was new to the publishing house. Receives 100+ queries yearly.
Submissions and Payment: Guidelines and catalogue available at website. Not accepting queries or unsolicited mss at this time. Check website for changes to this current submission policy.

Baker Trittin Press

P.O. Box 277
Winona Lake, IN 46590

Editor-in-Chief: Dr. Marvin G. Baker

Publisher's Interests
The books of Baker Trittin Press target children ages 8 to 13 (tweens) with middle-grade and young adult fiction, especially that which appeals to boys. The Christian company prefers books with Christian value lessons. 20% self-, subsidy-, co-venture, or co-op published material.
Website: www.bakertrittinpress.com

Freelance Potential
Published 8–10 titles in 2009: each was developed from an unsolicited submission. Of the 8–10 titles, 4 were by unpublished writers and 4 were by new authors.
Submissions and Payment: Guidelines available at website. Query. Accepts email queries to marvin@btconcepts.com. Responds in 3 months. Publication in 18 months. Royalty.

Bantam Books for Young Readers

1745 Broadway
New York, NY 10019

Editor

Publisher's Interests
Bantam Books for Young Readers, a Random House imprint,
focuses on media-driven and movie tie-in titles for the middle-
grade and young adult audience. Submissions are accepted
through literary agents only; but new and unagented writers
may submit their own material to Random House's Delacorte
Yearling Contest for a First Middle Grade Novel, or Delacorte
Press Contest for a First Young Adult Novel.
Website: www.randomhouse.com/kids

Freelance Potential
Published several titles in 2009.
Submissions and Payment: Guidelines available at website. No
simultaneous submissions. Accepts queries from agents only.
Response time and publication period vary. Royalty; advance.

Barbour Publishing

P.O. Box 719
Unionville, OH 44683

Submissions Editor

Publisher's Interests
Barbour offers children's fiction and nonfiction that embrace a
religious or inspirational theme. Its catalogue includes everything from concept books for toddlers to books for young
adults, as well as a number of fiction and nonfiction series for
adult readers. All submissions should present a conservative,
evangelical Christian worldview.
Website: www.barbourbooks.com

Freelance Potential
Published 25 titles in 2009.
Submissions and Payment: Guidelines and catalogue available at website. Query. Accepts hard copy and email queries
to submissions@barbourbooks.com. SASE. Responds in 4–6
months. Publication period varies. Royalty; advance.

Barron's Educational Series

250 Wireless Boulevard
Hauppauge, NY 11788

Acquisitions Editor: Wayne Barr

Publisher's Interests
Study materials and fiction for children of all ages are the
focus of this publisher.
Website: www.barronseduc.com

Freelance Potential
Published 260 titles (75 juvenile) in 2009: 12 were developed
from unsolicited submissions, 6 were by agented authors, and
225 were reprint/licensed properties. Receives 3,000 queries,
1,000 unsolicited mss yearly.
Submissions and Payment: Guidelines available. Send ms
with résumé for fiction. Query for nonfiction. Prefers email to
waynebarr@barronseduc.com (no attachments); will accept
hard copy. SASE. Responds to queries in 1–3 months, to mss
in 6–8 months. Publication in 2 years. Royalty; advance.

Bay Light Publishing

P.O. Box 3032
Mooresville, NC 28117

Owner: Charlotte Soutullo

Publisher's Interests
Bay Light Publishing is an award-winning publisher of Christian
children's books. It offers story picture books for children as
young as four years of age, as well as series titles for children
up to 10 years of age. Every book is designed to help readers
discover a Christ-centered life by inspiring, motivating, and
educating them through Bible-based stories, such as those
that are part of its "Thank You, God" series.
Website: www.baylightpub.com

Freelance Potential
Published 1 title in 2009. Receives 20 queries yearly.
Submissions and Payment: Query. Accepts hard copy and
simultaneous submissions if identified. SASE. Responds in
3–6 weeks. Publication in 1 year. Payment policy varies.

Baylor University Press

One Bear Place, #97363
Waco, TX 76798-7363

Director: Carey C. Newman

Publisher's Interests
Baylor University Press strives to serve the academic community by producing works that integrate faith and understanding. Its catalogue includes contemporary and scholarly works in religion, literature, philosophy, theology, ethics, history, and public life.
Website: www.baylorpress.com

Freelance Potential
Published 30–35 titles in 2009: 18 were developed from unsolicited submissions. Receives 120–180 queries yearly.
Submissions and Payment: Guidelines and catalogue available at website or with 9x12 SASE. Query. Accepts email queries to carey_newman@baylor.edu. Responds in 1 month. Publication in 9 months. Royalty, 10%.

Beacon Hill Press of Kansas City

2923 Troost Avenue
Kansas City, MO 64109

Submissions: Judi Perry

Publisher's Interests
This Christian publisher offers books for pastors, youth ministers, and parents to help young people develop spiritually.
Website: www.beaconhillbooks.com

Freelance Potential
Published 40 titles in 2009: 7 were developed from unsolicited submissions. Of the 40 titles, 10 were by unpublished writers and 10 were by authors who were new to the publishing house. Receives many queries and unsolicited mss yearly.
Submissions and Payment: Guidelines available via email to bhinquiry@nph.com. Catalogue available at website or with 9x12 SASE ($1 postage). Query or send ms. Accepts hard copy. SASE. Responds to queries in 1 month, to mss in 3–6 months. Publication in 12–18 months. Payment policy varies.

Bebop Books

95 Madison Avenue
New York, NY 10016

Submissions Editor

Publisher's Interests
The books found in this publisher's catalogue are geared to
beginning readers and are organized by reading level. All titles
are available in English and Spanish and many are multicultural
in content. An imprint of Lee & Low Books, it is currently not
reviewing queries or manuscripts. Writers are asked to check
the website periodically for changes.
Website: www.bebopbooks.com

Freelance Potential
Published few titles in 2009.
Submissions and Payment: Guidelines available at website
or with SASE during open submission periods only. Check
website for updates to this policy.

Beckham Publications

P.O. Box 4066
Silver Spring, MD 20914-4066

Acquisitions Editor

Publisher's Interests
This publisher specializes in multicultural, ethnic, and contemporary themes in works of fiction and nonfiction for children
and adults. 20% co-venture published material.
Website: www.beckhamhouse.com

Freelance Potential
Published 60 titles (4 juvenile) in 2009: 50 were developed
from unsolicited submissions. Receives 200 unsolicited mss
each year.
Submissions and Payment: Guidelines and catalogue available at website. Send complete ms with illustrations. Prefers
email to submit@beckhamhouse.com (Microsoft Word attachments); will accept hard copy. SASE. Responds in 6 weeks.
Publication in 2 months. Royalty.

Alexander Graham Bell Association for the Deaf and Hard of Hearing

3417 Volta Place NW
Washington, DC 20007-2778

Production/Editorial Manager: Melody Felzien

Publisher's Interests
As the most venerable membership organization advocating the use of spoken language by individuals with hearing loss or impairment, the Alexander Graham Bell Association for the Deaf and Hard of Hearing produces books and other publications on the latest research, medical advancements, and technology. It also publishes educational materials and some relevant fiction for children and young adults.
Website: www.agbell.org

Freelance Potential
Published 6 titles in 2009. Receives 150 queries yearly.
Submissions and Payment: Guidelines available. Query. Accepts hard copy. SASE. Responds in 3 months. Publication in 9–16 months. Royalty, to 10%.

The Benefactory

24 Pine Circle
Pembroke, MA 02359

Submissions: Randy Houk

Publisher's Interests
Protecting animals and the environment is the guiding theme of this specialty publisher. Its catalogue features true stories about abandoned pets as well as wild animals, written for children ages three to nine.
Website: www.thebenefactory.com

Freelance Potential
Published 15 titles in 2009: 2 were developed from unsolicited submissions. Of the 15 titles, 7 were by authors who were new to the publishing house. Receives 360 queries yearly.
Submissions and Payment: Most work is assigned. Guidelines available. Query. Accepts hard copy and email queries to rhouk@benefactory.biz. SASE. Responds in 6–8 weeks. Publication in 2 years. Royalty, 5%; advance.

BePuzzled

University Games Corporation
2030 Harrison Street
San Francisco, CA 94110

General Manager: Elise Gretch

Publisher's Interests
All the pieces of a mystery come together in the unique product offered by this specialty publisher: a puzzle that is accompanied by a 2,500- to 3,000-word mystery story. Stories have age-appropriate themes for children ages seven to nine, and therefore do not include violence, sex, drug use, profanity, or other adult content.
Website: www.ugames.com

Freelance Potential
Published 5–7 titles (2–4 juvenile) in 2009: each was developed from an unsolicited submission. Receives 500 queries yearly.
Submissions and Payment: Guidelines available. Query with short mystery sample. Accepts hard copy. SASE. Responds in 2 weeks. Publication in 1 year. World rights. Flat fee.

Bick Publishing House

307 Neck Road
Madison, CT 06443

President: Dale Carlson

Publisher's Interests
Bick Publishing House publishes "books on living" for teen readers. Nonfiction book topics include psychology, science, philosophy, relationships, and life choices. Science fiction is also offered.
Website: www.bickpubhouse.com

Freelance Potential
Published 2 titles in 2009: both were by agented authors. Receives 120 queries yearly.
Submissions and Payment: Guidelines and catalogue available. Query with outline/synopsis, table of contents, 3 chapters, and author biography. Accepts hard copy. SASE. Responds in 2 weeks. Publication in 1 year. Royalty, 10% of net; advance.

Birdsong Books

1322 Bayview Road
Middletown, DE 19709

President: Nancy Carol Willis

Publisher's Interests
Birdsong's publishing emphasis is on educational story picture books for children ages 3 to 12 about North American animals and their habitats. It publishes one book each year and currently seeks natural science and animal life cycle picture books and activity books about nature and the environment.
Website: www.birdsongbooks.com

Freelance Potential
Published 1 title in 2009: it was developed from an unsolicited submission. Receives 120 unsolicited mss yearly.
Submissions and Payment: Guidelines available at website. Send ms or book dummy with bio and market analysis. Accepts hard copy and simultaneous submissions. SASE. Responds in 3 months. Publication in 2–3 years. Payment policy varies.

John F. Blair, Publisher

1406 Plaza Drive
Winston-Salem, NC 27103

Acquisitions Committee

Publisher's Interests
John F. Blair specializes in regional books for adults and younger readers, with an emphasis on nonfiction categories such as history, travel, folklore, and biography. It publishes only one or two fiction titles each year, accepting only those somehow related to the southeastern U.S.
Website: www.blairpub.com

Freelance Potential
Published 15–20 titles in 2009.
Submissions and Payment: Guidelines available at website. Query with synopsis, first 2 chapters, and author bio for fiction; with outline, 30 sample pages, market analysis, and author bio for nonfiction. Accepts hard copy. SASE. Responds in 2 months. Publication period and payment policy vary.

Blazers

Capstone Press
151 Good Counsel Drive
Mankato, MN 55438

Submissions Editor

Publisher's Interests
Blazers, an imprint of Capstone Press, publishes high-interest nonfiction with low, first- to second-grade reading levels. Its titles are perfect for struggling readers and ELL students in grades three through nine.
Website: www.capstonepress.com

Freelance Potential
Published several titles in 2009. Receives several queries each year.
Submissions and Payment: Guidelines and catalogue available. Query with résumé and writing samples. Accepts hard copy. SASE. Responds in 1 month. Publication period varies. Flat fee.

Blooming Tree Press

P.O. Box 140934
Austin, TX 78714

Publisher/Managing Editor: Miriam Hees

Publisher's Interests
Publishing quality fiction and nonfiction books that create hope and encourage dreams for young readers and adults is the mission of Blooming Tree Press. It will accept submissions from agents only, but unpublished writers are invited to submit material for its annual Bloom Award. Details are available at the website.
Website: www.bloomingtreepress.com

Freelance Potential
Published 5–10 titles in 2009: all were by agented authors.
Submissions and Payment: Guidelines available at website. Agented authors only. Query. Accepts hard copy and email queries to bloomingtree@gmail.com. SASE. Response time and publication period vary. Royalty, 10%.

Blue Marlin Publications

823 Aberdeen Road
Bay Shore, NY 11706

Publisher: Francine Poppo Rich

Publisher's Interests
Blue Marlin Publications wants young readers to laugh as they learn. Stories teach the reader a simple lesson, and are geared to children up to the age of twelve. As a small, independent publisher, it offers a limited number of books each year.
Website: www.bluemarlinpubs.com

Freelance Potential
Plans to resume publishing (2 or more titles) in 2010. Receives 900 unsolicited mss yearly.
Submissions and Payment: Guidelines available at website. Query with synopsis and first 3 chapters; or send complete ms. Accepts hard copy and email queries to francinerich@ bluemarlinpubs.com. SASE. Responds in 3–9 months. Publication in 18 months. Royalty; advance, $1,000.

R. H. Boyd Publishing

P.O. Box 91145
Nashville, TN 37209-1145

Submissions

Publisher's Interests
In addition to fiction and nonfiction for children, this publisher offers books on religious history, education, parenting, and family issues—all from a Christian perspective and embracing Christian values. It also publishes inspirational stories, ministry aids, and an array of resources for religious education and Bible study.
Website: www.rhboydpublishing.com

Freelance Potential
Published several titles in 2009.
Submissions and Payment: Guidelines and catalogue available at website. Query with sample chapters; or send complete ms. Accepts hard copy. SASE. Responds in 2–4 months. Publication period varies. Royalty; advance.

Breakwater Books

100 Water Street, P.O. Box 2188
St. John's, Newfoundland A1C 6E6
Canada

Managing Director: Kim Pelley

Publisher's Interests
The culture, history, and natural resources of Newfoundland, Labrador, and the Maritime provinces of Canada are the focus of Breakwater Books. Fiction and nonfiction titles, including educational materials, are offered.
Website: www.breakwaterbooks.com

Freelance Potential
Published 14 titles (2 juvenile) in 2009. Receives 240 queries each year.
Submissions and Payment: Guidelines available at website. Query with author biography, synopsis, and 2–3 sample chapters. Availability of artwork improves chance of acceptance. Accepts hard copy. SAE/IRC. Responds in 4–6 months. Publication in 1 year. Royalty, 10%.

Brown Barn Books

119 Kettle Creek Road
Weston, CT 06883

Editor-in-Chief: Nancy Hammerslough

Publisher's Interests
High-quality fiction for children ages 12 and up fill the catalogue of Brown Barn Books, an imprint of Pictures of Record, Inc. Genres include mystery, suspense, and romance. Brown Barn Books is currently closed to submissions; check its website for changes to this policy.
Website: www.brownbarnbooks.com

Freelance Potential
Published 20 titles in 2009. Receives 600 queries yearly.
Submissions and Payment: Guidelines and catalogue available at website. Not reviewing queries or unsolicited mss at this time.

Caddo Gap Press

3145 Geary Boulevard
PMB 275
San Francisco, CA 94118

Publisher: Alan H. Jones

Publisher's Interests
This educational publisher produces periodicals and a small number of books each year. Everything in its catalogue focuses on the fields of teacher education, multicultural education, and the social foundations of education. It is proud of its reputation for supporting the voices of progressive and radical change in American and international education.
Website: www.caddogap.com

Freelance Potential
Published several titles in 2009. Receives 24 queries, 24 unsolicited mss yearly.
Submissions and Payment: Catalogue available at website. Query or send complete ms. Accepts hard copy. SASE. Response time and publication period vary. Royalty, 10%.

Carolina Wren Press

120 Morris Street
Durham, NC 27701

Editor: Andrea Selch

Publisher's Interests
This publisher offers mainly fiction and poetry that celebrate social groups and ethnicities that are not usually featured in children's literature. Its titles target children ages 5 through 12.
Website: www.carolinawrenpress.org

Freelance Potential
Published 3 titles (1 juvenile) in 2009: 1 was developed from an unsolicited submission. Receives 240 queries yearly.
Submissions and Payment: Guidelines available at website. Query with author biography, synopsis, and sample chapters. Accepts hard copy, email to carolina@carolinawrenpress.org (no attachments), and simultaneous submissions if identified. SASE. Responds in 6 months. Publication in 2 years. Honorarium, $1,000.

Carousel Press

P.O. Box 6038
Berkeley, CA 94706-0038

Publisher: Carole T. Meyers

Publisher's Interests
Travel writers have a home at Carousel Press, a publishing
house dedicated to travel guides and travel adventure books.
It has won awards for its books about traveling through
California and Europe, and camping. It is interested in books
for parents about traveling with a family.
Website: www.carouselpress.com

Freelance Potential
Published 1 title in 2009: it was written by an unpublished
writer. Receives 60 queries yearly.
Submissions and Payment: Guidelines and catalogue avail-
able at website. Query with synopsis and table of contents.
Accepts email to books@carouselpress.com (no attachments).
Responds in 1 month. Publication in 1 year. Royalty; advance.

Cascadia Publishing

126 Klingerman Road
Telford, PA 18969

Submissions: Michael A. King

Publisher's Interests
Cascadia publishes academic and theological books on
Anabaptist-related topics. Through its Dreamseekers imprint,
it publishes fiction, memoirs, poetry books, and books on
popular topics for young adults and adults.
Website: www.cascadiapublishinghouse.com

Freelance Potential
Published several titles in 2009.
Submissions and Payment: Guidelines and catalogue available at website. Query with résumé, synopsis, table of contents, and 1–2 sample chapters; explain why your book would
be a good fit for Cascadia. Accepts hard copy and email
queries to editor@cascadiapublishinghouse.com. SASE.
Responds in 2 months. Publication period varies. Royalty.

Chaosium

22568 Mission Boulevard, Suite 423
Hayward, CA 94541

Editor-in-Chief: Lynn Willis

Publisher's Interests
Chaosium produces young adult and adult role-playing games, supplementary material for games, and related books. It publishes stories of adventure, fantasy, and horror, often inspired by the great writers within those genres.
Website: www.chaosium.com

Freelance Potential
Published 15 titles in 2009. Of the 15 titles, 3 were by unpublished writers and 6 were by authors who were new to the publishing house. Receives 60+ queries yearly.
Submissions and Payment: Guidelines and catalogue available at website. Query with synopsis and writing samples. Accepts hard copy. SASE. Responds in 1–2 weeks. Publication in 1–2 years. Flat fee, $.03–$.05 per word.

Cinco Puntos Press

701 Texas Avenue
El Paso, TX 79901

Editor: Lee Byrd

Publisher's Interests
Spanish culture and language come together in this bilingual publisher's list of titles for children of all ages. Cinco Puntos Press offers fiction and nonfiction with a focus on Spanish folklore and history, as well as religious themes.
Website: www.cincopuntos.com

Freelance Potential
Published 10 titles in 2009.
Submissions and Payment: Writers' guidelines and catalogue available at website. Accepts phone calls to Lee Byrd at 915-838-1625 to discuss potential projects; manuscript must be complete prior to calling. No unsolicited queries or mss; no sample chapters before speaking with editor. Publication in 18–36 months. Royalty.

Conari Press

500 Third Street, Suite 230
San Francisco, CA 94107

Acquisitions Editor: Pat Bryce

Publisher's Interests
Publishing "books to live by" for young adults and adults,
Conari focuses on books about parenting, social issues, self-
help, spirituality, and personal empowerment.
Website: www.conari.com

Freelance Potential
Published 45 titles in 2009: 9 were developed from unsolicited
submissions, 36 were by agented authors, and 2 were reprint/
licensed properties. Receives 1,200 queries yearly.
Submissions and Payment: Guidelines and catalogue available at website. Query with author bio, table of contents,
3 sample chapters, synopsis, market analysis, and sample
artwork. Accepts hard copy. SASE. Responds in 3 months.
Publication in 18 months. Royalty; advance.

Conciliar Press

3112 Calle Rosales
Santa Barbara, CA 93105

Children's Book Project Manager: Jane G. Meyer

Publisher's Interests
Conciliar Press seeks submissions that enhance its mission of
communicating historic Orthodox Christianity to today's world.
These include toddler books, picture books, middle-grade
books, and young adult titles, in addition to those for adults.
At this time it is particularly interested in manuscripts about
Orthodox spirituality and contemporary life.
Website: www.conciliarpress.com

Freelance Potential
Published several titles in 2009.
Submissions and Payment: Guidelines and catalogue avail-
able at website. Query with first 3 chapters. Send complete
ms for picture books only. Accepts hard copy. SASE.
Responds in 3 months. Publication period varies. Royalty.

Continental Press

520 East Bainbridge Street
Elizabethtown, PA 17022

Managing Editor: Megan Bergonzi

Publisher's Interests
Continental Press is an educational publisher that focuses on instructional materials and textbooks for kindergarten through grade 12. It accepts submissions on classroom-tested reading, math, and test preparation materials.
Website: www.continentalpress.com

Freelance Potential
Published 100 titles in 2009: 2 were by authors who were new to the publishing house.
Submissions and Payment: Guidelines available at website. Query with program rationale, author biography, outline, and sample lesson, chapter, or unit; or send complete ms. Accepts hard copy. SASE. Responds in 6 months. Publication period and payment policy vary.

Course Crafters

3 Washington Square
Haverhill, MA 01830

CEO & Publisher: Lise Ragan

Publisher's Interests
English Language Learner and English as a Second Language textbooks, supplemental products, and some fiction are the purview of this specialty publisher. It is interested in multicultural and ethnic fiction specifically. Its titles are for students of all ages. It also publishes professional development titles for teachers and other education professionals. Freelance writers are encouraged to make queries.
Website: www.coursecrafters.com

Freelance Potential
Published 10–12 titles in 2009. Receives 20 queries yearly.
Submissions and Payment: Guidelines available. Query with clips. Accepts hard copy. SASE. Responds in 1 month. Publication in 1–2 years. Royalty. Flat fee.

Creative Bound International

151 Tansley Drive
Carp, Ontario K0A 1L0
Canada

Editor: Gail Baird

Publisher's Interests
Creative Bound International publishes "resources for personal growth and enhanced performance." All the titles in its catalogue, including those on topics related to parenting and family issues, are designed to promote healthy relationships through improved physical and emotional well-being.
Website: www.creativebound.com

Freelance Potential
Published 4 titles in 2009. Of the 4 titles, 3 were by authors who were new to the publishing house. Receives 120 queries each year.
Submissions and Payment: Guidelines and catalogue available at website. Query. Accepts hard copy. SAE/IRC. Responds in 2 months. Publication in 6–12 months. Royalty.

Creative Editions

P.O. Box 227
Mankato, MN 56002

Managing Editor: Aaron Frisch

Publisher's Interests
This children's book company, an imprint of the Creative Company, publishes high-quality fiction picture books that target libraries and schools. It is not accepting submissions at this time. Any submissions received will be neither reviewed nor returned. Check website for changes to this policy.
Website: www.thecreativecompany.us

Freelance Potential
Published 4 titles in 2009: 1 was by an agented author. Receives 40 queries yearly.
Submissions and Payment: Not reviewing queries or unsolicited mss at this time. Check website for the most current submission information.

Creative Paperbacks

P.O. Box 227
Mankato, MN 56002

Managing Editor: Aaron Frisch

Publisher's Interests
This imprint of the Creative Company publishes fiction and nonfiction for children in kindergarten through sixth grade. Genres include contemporary and historical fiction, and adventure. Nonfiction topics include history, geography, and science. Creative Paperbacks does not have plans for expansion at this time.
Website: www.thecreativecompany.us

Freelance Potential
Published several titles in 2009.
Submissions and Payment: Guidelines available. Query with manuscript sample. Accepts hard copy. SASE. Responds in 4–6 months. Publication in 2–4 years. Payment policy varies.

Creative With Words Publications

P.O. Box 223226
Carmel, CA 93922

Editor & Publisher: Brigitta Geltrich

Publisher's Interests
This publisher produces anthologies of a variety of genres from a variety of authors—including children. It accepts poetry and prose. Each issue has a set theme, as outlined at its website.
Website: http://members.tripod.con/CreativeWithWords

Freelance Potential
Published 12 titles in 2009: each was developed from an unsolicited submission. Of the 12 titles, 6 were by unpublished writers and 9 were by authors who were new to the publishing house. Receives 500–1,000 queries and unsolicited mss yearly.
Submissions and Payment: Guidelines available. Query or send complete ms. Accepts hard copy. SASE. Responds 1 month after anthology deadline. Publication period varies. No payment; 20–40% discount on 10+ copies purchased.

Cricket Books

P.O. Box 300
Peru, IL 61354

Submissions Editor

Publisher's Interests
Cricket Books publishes a variety of fiction and nonfiction titles for children of all ages. Its list ranges from silly pop-up books for preschool kids to novels for young adults. It is currently reviewing submissions only from writers who have been previously published by the company.
Website: www.cricketmag.com

Freelance Potential
Published 2 titles in 2009: each was assigned. Receives 36 unsolicited mss yearly.
Submissions and Payment: Guidelines and catalogue available at website. Authors previously published by Cricket Books may submit. Publication in 18 months. Royalty, to 10%; advance, $2,000+.

Darby Creek Publishing

7858 Industrial Parkway
Plain City, OH 43064

Submissions Editor

Publisher's Interests
Middle-grade and young adult readers are the target audience for this small publisher of fiction and nonfiction titles. It specializes in books that appeal to reluctant readers.
Website: www.darbycreekpublishing.com

Freelance Potential
Published 9 titles in 2009: 2 were developed from unsolicited submissions and 1 was by an agented author. Of the 9 titles, 1 was by an unpublished writer and 3 were by authors who were new to the publishing house. Receives 500+ queries, 1,000+ unsolicited mss yearly.
Submissions and Payment: Guidelines and catalogue available at website. Not accepting submissions at this time. Check website for changes to this policy.

May Davenport Publishers

26313 Purissima Road
Los Altos Hills, CA 94022

Publisher & Editor: May Davenport

Publisher's Interests
Anthologies, poems, coloring books, and short "read aloud" stories for use in kindergarten through grade 12 are the focus of May Davenport Publishers. It seeks positive and humorous stories, rather than tragic coming-of-age stories. New writers are welcome to submit their work.
Website: www.maydavenportpublishers.com

Freelance Potential
Published 1 title in 2009. It was developed from an unsolicited submission. Recieves 600 queries yearly.
Submissions and Payment: Guidelines available. Query. Prefers Macintosh disk submissions; will accept hard copy. SASE. Responds in 1–2 weeks. Publication in 1–2 years. Royalty, 15%. Flat fee.

Displays for Schools

1825 NW 22nd Terrace
Gainesville, FL 32605

Manager: Sherry DuPree

Publisher's Interests
Displays for Schools produces just that—educational exhibits for classroom use. Its materials are designed for all grade levels, as well as special education, religion classes, and adult education. A wide range of subjects are covered, and all materials are classroom-tested.
Website: www.displaysforschools.com

Freelance Potential
Published 4 titles (1 juvenile) in 2009: 2 were developed from unsolicited submissions. Receives 180 queries yearly.
Submissions and Payment: Guidelines available. Query with outline, synopsis, sample chapters, and brief author biography. Accepts hard copy. SASE. Responds in 2 months. Publication in 4–24 months. Royalty, 12%.

Diversion Press

P.O. Box 30277
Clarksville, TN 37040

Acquisitions Editor

Publisher's Interests
This publisher seeks children's picture books with morals, and young adult novels that depict adolescence in a positive light. In addition to contemporary, historical, and inspirational fiction for tweens and teens, it also publishes nonfiction for all age groups on such topics as current events, history, and social issues.
Website: www.diversionpress.com

Freelance Potential
Published 10–20 titles in 2009.
Submissions and Payment: Guidelines and catalogue available at website. Query with author bio. Accepts email queries to diversionpress@yahoo.com (no attachments). Responds in 1–3 months. Publication period varies. Royalty.

Dzanc Books

1334 Woodbourne Street
Westland, MI 48186

Editor: Dan Wickett

Publisher's Interests
Dzanc Books is a nonprofit publisher that seeks to publish books that don't fit neatly into the marketing niches of for-profit presses. It offers high-quality literary fiction in short story and novel form, as well as creative nonfiction.
Website: www.dzancbooks.org

Freelance Potential
Published 6 titles in 2009: 4 were developed from unsolicited submissions and 2 were by agented authors. Receives 100–150 queries yearly.
Submissions and Payment: Guidelines available at website. Query with 1–2 sample chapters. Accepts hard copy and email queries to submit@dzancbooks.org. SASE. Responds in 5–6 months. Publication period varies. Royalty; advance.

Eastgate Systems

134 Main Street
Watertown, MA 02472

Acquisitions Editor: Mark Bernstein

Publisher's Interests
Eastgate Systems seeks original fiction and nonfiction written in hypertext form for reading on the computer, geared toward the young adult reader. All Eastgate Systems' titles are published as CD-ROMs and disks; it does not publish print, downloadable, or e-books.
Website: www.eastgate.com

Freelance Potential
Published 2 titles in 2009. Receives 25 queries yearly.
Submissions and Payment: Guidelines and catalogue available at website. Send complete ms. Accepts disk submissions, email submissions to info@eastgate.com, and simultaneous submissions if identified. SASE. Responds in 4–6 weeks. Publication in 1 year. Royalty, 15%; advance.

Ecopress

Finney Company
8075 215th Street West
Lakeville, MN 55044

President: Alan E. Krysan

Publisher's Interests
Ecopress, an imprint of Finney Company, is interested in books that promote an awareness of the natural environment. It produces a few books for young readers.
Website: www.ecopress.com

Freelance Potential
Published 4 titles (3 juvenile) in 2009: 3 were developed from unsolicited submissions. Of the 4 titles, 2 were by unpublished writers and 3 were by authors who were new to the publishing house. Receives 96–120 queries yearly.
Submissions and Payment: Guidelines available at website. Query with 3–4 sample chapters and marketing ideas. Accepts hard copy. SASE. Responds in 8–10 weeks. Publication in 6–18 months. Royalty, 10%.

Edge Books

151 Good Counsel Drive
Mankato, MN 55438

Submissions Editor

Publisher's Interests
This imprint of Capstone Press focuses on books for struggling
and reluctant readers in grades three to nine. It publishes
high-interest nonfiction on extreme topics to capture the attention of its specific demographic. Currently, it is seeking submissions on extreme sports, dirt bikes, music, and science.
Most of its books are written on a work-for-hire basis.
Website: www.capstonepress.com

Freelance Potential
Published 47 titles in 2009.
Submissions and Payment: Guidelines and catalogue avail-
able at website. Query with résumé and clips, stating area of
expertise. Accepts hard copy. SASE. Responds in 1 month.
Publication period varies. Flat fee.

Encounter Books

900 Broadway
New York, NY 10003-1239

Acquisitions Editor

Publisher's Interests
Encounter Books publishes books on religion, public policy,
education, and current events for young adults. This publisher
considers the work of agented authors only.
Website: www.encounterbooks.com

Freelance Potential
Published 25–30 titles in 2009: each was by an agented
author and 8 were reprint/licensed properties. Receives
300–500 unsolicited mss yearly.
Submissions and Payment: Guidelines and catalogue available at website. Accepts submissions through literary agents
only. Query with outline and/or sample chapters. Accepts hard
copy. SASE. Response time, publication period, and payment
policy vary.

EOS

HarperCollins Children's Books
1350 Avenue of the Americas
New York, NY 10019

Editorial Department

Publisher's Interests
EOS is a HarperCollins imprint specifically focused on the teen
and young adult reader. It publishes a wide variety of genre
fiction, such as romance, mystery, adventure, fantasy, light
horror, and historical fiction. Many of its titles are part of a
series, for example, Books of Magic and Fire-Us. Prospective
writers must submit their work through a literary agent.
Website: www.harperteen.com

Freelance Potential
Published 130 titles in 2009.
Submissions and Payment: Guidelines available. Accepts
queries through literary agents only. No unsolicited submis-
sions. Accepts hard copy. SASE. Responds in 1 month.
Publication in 18–36 months. Royalty; advance.

Exclamation! Publishers

770 East Main Street, Suite 220
Lehi, UT 84043

President & Publisher: Denise E. Heap

Publisher's Interests
Exclamation! is primarily interested in receiving books on the
Holocaust, historical fiction, and nonfiction for ages 15 to 22.
Its anthologies present the best chance for publication.
Website: www.deheap.com/exclamation!_publishers.htm

Freelance Potential
Published 15 titles (10 juvenile) in 2009: 5 were developed
from unsolicited submissions. Of the 15 titles, 2 were by
unpublished writers and 3 were by authors who were new to
the publishing house. Receives 300–600 queries yearly.
Submissions and Payment: Guidelines available at website.
Query with résumé. Accepts hard copy and email queries to
exclamation.publishers@deheap.com (no attachments). SASE.
Responds in 4–6 weeks. Publication period varies. Royalty, 15%.

The Feminist Press

The Graduate Center
365 Fifth Avenue, Suite 5406
New York, NY 10016

Associate Editor: Anjoli Roy

Publisher's Interests
Feminist, multicultural, and ethnic issues are the focus of this publisher. Its catalogue includes nonfiction titles about modern and historical women, and works of fiction depicting strong women characters.
Website: www.feministpress.org

Freelance Potential
Published 16 titles in 2009: 2 were developed from unsolicited submissions and 12 were reprint/licensed properties. Of the 16 titles, 10 were by new authors. Receives 500 queries yearly.
Submissions and Payment: Guidelines and catalogue available at website. Query. Accepts 200-word email queries to editor@ feministpress.org ("Submission" in subject line). Responds in 2 weeks. Publication period varies. Royalty; advance.

Five Leaves Publications

P.O. Box 8786
Nottingham NG1 9AW
United Kingdom

Submissions Editor

Publisher's Interests
This independent publisher specializes in Jewish secular culture, social history, fiction, and poetry. It has a young adult list that includes a variety of fiction genres, and recently added crime stories to the mix. It has published a number of well-known authors, but also enjoys discovering writers at the beginning of their career. Most of its titles are commissioned.
Website: www.fiveleaves.co.uk

Freelance Potential
Published 15 titles in 2009
Submissions and Payment: Guidelines and catalogue available at website. Prefers query; will accept complete ms. Accepts hard copy. SASE. Responds if interested. Publication in 2 years. Royalty.

Franklin Watts

Scholastic Inc.
90 Old Sherman Turnpike
Danbury, CT 06816

Editor: Elizabeth Ward

Publisher's Interests
Franklin Watts, an imprint of Scholastic Library Publishing, offers a wide variety of reference, nonfiction, and some fiction books for children in preschool through high school. Its titles cover curriculum-based material in science and social studies, biographies, arts and crafts, and high-interest subjects, as well as some classics.
Website: www.scholasticlibrary.com

Freelance Potential
Published 191 titles in 2009. Receives 1,000+ queries yearly.
Submissions and Payment: Query with résumé, outline, and sample chapters. No unsolicited mss. Accepts hard copy. SASE. Responds in 3–5 weeks. Publication period and payment policy vary.

Gefen Publishing House

6 Hatzvi Street
Jerusalem 94386
Israel

Editor: Ilan Greenfield

Publisher's Interests
Gefen Publishing is one of Israel's leading publishers of Jewish books. For children, it is interested in Hebrew stories, prayer books, translations, and books about Israel and the Holocaust.
Website: www.gefenpublishing.com

Freelance Potential
Published 20 titles (4–5 juvenile) in 2009: most were developed from unsolicited submissions. Of the 20 titles, 19 were by unpublished writers and 12 were by authors new to the publishing house. Receives 240 queries, 100+ mss yearly.
Submissions and Payment: Guidelines available at website. Query or send complete ms. Accepts hard copy and simultaneous submissions if identified. SASE. Response time, publication period, and payment policy vary.

Graywolf Press

2402 University Avenue, Suite 203
St. Paul, MN 55114

Fiction/Nonfiction Editor: Katie Dublinski
Poetry Editor: Jeff Shotts

Publisher's Interests
Graywolf Press considers itself "A Rare Breed of Publisher," offering imaginative and thoughtful books. Titles that are appropriate for young adults reflect the work of essayists, literary critics, poets, and literary novelists, mostly with contemporary themes, as well as translations. It does not publish genre fiction, drama, self-help, or how-to books.
Website: www.graywolfpress.org

Freelance Potential
Published 27 titles in 2009. Receives 3,600 queries yearly.
Submissions and Payment: Guidelines and catalogue available at website. Send complete ms in January, May, and September only. Accepts hard copy. SASE. Responds in 4 months. Publication in 2 years. Royalty; advance.

Great Potential Press

P.O. Box 5057
Scottsdale, AZ 85261

Editor

Publisher's Interests
This publisher produces books and resource materials to guide parents and teachers through the process of supporting, encouraging, and challenging gifted students. It does not publish books targeting students themselves, but rather focuses on books that support those guiding the students.
Website: www.giftedbooks.com

Freelance Potential
Published 8 titles in 2009. Receives 120 queries yearly.
Submissions and Payment: Guidelines and catalogue available at website. Query with introduction, table of contents, 3 sample chapters, and market analysis. Accepts hard copy and queries through form available at website. SASE. Responds in 2 months. Publication period varies. Royalty.

Greene Bark Press

P.O. Box 1108
Bridgeport, CT 06601-1108

Associate Editor: Tara Maroney

Publisher's Interests
This publisher offers a range of materials, from concept books
to CD-ROMs, all designed to make learning fun. It looks for
imaginative stories, revolving around a theme, that foster reading comprehension. Bilingual material is also sought.
Website: www.greenebarkpress.com

Freelance Potential
Published 1 title in 2009. Receives 4,000 unsolicited mss
each year.
Submissions and Payment: Guidelines available. Catalogue
available at website. Send ms with illustrations and storyboard.
Prefers one story per submission. Accepts hard copy and simultaneous submissions if identified. SASE. Responds in 2–6
months. Publication in 12–18 months. Royalty, 10–15%.

Greenwillow Books

HarperCollins Children's Books
1350 Avenue of the Americas
New York, NY 10019

Editorial Department

Publisher's Interests
Greenwillow Books is an imprint of HarperCollins Publishers.
It was founded in 1974 as a publisher of high-quality picture
books, fiction, and novels for children in preschool through
high school. The books in its catalogue run the gamut from
funny stories that elicit giggles from toddlers to historical
novels for young adults. It also publishes a variety of children's poetry, including works from the first Children's Poet
Laureate, Jack Prelutsky.
Website: www.harperchildrens.com

Freelance Potential
Published 40 titles in 2009.
Submissions and Payment: Not currently accepting manu-
scripts or queries. Check website for changes to this policy.

Grosset & Dunlap

Penguin Group USA, Inc.
345 Hudson Street
New York, NY 10014

Editorial Department

Publisher's Interests
This company began more than 100 years ago, reprinting and mass-marketing popular novels and series of the time. Now an imprint of Penguin Group USA, Grosset & Dunlap focuses mainly on licensed properties, original paperback series, and in-house brands such as the Corduroy books and children's author Eric Carle.
Website: www.us.penguingroup.com

Freelance Potential
Published 175+ titles in 2009.
Submissions and Payment: Catalogue available at website. Query with outline and synopsis. Accepts hard copy. SASE. Responds in 4 months. Publication in 18–36 months. Royalty; advance.

Guardian Angel Publishing

12430 Tesson Ferry Road, #186
St. Louis, MO 63128

Submissions Editor

Publisher's Interests
This publisher is interested in books for children up to the age of 12. It publishes ebooks, print books, and DVDs, including chap books for tweens and faith-based stories. Its publishing topics include academic subjects, health, and animals.
Website: www.guardianangelpublishing.com

Freelance Potential
Published 50 titles in 2009: 45 were developed from unsolicited submissions. Receives 120 queries, 1,200–2,400 mss yearly.
Submissions and Payment: Guidelines and catalogue available at website. Query or send complete ms with genre description and word count. Accepts email to editorial_staff@ guardianangelpublishing.com. Responds in 2 months. Publication period varies. Royalty, 30%.

Hampton-Brown Books

26385 Carmel Rancho Boulevard
Carmel, CA 93923

Special Projects Coordinator

Publisher's Interests
Hampton-Brown publishes books for the education of linguistically and culturally diverse students in middle school and high school. Guides for reading and language arts teachers in English as a Second Language programs are one of this publisher's specialties.
Website: www.ngsp.com

Freelance Potential
Published 220 titles (165 juvenile) in 2009: 110 were reprint/licensed properties. Receives 130+ queries yearly.
Submissions and Payment: Guidelines and catalogue available at website. Query with synopsis. Accepts hard copy. SASE. Responds in 3–6 months. Publication period varies. Flat fee.

Hancock House

1431 Harrison Avenue
Blaine, WA 98230

Submissions

Publisher's Interests
This independent publisher focuses on regional titles regarding the northwestern region of North America, with an emphasis on history, native culture, and nature for young adults and adults. Its catalogue contains nature guides, books on wildlife and history, and biographies—all pertaining to the region.
Website: www.hancockhouse.com

Freelance Potential
Published 8–10 titles in 2009.
Submissions and Payment: Guidelines and catalogue available at website. Query with synopsis and 1–3 sample chapters. Accepts hard copy and email queries to submissions@ hancockhouse.com. SASE. Response time, publication period, and payment policy vary.

Harbour Publishing

P.O. Box 219
Madeira Park, British Columbia V0N 2H0
Canada

Editors: Howard White & Silas White

Publisher's Interests
Canadian authors only are featured in the catalogue of this publisher. Books on regional topics, focusing on the west coast of British Columbia, include fiction and nonfiction titles for all ages.
Website: www.harbourpublishing.com

Freelance Potential
Published 25 titles (1–2 juvenile) in 2009. Receives 1,000 queries yearly.
Submissions and Payment: Canadian authors only. Guidelines available at website. Query with outline, brief author biography, publication credits, and sample chapter. Accepts hard copy. SASE. Responds in 2 months if interested. Publication period varies. Royalty; advance, negotiable.

Harcourt Religion Publishers

6277 Sea Harbor Drive
Orlando, FL 32887

Submissions Editor

Publisher's Interests
This publisher provides practical, user-friendly resources for the Catholic educational market. Its goal is to assist children and adults in the formation of their faith while reflecting the authentic values of the Catholic Church.
Website: www.harcourtreligion.com

Freelance Potential
Published 30 titles (5 juvenile) in 2009. Of the 30 titles, 2 were by unpublished writers and 4 were by authors who were new to the publishing house. Receives 30–35 queries yearly.
Submissions and Payment: Guidelines available. Query with résumé, outline, and 3 sample chapters. Accepts hard copy. SASE. Responds in 3–6 months. Publication in 1 year. Royalty. Flat fee.

HarperFestival

1350 Avenue of the Americas
New York, NY 10019

Editorial Department

Publisher's Interests
This imprint of HarperCollins focuses its publishing efforts on
the very youngest of book lovers—children under the age of
seven. It produces board books, novelty books, and picture
books that feature engaging characters and entertain young
minds. It does not accept manuscripts or queries from
unagented authors.
Website: www.harpercollinschildrens.com

Freelance Potential
Published 120 titles in 2009.
Submissions and Payment: Writers' guidelines available.
Accepts queries through literary agents only. Accepts hard
copy. SASE. Responds in 1 month. Publication in 18 months.
Royalty; advance.

HarperTeen

1350 Avenue of the Americas
New York, NY 10019

Editorial Department

Publisher's Interests
Fiction and nonfiction targeting teenage readers is the focus of
this imprint of HarperCollins. HarperTeen accepts a variety of
genres, from sassy beach reads to compelling novels that
offer a glimpse into the lives of troubled teens. It also publishes nonfiction titles on a variety of subjects that appeal to
young adult readers, such as sports, contemporary social
issues, and religion. It does not work with unagented authors.
Website: www.harperteen.com

Freelance Potential
Published 130 titles in 2009.
Submissions and Payment: Guidelines available. Accepts
queries through agents only. Responds in 1 month.
Publication in 18 months. Royalty; advance.

Harvard Common Press

535 Albany Street
Boston, MA 02118

Senior Editor: Valerie Cimino

Publisher's Interests
Books for parents, including parents-to-be and adoptive parents, are the specialty of Harvard Common Press. Topics range from prenatal care to toddler issues.
Website: www.harvardcommonpress.com

Freelance Potential
Published 12 titles in 2009. Receives 250 queries yearly.
Submissions and Payment: Writers' guidelines and catalogue available at website. Query with résumé, outline, 1–2 sample chapters, and market analysis. Accepts hard copy, email queries to editorial@harvardcommonpress.com (no attachments), and simultaneous submissions if identified. SASE. Responds in 1–3 months. Publication period varies. Royalty, 5%; advance, $2,500.

High Noon Books

20 Commercial Boulevard
Novato, CA 94949

Acquisitions Editor

Publisher's Interests
This imprint of Academic Therapy Publications produces books for struggling readers ages 8 to 16, and those who teach them. These include leveled chapter books with carefully controlled vocabulary, simple sentence structures, connected text (read: not picture books), engaging content, and "a look that is anything but babyish." Its Sound Out line of phonics-based chapter books targets students reading at the low first-grade level.
Website: www.highnoonbooks.com

Freelance Potential
Published 10 titles in 2009.
Submissions and Payment: Query with synopsis and author bio. Accepts hard copy. SASE. Response time varies. Publication period varies. Flat fee.

History Publishing Company

P.O. Box 700
Palisades, NY 10964

Editor: Don Bracken

Publisher's Interests
History Publishing Company seeks to inspire an appreciation
and understanding of the world today. It continues to seek
queries for books for young adults that focus on solutions to
the problems stemming from current events.
Website: www.historypublishingco.com

Freelance Potential
Published 12 titles in 2009. Of the 12 titles, 3 were by unpub-
lished writers and 12 were by authors who were new to the
publishing house. Receives 100 queries yearly.
Submissions and Payment: Guidelines available at website.
Query with 2–3 sample chapters for complete manuscripts;
query with résumé for book ideas. Accepts hard copy. SASE.
Responds in 2–4 months. Publication period varies. Royalty.

Hodder Education

338 Euston Road
London NW1 3BH
United Kingdom

Editorial Assistants: Zoe Duncan & Naomi Pottesman

Publisher's Interests
Formerly known as Hodder Children's Books, Hodder
Education provides materials supporting curriculum in almost
every subject at almost every level, including textbooks for
medical and nursing students.
Website: www.hoddereducation.co.uk

Freelance Potential
Published 500 titles in 2009: 10 were developed from unsolicited submissions, 400 were by agented authors, and 20
were reprint/licensed properties. Receives 300 queries yearly.
Submissions and Payment: Guidelines available. Prefers
agented submissions. Query with synopsis. Accepts hard copy.
SAE/IRC. Responds in 3–6 months. Publication in 12–18
months. Royalty; advance. Flat fee.

Hohm Press

P.O. Box 2501
Prescott, AZ 86302

Editor: Dasya Zuccarello

Publisher's Interests
Hohm Press publishes books that provide alternatives to materialistic values, and promote self-awareness and compassion. Although many of its books are targeted toward adults, it also publishes several books for children. Hohm Press prefers to work with unagented authors.
Website: www.hohmpress.com

Freelance Potential
Published 12 titles (1 juvenile) in 2009: 2 were developed from unsolicited submissions. Receives 300 queries yearly.
Submissions and Payment: Guidelines and catalogue available at website. Query with sample pages. Accepts hard copy. SASE. Response time and publication period vary. Royalty, 10% of net.

Hyperion Books for Children

114 Fifth Avenue, 14 Floor
New York, NY 10011

Submissions Editor

Publisher's Interests
Publishing children's and young adult books since 1991, Hyperion Books for Children has something for every age and interest. It publishes board and novelty books for little ones, middle-grade titles, and novels for teens, as well as a large number of book series that target several age levels. This publisher does not accept unsolicited manuscripts or queries from unagented authors.
Website: www.hyperionbooksforchildren.com

Freelance Potential
Published 100 titles in 2009: each was by an agented author.
Submissions and Payment: Guidelines and catalogue available at website. Accepts queries and mss through literary agents only.

Ideals Publications

2636 Elm Hill Pike, Suite 120
Nashville, TN 37214

Submissions Editor

Publisher's Interests
Ideals, owned by Guideposts, has been publishing books
since 1944. Its children's list contains fiction and nonfiction
titles in a variety of topics and genres, including holidays,
biblical themes, and patriotic and biographical themes. Ideals
Publications is currently closed to submissions; changes to
this policy will be posted at the website.
Website: www.idealsbooks.com

Freelance Potential
Published 50 titles in 2009. Receives 480–600 mss yearly.
Submissions and Payment: Guidelines and catalogue available at website. Not reviewing queries or unsolicited mss at
the current time.

Illumination Arts

13256 Northup Way, Suite 9
Bellevue, WA 98005

President: John Thompson

Publisher's Interests
Inspirational picture books for children can be found in this
publisher's catalogue. It is currently closed to submissions;
refer to the website for updates.
Website: www.illumin.com

Freelance Potential
Published 1 title in 2009: it was developed from an unsolicited
submission and was by an unpublished writer who was new
to the publishing house. Receives 2,280 unsolicited mss
each year.
Submissions and Payment: Guidelines available. Not accepting submissions at this time. Check website for updates to
this policy before submitting.

Images Unlimited

P.O. Box 305
Maryville, MO 64468

President: Lee Jackson

Publisher's Interests
Images Unlimited publishes children's educational books on a range of topics under its Snaptail Press division. It is currently seeking biography submissions for Native American children in second and fourth grades. 50% self-, subsidy-, co-venture, or co-op published material.
Website: www.imagesunlimitedpub.com

Freelance Potential
Published 2 titles in 2009. Of the two titles, 1 was by an unpublished writer and 1 was by an author who was new to the publishing house. Receives 5 queries yearly.
Submissions and Payment: Guidelines available. Query. Accepts hard copy. SASE. Responds in 1 month. Publication in 6 months. Royalty; advance.

Immortal Books

P.O. Box 5123
South Murwillumbah 2484
Australia

Director: Dr. David Vickers-Shand

Publisher's Interests
This publisher offers children's chapter books and novels focusing on anthroposophy, biodynamic agriculture, eurythmy, and Waldorf education. 25% subsidy-published material.
Website: www.immortalbooks.com.au

Freelance Potential
Published 5 titles (3 juvenile) in 2009. Of the 5 titles, 1 was by an unpublished writer and 3 were by authors who were new to the publishing house. Receives 6 unsolicited mss yearly.
Submissions and Payment: Guidelines and catalogue available at website. Send complete ms. Accepts email submissions to info@immortalbooks.com.au (Microsoft Word attachments). Responds in 3–4 weeks. Publication in 3–6 months. Payment policy varies.

Innovative Kids

18 Ann Street
Norwalk, CT 06854

Publisher: Shari Kaufman

Publisher's Interests
This publisher's motto, "More fun means more learning,"
guides the design of each title in its catalogue. From books to
games, puzzles, and toys, Innovative Kids' products combine
education and entertainment for children up to age ten.
Website: www.innovativekids.com

Freelance Potential
Published 50 titles in 2009. Of the 50 titles, 20 were by
authors who were new to the publishing house. Receives
200 queries, 200 unsolicited mss yearly.
Submissions and Payment: Guidelines available at website.
Query or send complete ms with dummy. Accepts hard copy.
Does not return mss. Response time and publication period
vary. Flat fee.

InQ Publishing

P.O. Box 10
North Aurora, IL 60542

Editor: Jana Fitting

Publisher's Interests
Middle-grade readers are the audience for this publisher of
educational books on health, safety, and genealogy. Its catalogue also includes games and activity books for use by
babysitters and childcare providers.
Website: www.inqbooks.com

Freelance Potential
Published 3 titles (2 juvenile) in 2009. Of the 3 titles, 1 was
by an unpublished writer and 1 was by an author who was
new to the publishing house. Receives 12–24 queries yearly.
Submissions and Payment: Catalogue available at website.
Query with writing samples. No unsolicited mss. Accepts hard
copy. SASE. Responds in 6 weeks. Publication in 18 months.
Payment policy varies.

Interlink Publishing Group

46 Crosby Street
Northampton, MA 01060

Editorial Director: Pam Thompson

Publisher's Interests
Interlink Publishing Group focuses on multicultural and ethnic themes of the global community. It offers both fiction and nonfiction for all ages, including poetry and biographies.
Website: www.interlinkbooks.com

Freelance Potential
Published 61 titles (3 juvenile) in 2009: 8 were developed from unsolicited submissions, 8 were by agented authors, and 17 were reprint/licensed properties. Receives 1,800 queries each year.
Submissions and Payment: Guidelines and catalogue available at website or with 9x12 SASE. Query. Accepts hard copy. SASE. Responds in 1–24 weeks. Publication in 18–24 months. Royalty, 6–7% of retail; small advance.

January Productions

116 Washington Avenue
Hawthorne, NJ 07507

Creative Director: Barbara Peller

Publisher's Interests
This publisher produces curriculum-based books and other materials for libraries and schools serving students four to twelve years of age. It specializes in high interest/low reading level titles in both fiction and nonfiction, covering a variety of subjects and themes.
Website: www.edimpressions.com

Freelance Potential
Plans to resume publishing (1 or more titles) in 2010.
Receives 20 queries, 20 unsolicited mss yearly.
Submissions and Payment: Catalogue available at website. Prefers query with outline/synopsis; will accept complete ms with résumé. Accepts hard copy. SASE. Response time and publication period vary. Flat fee, $325–$375.

Journey Stone Creations

3533 Danbury Road
Fairfield, OH 45014

Editor: Janet Kelly

Publisher's Interests
Children's picture books, including the popular Touch and
Learn titles, are published by Journey Stone Creations. Its
goal is to reach children with positive and life changing information. Most of its books are written for specific clients on a
work-for-hire basis.
Website: www.jscbooks.com

Freelance Potential
Published 10 titles in 2009. Receives 3,000 queries yearly.
Submissions and Payment: Guidelines and catalogue avail-
able at website. Query with author biography. Accepts email
queries to info@jscbooks.com. Responds in 1 week.
Publication period and payment policy vary.

Jump at the Sun

114 Fifth Avenue
New York, NY 10011

Acquisitions

Publisher's Interests
Jump at the Sun, an imprint of Disney Enterprises, focuses
on the experiences—past and present—of African Americans.
It publishes fiction and nonfiction in board and novelty book
formats, picture and chapter books, and novels for young
adult readers. It also publishes biographies and photo-essays.
Only agented authors appear in this publisher's catalogue
of titles.
Website: www.jumpatthesun.com

Freelance Potential
Published 4 titles in 2009: each was by an agented author.
Submissions and Payment: Guidelines and catalogue available at website. Accepts submissions from agented authors
only. Royalty; advance.

Kaplan Publishing

1 Liberty Plaza, 24th Floor
New York, NY 10006

Editorial Department

Publisher's Interests
Kaplan Publishing is known for its reliable test preparation
materials for high school and college students, as well as professional development resources. What may be news to some
is that this publisher also produces educational materials,
including workbooks and study guides, for younger students in
kindergarten through grade six. Its books cover a variety of
subjects, including history and language arts.
Website: www.kaplanpublishing.com

Freelance Potential
Published 200 titles in 2009.
Submissions and Payment: Guidelines available. Query.
Accepts email queries to kaplaneditorial@kaplan.com.
Response time and publication period vary.

Kregel Publications

P.O. Box 2607
Grand Rapids, MI 49501-2607

Acquisitions Editor

Publisher's Interests
Christian themes and topics are the sole focus of Kregel
Publications. Both fiction and nonfiction titles are published,
for children and adults, and are marketed to the evangelical
Christian market.
Website: www.kregelpublications.com

Freelance Potential
Published 60 titles (8 juvenile) in 2009: 50 were by agented
authors and 10 were reprint/licensed properties. Of the 60
titles, 6 were by unpublished writers and 24 were by authors
who were new to the publishing house.
Submissions and Payment: Accepts queries through literary
agents and Christian manuscript-screening services only.
Guidelines available at website. Response time varies. Royalty.

Laredo Publishing

465 Westview Avenue
Englewood, NJ 07631

Editor: Raquel Benatar

Publisher's Interests
Books for children and young readers remains the focus of
this publisher. It is interested in biographies of extraordinary
people, bilingual trade books, multicultural fiction, and stories
about nature and the heritage of North and South America.
50% self-, subsidy-, co-venture, or co-op published material.
Website: www.renaissancehouse.net

Freelance Potential
Published 10 titles (6 juvenile) in 2009. Receives 250 queries,
350 unsolicited mss yearly.
Submissions and Payment: Catalogue available at website.
Query with synopsis; or send complete ms. Accepts email sub-
missions to laredo@renaissancehouse.net (no attachments).
Response time and publication period vary. Royalty.

Leadership Publishers Inc.

P.O. Box 83581
Des Moines, IA 50301-8358

Owner/Publisher: Dr. Lois Roets

Publisher's Interests
This publisher specializes in books, reports, and programs for
teachers and administrators involved in gifted and talented
educational programs. It was founded by Lois Roets, a noted
educational consultant and resource specialist. At the present
time, it is not reviewing queries or manuscripts. Check the
website for changes to this current policy.
Website: www.leadershippublishers.com

Freelance Potential
Published 1 title in 2009. Receives 12 queries yearly.
Submissions and Payment: Catalogue available at website.
Not reviewing queries or unsolicited mss at this time.

Lighthouse Publishing

5531 Dufferin Drive
Savage, MN 55378

Submissions Editor: Chris Wright

Publisher's Interests
This multi-media company offers Christian-themed books.
50% self-, subsidy-, co-venture, or co-op published material.
Website: www.lighthousechristianpublishing.com

Freelance Potential
Published 50 titles (30 juvenile) in 2009: 45 were developed
from unsolicited submissions and 5 were by agented authors.
Of the 50 titles, all were by authors who were new to the pub-
lishing house. Receives 144–180 unsolicited mss yearly.
Submissions and Payment: Guidelines available at website.
Send complete ms. Accepts email submissions to info@
lighthousechristianpublishing.com (Microsoft Word attach-
ments). Responds in 6–8 weeks. Publication in 3–4 months.
Royalty, 50% of net.

Liturgical Press

St. John's Abbey
P.O. Box 7500
Collegeville, MN 56321-7500

Editorial Director: Hans Christoffersen

Publisher's Interests
This long-time publisher of Catholic missals, Bible study
guides, and sacramental literature also offers religious education materials, prayer books, and fiction titles for children. It
offers bilingual and multicultural books as well. All titles are
designed to proclaim the Good News of Jesus Christ.
Website: www.litpress.org

Freelance Potential
Published 80 titles (10 juvenile) in 2009.
Submissions and Payment: Guidelines and catalogue available at website. Query with synopsis, outline, and sample
chapter. Accepts hard copy and email queries to hchristoffe@
osb.org. SASE. Responds in 3–4 months. Publication in 18–24
months. Royalty.

Lollipop Power Books

120 Morris Street
Durham, NC 27701

Children's Book Editor

Publisher's Interests
Dedicated to publishing quality writing, especially by writers historically neglected by mainstream publishing, Lollipop Power Books produces nontraditional children's books with multicultural themes.
Website: www.carolinawrenpress.org

Freelance Potential
Published 1 title in 2009: it was developed from an unsolicited submission.
Submissions and Payment: Guidelines available at website. Query with author bio, synopsis, and sample chapters. Accepts hard copy and email queries to carolina@carolinawrenpress.org. SASE. Responds in 3 months. Publication in 2 years. Flat fee, $1,000 honorarium.

Longacre Press

P.O. Box 5340
Dunedin, New Zealand

Acquisitions Editor

Publisher's Interests
This independent publisher of middle-grade and young adult fiction looks for authors who have an individual voice and a good story to tell. Its catalogue features mystery; suspense; and contemporary, inspirational, multicultural, and regional fiction. It also publishes regional nonfiction focusing on southern New Zealand.
Website: www.longacre.co.nz

Freelance Potential
Published 5–10 titles in 2009.
Submissions and Payment: Guidelines and catalogue available at website. Query with synopsis, 2 sample chapters, and author bio. Accepts hard copy. SASE. Responds in 2–4 months. Publication period varies. Payment policy varies.

The Love and Logic Press

2207 Jackson Street
Golden, CO 80401-2300

Publisher

Publisher's Interests
This publisher's books, audiocassettes, and CD-ROMs are
designed to make parenting and teaching fun and rewarding
instead of stressful and chaotic. Its materials offer practical
tools and techniques that help parents and educators achieve
respectful and healthy relationships with their children. Topics
include sibling rivalry, stepfamilies, adoption, behavioral problems, and stress reduction.
Website: www.loveandlogic.com

Freelance Potential
Published 8 titles in 2009. Receives 30 queries yearly.
Submissions and Payment: Catalogue available at website.
Send résumé. No queries or mss. All work is done on assign-
ment only.

The Lutterworth Press

P.O. Box 60
Cambridge CB1 2NT
United Kingdom

Managing Editor: Adrian Brink

Publisher's Interests
Lutterworth Press publishes religious and other nonfiction
books that emphasize moral values. Although it has offered
children's books in the past, it has cut back on its juvenile list
and is no longer reviewing submissions for young readers.
Website: www.lutterworth.com

Freelance Potential
Published 20 titles (2 juvenile) in 2009. Receives 360 queries
each year.
Submissions and Payment: Guidelines and catalogue available at website. Query with outline, table of contents, and
1–2 sample chapters. Availability of artwork improves chance
of acceptance. Accepts hard copy. SAE/IRC. Responds in 2
months. Publication period varies. Royalty.

Manor House Publishing

452 Cottingham Crescent
Ancaster, Ontario L9G 3V6
Canada

President/CEO: Mike Davie

Publisher's Interests
Offering fiction and nonfiction works for young adults and
adults, this publisher prefers to work with Canadian writers. Its
current needs include well-written business and self-help
books for a wide audience.
Website: www.manor-house.biz

Freelance Potential
Published 6 titles in 2009: 5 were by authors who were new to
the publishing house. Receives 50 queries yearly.
Submissions and Payment: Canadian authors preferred.
Guidelines available at website. Query with synopsis, author
biography, and first 3 chapters. Accepts email submissions to
mike_davie@execs.com. Responds only if interested.
Publication period varies. Royalty; advance.

Mapletree Publishing Company

72 North Wind River Road
Silverton, ID 83867-0446

Manuscript Submissions

Publisher's Interests
This imprint of WindRiver Publishing specializes in quality publications that support homeschooling, child development, and
family values. It offers fiction and nonfiction, including mysteries and historical fiction for young adults.
Website: www.mapletreepublishing.com

Freelance Potential
Published 6 titles in 2009. Of the 6 titles, 2 were by unpublished writers and 3 were by authors who were new to the
publishing house. Receives 500 queries yearly.
Submissions and Payment: Guidelines available. Query with
3–4 sample chapters and market information. Prefers submissions through website; will accept hard copy. SASE. Responds
in 4–6 months. Publication period varies. Royalty, 15%.

Marlor Press

4304 Brigadoon Drive
St. Paul, MN 55126

Editorial Director: Marlin Bree

Publisher's Interests
Marlor Press publishes trade paperback nonfiction books for children, as well as books on boating, traveling, and family life. Among its traveling titles are family travel guides to locations throughout the U.S. and Europe. It does not accept fiction or poetry.

Freelance Potential
Published 1 title in 2009: it was by an unpublished author who was new to the publishing house. Receives 100+ queries each year.
Submissions and Payment: Query with résumé, outline, description of target audience, and market analysis. No unsolicited mss. Accepts hard copy. SASE. Response time varies. Publication in 1 year. Royalty, 8–10% of net.

Maupin House

2416 NW 71 Place
Gainesville, FL 32653

Editor: Emily Raij

Publisher's Interests
Maupin House offers professional resources in writing and language arts for teachers of kindergarten through grade 12. It seeks grassroots solutions from teachers and former teachers.
Website: www.maupinhouse.com

Freelance Potential
Published 8 titles in 2009: 7 were developed from unsolicited submissions. Of the 8 titles, 3 were by authors who were new to the publishing house. Receives 120–240 queries yearly.
Submissions and Payment: Catalogue available at website. Query with résumé, publishing credits, table of contents, and sample chapter. Accepts email queries to publisher@ maupinhouse.com. Responds in 1 week. Publication in 12–18 months. Royalty, 5–10%.

Mayhaven Publishing

803 Buckthorn Circle
P.O. Box 557
Mahomet, IL 61853

Editor/Publisher: Doris Wenzel

Publisher's Interests
For 20 years, Mayhaven Publishing has been offering young
readers illustrated novels, biographies, poetry, and books
about history. 50% co-op published material.
Website: www.mayhavenpublishing.com

Freelance Potential
Published 14 titles (7 juvenile) in 2009: all were developed
from unsolicited submissions and 1 was by an agented author.
Of the 14 titles, 4 were by unpublished writers and 2 were by
authors who were new to the publishing house. Receives 720
queries yearly.
Submissions and Payment: Guidelines available. Query
with 3 sample chapters. Accepts hard copy. SASE. Responds
in 3–9 months. Publication in 9–12 months. Royalty.

The McDonald & Woodward Publishing Company

431-B East College Street
Granville, OH 43023

Submissions: Jerry McDonald

Publisher's Interests
The McDonald & Woodward Publishing Company's mission is
to publish books about natural and cultural history—as broadly
defined—for middle-grade, young adult, and adult readers.
Website: www.mwpubco.com

Freelance Potential
Published 7 titles in 2009: 5 were developed from unsolicited
submissions. Of the 7 titles, 1 was by an unpublished writer
and 6 were by authors who were new to the publishing house.
Receives 60 queries yearly.
Submissions and Payment: Guidelines available at website.
Query. Accepts hard copy and email queries to mwpubco@
mwpubco.com. SASE. Responds in 1 month. Publication period
varies. Royalty, 10%.

Milet Publishing

333 North Michigan Avenue, Suite 530
Chicago, IL 60601

Editorial Director

Publisher's Interests
Multicultural, artistic, innovative, and unique are some of the
words this publisher uses to describe the children's books in
its catalogue. It is not currently reviewing submissions; check
the website periodically for updates to this policy.
Website: www.milet.com

Freelance Potential
Published 9 titles in 2009: 1 was by an agented author. Of the
9 titles, 2 were by authors who were new to the publishing
house. Receives 300 queries, 600 unsolicited mss yearly.
Submissions and Payment: Guidelines and catalogue available at website. Not accepting queries or manuscripts at this
time. Check website for changes to this policy.

Modern Publishing

155 East 55th Street
New York, NY 10022

Editorial Director: Kathy O'Hehir

Publisher's Interests
Modern Publishing produces picture storybooks, beginning
readers, novelty and board books, and activity books and
puzzles for children ages two through ten. It publishes some
Spanish bilingual titles.
Website: www.modernpublishing.com

Freelance Potential
Published 300 titles in 2009. Receives 75 queries and unsolicited mss yearly.
Submissions and Payment: Guidelines available. Query with
outline/synopsis; or send complete ms. Accepts hard copy
and simultaneous submissions if identified. SASE. Responds
in 2 months. Publication period varies. Royalty, by arrangement. Flat fee.

Morning Glory Press

6595 San Haroldo Way
Buena Park, CA 90620-3748

President: Jeanne Lindsay

Publisher's Interests
The self-help and educational books found in this publisher's catalogue are geared to pregnant and parenting teens, covering such topics as prenatal health, childbirth, newborn care, life skills, and single parenting. Morning Glory Press also publishes material for teen fathers and social workers, as well as a small number of picture books about adoption and absentee fathers, and a fiction series about teens in crisis.
Website: www.morningglorypress.com

Freelance Potential
Published 1–2 titles in 2009. Receives 20 queries yearly.
Submissions and Payment: Query. Accepts hard copy. SASE. Responds in 1–3 months. Publication in 6–8 months. Royalty; advance, $500.

National Resource Center for Youth Services

The University of Oklahoma Outreach
4502 East 41st Street, Building 4W
Tulsa, OK 74135

Associate Director: Kristi Charles

Publisher's Interests
This publisher's catalogue features manuals and workbooks for youth service professionals, as well as books on sensitive issues for troubled teens. Designed to motivate, inspire, and guide, these titles cover such topics as teen pregnancy, domestic violence, and conflict resolution.
Website: www.nrcys.ou.edu

Freelance Potential
Published 5 titles in 2009: 1 was by an unpublished writer and 3 were by authors who were new to the publishing house. Receives 5–10 queries yearly.
Submissions and Payment: Guidelines available. Query with outline and 1–3 sample chapters. Accepts hard copy. SASE. Responds in 1–3 months. Publication in 8–18 months. Royalty.

Natural Heritage Books

P.O. Box 95, Station O
Toronto, Ontario M4A 2MB
Canada

Publisher Emeritus: Barry Penhale

Publisher's Interests
Natural Heritage Books, part of the Dundurn Group, publishes books on Canada's history, heritage, culture, environment, and natural history. It also publishes biographies. Its titles are geared toward middle-grade and high school readers, and are noted for their high quality.
Website: www.naturalheritagebooks.com

Freelance Potential
Published 20 titles in 2009. Receives 100+ queries yearly.
Submissions and Payment: Writers' guidelines and catalogue available at website. Query with résumé, synopsis, table of contents, and 3 sample chapters. Accepts hard copy. SAE/IRC. Responds in 3–6 months. Publication in 1–2 years. Royalty; advance.

Nelson Education

1120 Birchmount Road
Toronto, Ontario M1K 5G4
Canada

Submissions

Publisher's Interests
As a leading provider of books and online resources for the Canadian educational publishing market, Nelson Education offers material covering the full range of subject matter for students in kindergarten through high school. It also publishes material for literacy programs for at-risk students. While submissions through agents are preferred, qualified writers may submit directly.
Website: www.nelson.com

Freelance Potential
Published 60 titles in 2009. Receives 100 queries yearly.
Submissions and Payment: Query. Prefers queries submitted through literary agents. Accepts hard copy. SAE/IRC. Responds in 6–12 months. Publication period and payment policy vary.

Newmarket Press

18 East 48th Street, 15th Floor
New York, NY 10017

Editor: Shannon Berning

Publisher's Interests
Newmarket Press' focus is on nonfiction titles within the parenting, health, nutrition, history, personal finance, and self-help categories. It also publishes biographies. At this time, the company is closed to submissions.
Website: www.newmarketpress.com

Freelance Potential
Published 45 titles in 2009: most were by agented authors. Receives 1,200 queries yearly.
Submissions and Payment: Guidelines available at website. Not reviewing queries or mss at this time. Please refer to website for changes to this policy.

New Voices Publishing

P.O. Box 560
Wilmington, MA 01887

Editor

Publisher's Interests
Kids Terrain, Inc., a company that produces "resources for family, work, and school," extends its mission through its New Voices Publishing house. The books it publishes address topics such as self-esteem, coping with real-life situations, respect for others, and multicultural issues. It also offers author-assisted publishing services to emerging writers.
Website: www.kidsterrain.com

Freelance Potential
Published 2 titles in 2009: 1 was developed from an unsolicited submission.
Submissions and Payment: Guidelines and catalogue available at website. Query. Accepts hard copy. SASE. Responds in 1–2 months. Publication in 12–18 months. Royalty, 10–15%.

New World Library

14 Pamaron Way
Novato, CA 94949

Submissions Editor: Jonathan Wickmann

Publisher's Interests
For more than thirty years, New World Library has offered books that reflect its dedication to social and environmental awareness. Personal growth, creativity, and spiritual and physical well-being are the themes that run through its publications for children and adults alike. It also offers parenting and education titles.
Website: www.newworldlibrary.com

Freelance Potential
Published 35 titles in 2009. Receives many queries yearly.
Submissions and Payment: Guidelines available at website. Query. Prefers email queries to submit@newworldlibrary.com; will accept hard copy and simultaneous submissions. SASE. Responds in 2–3 months. Publication in 12–18 months.

Nickname Press

Box 454, 39 Queen Street
Cobourg, Ontario K9A 1M0
Canada

Editor: Heather Jopling

Publisher's Interests
Nickname Press is a small, independent publisher of books for young children. It offers easy-to-read and story picture books that incorporate multiculturalism, ethnic diversity, social issues, and nontraditional family types.
Website: www.nicknamepress.com

Freelance Potential
Published 2 titles in 2009. Receives 12–20 queries yearly.
Submissions and Payment: Guidelines and catalogue available at website. Query with outline and synopsis. Accepts hard copy and email queries to info@nicknamepress.com. SASE. Responds in 2 months. Publication period varies. Royalty.

Nomad Press

2456 Christian Street
White River Junction, VT 05001

Editor: Susan Kahan

Publisher's Interests
This independent publisher focuses on books about science, social studies, and the environment that spark the interest of young readers. Its titles target readers ages 6 to 13.
Website: www.nomadpress.net

Freelance Potential
Published 10–12 titles in 2009: 3 were by unpublished writers and 7 were by authors who were new to the publishing house. Receives 30 queries yearly.
Submissions and Payment: Guidelines and catalogue available at website. Query with résumé and list of publishing credits. Accepts hard copy and email queries to info@ nomadpress.net. SASE. Responds in 2–4 weeks. Publication in 6–18 months. Royalty. Flat fee.

Ocean Publishing

P.O. Box 1080
Flagler Beach, FL 32136-1080

Editor: Jake Wilson

Publisher's Interests
This small press specializes in titles about nature, the environment, and conservation. It also offers children's picture books, mysteries, histories, and how-to books. Ocean Publishing markets its books to a wide age range.
Website: www.ocean-publishing.com

Freelance Potential
Published 3 titles in 2009. Of the 3 titles, 1 was by an unpublished writer and 1 was by an author who was new to the publishing house. Receives 400 queries yearly.
Submissions and Payment: Guidelines available at website. Query with clips. Accepts hard copy and simultaneous submissions if identified. SASE. Responds in 1 month. Publication in 6 months. Royalty, 5–8%; advance, to $250.

Optimum Publishing Company

10 Highland Drive, Box 524
Maxville, Ontario K0C 1T0
Canada

Submissions: Michael Baxendale

Publisher's Interests
This publisher's catalogue offers a wide range of nonfiction
titles for all ages, including biographies, true crime stories,
self-help, and parenting and childcare books. Cookbooks also
appear on its list. In business since 1967, it is always on the
lookout for undiscovered talent. New writers are encouraged
to submit material.
Website: www.optimumbooks.com

Freelance Potential
Published 10–20 titles in 2009. Receives 300 queries yearly.
Submissions and Payment: Query with outline and
sample chapters. Accepts email queries only to info@
optimumbooks.com. Response time varies. Publication
period varies. Royalty, 10%.

Orbit Books

Hachette Book Group
237 Park Avenue
New York, NY 10017

Editorial Department

Publisher's Interests
The Orbit Book imprint of Hachette Book Group publishes
science fiction and fantasy for adults, with some work appropriate for young adults. The full-spectrum of these genres is
represented in its catalogue—from action-packed urban fan-
tasies to futuristic thrillers. While new writers may be included
on its list of authors, only agented submissions will be considered for publication.
Website: www.orbitbooks.net

Freelance Potential
Published 40 titles in 2009.
Submissions and Payment: Accepts submissions from
agented authors only. Responds in 2–6 months. Publication
period varies. Royalty; advance.

Orchard House Press

7419 Ebbert Drive SE
Port Orchard, WA 98367

Senior Editor: Chris K. A. DiMarco

Publisher's Interests
Formerly called Windstorm Creative, this publisher aims to
produce timeless books and games in a variety of genres that
entertain and enrich its readers. It welcomes strongly-written
and well-paced submissions from authors who have familiar-
ized themselves with its titles and submission process.
Website: www.orchardhousepress.com

Freelance Potential
Published 100 titles in 2009: 95 were developed from unsolicited submissions. Receives 3,000+ queries yearly.
Submissions and Payment: Guidelines, required submission
form, and label available at website. Query with chapter-by-
chapter synopsis. Accepts hard copy. SASE. Responds in 1-3
months. Publication in 18 months. Royalty, 15%.

Our Child Press

P.O. Box 4379
Philadelphia, PA 19118

President: Carol Perrott

Publisher's Interests
Our Child Press publishes fiction and nonfiction books about
adoption. Its titles are designed for the children, parents and
parents-to-be, and others involved in the process.
Website: www.ourchildpress.com

Freelance Potential
Published 2 titles (1 juvenile) in 2009: both were developed
from unsolicited submissions. Of the 2 titles, 1 was by an
unpublished writer and 1 was by an author who was new to
the publishing house. Receives 240 queries, 216 unsolicited
mss yearly.
Submissions and Payment: Guidelines available. Query with
outline/synopsis; or send complete ms. Accepts hard copy.
SASE. Responds in 1–3 months. Publication in 1 year. Royalty.

Oxford University Press

School & Young Adult Department
198 Madison Avenue
New York, NY 10016-4314

Editor

Publisher's Interests
Classic tales, thoroughly researched histories and biographies, and educational titles are published by the School & Young Adult Department of this scholarly publishing house.
Website: www.us.oup.com

Freelance Potential
Published 100+ titles (10 juvenile) in 2009: 20 were developed from unsolicited submissions.
Submissions and Payment: Guidelines and catalogue available at website. Query with résumé, synopsis, table of contents, and sample chapter. Send query to appropriate editor; see website for list of editors. Accepts hard copy. SASE. Responds in 3–6 months. Publication period varies. Royalty; advance.

Pacific View Press

P.O. Box 2897
Berkeley, CA 94702

Acquisitions Editor: Pam Zumwalt

Publisher's Interests
This cooperatively owned small press has a growing list of multicultural nonfiction for children and adults. Its children's books focus on the culture and history of Pacific Rim nations. At this time, it is primarily interested in titles for children ages 11 through 13 about Chinese history. 40% self-, subsidy-, co-venture, or co-op published material.
Website: www.pacificviewpress.com

Freelance Potential
Published 2 titles in 2009. Receives many queries yearly.
Submissions and Payment: Guidelines available. Query with outline and sample chapters. No unsolicited mss. Accepts hard copy. SASE. Responds in 1 month. Publication period varies. Royalty, 8–10%; advance, $500–$1,000.

Palari Books

P.O. Box 9288
Richmond, VA 23227

Submissions Editor: David Smitherman

Publisher's Interests
The Virginia region is the main focus of this publisher's hard-cover and trade paperback titles. Palari Books is currently closed to submissions; interested writers should check the website for changes to this policy.
Website: www.palaribooks.com

Freelance Potential
Published 4 titles in 2009: 2 were developed from unsolicited submissions and 1 was by an agented author. Receives 1,200 queries yearly.
Submissions and Payment: Guidelines available at website. Not reviewing queries or unsolicited mss at this time.

Parachute Press

322 Eighth Avenue, Suite 500
New York, NY 10001

Submissions Editor

Publisher's Interests
Parachute Press produces books that are appealing to kids and can also be embraced by teachers and parents. The Goosebumps and Mary-Kate & Ashley series are among its offerings. Agented authors are preferred.
Website: www.parachutepublishing.com

Freelance Potential
Published 70 titles in 2009: 10 were developed from unsolicited submissions and 50 were by agented authors.
Submissions and Payment: Work-for-hire guidelines available. Send résumé with 1- to 5-page writing sample. Accepts unsolicited mss from agents only. No simultaneous submissions. Accepts hard copy. SASE. Response time varies. Publication in 9 months. Flat fee, $3,000–$4,000.

PCI Education

P.O. Box 34270
San Antonio, TX 78265

Product Submission Editor

Publisher's Interests
PCI Education publishes instructional materials for students
with a wide range of special needs, from developmentally disabled children to struggling readers and ESL students. It seeks
manuscripts for all grade levels that combine research-based
insights with best classroom practices.
Website: www.pcieducation.com

Freelance Potential
Published several titles in 2009.
Submissions and Payment: Guidelines and catalogue available at website. Query or send complete ms with author bio,
page count, description of target audience, and market analysis. Accepts hard copy. SASE. Responds in 2–4 months.
Publication period varies. Payment policy varies.

Peartree

P.O. Box 14533
Clearwater, FL 33766

Publisher: Barbara Birenbaum

Publisher's Interests
Specializing in fiction and nonfiction books for children in the
elementary and middle grades, this independent publisher
covers topics such as animals, nature, and historical and contemporary fiction. It also offers parenting, legal education, and
self-help titles for adults. 50% self-, subsidy-, co-venture, or
co-op published material.

Freelance Potential
Published 5+ titles (2 juvenile) in 2009. Of the 5+ titles, 2
were by unpublished writers and 1 was by a new author.
Receives 30–50 queries, 25 unsolicited mss yearly.
Submissions and Payment: Guidelines available. Query or
send complete ms. Accepts hard copy. SASE. Responds in
6–8 weeks. Publication in 1 year. Payment policy varies.

Pebble Books

151 Good Counsel Drive
Mankato, MN 55438

Editorial Department

Publisher's Interests
Pebble Books, an imprint of Capstone Press, offers children in kindergarten through second grade a colorful and easy-to-read introduction to a variety of subjects, including science and social studies. Its catalogue of titles is organized by reading and interest level. Pebble Books also offers some biographies and bilingual titles.
Website: www.capstonepress.com

Freelance Potential
Published several titles in 2009.
Submissions and Payment: Guidelines available. Catalogue available at website. Query with résumé and nonfiction writing samples. Accepts hard copy. SASE. Responds in 1 month. Publication period varies. Flat fee.

Penguin Books Canada Limited

90 Eglinton East, Suite 700
Toronto, Ontario M4P 2Y3
Canada

Editorial Department

Publisher's Interests
All of the titles in this publisher's catalogue are written by Canadian authors and focus on Canadian themes. The children's books it publishes comprise a small portion of its list, and include picture books, easy-to-read books, middle-grade fiction, and young adult novels. It also publishes books about Canada's history.
Website: www.penguin.ca

Freelance Potential
Published 80 titles (14 juvenile) in 2009: each was by an agented author.
Submissions and Payment: Canadian authors only. Send complete ms. Accepts hard copy. SASE. Responds in 1 month. Publication in 1–2 years. Royalty, 8–10%.

Perspectives Press

P.O. Box 90318
Indianapolis, IN 46290-0318

Editor: Pat Johnston

Publisher's Interests
This publisher specializes in books about infertility and its
alternatives, including adoption. Its goal is to promote understanding of the issues for those experiencing these situations.
Website: www.perspectivespress.com

Freelance Potential
Published 2 titles in 2009: both were developed from unsolicited submissions. Of the 2 titles, both were by unpublished
writers who were new to the publishing house. Receives 1–3
queries yearly.
Submissions and Payment: Guidelines available at website.
Query with résumé and outline. Accepts hard copy. SASE.
Responds in 1 month. Publication in 12–18 months. Payment
policy varies.

Phaidon Press

180 Varick Street, 14th Floor
New York, NY 10014

Editorial Submissions

Publisher's Interests
This art book publisher produces titles related to the visual
and performing arts, fashion, film, travel, cookery, and architecture. Its catalogue lists a small number of illustrated story
books, as well as arts and crafts books, for children.
Website: www.phaidon.com

Freelance Potential
Published 20+ titles (3 juvenile) in 2009: 10 were developed
from unsolicited submissions. Receives 120–240 queries
each year.
Submissions and Payment: Guidelines available at website.
Query with résumé, table of contents, and description of
target audience. Accepts hard copy. SASE. Responds in
4 months. Publication period varies. Royalty; advance.

Piano Press

P.O. Box 85
Del Mar, CA 92014-0085

Editor: Elizabeth C. Axford

Publisher's Interests
Piano Press publishes books (including poetry and short sto-
ries) and resource materials for music teachers and students.
Website: www.pianopress.com

Freelance Potential
Published 10 titles (5 juvenile) in 2009: 1–5 were developed
from unsolicited submissions. Of the 10 titles, 3 were by
unpublished writers and 7 were by authors new to the publishing house. Receives 360 queries, 60 unsolicited mss yearly.
Submissions and Payment: Guidelines and catalogue available at website. Query for prose. Send complete ms for poetry.
Accepts hard copy, disk submissions (Microsoft Word), and
email submissions to pianopress@pianopress.com. SASE.
Responds in 2–4 months. Publication in 1 year. Royalty.

Picture Me Press LLC

1566 Akron-Peninsula Road
Akron, OH 44313

Submissions Editor

Publisher's Interests
The books from Picture Me Press are designed to make learning fun. Titles include interactive concept books, picture
books, and novelty/board books for very young children. Both
fiction and nonfiction are offered. Its Picture Me Pretend
books include removable, wearable headgear for role-play fun.
Other formats include die-cut shapes, pull-tabs, stickers, and
slots for photographs.
Website: www.playhousepublishing.com

Freelance Potential
Published 10–15 titles in 2009.
Submissions and Payment: Guidelines available. Query.
Accepts hard copy. SASE. Response time and publication
period vary. Royalty; advance.

Piñata Books

Arte Publico Press
452 Cullen Performance Hall, University of Houston
Houston, TX 77204

Submissions Editor

Publisher's Interests
This children's imprint of Arte Publico Press is dedicated to producing books for children and young adults that authentically and realistically portray themes, characters, and customs that are unique to U.S. Hispanic culture. It is currently seeking picture books and YA novels.
Website: www.latinoteca.com

Freelance Potential
Published 10–20 titles in 2009.
Submissions and Payment: Guidelines and catalogue available. Accepts queries by hard copy and unsolicited mss through the website only. SASE. Responds in 2–4 months. Publication in 2 years. Royalty.

Pippin Press

Gracie Station Box 1347
229 East 85th Street
New York, NY 10028

Publisher: Barbara Francis

Publisher's Interests
Publishing character-driven fiction and nonfiction for children under 10, Pippin is particularly interested in historical fiction chapter books and memoirs for ages 6 through 10. Topics of interest include East African culture and animals.

Freelance Potential
Published 2–3 titles in 2009: 2–3 were developed from unsolicited submissions. Of the 2–3 titles, 1–2 were by unpublished writers and 2–3 were by authors who were new to the publishing house. Receives 600–720 queries yearly.
Submissions and Payment: Guidelines available. Query with 1-page synopsis and sample chapter. Accepts hard copy; mark envelope "Query Enclosed." SASE. Responds in 1 month. Publication in 1–2 years. Royalty; advance.

The Place in the Woods

3900 Glenwood Avenue
Golden Valley, MN 55422

Editor: Roger Hammer

Publisher's Interests
This small, specialty publisher offers books for a multicultural
market including, but not limited to, African American, Hispanic
and Latino, Asian American, and Native American readers.
Books about persons with disabilities are also featured. It publishes uplifting stories that feature individuals overcoming adversity, and that call attention to contributions by minorities.

Freelance Potential
Published 2 titles (1 juvenile) in 2009: both were developed
from unsolicited submissions. Of the 2 titles, both were by
unpublished writers. Receives 1,200 unsolicited mss yearly.
Submissions and Payment: Guidelines and catalogue available. Send complete ms. Accepts hard copy. SASE. Responds
in 1 month. Publication in 2–3 years. Royalty. Flat fee.

Pleasant St. Press

P.O. Box 520
Raynham Center, MA 02768

Editor: Jean M. Cochran

Publisher's Interests
Picture books for children from birth through age eight are the
specialty of this publisher, which has titles covering just about
every topic. It is not accepting written material at this time,
but will review art submissions.
Website: www.pleasantstpress.com

Freelance Potential
Published 8 titles in 2009: each was developed from an unsolicited submission. Of the 8 titles, 7 were by unpublished writers and 7 were by authors who were new to the publishing
house. Receives 500 queries yearly.
Submissions and Payment: Guidelines and catalogue available at website. Not accepting submissions at this time; check
website for changes to this policy.

Pogo Press

Finney Company
8075 215th Street West
Lakeville, MN 55044

President: Alan E. Krysan

Publisher's Interests
Established in 1986, this imprint of Finney Company publishes books on history, the arts, pop culture, and the travel odyssey. Many of its adult titles also appeal to young adults.
Website: www.pogopress.com

Freelance Potential
Published 3 titles in 2009: each was developed from an unsolicited submission. Of the 3 titles, each was by an unpublished writer who was new to the publishing house. Receives 96–120 queries yearly.
Submissions and Payment: Guidelines and catalogue available at website. Query with 3–4 sample chapters and marketing plan. Accepts hard copy. SASE. Responds in 10–12 weeks. Publication in 6–18 months. Royalty, 10%.

Prep Publishing

1110 1/2 Hay Street, Suite C
Fayetteville, NC 28305

Editor: Anne McKinney

Publisher's Interests
Prep Publishing specializes in books related to careers and job hunting, as well as fiction and nonfiction. Its catalogue includes books on Judeo-Christian themes, biographies, and mysteries for a general audience.
Website: www.prep-pub.com

Freelance Potential
Published 3 titles in 2009: 1 was by an author who was new to the publishing house. Receives 1,000 queries, 400 unsolicited mss yearly.
Submissions and Payment: Guidelines and catalogue available at website. Query with synopsis; or send complete ms with $350 reading fee. Accepts hard copy. SASE. Responds in 3 months. Publication in 18 months. Royalty, 6–14%.

Purple Sky Publishing

P.O. Box 12013
Parkville, MO 64152

Submissions Editor: Thad W. Pealer

Publisher's Interests
Innovation and imagination are brought together in the books published by this small, independent publisher of fiction, children's story picture books, and poetry.
Website: www.purpleskypublishing.com

Freelance Potential
Published 4 titles in 2009. Of the 4 titles, 1 was by an unpublished writer and 2 were by authors who were new to the publishing house. Receives 300 queries yearly.
Submissions and Payment: Guidelines and catalogue available at website. Query with author biography, synopsis, and market analysis. Accepts email queries to admin@ purpleskypublishing.com. Responds in 1 week. Publication period varies. Royalty.

PUSH

557 Broadway
New York, NY 10012

Editor: David Levithan

Publisher's Interests
As Scholastic's teen imprint, PUSH publishes fiction that reflects and respects today's young adult reader. Stories with contemporary themes and issues, as well as historical and multicultural fiction, are featured in its list of titles. The PUSH Novel Contest for aspiring writers is the source of some of the material published.
Website: www.thisispush.com

Freelance Potential
Published 5 titles in 2009. Of the 5 titles, 2 were by authors who were new to the publishing house.
Submissions and Payment: Catalogue available at website. Query. Accepts hard copy. SASE. Response time varies. Publication period and payment policy vary.

QED

226 City Road
London, EC1V 2TT
United Kingdom

Editor: Amanda Askew

Publisher's Interests
QED Publishing focuses on educational fiction and nonfiction books for children up to age 12. Its subjects include literacy, math, science, history, art, technology, and the environment. It seeks books that are as entertaining as they are educational.
Website: www.qed-publishing.co.uk

Freelance Potential
Published 80 titles in 2009: 15 were by unpublished writers and 6 were by new authors. Receives 50–100 queries yearly.
Submissions and Payment: Guidelines available. Catalogue available at website. Query with clips. Accepts hard copy and email to amandaa@quarto.com. Availability of artwork improves chance of acceptance. SAE/IRC. Response time and publication period vary. Royalty. Flat fee.

Quixote Press

3544 Blakslee Street
Wever, IA 52658

President: Bruce Carlson

Publisher's Interests
"Books from the Heartland of America" is the slogan of this publisher. Quixote Press publishes regional fiction and nonfiction, particularly folktales and ghost stories, as well as offbeat cookbooks and pioneer memoirs. Many of its titles are humorous in their approach.

Freelance Potential
Published 30 titles (20 juvenile) in 2009: 15–20 were developed from unsolicited submissions and 2–3 were by agented authors. Of the 30 titles, most were by unpublished writers. Receives 300–360 queries, 120–180 unsolicited mss yearly.
Submissions and Payment: Query or send ms. Accepts hard copy and simultaneous submissions if identified. SASE. Responds in 1 week. Publication in 2–24 months. Royalty.

Rainbow Books

P.O. Box 430
Highland City, FL 33846-0430

Editorial Director: Betsy Lampe

Publisher's Interests
Rainbow Books publishes nonfiction titles for middle-grade readers that aim to help them cope with the difficult teen years, including self-help and how-to books.
Website: www.rainbowbooksinc.com

Freelance Potential
Published 28 titles (4 juvenile) in 2009: 26 were developed from unsolicited submissions and 2 were by agented authors. Of the 28 titles, 18 were by unpublished writers and 20 were by new authors. Receives 300–420 queries yearly.
Submissions and Payment: Guidelines and catalogue available at website. Query. Accepts hard copy and email to submissions@rainbowbooksinc.com (no attachments). SASE. Responds in 6 weeks. Publication in 1 year. Royalty; advance.

Randall House Publications

114 Bush Road
Nashville, TN 37217

Acquisitions Editor: Michelle Orr

Publisher's Interests
Sunday school curriculum for children of all ages, as well as for adults, is offered by this specialty publisher. Also offered are reference materials and devotionals.
Website: www.randallhouse.com

Freelance Potential
Published 15 titles in 2009: 3 were developed from unsolicited submissions and 2 were by agented authors. Of the 15 titles, 2 were by unpublished writers and 3 were by new authors. Receives 1,000+ queries yearly.
Submissions and Payment: Guidelines available at website. Query. Accepts hard copy and email queries via website. SASE. Responds in 3 months. Publication in 12–14 months. Royalty, 10–14%; advance, $1,000–$2,000.

Rand McNally

8255 North Central Park
Skokie, IL 60076

Editorial Director: Laurie Borman

Publisher's Interests
Rand McNally offers educational resources in various formats for children ages 4 to 12 in the subjects of geography, social studies, and history; it also offers a subscriber-based website for teachers. It works only with experienced education writers on a work-for-hire basis.
Website: www.randmcnally.com/education

Freelance Potential
Published 8–10 titles in 2009: most were by unpublished writers and 1–2 were by authors who were new to the publishing house. Receives 12–24 queries yearly.
Submissions and Payment: Send résumé only. All work is assigned. Response time, publication period, and payment policy vary.

Random House Children's Books

61-63 Uxbridge Road
Ealing, London W5 5SA United Kingdom

Picture Books: Hannah Featherstone
Fiction: Naomi Wood

Publisher's Interests
Books for children of all ages are published by this London-based division of Random House. Its titles run the gamut from genre fiction such as adventure, mystery, fantasy, humor, and suspense to joke books, poetry collections, and activity books to nonfiction books on a variety of topics. Agented authors may send work for consideration.
Website: www.kidsatrandomhouse.co.uk

Freelance Potential
Published 200+ titles in 2009: most were by agented authors. Receives 3,000 queries yearly.
Submissions and Payment: Guidelines available. Accepts submissions from agented authors only. Publication in 1–2 years. Royalty; advance.

Rayo

HarperCollins Children's Books
1350 Avenue of the Americas
New York, NY 10019

Executive Editor: Adriana Dominguez

Publisher's Interests
Latino culture and language are highlighted in the books of this HarperCollins imprint. Its list of titles includes bilingual, Spanish-language, and English-language picture books, media tie-ins, board books, and middle-grade books, as well as Spanish-language translations of classic children's literature. It seeks young adult novels written in English by Latino authors.
Website: www.harpercollinschildrens.com

Freelance Potential
Published 20 titles in 2009: all were by agented authors. Receives 24 queries yearly.
Submissions and Payment: Accepts submissions through literary agents only. Response time, publication period, and payment policy vary.

Red Rock Press

459 Columbus Avenue, Suite 114
New York, NY 10024

Creative Director

Publisher's Interests
This publisher specializes in highly illustrated and entertaining gift books for children, as well as home, cooking, and style books for adults.
Website: www.redrockpress.com

Freelance Potential
Published 6 titles (1 juvenile) in 2009: 2 were developed from unsolicited submissions. Of the 6 titles, 1 was by an unpublished writer. Receives 800 unsolicited mss yearly.
Submissions and Payment: Prefers agented submissions. Send complete ms with marketing plan. Accepts hard copy. SASE. Responds in 2–4 months. Publication in 18 months. Royalty; advance. Flat fee.

Red Wheel

500 Third Street, Suite 230
San Francisco, CA 94107

Acquisitions Editor: Pat Bryce

Publisher's Interests
Self-help and inspirational books that are of interest to young
adults and adults are the mainstay of this imprint from Red
Wheel/Weiser.
Website: www.redwheelweiser.com

Freelance Potential
Published 50 titles in 2009: 10 were developed from unsolicited
submissions and 30 were by agented authors.
Submissions and Payment: Guidelines and catalogue available at website. Query with author biography, table of contents, 3 sample chapters, synopsis, market analysis, and samples of artwork. Accepts hard copy. SASE. Responds in 3
months. Publication in 18 months. Royalty; advance.

River's Bend Press

P.O. Box 606
Stillwater, MN 55082

Editor

Publisher's Interests
River's Bend Press specializes in publishing books of fiction
and nonfiction that focus on social issues and events of historical significance. While its titles are not specifically geared
toward children, River's Bend will consider those works that
may hold some appeal to younger readers.
Website: www.riversbendpress.com

Freelance Potential
Published 2 titles in 2009: both were developed from unsolicited submissions. Receives 600 queries yearly.
Submissions and Payment: Guidelines and catalogue available at website. Query with 3 chapters. Accepts hard copy.
SASE. Responds in 2 months. Publication period and payment
policy vary.

Robbie Dean Press

2910 East Eisenhower Parkway
Ann Arbor, MI 48108

Owner: Dr. Fairy Hayes-Scott

Publisher's Interests
This independent publisher is "determined to make a difference" in the lives of its teen and young adult readers by offering books that address the pressing issues in their lives.
Website: www.robbiedeanpress.com

Freelance Potential
Published 5–10 titles (3 juvenile) in 2009: each was developed from an unsolicited submission. Of the 5–10 titles, each was by an unpublished writer. Receives 5 queries, 5 unsolicited mss yearly.
Submissions and Payment: Query for nonfiction; send complete ms for fiction. Accepts hard copy and disk submissions (Microsoft Word). SASE. Responds to queries in 2 days; to mss in 2 months. Publication in 9 months. Royalty, 10–20%.

Robinswood Press

30 South Avenue
Stourbridge, West Midlands DY8 3XY
United Kingdom

Editor: Sally Connolly

Publisher's Interests
Robinswood Press publishes books that are designed to foster a love of reading and writing, many of which specifically target young readers with difficulties in those areas.
Website: www.robinswoodpress.com

Freelance Potential
Published 12 titles in 2009: 10 were developed from unsolicited submissions and 2 were by agented authors. Of the 12 titles, 2 were by unpublished writers and 3 were by authors new to the publishing house. Receives 360 queries yearly.
Submissions and Payment: Guidelines available at website. Query with synopsis and author bio. Accepts email queries to publishing@robinswoodpress.com (no attachments). Responds in 4–6 weeks. Publication period and payment policy vary.

Rose Publishing

4733 Torrance Boulevard, Suite 259
Torrance, CA 90503

Acquisitions Editor: Lynette Pennings

Publisher's Interests
This publisher produces easy-to-use Bible study and reference
materials including wall charts, maps, and timelines. It follows
conservative evangelical Christian views.
Website: www.rose-publishing.com

Freelance Potential
Published 25 titles in 2009. Of the 25 titles, 2–3 were by
authors who were new to the publishing house.
Submissions and Payment: Catalogue available at website
or with 9x12 SASE (4 first-class stamps). Query with sketch
of proposed chart or poster. Accepts hard copy, email to
rosepubl@aol.com (no attachments), and simultaneous submissions if identified. Does not return materials. Responds in
2–3 months. Publication in 18 months. Flat fee.

RP Graphics

Reagent Press
P.O. Box 362
East Olympia, WA 98540-0362

Associate Publisher: Thomas Green

Publisher's Interests
This imprint of Reagent Press publishes science fiction and
fantasy graphic novels for children, teens, and adults. Its list
includes original graphic novels as well as graphic novels of
Reagent Press' proven best-selling science fiction titles. It is
eager to work with emerging graphic novel artists and writers,
especially those who understand the working of a small, independent press.
Website: www.reagentpress.com

Freelance Potential
Published 3–6 titles in 2009.
Submissions and Payment: Guidelines available at website.
Query. Accepts hard copy. SASE. Responds in 1–2 months.
Publication in 6–12 months. Royalty; advance.

Sandcastle Books

3 Church Street, Suite 500
Toronto, Ontario M5E 1M2
Canada

Submissions Editor

Publisher's Interests
Canadian themes, in both nonfiction and genre fiction, are
published by Sandcastle Books. Its titles are geared toward
children ages 8 through 13.
Website: www.dundurn.com

Freelance Potential
Published 9 titles in 2009. Receives 200 queries, 300 unsolicited mss yearly.
Submissions and Payment: Canadian authors only.
Guidelines available. Query with 250-word synopsis, résumé,
3 sample chapters, and word count (include table of contents
for nonfiction); or send complete ms. Accepts hard copy.
SASE. Responds to nonfiction submissions in 2–3 months, to
fiction in 6–8 months. Publication period varies. Advance.

Sandcastle Publishing

1723 Hill Drive
P.O. Box 3070
South Pasadena, CA 91030

Acquisitions: Renee Rolle-Whatley

Publisher's Interests
The books from Sandcastle Publishing aim to help children
and young adults develop their potential and improve literacy
through participation in the performing arts. Skits, monologues, and read-aloud plays, as well as early reader fiction
are among the company's offerings. It does not accept unsolicited manuscripts.
Website: www.childrenactingbooks.com

Freelance Potential
Published 2 titles in 2009. Receives 200 queries yearly.
Submissions and Payment: Guidelines available. Query
with résumé. No unsolicited mss. Accepts hard copy. SASE.
Responds in 2–3 months. Publication period and payment
policy vary.

Santillana USA Publishing Company

2105 NW 86th Avenue
Doral, FL 33122

Editorial Director: Mario Castro

Publisher's Interests
English as a second language and Spanish as a foreign language books are the mainstay of the Santillana USA Publishing Company. Material is geared toward student readers in kindergarten through high school. Bilingual and dual language nonfiction titles cover subjects such as history, science, and mathematics. Literary works are also offered in both languages. French and Portuguese language materials for middle and high school readers are also published.
Website: www.santillanausa.com

Freelance Potential
Published 10 titles in 2009. Receives 60+ queries yearly.
Submissions and Payment: Not accepting queries or unsolicited manuscripts at this time.

Scholastic Canada Ltd

604 King Street West
Toronto, Ontario M5V 1E1
Canada

Editor

Publisher's Interests
The work of Canadian authors only is published by this division of Scholastic Inc. Its catalogue features titles for children of all ages, most specializing in Canadian themes and topics. A wide variety of genres, including adventure, suspense, mystery, and historical and realistic fiction, are published.
Website: www.scholastic.ca

Freelance Potential
Published 80–100 titles in 2009. Of the 80–100 titles, 3 were by authors who were new to the publishing house.
Submissions and Payment: Canadian authors only. Guidelines and catalogue available at website. Not accepting queries or unsolicited manuscripts at this time. Check the website or call 905-887-7323, extension 4308, for changes to this policy.

School Specialty Publishing

W6316 Design Drive
Greenville, WI 54942

Submissions Editor

Publisher's Interests
Books for homeschool and classroom teachers are provided
by School Specialty Publishing. Its curriculum-based titles
for parents and educators cover subject areas such as social
studies, mathematics, science, and language arts. Its imprint,
Gingham Dog Press, offers titles for emergent readers in the
form of picture books and activity books.
Website: www.schoolspecialty.com

Freelance Potential
Published 425–450 titles (400 juvenile) in 2009. Receives
400 unsolicited mss yearly.
Submissions and Payment: Writers' guidelines and catalogue
available. Not accepting queries or unsolicited manuscripts at
this time.

School Zone Publishing

1819 Industrial Drive
P.O. Box 777
Grand Haven, MI 49417

Editor

Publisher's Interests
School Zone Publishing offers a full line of children's educational products for use in the school and home classroom.
Its grade-leveled workbooks cover all curriculum areas for
students in preschool through the elementary grades. This
publisher also produces flash cards, games, and computer
software. Its "Bilingual Get Ready!" titles cover mathematics
as well as language skills.
Website: www.schoolzone.com

Freelance Potential
Published 5–6 titles in 2009. Receives 100 queries yearly.
Submissions and Payment: Query with résumé and writing
samples. Response time and publication period vary. Flat fee.

Seven Stories Press

140 Watts Street
New York, NY 10013

Editorial Department

Publisher's Interests
This independent book publisher offers works of imagination as well as political titles, including biographies, that address issues not usually covered by traditional, mainstream publishing houses. While most of its offerings are for adult readers, Seven Stories Press seeks to include graphic novels for young adults on its list of titles.
Website: www.sevenstories.com

Freelance Potential
Published 20–30 titles in 2009.
Submissions and Payment: Guidelines and catalogue available at website. Query with sample chapters. Accepts hard copy. SASE. Responds in 2–4 months. Publication in 18 months. Royalty.

Silver Dolphin Books

10350 Barnes Canyon Road, Suite 100
San Diego, CA 92121

Submissions Editor

Publisher's Interests
Silver Dolphin Books publishes activity, novelty, and educational nonfiction books for preschoolers through age 12. These include the popular Maurice Pledge and Snappy Sounds series books for younger children and the highly interactive Robotic Animal and Uncover series for older children.
Website: www.silverdolphinbooks.com

Freelance Potential
Published 44 titles in 2009. Receives 50+ queries yearly.
Submissions and Payment: Published authors only. Guidelines and catalogue available at website. Query with outline and sample chapters. Accepts hard copy. Availability of artwork improves chance of acceptance. SASE. Responds in 1–3 months. Publication period and payment policy vary.

Smith & Sons

177 Lyme Road
Hanover, NH 03755

Editor: Marisa Kraus

Publisher's Interests
Middle-grade and young adult fiction are the mainstay of this division of Smith & Kraus, which was started in 2007. Writers are encouraged to send in their adventure, fantasy, and science fiction submissions that will thrill and capture the imaginations of tweens.
Website: www.smithandkraus.com

Freelance Potential
Published 1 title in 2009: it was developed from an unsolicited submission.
Submissions and Payment: Guidelines available at website. Query with brief bio, synopsis, and sample chapters. Accepts email queries to sandk@sover.net. Responds in 1–2 months. Publication in 1 year. Royalty; advance. Flat fee.

Snap Books

Capstone Press
151 Good Counsel Drive
Mankato, MN 55438

Submissions Editor

Publisher's Interests
This imprint from Capstone Press offers hip, high-interest nonfiction for girls in grades three through nine. Snap Books covers topics including babysitting, cheerleading, health, fitness, social issues, peer pressure, and crafts.
Website: www.capstonepress.com

Freelance Potential
Published several titles in 2009. Receives several queries each year.
Submissions and Payment: Guidelines and catalogue available. Query with résumé and writing samples. Accepts hard copy. SASE. Responds in 1 month. Publication period varies. Flat fee.

Southern Early Childhood Association

1123 South University, Suite 255
Little Rock, AR 72204

Editor: Janet B. Stivers

Publisher's Interests
Books by this publisher address both the continuing interests
of early childhood professionals as well as emerging ideas and
issues in the field. Its audience typically includes teachers of
young children, families, group child care providers, administrators, teacher educators, social workers, education policy
makers, and researchers.
Website: www.southernearlychildhood.org

Freelance Potential
Published 2–3 titles in 2009: each was assigned. Receives
20 unsolicited mss yearly.
Submissions and Payment: Guidelines and catalogue avail-
able at website. Query with clips. Accepts hard copy. SASE.
Response time and publication period vary. Royalty, 10%.

Spinner Books

University Games Corporation
2030 Harrison Street
San Francisco, CA 94110

Product Manager

Publisher's Interests
Spinner Books, a division of University Games Corporation,
publishes activity- and game-based books for children ages six
and older. The books they produce can be read and played,
thus providing social interaction as well as education. New
titles include *Five Little Monkeys Jumping on the Bed* and *The
Dangerous Book for Boys Magic Kit.*
Website: www.universitygames.com

Freelance Potential
Published 8 titles (5 juvenile) in 2009: each was assigned.
Receives 20 queries yearly.
Submissions and Payment: Guidelines available. Catalogue
available at website. Query. Accepts hard copy. SASE. Responds
in 3 months. Publication in 6–9 months. Royalty, 5–10%.

Stackpole Books

5067 Ritter Road
Mechanicsburg, PA 17055

Publisher: Judith Schnell

Publisher's Interests
Outdoor sports, birding, and regional travel in the Mid-Atlantic states are the main themes found in the titles published by Stackpole Books.
Website: www.stackpolebooks.com

Freelance Potential
Published 130 titles in 2009: 30 were developed from unsolicited submissions. Of the 130 titles, 65 were by unpublished writers. Receives 1,000 queries yearly.
Submissions and Payment: Catalogue available at website. Query with clips. Accepts hard copy and simultaneous submissions if identified. Availability of artwork improves chance of acceptance. SASE. Responds in 1 month. Publication in 2 years. Royalty; advance.

Success Publications

3419 Dunham Road
Warsaw, NY 14569

Submissions Editor: Dana Herbison

Publisher's Interests
Success Publications is an independent publisher offering teens and young adults a variety of how-to books on crafts, hobbies, and entertainment. Prospective authors are encouraged to review the publisher's catalogue before submitting.

Freelance Potential
Published 57 titles (2 juvenile) in 2009. Receives 300 unsolicited mss yearly.
Submissions and Payment: Guidelines and catalogue available. Send complete ms with synopsis, table of contents, and author biography. Accepts hard copy and simultaneous submissions if identified. Availability of artwork improves chance of acceptance. SASE. Responds in 2 weeks. Publication in 3 months. Payment policy varies.

Sumach Press

1415 Bathurst Street, Suite 202
Toronto, Ontario M5R 3H8
Canada

Submissions Editor

Publisher's Interests
As a small, independent, feminist press, this publisher is very
selective in choosing its manuscripts. It looks for non-sexist,
non-racist stories that relate to young people's lives today—
including contemporary, literary, and multicultural fiction;
adventure; mystery; suspense; and drama. It also publishes
nonfiction books pertaining to women's issues.
Website: www.sumachpress.com

Freelance Potential
Published 9–10 titles in 2009.
Submissions and Payment: Send complete ms for young
adult fiction. Query with sample chapter and outline/synopsis
for nonfiction. Accepts hard copy. SASE. Responds in 3–4
months. Publication period varies. Payment policy varies.

Sunburst Technology

1550 Executive Drive
Elgin, IL 60123

Product Manager: Mollyann Hufford

Publisher's Interests
Educational resources for kindergarten through high school
are the mainstay of this publisher. Its offerings are available in
print, Web-enabled, Web-based network, and individual software versions. Keyboarding, math, science, and reading, as
well as conflict resolution and career guidance, are some of
the topics covered.
Website: www.sunburst.com

Freelance Potential
Published 6 titles in 2009. Receives 1,500 queries yearly.
Submissions and Payment: Query with résumé and writing
samples. Accepts product concept proposals with accompanying graphics. SASE. Responds in 3–6 weeks. Publication period
and payment policy vary.

The Templar Company

The Granary, North Street
Dorking, Surrey RH4 1DN
United Kingdom

Submissions: Rebecca Spiers

Publisher's Interests
This publisher features picture books, novelty titles, fiction, and some nonfiction in its catalogue.
Website: www.templar.co.uk

Freelance Potential
Published 60 titles in 2009: 1 was developed from an unsolicited submission and 12 were by agented authors. Of the 60 titles, 6 were by unpublished writers and 12 were by authors who were new to the publishing house. Receives 300 queries, 400 unsolicited mss yearly.
Submissions and Payment: Guidelines available. Query with synopsis; or send complete ms. Accepts hard copy. SAE/IRC. Responds to queries in 2 weeks, to mss in 3–4 months. Publication period and payment policy vary.

Thistledown Press

633 Main Street
Saskatoon, Saskatchewan S7H OJ8
Canada

Submissions Editor: Allan Forrie

Publisher's Interests
All of the books published by Thistledown Press are written by Canadian authors. It offers juvenile and young adult titles in a variety of genres.
Website: www.thistledownpress.com

Freelance Potential
Published 18 titles in 2009. Of the 18 titles, 7 were by unpublished writers and 10 were by authors who were new to the publishing house. Receives 600 queries yearly.
Submissions and Payment: Canadian authors only. Writers' guidelines and list of new titles available at website. Query with outline, sample chapter, and brief author biography. Accepts hard copy. SASE. Responds in 4 months. Publication in 1 year. Royalty.

Ticktock Media Limited

The Old Sawmill, 103 Goods Station Road
Tunbridge Wells, Kent TN1 2DP
United Kingdom

Editor: Melissa Fairley

Publisher's Interests
An independent publisher, Ticktock Media Limited strives to produce a diverse list of titles for children from birth to age 16. It is currently publishing nonfiction only, but will be accepting fiction in the near future. Thus, prospective authors are encouraged to query regarding works of fiction.
Website: www.ticktock.co.uk

Freelance Potential
Published 130 titles in 2009.
Submissions and Payment: All work is assigned. Guidelines available by email request to info@ticktock.co.uk. Query with résumé. Accepts hard copy and email queries to info@ticktock.co.uk. Response time varies. Publication in 1–2 years. Payment policy varies. Royalty.

Touchwood Editions

340-1105 Pandora Avenue
Victoria, British Columbia V8V 3P9
Canada

Associate Publisher: Ruth Linka

Publisher's Interests
This publisher offers historical fiction and mysteries. Nonfiction topics include food and art.
Website: www.touchwoodeditions.com

Freelance Potential
Published 20 titles (1 juvenile) in 2009: 8 were developed from unsolicited submissions and 2 were by agented authors. Of the 20 titles, 5 were by unpublished writers and 5 were by new authors. Receives 350 queries yearly.
Submissions and Payment: Guidelines and catalogue available at website. Query with 200-word synopsis, market analysis, illustration list, author bio, table of contents, and 2–3 sample chapters. Accepts hard copy. SAE/IRC. Response time, publication period, and payment policy vary.

Turtle Press

P.O. Box 34010
Santa Fe, NM 87594-4010

Editor: Cynthia Kim

Publisher's Interests
Training guides, instructional books, and DVDs on martial arts are the specialty of this publisher. Its material covers taekwondo, tai chi, tang soo do, and shaolin kung fu.
Website: www.turtlepress.com

Freelance Potential
Published 8 titles in 2009: 1 was developed from an unsolicited submission. Of the 8 titles, 2 were by unpublished writers and 2 were by authors who were new to the publishing house. Receives 480 queries yearly.
Submissions and Payment: Guidelines and catalogue available at website. Query. Accepts hard copy. SASE. Responds in 2–3 weeks. Publication period varies. Royalty, 10%; advance, $500–$2,000.

Tyrannosaurus Press

5486 Fairway Drive
Zachary, LA 70791

Submissions Editor: Roxanne Reiken

Publisher's Interests
Speculative fiction for young adults and adults—including fantasy, science fiction, and horror—is at the core of this company's publishing program.
Website: www.tyrannosauruspress.com

Freelance Potential
Published 2 titles in 2009: 1 was by an unpublished writer and 1 was by a new author. Receives 300 queries yearly.
Submissions and Payment: Guidelines and catalogue available at website. Query with cover letter, author credentials, word count, and description of target audience. Prefers email queries to info@tyrannosauruspress.com (no attachments); will accept hard copy. SASE. Responds in 3 months. Publication in 1–2 years. Royalty, 10% of gross.

Unity House

Unity School of Christianity
1901 NW Blue Parkway
Unity Village, MO 64065-0001

Submissions

Publisher's Interests
Spiritual titles based on Unity principles, as well as inspirational books on self-help, psychology, and practical spirituality for adults and children, are found in Unity House's catalogue. It is currently not reviewing children's material or fiction. Check website for updates.
Website: www.unityonline.org

Freelance Potential
Published 6 titles in 2009. Of the 6 titles, most were by authors who were new to the publishing house. Receives 450 queries yearly.
Submissions and Payment: Guidelines and catalogue available at website. Query with proposal. Accepts hard copy. SASE. Responds in 6 months. Publication in 11 months. Royalty.

VanderWyk & Burnham

1610 Long Leaf Circle
St. Louis, MO 63146

Acquisitions Editor

Publisher's Interests
VanderWyk & Burnham's books are designed to "promote learning, compassion, and self-reliance, and to make a difference in people's lives." To that end, this publisher focuses on education, family and social issues, and personal growth, mostly in nonfiction works.
Website: www.VandB.com

Freelance Potential
Plans to resume publishing (1 or more titles) in 2010. Receives 60–100 queries yearly.
Submissions and Payment: Guidelines and catalogue available at website. Query. Accepts email queries to info@VandB.com. Response time varies. Publication in 1–2 years. Royalty; advance, to $2,000.

Volcano Press

P.O. Box 270
Volcano, CA 95689

Publisher Emerita: Ruth Gottstein

Publisher's Interests
A variety of nonfiction titles comprise the Volcano Press catalogue, which emphasizes women's health and social issues
regarding women and children. Some titles about California
history also appear on its list. Queries regarding children's
books, while not expressly encouraged, are welcome.
Website: www.volcanopress.com

Freelance Potential
Published 3 titles in 2009. Receives 24–48 queries yearly.
Submissions and Payment: Catalogue available at website.
Query with outline, sample chapters, and marketing analysis.
Prefers email queries to ruth@volcanopress.com; will accept
hard copy. SASE. Responds in 2 months. Publication period
varies. Royalty; advance.

WestSide Books

Submission Editor

Publisher's Interests
WestSide Books is a publisher of fiction for young adults. The
books from this publisher illustrate the diverse and complicated
lives of today's teenagers. It is currently seeking edgy novel
submissions that reflect the real issues and situations that
teenagers contend with daily.
Website: www.westside-books.com

Freelance Potential
Published 9 titles in 2009.
Submissions and Payment: Guidelines available at website.
Query with synopsis, first 25 pages, and author bio. Accepts
email queries to submissions@westside-books.com. Responds
in 2 months. Publication period varies. Royalty.

Whiskey Creek Press

P.O. Box 51052
Casper, WY 82605-1052

Submissions

Publisher's Interests
This publisher produces ebook and trade paperback fiction
and nonfiction titles in all subject areas and genres for young
adults and adults. While actively seeking all types of books, it
is especially interested in reviewing romance, science fiction,
and fantasy titles.
Website: www.whiskeycreekpress.com

Freelance Potential
Published 15–20 titles in 2009.
Submissions and Payment: Guidelines and catalogue avail-
able at website. Send complete ms (60,000–80,000 words).
Accepts email submissions to subs@whiskeycreekpress.com.
Responds in 3–4 months. Publication period varies. Royalty.

Wild Child Publishing

P.O. Box 4897
Culver City, CA 90231-4897

Submissions: Marci Baun

Publisher's Interests
Publishing ebooks as well as books in print has been the focus
of Wild Child Publishing since 1999. It accepts fiction and nonfiction titles on an array of topics and in many genres. Its readership includes middle-grade readers through octogenarians.
Website: www.wildchildpublishing.com

Freelance Potential
Published 25–30 titles (1 juvenile) in 2009: 20 were developed
from unsolicited submissions and 2 were by agented authors.
Submissions and Payment: Guidelines and catalogue available at website. Query with synopsis. Accepts email queries
to mgbaun@wildchildpublishing.com. Response time and
publication period vary. Royalty, 40% on e-books, 10% on
print books.

WindRiver Publishing

72 North WindRiver Road
Silverton, ID 83867-0446

Editor-in-Chief: Gail Howick

Publisher's Interests
A variety of fiction genres for children is offered by WindRiver Publishing, including science fiction, mystery, romance, and historical fiction. It also publishes books on homeschooling.
Website: www.windriverpublishing.com

Freelance Potential
Published 6 titles (1 juvenile) in 2009. Of the 6 titles, 1 was by an unpublished writer and 2 were by authors who were new to the publishing house. Receives 1,000 queries yearly.
Submissions and Payment: Guidelines available at website. Query with 3–4 chapters, synopsis, and market info. Prefers submissions of proposals via website. Accepts hard copy and simultaneous submissions if identified. SASE. Responds in 4–6 months. Publication period varies. Royalty, 15% of net.

Paula Wiseman Books

Simon & Schuster
1230 Avenue of the Americas
New York, NY 10020

Submissions Editor

Publisher's Interests
An imprint of Simon & Schuster, Paula Wiseman Books produces fiction and nonfiction titles for children from preschool through young adult. Picture books, novelty books, and board books are among the categories in its catalogue. Unsolicited queries may be sent for review; however, the imprint prefers to receive agented submissions.
Website: http://kids.simonandschuster.com

Freelance Potential
Published several titles in 2009.
Submissions and Payment: Guidelines available. Send complete ms for picture books. Query with sample chapter for all other submissions. Accepts hard copy. SASE. Responds in 4 months. Publication in 18–24 months. Royalty; advance.

Wizards of the Coast

P.O. Box 707
Renton, WA 98057-0707

Submissions Editor

Publisher's Interests
This publisher features high-quality science fiction and fantasy books for both young adults and adults. Role-playing guides and games are also included in the mix.
Website: www.wizards.com

Freelance Potential
Published 46 titles in 2009: 11 were by agented authors. Of the 46 titles, 6 were by unpublished writers and 9 were by authors who were new to the publishing house. Receives 200+ queries yearly.
Submissions and Payment: Guidelines and catalogue available at website. Check website for open submission periods. Query with synopsis. Accepts hard copy. SASE. Response time, publication period, and payment policy vary.

Wordsong

813 Church Street
Honesdale, PA 18431

Submissions Editor

Publisher's Interests
As one of the only imprints in children's publishing dedicated to poetry, Wordsong uses a variety of poetry books to connect young readers to the melody and emotion of poems. Its list ranges from the silly to the serious, and includes poetry on all topics as long as the story has lasting value. Wordsong is an imprint of Boyds Mills Press.
Website: www.wordsongpoetry.com

Freelance Potential
Published 9 titles in 2009. Receives 300–360 mss yearly.
Submissions and Payment: Guidelines and catalogue available at website. Send complete ms. Accepts hard copy. SASE. Responds in 3 months. Publication period varies. Royalty; advance. Flat fee.

World Book, Inc.

233 North Michigan Avenue, Suite 200
Chicago, IL 60601

Associate Director, Supplementary Publications: Scott Thomas

Publisher's Interests
The research materials offered by World Book include encyclopedias, reference books, supplements, and multimedia educational resources for children of all ages. Available in both print and electronic formats, its titles cover such categories as geography, nature, science, language, and social studies.
Website: www.worldbook.com

Freelance Potential
Published 3 multi-volume titles in 2009.
Submissions and Payment: Guidelines and catalogue available at website. Query with outline/synopsis. Accepts hard copy and simultaneous submissions if identified. SASE. Responds in 1–2 months. Publication in 18 months. Payment policy varies.

YMAA Publication Center

P.O. Box 480
Wolfeboro, NH 03894

Director: David Ripianzi

Publisher's Interests
This publisher seeks nonfiction and fiction that is supported by some aspect of martial arts or Asian culture. Its catalogue features titles that embrace Qigong, philosophy, martial arts, and Asian medicine and healing arts.
Website: www.ymaa.com

Freelance Potential
Published 8 titles in 2009: 2 were by agented authors and 1 was by an author who was new to the publishing house. Receives 100+ queries yearly.
Submissions and Payment: Guidelines and catalogue available at website. Query with clips and sample chapter; or send complete ms. Accepts hard copy. SASE. Responds in 1–3 months. Publication in 12–18 months. Royalty, 10%.

Zaner-Bloser Educational Publishers

Dublin Road
P.O. Box 16764
Columbus, OH 43216

Senior Vice President of Editorial: Marytherese Croarkin

Publisher's Interests
Zaner-Bloser, a division of the much-respected Highlights for Children, publishes literacy-leveled books for students in preschool through grade six. Its books are fun for readers and help teachers achieve best practices in reading instruction with a variety of curriculum-based activities. All titles focus on developing fluent reading, covering topics such as mathematics, science, social studies, Spanish, and language arts.
Website: www.zaner-bloser.com

Freelance Potential
Published 200+ titles in 2009.
Submissions and Payment: Catalogue available at website. Query with résumé and clips. Accepts hard copy. SASE. Response time and publication period vary. Flat fee.

Zonderkidz

5300 Patterson SE
Grand Rapids, MI 49530

Acquisitions

Publisher's Interests
Christian books, both fiction and nonfiction, are published by this children's imprint of Zondervan. It is currently looking for picture books, board books, juvenile fiction and nonfiction, young adult fiction and nonfiction, and Bible stories.
Website: www.zondervan.com

Freelance Potential
Published 150 titles (40 juvenile) in 2009: 120 were by agented authors and 3 were reprint/licensed properties. Of the 150 titles, 1 was by an unpublished writer and 5 were by authors who were new to the publishing house.
Submissions and Payment: Guidelines available. Query. Accepts hard copy. SASE. Response time varies. Publication period varies. Royalty; advance.

Contests
and Awards

Selected Contests & Awards

Whether you enter a contest for unpublished writers or submit your published book for an award, you will have an opportunity to have your book read by established writers and qualified editors. Participating in a competition can increase recognition of your writing and possibly open more doors for selling your work. If you don't win and the winning entry is published, try to read it to see how your work compares with its competition.

To be considered for the contests and awards that follow, your entry must fulfill all of the requirements mentioned. Most are looking for unpublished article or story manuscripts, while a few require published works. Note special entry requirements, such as whether or not you can submit the material yourself, need to be a member of an organization, or are limited in the number of entries you can send. Also, be sure to submit your article or story in the standard manuscript submission format.

For each listing, we've included the address, the contact, a description, the entry requirements, the deadline, and the prize. In some cases, the 2010 deadlines were not available at press time. We recommend that you write to the addresses provided and ask for an entry form and the contest guidelines, which usually specify the current deadline.

Abilene Writers Guild Annual Contest

Barbara Darnall
726 Davis Drive
Abilene, TX 79605

Description
Open to all writers, this annual contest presents awards in seven categories including children's stories for readers ages 3–8; novels; young adult; and inspirational fiction.
Website: http://abilenewritersguild.org
Length: Varies for each category.
Requirements: Entry fee, $10 for novel categories; $5 for all other categories. Accepts hard copy. Author's name should not appear on manuscript. Include a cover letter with author's name, address, telephone number, and email in the upper left corner.
Prizes: First-place winners in each category receive $100. Second- and third-place winners in each category receive $65 and $35, respectively.
Deadline: Entries are accepted between September 1 and October 31.

Arizona Authors Association Literary Contests

Contest Coordinator
6145 W. Echo Lane
Glendale, AZ 85302

Description
Sponsored by the Arizona Authors Association, these contests have categories for both published and unpublished material.
Website: www.azauthors.com/contest_index.html
Length: Varies for each category.
Requirements: Entry fees range from $15 to $30 depending on category. Submit first 25 pages for novel entries. Accepts hard copy. Author's name should not be included on unpublished manuscripts. Include a cover letter with author's name, address, and telephone number. Visit the website for a complete list of submission guidelines for each category.
Prizes: First-place winners in each category receive a cash award of $100. Winner in the unpublished novel category receives a publication contract with AuthorHouse.com.
Deadline: Entries are accepted between January 1 and July 1.

Atlantic Writing Competition

Writers' Federation of Nova Scotia
1113 Marginal Road
Halifax, Nova Scotia B3H 4P7
Canada

Description
This competition is open to writers living in Atlantic Canada and accepts entries of YA novels, short stories, poetry, writing for children, and magazine articles/essays. It accepts previously unpublished, original work only.
Website: www.writers.ns.ca
Length: Varies for each category.
Requirements: Entry fees: novel category, $25; all other categories, $15. WFNS members receive a $5 discount on entry fees. Published authors may not enter the competition in the genre in which they have been published. Limit one entry per category. Accepts hard copy. Guidelines available at website.
Deadline: December 5.
Prizes: First- through third-place winners in each category receive cash awards ranging from $50 to $200.

Autumn House Poetry and Fiction Contests

Autumn House Press
P.O. Box 60100
Pittsburgh, PA 15211

Description
This annual contest is sponsored by Autumn House Press and accepts collections of poetry and fiction entries. All fiction genres are welcome.
Website: www.autumnhouse.com
Length: Poetry collections, 50–80 pages. Fiction, 200–300 pages.
Requirements: Entry fee, $25. Accepts hard copy. Visit the website for complete competition guidelines. Include an SASE for contest results.
Prizes: Winning entries are published by Autumn House Press with a $1,000 advance against royalties. All entries will be considered for publication by Autumn House.
Deadline: June 30.

AWP Award Series

George Mason University
MS 1E3
Fairfax, VA 22030-4444

Description
This award series is held annually and accepts entries of fiction, creative nonfiction, and poetry. It is open to all writers.
Website: www.awpwriter.org
Length: Varies for each category.
Requirements: Accepts hard copy. Author's name should not appear on manuscript. Include a cover letter with author's name, address, telephone number, and email in upper left corner.
Prizes: Winners receive a $2,000 cash honorarium and publication of their book by the University of Pittsburgh Press, University of Massachusetts Press, or University of Georgia Press.
Deadline: Ongoing.

Doris Bakwin Award

Carolina Wren Press
120 Morris Street
Durham, NC 27701

Description
Carolina Wren Press sponsors this contest that seeks fiction or nonfiction submissions on any subject written by women. It encourages submissions from both new and experienced writers. This competition is open to previously unpublished manuscripts only.
Website: www.carolinawrenpress.org
Length: 150 to 500 pages.
Requirements: Entry fee, $20. Multiple entries are accepted. Accepts hard copy with disk (Microsoft Word or text files) only. Visit website for complete guidelines.
Prizes: Winners receive cash awards ranging from $150 to $600.
Deadline: December 1.

Josiah Bancroft Sr. Novel Contest

Attn. Dr. Dana Thomas
Writers' Festival Contests
4501 Capper Road
Jacksonville, FL 32218

Description
This contest welcomes original, unpublished submissions in all
genres of fiction. It is held annually as part of the Florida First
Coast Writers' Festival.
Website: www.fccj.org
Length: First 100 pages.
Requirements: Entry fee, $45. Accepts hard copy. Submit
two copies of entry; include a brief summary. Visit the website
for complete guidelines.
Prizes: First-place winners receive $700 and consideration for
publication by a major publishing house. Second- and third-place
winners receive $200 and $100, respectively.
Deadline: Ongoing.

The *Boston Globe–Horn Book* Awards

Horn Book
56 Roland Street, Suite 200
Boston, MA 02129

Description
These prestigious awards honor excellence in literature for children and young adults. A committee of three judges evaluates
books submitted by United States publishers and selects winners on the basis of overall creative excellence.
Website: www.hbook.com
Length: No length requirements.
Requirements: No entry fee. Publishers may submit books
from each of their juvenile imprints in the following categories:
fiction or poetry, nonfiction, and picture books. Eligible titles
will have been published in the year preceding the contest. Visit
the website for complete guidelines, or send an SASE.
Prizes: Winner receives $500 and an engraved silver bowl.
Honor books may also be named.
Deadline: May 15.

CNW/FFWA Florida State Writing Competition

CNW/FFWA
P.O. Box A
North Stratford, NH 03590

Description
This competition is open to all writers and accepts entries in four divisions: nonfiction, fiction, children's literature, and poetry. Each division has its own sub-categories to further narrow the genres of writing.
Website: www.writers-editors.com
Length: Varies for each category.
Requirements: Entry fees range from $3–$10 for members and $5–$20 for non-members. Multiple entries are accepted. Use paper clips only; no staples. Author's name should not appear on manuscript. Send an SASE or visit the website for category-specific guidelines and entry forms.
Prizes: First- through third-place winners in each category will receive cash prizes ranging from $50 to $100.
Deadline: March 15.

Delacorte Dell Yearling Contest for a First Middle-Grade Novel

Random House
1745 Broadway, 9th Floor
New York, NY 10019

Description
This annual contest looks for exemplary submissions of contemporary or historical fiction targeting the 9 to 12 age group. All entries must have a North American setting. The contest is open to writers from the U.S. and Canada only.
Website: www.randomhouse.com/kids/writingcontests/
Length: 96–160 typewritten pages.
Requirements: No entry fee. Accepts hard copy. No simultaneous submissions or foreign-language translations. Include a brief plot summary and cover letter. Include an SASE for return of manuscript.
Prizes: Winner receives a book contract including an advance of $7,500 and a cash prize of $1,500.
Deadline: Entries must be postmarked between April 1 and June 30.

Delacorte Press Contest for a First Young Adult Novel

Random House
1745 Broadway, 9th Floor
New York, NY 10019

Description
Encouraging writers to experiment in the contemporary young adult fiction genre, this contest is sponsored by Random House. It is open to residents of the U.S. and Canada who have not yet been published in this genre.
Website: www.randomhouse.com/kids/writingcontests/
Length: 100–224 typewritten pages.
Requirements: No entry fee. Accepts hard copy. No simultaneous submissions or foreign-language translations. Include a brief plot summary and cover letter. Include an SASE for return of manuscript.
Prizes: Winner receives a book contract including an advance of $7,500 and a cash prize of $1,500.
Deadline: Entries must be postmarked between October 1 and December 31.

Shubert Fendrich Memorial Playwriting Contest

Pioneer Drama Service
P.O. Box 4267
Englewood, CO 80155

Description
In honor of the founder of Pioneer Drama Service, Shubert Fendrich, this annual contest encourages the development of high-quality drama for educational and community theaters. It is open to all writers.
Website: www.pioneerdrama.com
Length: Running time of 20 to 90 minutes.
Requirements: No entry fee. Accepts hard copy and email submissions to playwrights@pioneerdrama.com. Include a cover letter, synopsis, cast list, proof of production, number of sets and scenes, and musical score, if applicable.
Prizes: Winner receives a contract for publication and a cash advance of $1,000.
Deadline: March 1.

Genesis Contest

American Christian Fiction Writers

Description
This annual contest is for members of the American Christian Fiction Writers who have not published young adult or adult fiction in the last seven years. It accepts manuscripts in several categories including young adult, suspense/thriller, historical fiction, and chick lit.
Website: www.acfw.com
Length: First 15 pages.
Requirements: Check website for entry fees and email addresses by category. No hard copy submissions. Submit first 15 pages of novel with manuscript synopsis. Accepts 100 entries per category.
Prizes: Winners receive a plaque and first choice for an editor/agent appointment at the ACFW Annual Conference.
Deadline: March 1.

Paul Gillette Memorial Writing Contest

Pikes Peak Writers
416 Austin Bluff Pkwy, #246
Colorado Springs, CO 80918

Description
Encouraging writers to focus on producing a marketable project, this annual contest is open to unpublished writers of short stories and book-length fiction. Entries are accepted in the categories of mystery; romance; historical, mainstream, and science fiction; children's and young adult novels.
Website: www.ppwc.net
Length: Varies for each category.
Requirements: Entry fee, $30 for members; $40 for non-members. Accepts hard copy. All entries must be accompanied by an entry form, a cover letter, and two copies of manuscript. Guidelines available at website.
Prizes: First-place winner in each category receives $100. Second-place winner in each category receives $50.
Deadline: November 1.

The Barbara Karlin Grant

Barbara Karlin Grant Committee c/o Q. L. Pearce
884 Atlanta Court
Claremont, CA 91711

Description
This grant was established by the Society of Children's Book Writers and Illustrators to encourage the work of aspiring picture book writers. It is open to members of the SCBWI who have not yet published a picture book. Original short stories, nonfiction, or re-tellings of fairy tales, folktales, or legends are eligible for consideration.
Website: www.scbwi.org
Length: 8 pages.
Requirements: No entry fee. Requests for application may be made beginning October 1 of each year. Instructions and complete guidelines are sent with application forms.
Prizes: Cash grants of $1,500 and $500 are awarded.
Deadline: Entries are accepted between February 15 and March 15.

Maryland Writers' Association Novel Contest

P.O. Box 65
Pylesville, MD 21132-0065

Description
Open to all writers, this contest encourages aspiring authors by providing a reputable literary critique and contest experience. Entries must be completed, English-language works of fiction that are currently not under contract by an agent or publisher.
Website: www.marylandwriters.org
Length: 50,000 words minimum.
Requirements: Entry fee, $35 for members; $38 for non-members. Accepts hard copy. Visit the website or send an SASE for complete guidelines.
Prizes: The overall contest winner receives a cash award of $150. First-place winners in each category receive a cash award of $100.
Deadline: February 28.

Mayhaven Awards for Children's Fiction

P.O. Box 557
Mahomet, IL 61853

Description
Mayhaven Publishing sponsors this annual contest that is open to original, previously unpublished fiction manuscripts. All submissions must be written in English.
Website: www.mayhavenpublishing.com
Requirements: Entry fee, $50. Applications are available with an SASE or at the website. Accepts hard copy. Multiple entries are accepted. Manuscripts will not be returned. Send an SASE or visit the website for more information.
Prizes: First-place winner receives publication of their manuscript and royalties on sales. Second- and third-place winners receive cash prizes of $200 and $100, respectively.
Deadline: December 31.

Milkweed Prize for Children's Literature

Milkweed Editions
1011 Washington Ave. South, Suite 300
Minneapolis, MN 55415-1246

Description
This annual competition looks for high-quality manuscripts for readers ages 8 to 13 for its children's book publishing program. Entries should embody humane values and contribute to cultural understanding.
Website: www.milkweed.org
Length: 90–200 typewritten pages.
Requirements: No entry fee. Entries must have been accepted for publication by Milkweed during the calendar year, and been written by a writer not previously published by Milkweed. Picture books and collections of stories are not eligible. All entries must follow Milkweed's usual submission guidelines. Visit the website or send an SASE for further information.
Prizes: Winners receive a $10,000 cash advance on royalties.
Deadline: Ongoing.

Minotaur Books/MWA Competition

St. Martin's Minotaur
175 Fifth Avenue
New York, NY 10010

Description
Open to writers who have not yet published a novel, this competition accepts original, book-length manuscripts in which murder or another serious crime is at the heart of the story.
Website: www.mysterywriters.org
Length: No less than 220 pages (60,000 words).
Requirements: Limit one entry per competition. Send an SASE for an official entry form. Include a cover letter with author bio and contact information.
Prizes: Winner receives a standard publishing contract from St. Martin's Press/Minotaur Books. After execution of the standard form author's agreement by both parties, the winner will receive a $10,000 advance against royalties.
Deadline: November 30.

National Children's Theatre Festival Competition

Actors' Playhouse at the Miracle Theatre
280 Miracle Mile
Coral Gables, FL 33134

Description
This competition invites the submission of original scripts for musicals to be judged by a distinguished panel from both professional and academic theatre. All entries should target the 5–12 age group, but plays that are appealing to both children and adults are preferred.
Website: www.actorsplayhouse.org
Length: Running time, 45–60 minutes.
Requirements: Entry fee, $10 per submission. Multiple entries are accepted. Accepts hard copy. Include an SASE for return of manuscript. Guidelines available at website.
Prizes: Winner receives a cash prize of $500 and a full production of their play.
Deadline: April 1.

Newbery Medal Award

American Library Association
50 East Huron
Chicago, IL 60611

Description
The Newbery Medal Award is presented annually to an author
who has made a distinguished contribution to American literature for children published in the U.S. Eligible authors must be
citizens or residents of the U.S.
Website: www.ala.org
Length: No length limit.
Requirements: No entry fee. Multiple submissions are
accepted. All entries must have been published in the year
preceding the contest. Guidelines available at website.
Prizes: The Newbery Medal is awarded to the winner. Honor
books may also be named.
Deadline: December 31.

New Voices Award

Attn. New Voices Award
Lee & Low Books
95 Madison Avenue
New York, NY 10016

Description
This annual award, sponsored by Lee & Low Books, is pre-
sented for a picture book manuscript by an author of color.
The competition is open to U.S. residents who have not pub-
lished a children's picture book. All entries should target chil-
dren ages 2 through 10 and may be either fiction or nonfic-
tion that addresses the needs of children of color.
Website: www.leeandlow.com
Length: To 1,500 words.
Requirements: No entry fee. Limit 2 entries per competition.
Accepts hard copy. Guidelines available at website.
Prizes: Winner receives a cash grant of $1,000 and a stan-
dard publishing contract from Lee & Low Books. An honor
grant of $500 will also be awarded.
Deadline: December 31.

Once Upon a World Book Award

Museum of Tolerance
1399 S. Roxbury Drive
Los Angeles, CA 90035-4709

Description
The Simon Wiesenthal Center & Museum of Tolerance sponsors this award to honor children's books targeting the 6 to 10 age group. Entries should promote acceptance, tolerance, and communication among people while demonstrating the importance of history. It accepts entries of fiction, nonfiction, or poetry.
Website: www.wiesenthal.com/library/award.cfm
Length: No length limit.
Requirements: No entry fee. All entries must have been published in the year preceding the contest. A nomination form must accompany each submission. Guidelines and nomination form available at website.
Prizes: Winners receive a cash award of $1,000.
Deadline: April 1.

Pacific Northwest Writers Association Literary Contests

PMB 2717
1420 NW Golman Boulevard, Suite 2
Issaquah, WA 98027

Description
These annual contests offer prizes in several categories including juvenile/young adult novel; nonfiction book; juvenile memoir; and short story. Only original, previously unpublished material is eligible for submission.
Website: www.pnwa.org
Length: Varies for each category.
Requirements: Entry fee, $35 for members; $50 for nonmembers. Multiple entries are accepted. Accepts hard copy. All entries must include an official entry form. Submit 2 copies of each entry. Guidelines and category information available at website.
Prizes: Winners receive cash awards ranging from $150 to $600.
Deadline: February 20.

San Antonio Writers Guild Annual Contest

P.O. Box 100717
San Antonio, TX 78201-8717

Description
Open to all writers, this annual contest offers prizes in five categories: first chapter of a novel; first chapter of a nonfiction book; memoir; poetry; and short story.
Website: www.sawritersguild.com
Length: Varies for each category.
Requirements: Entry fee, $10 for SAWG members; $15 for nonmembers. Accepts hard copy. Include an SASE for winners' list. Visit the website for complete guidelines and specific category information.
Prizes: Winners in each category receive a cash award and possible publication.
Deadline: October 15.

Kay Snow Writing Contest

Willamette Writers
9045 SW Barbour Boulevard, Suite 5A
Portland, OR 97219-4027

Description
This annual contest looks to help writers reach professional goals. It offers awards in several categories including juvenile writing, fiction, nonfiction, and screenwriting.
Website: www.willamettewriters.com
Length: Varies for each category.
Requirements: Entry fee, $10 for members; $15 for nonmembers. Submit 3 copies of each entry. Author's name must not appear on manuscript. Request complete contest guidelines or visit website for additional information.
Prizes: Cash prizes ranging from $50 to $300 are awarded in each category. A Liam Callen award will also be presented to the best overall entry with a cash prize of $500.
Deadline: April 23.

SouthWest Writers Contests

Southwest Writers Workshop
3721 Morris NE
Albuquerque, NM 87111

Description

These contests are sponsored by the SouthWest Writers and present awards in several categories including middle-grade novel, young adult novel, children's picture book, and nonfiction book.

Website: www.southwestwriters.com

Length: Varies for each category.

Requirements: Entry fee, $29 for members; $39 for non-members. Submit 2 copies of each entry. Each entry must be accompanied by an official entry form. Author's name should appear on the entry form only. Multiple entries are accepted. All entries must be typed. Send an SASE for complete contest guidelines and official entry form, or visit the website.

Prizes: Cash prizes range from $50–$150.

Deadline: May 1.

Surrey International Writers' Conference Writing Contest

Unit 400, 9260-140 Street
Surrey, British Columbia
Canada

Description

Open to all writers over the age of 18, this annual contest offers prizes in the categories of nonfiction, short story, poetry, and writing for young people.

Website: www.siwc.ca

Length: Nonfiction and writing for young people, to 1,500 words. Short stories, 3,500–5,000 words. Poetry, to 36 lines.

Requirements: Entry fee, $15. Multiple entries are accepted. Accepts hard copy and email entries to contest@siwc.ca. Author's name should not appear on manuscript. Include a cover letter with author's name and contact information.

Prizes: First-place winners in each category receive a cash award of $1,000. Honorable mentions receive a cash award of $150.

Deadline: September 5.

Tennessee Williams One-Act Play Competition

938 Lafayette Street, Suite 514
New Orleans, LA 70113

Description

The Tennessee Williams One-Act Play Competition recognizes excellence in one-act plays. It is open to all writers and accepts previously unpublished work only.
Website: www.tennesseewilliams.net
Length: One act, no more than one hour in length.
Requirements: Entry fee, $25. Multiple entries are accepted. Accepts hard copy. Entries must include an entry form, available at website. Send an SASE or visit the website for further guidelines.
Prizes: Winner receives a cash prize of $1,500 and a staged reading of their play at an annual literary festival. Second- and third-place winners receive $200 and $100, respectively.
Deadline: November 16.

Work-in-Progress Grants

The Society of Children's Book Writers and Illustrators
8271 Beverly Boulevard
Los Angeles, CA 90048

Description

The Society of Children's Book Writers and Illustrators presents five grants annually to assist children's book writers in the completion of a project. Grants are awarded in the categories of general work-in-progress; contemporary novel for young people; nonfiction research; and unpublished author.
Website: www.scbwi.org
Length: 750-word synopsis and writing sample from an entry that is no longer than 2,500 words.
Requirements: No entry fee. Requests for applications may be made beginning October 1 each year. Instructions and complete guidelines are sent with application forms.
Prizes: Cash grants of $1,500 and $500 are awarded in each of the categories.
Deadline: March 15.

Writers' League of Texas Annual Novel Manuscript Contest

611 S. Congress Avenue, Suite 130
Austin, TX 78704

Description
This annual novel contest accepts entries in the categories of mainstream fiction; children/middle-grade; young adult; mystery/thriller; science fiction; historical/Western; and romance. This competition accepts previously unpublished entries only.
Website: www.writersleague.org
Requirements: Entry fee, $50. Send one-page synopsis along with the first 10 pages of your novel. Include an entry form with manuscript. Send an SASE or visit the website for guidelines.
Prizes: Winner in each category is invited to a one-on-one meeting with an agent at the Writers' League of Texas Agents and Editors Conference in June. Cash prizes are also awarded.
Deadline: Visit website for current deadline.

Writing for Children Competition

90 Richmond Street, Suite 200
Toronto, Ontario M5C 1P1
Canada

Description
Open to Canadian citizens who have not yet published a book, this contest is held annually. Its purpose is to discover new talent and promote new writers of children's literature.
Website: www.writersunion.ca
Length: To 1,500 words.
Requirements: Entry fee, $15. Multiple entries are accepted. Accepts hard copy. Manuscripts will not be returned. Send an SASE or visit the website for more information.
Prizes: Winner receives a cash prize of $1,500. Winning entries will be submitted to several children's publishers.
Deadline: April 24.

Indexes

2010 Market News

New Listings

Abbeville Family
Abilene Writers Guild Annual
    Contest
Academic Therapy
    Publications
The Alternate Press
Ambassador International
Arizona Authors Association
    Literary Contests
August House Publishers
Autumn House Poetry and
    Fiction Contests
AWP Award Series
Josiah Bancroft Sr. Novel
    Contest
Barbour Publishing
John F. Blair, Publisher
Blazers
R. H. Boyd Publishing
Capstone Publishers Fiction
    Division
Capstone Publishers
    Nonfiction Division
Cascadia Publishing
Conciliar Press
Diversion Press
Edge Books
Elva Resa Publishing
Five Leaves Publications
Go Teach It
Guardian Angel Publishing
Gumboot Books
Hancock House
High Noon Books

Hodder Education
Hohm Press
Kane Miller
Longacre Press
Mapletree Publishing
    Company
The McDonald & Woodward
    Publishing Company
Minotaur Books/MWA
    Competition
Optimum Publishing
    Company
Orchard House Press
PCI Education
Pick-a-WooWoo Publishers
Picture Window Books
Mathew Price Ltd.
Random House Children's
    Publishing (USA)
Reagent Press Books for
    Young Readers
San Antonio Writers Guild
    Annual Contest
Snap Books
Sumach Press
Surrey International Writers'
    Conference Writing Contest
Ticktock Media Ltd
WestSide Books
Whiskey Creek Press
Wild Child Publishing
YouthLight, Inc.

2010 Market News

Deletions/Name Changes

Abbeville Kids: See listing for Abbeville Family

Ambassador-Emerald International: See listing for Ambassador International

Avisson Press: Removed at editor's request

Boardwalk Books: See listing for Dundurn Group

Bridgestone Books: No longer publishing

Cornerstone Press Chicago: Unable to contact

Joanna Cotler Books: Unable to contact

Creative Book Publishing: Removed at editor's request

Evan-Moor Educational Publishers: Not using outside submissions

First Second Books: Removed at editor's request

Laura Geringer Books: Imprint ceased publication

Great Plains Publications: Unable to contact

Kaplan InterActive: Unable to contact

Kids Play: No longer publishing

KRBY Creations, LLC: Removed at editor's request

Melanie Kroupa Books: Imprint ceased publication

LangMarc Publishing: No longer publishing

Lark Books: Unable to contact

Luna Rising: No longer publishing

Maple Tree Press: Merged into Owl Kids Books

Mitten Press: Removed at editor's request

Moody Publishers: Removed at editor's request

Mount Olive College Press: Unable to contact

NorthWord Books for Young Readers: No longer publishing

Novalis: Unable to contact

Rising Moon: No longer publishing

Sports Publishing Inc.: No longer publishing

Megan Tingley Books: Imprint ceased publication

Two-Can Publishing: No longer publishing

Windswept House Publishers: Removed at editor's request

Wish Publishing: Removed at editor's request

Category Index

T o help you find the appropriate market for your query or manuscript, we have compiled a selective index of publishers according to the types of books they currently publish.

If you don't find a category that exactly fits your material, try a broader term that covers your topic. For example, if you have written a middle-grade biography, look through the list of publishers for both Middle-Grade (Nonfiction) *and* Biography. If you've written a young adult mystery, look under Mystery/Suspense *and* Young Adult (Fiction). Always check the publisher's listing for explanations of specific needs.

For your convenience, we have listed all of the categories that are included in this index.

Activity Books
Adventure
Animals/Pets
Bilingual (Fiction)
Bilingual (Nonfiction)
Biography
Board Books
Canadian Publishers
Chapter Books (Fiction)
Chapter Books (Nonfiction)
Concept Books
Contemporary Fiction
Crafts/Hobbies
Current Events
Drama
Early Picture Books (Fiction)
Early Picture Books (Nonfiction)
Easy-to-Read (Fiction)
Easy-to-Read (Nonfiction)
Education/Resource Material
Fairy Tales
Fantasy

Folklore/Folktales
Geography
Gifted Education
Health/Fitness
High Interest/ Low Vocabulary
Historical Fiction
History
Horror
How-to
Humor
Inspirational Fiction
Language Arts
Mathematics
Middle-Grade (Fiction)
Middle-Grade (Nonfiction)
Multicultural/ Ethnic (Fiction)
Multicultural/Ethnic (Nonfiction)
Mystery/Suspense
Nature/ Environment
Parenting
Photo-Essays
Picture Books (Fiction)
Picture Books (Nonfiction)
Plays

Reference Books
Regional (Fiction)
Regional (Nonfiction)
Religious (Fiction)
Religious (Nonfiction)
Romance
Science Fiction
Science/Technology
Self-Help
Series
Social Issues
Social Sciences
Special Education
Sports (Fiction)
Sports (Nonfiction)
Story Picture Books (Fiction)
Story Picture Books (Nonfiction)
Toddler Books (Fiction)
Toddler Books (Nonfiction)
Travel
Western
Young Adult (Fiction)
Young Adult (Nonfiction)

Board Books

Canadian Publishers

Chapter Books (F)

Chapter Books (NF)

Early Picture Books (NF)

586

Fairy Tales

Early Picture Books (NF)

Easy-to-Read (F)

Easy-to-Read (NF)

Education/Resource Mate[rials]

Parenting

Photo-Essays

Picture Books (F)

Picture Books (NF)

Plays

Reference Books

607

Publisher and Contest Index

If you do not find a particular publisher, turn to page 575 for a list of deletions and name changes.

★ indicates a newly listed publisher or contest